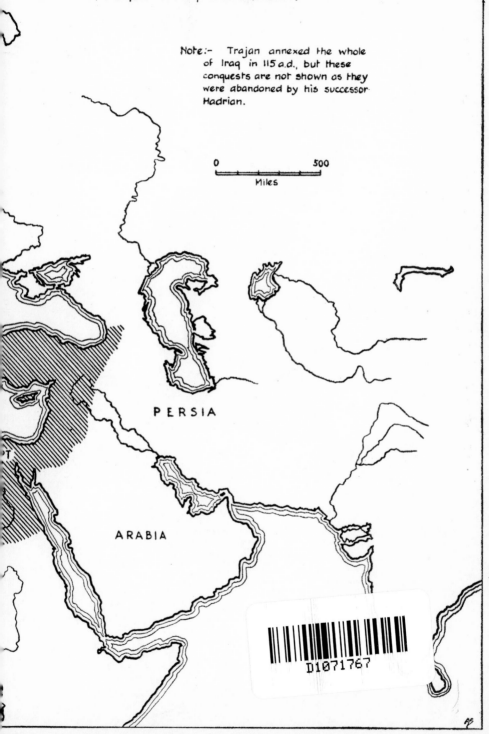

THE ROMAN EMPIRE
AT ITS GREATEST EXTENT (100A.D)
(Compare with map inside Back Cover)

Note:-   Trajan annexed the whole
of Iraq in 115 a.d., but these
conquests are not shown as they
were abandoned by his successor
Hadrian.

0   500

Miles

PERSIA

ARABIA

The Empire of the Arabs

THE EMPIRE
OF THE ARABS

Lieutenant-General
SIR JOHN GLUBB

> Man's history is by far the most wonderful thing
> in the Universe of which any news has come
> through to us... The story of man is far more
> wonderful than the wonders of physical science.
> It is a mystery unsolved, yet it is solid fact. It is
> divine, diabolic—in short, human.
>
> G. M. TREVELYAN

PRENTICE-HALL, INC.
ENGLEWOOD CLIFFS, NEW JERSEY

PRINTED IN GREAT BRITAIN

Preface

MY previous book, *The Great Arab Conquests*, dealt with the sudden rise of the Arab people in twenty-five years to the position of one of the world's Great Powers. The present work tells the story of the two hundred years during which that Arab Empire was the dominant Power in the world. In Chapter I, I have briefly summarized the life of Muhammad and the story of the first twenty-five years of the conquests, for the benefit of readers who have not read *The Great Arab Conquests*.

We live in times during which the idea of empire has been the subject of world-wide controversy. It is a remarkable fact that the Arabic-speaking peoples, whose imperial history is recorded in these pages, have been in recent years amongst the most virulent opponents of empires, as though they themselves had not been at one time one of history's greatest Imperial Powers. Thus we find that, at any given time, the leading nations defend the principle of empire, while the idea is denounced by those who happen to be out of power at the particular moment in question. A few centuries later, when the balance of power has changed, those nations which were formerly imperialists have become the enemies of empire, while those newly risen to power are transformed into the defenders of the very principle which they previously denounced. In other words, most of the views expressed on this subject seem to have been coloured by the particular situation of each nation at a special moment of its history. The history of the Arabs is of especial interest now that they are once more playing an important rôle in world affairs. In addition, however, their imperial record, dealing with one of the greatest empires of the past, may assist us also in forming a more far-sighted estimate of international leadership in general.

For various reasons, the word empire today conveys to many people an idea of injustice, of the oppression of weak nations by those physically more powerful. In order to avoid such a prejudiced assumption, I propose, for the moment, to avoid the word empire and to substitute for it that of international leadership.

When we make use of this wider expression, we find that there have always, at any one moment, been one or two leading nations, which, in their time, were admired, or at least tacitly imitated, by the others. Moreover this phase of leadership has passed from one nation to another in rotation, and, in historical times, no nation has ever yet enjoyed it twice. We may perhaps mention the early Egyptians, Assyrians, Babylonians and particularly the Persians under the Achaemenid dynasty from 550 B.C. to 330 B.C. But the Greeks are probably the earliest who still seem to live in our thought today. A remarkable aspect of Greek leadership was that it never took the political form of a single empire, except for a very few years in the lifetime of Alexander. Owing to local and accidental circumstances, the empire broke up on his death, but Greek dynasties, Greek thought and Greek methods of war nevertheless dominated a large part of the world for at least three centuries.

Greek pre-eminence gave way to Roman, and Roman ideas, Roman fashions and Roman armies held undisputed leadership for some four centuries. After two hundred years of confusion, the Arabs emerged as the international leaders, remaining the most powerful empire of their time from A.D. 650 to 850. After the commencement of their decline, they remained the leaders in thought and science for five centuries more.

When the Arabic-speaking peoples fell behind, they had already passed on the torch of art, learning, science and industry to Western Europe. Here the lead was first assumed by the Holy Roman Empire, then by Spain, France and Britain in that order. In our own lifetime, we have seen the leadership moving on to the United States and Russia.

As in all human phenomena, the details of these successive empires vary. Yet, even if we admit these variations, we seem to notice certain general laws operating in this field of international leadership.

Whatever may be the details of the methods by which the leading nation of its day influences its weaker contemporaries, there always seems to be an element of strength involved. Whether or not the great nation imposes its rule by military occupation, it is always power which produces imitation. France, for example, did not conquer a vast extent of territory in the seventeenth and eighteenth centuries, yet French became the diplomatic language of the world, French officers were engaged to train the armies of other nations, French furniture, French fashions, French literature and French cooking were everywhere supreme. In our own times, the United States has not imposed military occupation on many other nations, yet American slang, American clothes, American music and American architecture have spread all over the world. We can scarcely claim that this is due to the fact that they are intrinsically better than anything which could be produced anywhere else. There is obviously something in human nature which causes us to imitate the thought and the mannerisms of those who are physically strong.

The general disapproval of imperial conquest which is now in vogue in the West is doubtless a temporary phenomenon. At the beginning of the present century, Germany and Italy felt themselves inferior to Britain because they had no colonies. Then Britain felt herself inferior to others, precisely because she *had* colonies. If we can divest ourselves for the moment of these temporary fashions, can we form any estimate of the place of military conquest in history?

If it be true that one nation after another has held the lead in art, learning and science, there can be no doubt that, throughout history, military conquest has been the principal means by which the torch of leadership has been passed on. The conquests of Alexander spread Greek thought over the Middle East. The military empire of Rome, though sometimes brutal in action, gave civilization to innumerable backward races. When Rome collapsed, the Arabs were just in time to snatch the fallen torch. As these pages show, the immediate result seemed to be to plunge the West once more into barbarism, but before the Arabs fell, they handed back the trust to Europe with interest.

Perhaps more remarkable still is the frequency with which the mantle of leadership falls on the shoulders of a colony of its predecessor. Thus the Arabs derived much of their knowledge from Syria, Egypt and North Africa, hitherto colonies (in the modern, not in the Latin, sense) of Rome. Spain, conquered by the Arabs, was to succeed them as a great empire, when the Muslims were driven out. The U.S.A., today's leader, began as a colony of Britain, her predecessor.

Looking at the subject from this angle, we can form a broader conception of "imperialism" than can be derived from the short-lived political slogans of our own time. But if we are to achieve this wider conception of empire, we must conceive the passing on of international leadership as a continual process which we can trace from the beginning of history. But here is the rub, for, during the last five hundred years, we have deliberately omitted all mention of the Arabs from our history books. Thus the continuous development of the human race, in which lies most of the interest and significance of history, is hidden from us. Our piecemeal methods of learning history have made such a long-term conception impossible. After the appearance of Islam, Christians and Muslims were at war with one another in the Mediterranean for a thousand years. It was during this period that our educational system was established, with its historical studies deliberately limited to Greece and Rome and intentionally omitting any reference to the Arabs.

The warfare between Christendom and Islam was not due to any innate mutual repulsion between the two religions. On the contrary, they were religions so closely related that Islam has more than once been designated by Christian divines as a mere Christian heresy. This unending warfare was probably due to two factors. Firstly the Qoran and the Prophet Muhammad, under entirely different circumstances, had stated that it was the duty of Muslims to fight against unbelievers. (When these orders were issued, the unbelievers were the idol-worshipping Arabs.) The second cause was mere geographical propinquity, the nearness of Constantinople to Damascus and the competition for control of the Mediterranean.

However this may be, the thousand years of hostility resulted in Europe's devotion to Greece and Rome to the exclusion of the Arab world. Greek and Latin became the languages of the learned, Greek and Roman history and legend were part of a gentleman's education, but historical teaching stopped short at Trajan or the Antonines and jumped to Charlemagne or William the Conqueror. Not a word about the mighty Empire of the Arabs was admitted to our textbooks.

In the last two centuries, with increasing ease of travel, many Europeans have met and become intimate with Muslims. The majority, however, finding the Islamic nations comparatively weak today, have assumed in all good faith that they have always been so, never having been taught at school that the Arabs also, like the Romans, had a long imperial past.

The deliberate boycott of Arab history which took place in Europe at the time of the Renaissance has not only prevented us from understanding the Middle East. It has also made the history of Europe incomprehensible. When I say to Europeans that our ignorance of Arab history is due to political hostility many years ago, they usually reply, "Yes, of course, the Crusades." In fact, as I hope this book may help to prove, the Crusades were only a late and indeed to some extent a minor incident. It was Muslim naval command of the Mediterranean which inflicted the greatest injury on Europe.

The Arabs began to dispute Byzantine sea power in 650 and Muslim ships, commonly known as the Barbary pirates, continued to make navigation unsafe in the Mediterranean until about a hundred and fifty years ago. A tradition of hostility lasting more than a thousand years inevitably left many prejudices.

Now, however, that the world has become so small, these prejudices must disappear. The history of the Arab Empire is as necessary to our education today as is an outline knowledge of the development of Greece and Rome. It is time for us impartially to assess the Arab contribution to the history of mankind, a process which will enable us more correctly to view the historical development of the human race as a continuous whole. If this book can in any way assist such a juster and broader conception of the past, I shall be amply rewarded.

J. B. G.

Mayfield,
Sussex.

Author's Note

THE greater part of the material for this book has been derived from the original Arab historians, but I have also made use of works by many European scholars, particularly in English and French. In the compilation of several of the maps I have derived much help from *The Lands of The Eastern Caliphate* and, in the two plans of the city of Baghdad, of *Baghdad Under the Abbasid Caliphate*. Both works are by Guy Le Strange.

In writing Arabic names, I have used the spelling which seemed to me the most likely to enable the English reader to pronounce them correctly. In the use of place names, I have been, I am afraid, equally arbitrary. In the case of names already familiar to the English reader, I have used the best known forms, such as Constantinople, Damascus, Jerusalem. Otherwise I have tried to use the Arabic forms. The Arabs, however, have the habit of inserting the definite article al, the, in some names and not in others. Thus Lebanon, Syria and Egypt have no article, but they say the Iraq, the Jordan, the Yemen. For simplicity I have omitted these articles.

There are two peculiarities of Arabic personal names which may be mentioned. The first is the Arab habit of calling a man the father of his first-born son. Thus a man may have the name of—let us say—Abdulla. He marries and his wife bears a son, whom they name Muhammad. Thereafter the father may either be called Abdulla or Abu Muhammad, the father of Muhammad.

A second peculiarity of Arabic names is the habit of calling a man the servant of God. The word for a servant or slave is abid. Thus we have Abdulla —Abid Allah—the servant of God. But instead of using the word Allah, one of the attributes of God is often used— Servant of the Conqueror, Servant of the Generous, Servant of the Compassionate. Here the definite article "the" is included in the name, as in Abid al Rahman, Servant of the Merciful, Abid al Aziz, Servant of the Beloved. In all these instances, the Conqueror, the Generous, the Compassionate, the Merciful are synonyms for God. It has become customary in English to write Abdul Rahman, Abdul Aziz, instead of Abid al Rahman and so on. English people at times imagine Abdul Rahman to be a personal name and a family name like Tom Jones. They accordingly address such an individual as Abdul if they wish to be familiar or as Mister Rahman if they wish to be more polite. The result is somewhat ludicrous, for Abdul is not a word but the first half of a phrase—servant of the . . . —and Rahman means Merciful God.

The poetry presents a major problem to anyone seeking to depict Arab civilization twelve hundred years ago. Poetry played so important a part in the lives of the Arabs that to omit it in English would be to leave out an essential portion of the picture. Even the most down-to-earth Arab historian of the period included page after page of poetry in his narrative. Arabic poems were characterized by perfect form, rhyme and measure rather than by profound thought. Thus to translate them literally into halting English prose is almost worse than to omit them. Professor Nicholson is *facile princeps* in this field and where any piece of poetry has been put into English verse by him, we are on safe ground. In the case of any poems not translated by him, I have simply had to do the best I could.

This question of poetry leads me on to another. To any people living in their own country, other nations often appear hard, cruel and hostile. Our idea of an Arab may be that of a sinister, bearded warrior, apt at cutting throats. Or we may take a more modern view and visualize him as a smooth but treacherous politician with a penchant for the communists. In reality they are a passionate and a warm-hearted people. Arab life is full of laughter and tears rather than of bloodshed and avarice. In the words of an American professor, recently returned from the Middle East, "they are the most lovable people in the world." It is difficult to do justice to these qualities in an historical narrative.

I must once again express my gratitude to the library of the School of Oriental and African Studies of the University of London for the loan of books in Arabic, and to the Public Library of Tunbridge Wells for help in borrowing various works in English from libraries in different parts of this country.

Contents

Contents

List of Maps

I

Muhammad and the Early Conquests

"As a prophet and reformer of his people Muhammad could not be otherwise than a revolutionary; for his religious propaganda introduced not only a complete change in the political situation but also had an equally important bearing on the social conditions. For his followers he was all in all. He remained ever true to the principle, set up by him, of the equality and close brotherhood of all Muslims."   Von Kremer, *The Orient under the Caliphs*

With the Qoran in one hand and the scimitar in the other, the impetuous and indomitable Arab achieved a series of splendid victories unparalleled in the history of nations, for in the short space of eighty years that mighty range of Saracenic conquest embraced a wider extent of territory than Rome had mastered in the course of eight hundred.   Ockley, *History of the Saracens*

Be not afraid nor dismayed . . . For the battle is not yours but God's.
II *Chronicles* XX, 15

I

MUHAMMAD AND THE EARLY CONQUESTS

IT was the inauguration of the Muslim religion by Muhammad, the Arabian
Prophet, which first raised the Arabs to the rank of a great nation. Previous
to this event, which occurred in the first half of the seventh century A.D.,
the Arab race was to be found only in the deserts of the Arabian peninsula.
The great majority of Arabs were members of nomadic tribes, breeders of
sheep, camels and horses, who led a wandering life in the vast steppes of the
desert. Such an existence makes education, even literacy, well nigh impossible, and the ancient empires, whether Egyptians, Babylonians, Persians or
Romans, normally regarded the backwardness of the Arabs with some contempt. In spite of this, however, Arabia has always been important owing to
its geographical situation. The countries which lie on the shores of the Indian
Ocean and those which surround the Mediterranean enjoy entirely different
climates and, as a result, produce different products, which they desire to
exchange with one another. The defile leading from the Indian Ocean to the
Mediterranean lies across the Arabian peninsula or up the narrow seas—the
Red Sea and the Persian Gulf—which wash its shores. Further north, the
route between India and Europe is blocked by the deserts and mountains of
Persia, further south by the jungles and deserts of Africa. Thus, although
most of Arabia consisted of desert, trade routes crossed the peninsula bearing
the priceless commodities and luxuries of the East, and along these lines of
communication sprang up rich commercial cities, inhabited by wealthy and
sophisticated Arab merchants.

In classical times, the world was divided between east and west as it is
today, Rome representing the West and Persia the East. The Western Roman
Empire collapsed in A.D. 475, leaving Byzantium to support the cause of
Europe against Asian Persia. The two empires were constantly engaged in the
struggle for supremacy, whether in actual hot war or, in the intervals of
nominal peace, in commercial rivalry, intrigue and propaganda. The frontier
between Byzantium and Persia ran from the Upper Euphrates to the
Caucasus, leaving the Arabs on the south in contact with both of the Great
Powers. In A.D. 602, a desperate war broke out between the two empires,
lasting for twenty-six years. When peace was eventually made in A.D. 628,
both states were utterly exhausted, devastated and bankrupt.

*　　*　　*

The Prophet Muhammad had been born in A.D. 570 in Mecca, a town which
depended for its livelihood on the trade caravans from India to the Mediterranean. In 610,[1] at the age of 40, he saw the Archangel Gabriel in a vision

1. The letters A.D. will be omitted henceforward, all dates being anno domini.

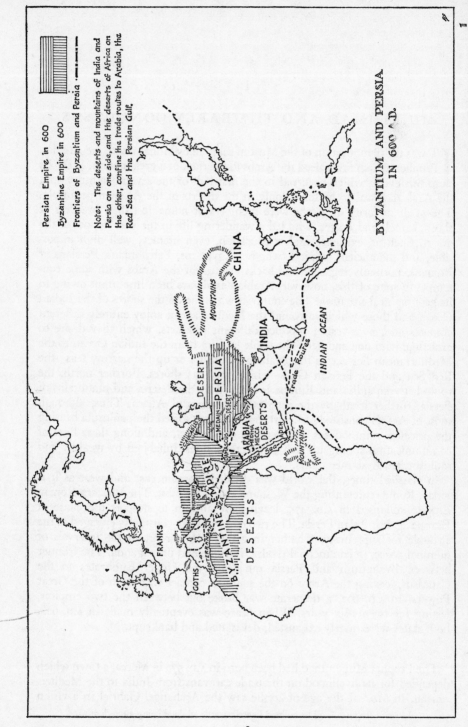

BYZANTIUM AND PERSIA
IN 600 A.D.

Persian Empire in 600

Byzantine Empire in 600

Frontiers of Byzantium and Persia

Note: The deserts and mountains of India and Persia on one side, and the deserts of Africa on the other, confine the trade routes to Arabia, the Red Sea and the Persian Gulf.

and three years later received an order to preach. Muhammad did not claim to expound a new religion. He alleged that the true faith was identical with that practised by the Patriarch Abraham, which, however, had become corrupted from its original purity by both the Jews and the Christians. God had sent him to restore the religion of Abraham in its original form. Both Judaism and Christianity had already commenced to penetrate Arabia, but the Prophet   have learnt more from the Jews than from the followers of Christ. Indeed, ... a result of his desire to put the clock back to Abraham, his preaching bore considerable resemblance to that of an Old Testament prophet.

The town of Mecca was ruled, and to a large extent inhabited, by the tribe of Quraish, which, however, did not obey the orders of a single chief but was divided into several, mutually hostile, clans. The leadership had, for two or three generations before Muhammad, been disputed between the rival families of Beni U   iya and Beni Hashim, to the latter of which the Prophet belonged. In addition to being a commercial stageing post for caravans, Mecca was regarded by the Arabs, most of whom were idolaters, as a sacred city. In the middle of the town stood the Kaaba, a small cubical building said to have housed at that time three hundred and sixty-five idols. On a certain day every year, tribesmen from all over Arabia foregathered to perform a pilgrimage to this idolatrous shrine. Quraish were proud of their position as guardians of so holy a temple and, being essentially merchants, took advantage of the pilgrimage crowds to hold fairs and to transact some profitable business.

Muhammad in his preaching denounced idols, and proclaimed the existence of one sole God, who would come one day to judge the world, welcoming the faithful to Paradise and condemning the wicked to hell-fire. Such a faith seemed to the Meccans to be calculated to destroy the fame of their sanctuary and thereby also to injure their commerce. Ten years of the Prophet's teaching in Mecca resulted in only sixty or seventy converts, who were subjected to contempt, ostracism and sometimes even persecution, by the outraged citizens. Muhammad himself was mocked and humiliated, though fear of his clan, Beni Hashim, prevented his enemies from actually assassinating him. Eventually in 622 he concluded an agreement with a party of pilgrims from Medina, a town two hundred and fifty miles north of Mecca, who undertook to give sanctuary to him and to his followers. In the course of the following few weeks, the Prophet[2] and his converts succeeded in slipping inconspicuously one by one out of Mecca and in taking refuge in Medina, where Muhammad arrived on 28th June, 622. The inhabitants of Medina proved to be far more receptive than the Meccans had been to Muhammad's teaching. Soon the Medina Muslims greatly exceeded the Meccan emigrants in numbers. The Apostle, who had a pleasant facility for bestowing nicknames, called the Medinis the Helpers and his Meccan fellow-exiles the Emigrants.

The majority of the Meccan fugitives had been obliged to escape by stealth, leaving all or most of their worldly property behind them. Many found themselves destitute in Medina. Quraish, as has already been noticed, lived by

2. Muhammad was known both as the Apostle of God and as the Prophet. I have used both designations.

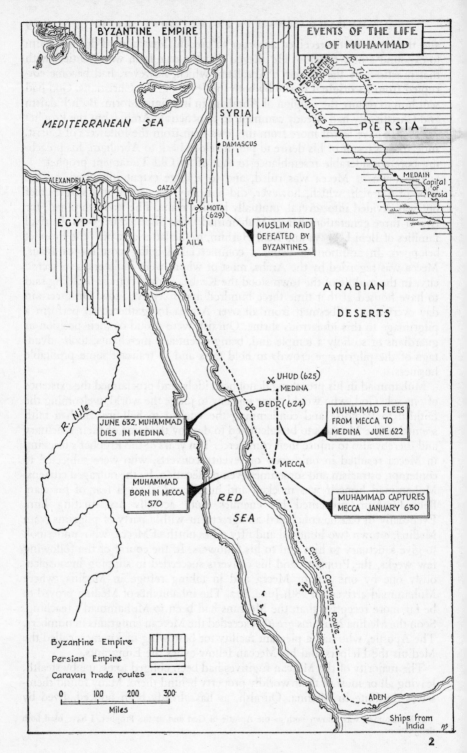

EVENTS OF THE LIFE
OF MUHAMMAD

BYZANTINE EMPIRE

MEDITERRANEAN SEA

PERSIA

SYRIA

DAMASCUS

ALEXANDRIA

GAZA

MOTA
(629)

AILA

EGYPT

MEDAIN
Capital of
Persia

MUSLIM RAID
DEFEATED BY
BYZANTINES

ARABIAN

DESERTS

R. Nile

UHUD (625)
MEDINA

BEDR (624)

JUNE 632. MUHAMMAD
DIES IN MEDINA

MUHAMMAD FLEES
FROM MECCA TO
MEDINA JUNE 622

MECCA

MUHAMMAD
BORN IN MECCA
570

RED
SEA

MUHAMMAD CAPTURES
MECCA JANUARY 630

Camel Caravan Route

Byzantine Empire
Persian Empire
Caravan trade routes

0   100   200   300
Miles

ADEN

Ships from
India

2

20

their caravan trade, to Aden in one direction, to Egypt and Syria in the other. The route to the north passed between Medina and the sea. If the Muslim Emigrants could plunder the Meccan caravans, they would retrieve their fortunes at the expense of their fellow citizens who had driven them from their homes.

In January 624, a large and wealthy Meccan caravan was expected to pass Medina returning from Syria. The Prophet determined to seize and plunder it. The leader of the caravan was a certain Abu Sofian, the chief of Beni Umaiya, long the rivals of Muhammad's clan, Beni Hashim. Abu Sofian was an experienced caravan leader. While still in Syria, he received word of the intentions of the Muslims and sent a fast camel-rider to Mecca, calling upon Quraish to despatch a force to meet him and escort him past Medina.

Early in January 624, Muhammad with some three hundred Muslim converts set out from Medina for the springs of Bedr, where he hoped to intercept the caravan two days later. Abu Sofian, however, was too clever. He suddenly changed his course, bypassed Bedr at night, and pressed on to Mecca by forced marches. Meanwhile, however, a thousand warriors had set out from Mecca to meet and escort the caravan. When the Muslims reached Bedr they were suddenly confronted by this force three times their own strength. A battle ensued in which the Muslims were completely victorious, although outnumbered by three to one. As a result, Muhammad's prestige soared and more and more converts joined his religion.

The threat to their northern trade route placed the livelihood of the Meccans in jeopardy, and in 625 they marched to Medina with three thousand men in order to deal with the Muslims once and for all. Against this force, the Prophet could muster only some seven hundred. A pitched battle was fought at Uhud just outside the town and the Muslims were utterly defeated, Muhammad himself being wounded. The remnant of the believers, carrying the Prophet between them, took refuge on a rocky hill north of Medina. The Meccans, who were commanded by Abu Sofian, did not, however, seal their victory by occupying Medina but returned to Mecca.

Muhammad was not discouraged. Many of the neighbouring nomadic tribes joined the Muslims, and his fame continued to spread. The population of Medina was half Arab and half Jewish. By driving out the Jews, the Apostle was able to provide money, houses and land for the Emigrants from Mecca. In 627, Quraish once more marched on Medina under the leadership of Abu Sofian of Beni Umaiya, who had now become Muhammad's principal enemy. This time the Muslims defended the city, refusing to give battle outside. After besieging them in vain for some three weeks, Abu Sofian abandoned the attempt and returned to Mecca.

The tide had now turned. Many bedouin tribes professed loyalty to the Prophet while public opinion in Mecca began also to change in his favour. At length, in January 630, six years after the Battle of Bedr, Muhammad marched on his native town at the head of ten thousand followers. The city was occupied without opposition, Abu Sofian announced his conversion to Islam and the Kaaba was cleansed of its three hundred and sixty-five idols. The Apostle, however, stated that the idol shrine was the House of God and had been founded by Abraham. The Meccans had sinned in placing idols in the temple but now that it had been purged of idols, it was once more the House of the One God and pilgrimage to it was incumbent on all Muslims. When they understood that their city would still remain a centre for pilgrimage, the Meccans abandoned their opposition. The city of Mecca increased in fame and prosperity through the triumph of Islam. Muhammad, however, returned to Medina, which he continued to use as his headquarters.

After the fall of Mecca, Muhammad became the greatest power in Arabia and delegations arrived from all over the peninsula to make submission to him and to accept the religion of Islam. In June 632, however, he fell ill, possibly of pneumonia, and died ten days later in Medina.

*   *   *

The idol-worshipping Arabs early in the seventh century were ripe for a higher religion, and indeed Judaism and Christianity were already spreading among them. By basing his religion on that of Abraham, the Prophet gave an Old Testament flavour to Islam. The spread of religion by war and the belief that the massacre of unbelievers is pleasing to an angry Divinity can be justified by many passages from the first five books of the Bible and would harmonize with the rough and warlike character of the Arabian tribes. In spite, however, of his advocacy of violence against those whom he denounced as the enemies of God, the Prophet appears to have been by nature of a kind and even an affectionate temperament, and was particularly devoted to children. He was not by any means of a martial disposition and took little interest in military operations.

The portions of the Qoran revealed in Mecca during the years of failure and persecution bear the marks of genuine and deep emotion. In later life, however, whether he so desired or not, he found himself transformed into a politician and a ruler, and the later chapters of the Qoran consist to an increasing extent of laws and administrative matters.

The mystery of the extraordinary enthusiasm provoked by Islam at the time of its appearance can only be explained by reference to the personality of the Prophet himself. Whatever qualities he may have possessed or whatever actions he may have performed, there can be no doubt that there was something about him which inspired in his followers a passionate devotion.

*   *   *

When Muhammad died in June 632, his closest friend and confidant, a certain Abu Bekr, was acknowledged as his successor, though not without opposition, for the Apostle had left no instructions regarding the leadership after his death. The fact that, to many Arabs, Islam meant Muhammad and little more, is emphasized by the fact that, as soon as his death became known, the great majority of the tribes renounced their allegiance. This revolt against Islam is known in history as the Apostasy. Abu Bekr, a frail little old man with a slight stoop, nevertheless rose to the occasion. Summoning all loyal Muslims to his banner, he despatched a force of some four thousand men into Central Arabia, under the command of a veteran Quraish warrior, Khalid

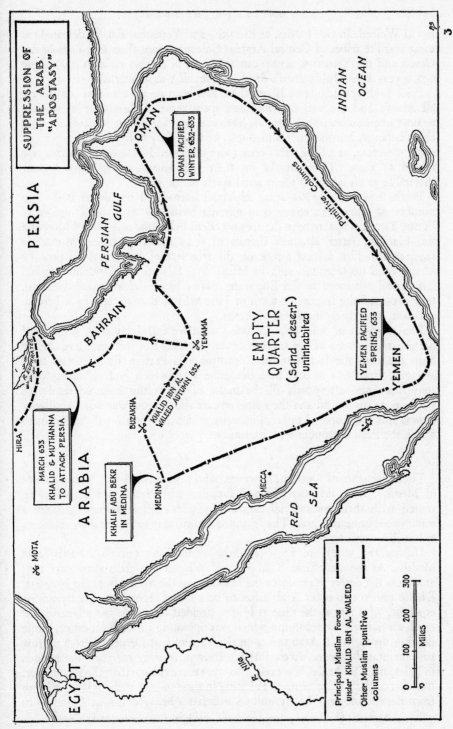

SUPPRESSION OF
THE ARAB
"APOSTASY"

PERSIA

INDIAN OCEAN

OMAN

OMAN PACIFIED
WINTER, 652-635

PERSIAN GULF

Punitive Columns

BAHRAIN

EMPTY QUARTER
(Sand desert)
uninhabited

R. EUPHRATES

HIRA

MARCH 633
KHALID & MUTHANNA
TO ATTACK PERSIA

YEMAMA

KHALID IBN AL
WALEED AUTUMN 632

BUZAKHA

YEMEN PACIFIED
SPRING, 633

YEMEN

ARABIA

KHALIF ABU BEKR
IN MEDINA

MEDINA

MECCA

RED SEA

MOTA

EGYPT

Nile

Principal Muslim force
under KHALID IBN AL WALEED

Other Muslim punitive
columns

0   100   200   300
Miles

ibn al Waleed. In two battles, at Buzakha and Yemama, Khalid defeated the most warlike tribes of Central Arabia. Columns were then sent to Bahrain, Oman and the Yemen to stamp out any signs of further resistance. By June 633, a year after Muhammad's death, the revolt was at an end.

Prior to the preaching of Islam, there had been no government controlling all Arabia and the various tribes had spent most of their time in warfare against one another. Muhammad, however, had forbidden Muslims to fight other believers but had proclaimed it to be their duty to fight the heathen. As soon, therefore, as all the tribes once more professed Islam, tribal warfare was bound to cease. Thus attacks on their non-Muslim neighbours became inevitable as an outlet to the martial spirit of the tribes.

In the lower Euphrates area, the Arab nomads of the desert had for a number of years been engaged in guerilla hostilities with the Kingdom of Persia. The principal tribe in the area was Beni Bekr, under its chief Muthanna ibn Haritha. After Khalid's defeats of the "apostate" tribes, Muthanna suggested to him a joint attack on the frontiers of Persia. Abu Bekr, the khalif,[3] had no objection and, in March 633, Khalid and Muthanna joined hands and advanced to the Euphrates. After twice defeating the Persians, they captured the important town of Hira which, though held by a Persian garrison, was largely inhabited by Arabs.

Persia, which in those days included what we call today Iraq, was one of the greatest Powers of the seventh century world. But reference has already been made to the fact that the Byzantine and Persian Empires had been engaged, from 602 to 628, in a desperate war, which had exhausted both countries. Soon afterwards all the males of the ruling Sassanid family of Persia were massacred and the whole empire slipped into chaos and civil war. It was this condition of internal anarchy which had permitted the Arabs to attack the Persian frontier with impunity.

*   *   *

The merchants of Quraish, however, who now formed the "government" in Medina, were interested in and familiar with Syria, which they often visited with their commercial caravans, whereas Persia seemed to them a remote and unknown area. They decided accordingly to devote their resources to hostilities against Byzantium.

During the winter of 633–634, three columns set out northwards from Medina. At the same time Khalid ibn al Waleed was ordered to leave Iraq and cross the desert to reinforce the Muslims on the Syrian front. In May 634, Khalid joined two other Arab columns near Deraa. Heraclius, the Byzantine emperor, who was at the time at Homs, decided to assume the offensive and crush an isolated Arab column which was operating in south Palestine, while holding up the main Arab forces on the Yarmouk at Deraa, where a narrow pass facilitated defence. Accordingly a Byzantine army marched southwards to Palestine. The Arabs, however, who were more mobile than the Byzantines, transferred their main army to Palestine in time to save their isolated column from destruction and the Byzantines suffered a heavy defeat at Ajnadain in

3. The word khalif merely means successor, that is, the successor of Muhammad.

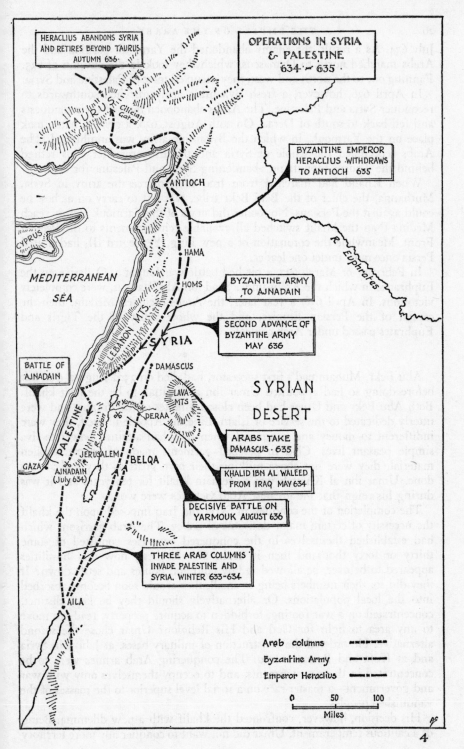

OPERATIONS IN SYRIA
& PALESTINE
634 ~ 635

HERACLIUS ABANDONS SYRIA
AND RETIRES BEYOND TAURUS
AUTUMN 636.

TAURUS MTS.

Cilician Gates

ANTIOCH

BYZANTINE EMPEROR
HERACLIUS WITHDRAWS
TO ANTIOCH 635

CYPRUS

MEDITERRANEAN
SEA

HAMA

HOMS

BYZANTINE ARMY
TO AJNADAIN

LEBANON MTS.

SYRIA

SECOND ADVANCE OF
BYZANTINE ARMY
MAY 636

DAMASCUS

BATTLE OF
AJNADAIN

LAVA
MTS.

SYRIAN

DESERT

R. Euphrates

PALESTINE

R. Yarmouk

DERAA

R. Jordan

ARABS TAKE
DAMASCUS · 635

JERUSALEM

BELQA

KHALID IBN AL WALEED
FROM IRAQ MAY 634

GAZA

AJNADAIN
(July 634)

DECISIVE BATTLE ON
YARMOUK AUGUST 636

THREE ARAB COLUMNS
INVADE PALESTINE AND
SYRIA, WINTER 633-634

AILA

Arab columns
Byzantine Army
Emperor Heraclius

0   50   100

Miles

4

July 634. As a result, the enemy abandoned the Yarmouk position and the Arabs marched north to Damascus, which they took in the autumn of 635. Fanning out to the north and west, they occupied most of Palestine and Syria.

In April 636, however, a fresh Byzantine army marched southwards to reconquer Syria and Palestine. The Arabs abandoned most of their conquests and fell back to south of Deraa. On 20th August, 636, a general battle took place on the Yarmouk, in which the Byzantine army was annihilated. The Arabs reoccupied the whole of Syria and the Emperor Heraclius retired behind the Taurus mountains, abandoning Syria and Palestine for ever.

When Khalid had marched from Iraq to reinforce the army in Syria, Muthanna, the chief of the Beni Bekr tribe, was left to carry on as best he could against the Persians. No sooner did news of the Yarmouk victory reach Medina than the khalif switched all available reinforcements to the Persian Front. Meanwhile the coronation of a new king, Yezdegird III, had united Persia once more under one leader.

In February or March 637, a pitched battle was fought at Qadasiya on the Euphrates, in which the Arabs under Saad ibn Abi Waqqas, were completely victorious. In April 638, a year later, the Arabs occupied Medain, then the capital of the Persian Empire, and the whole valley of the Tigris and Euphrates passed under Arab control.

*   *   *

Abu Bekr, Muhammad's first successor, had died on 23rd August, 634, but before doing so had appointed Umar ibn al Khattab to be the next khalif. Both Abu Bekr and Umar had been close intimates of the Prophet and were utterly dedicated to the service of Islam. Like the Apostle himself, they were indifferent to money and continued when they had attained power to live simple peasant lives. Clad in patched garments made of coarse woollen material, they were not above milking their own goats as they had always done. Umar ibn al Khattab was to remain khalif for ten years and it was during his reign that the greatest Arab victories were won.

The completion of the conquest of Syria and Iraq imposed upon the khalif the necessity of certain major decisions of policy. The Arab garrisons which had established themselves in the conquered countries consisted of some thirty or forty thousand men in each. Should these, now that hostilities appeared to be over, be allowed to buy land and houses and settle down? If they did so, their numbers being so small, they would soon become absorbed into the local populations. Or alternatively should they be kept distinct, concentrated on a war footing, forbidden to acquire property, ready to move to any area to fight for God and His Religion? Umar chose the second alternative. He ordered the construction of military bases, at Jabiya in Syria and at Kufa and Basra in Iraq. The conquering Arab armies were to be concentrated in these cantonments, and to occupy themselves only with war and government—a master-race on a social level superior to the masses of the vanquished peoples.

His decision, however, confronted the khalif with a new dilemma. Being of a cautious temperament, Umar did not want to conquer any more territory

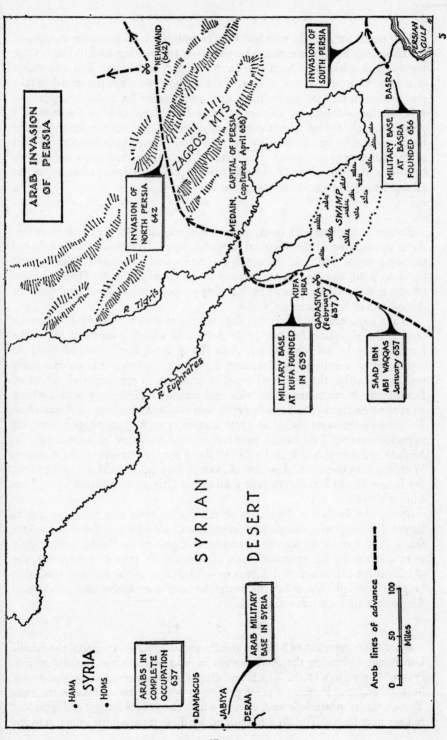

ARAB INVASION OF PERSIA

INVASION OF SOUTH PERSIA

INVASION OF NORTH PERSIA 642

NEHAWAND (642)

ZAGROS MTS

MEDAIN, CAPITAL OF PERSIA (captured April 658)

PERSIAN GULF

BASRA

MILITARY BASE AT BASRA FOUNDED 656

R Tigris

SWAMP

KUFA

HIRA

QADASIYA (February 657)

MILITARY BASE AT KUFA FOUNDED IN 659

SAAD IBN ABI WAQQAS January 657

R Euphrates

SYRIAN   DESERT

SYRIA

HAMA

HOMS

ARABS IN COMPLETE OCCUPATION 637

DAMASCUS

JABIYA

DERAA

ARAB MILITARY BASE IN SYRIA

Arab lines of advance ▪▪▪▪

0   50   100

Miles

at least until that already won had been consolidated. Hitherto the plunder of the conquests had been divided between the troops after each battle, except for one-fifth which had been sent to the treasury in Medina. But a cessation of conquest meant the end of loot. If the soldiers were not permitted to take part in commerce or agriculture, they must needs be paid, an operation necessitating a census of all the Arabs, a formidable task in the case of a people scarcely any of whom could read or write. The money for the pay of the army was to be obtained by the collection of a poll-tax from every man of the conquered provinces. If a man of the vanquished races voluntarily became a Muslim, he was to be excused the poll-tax but no pressure was put on the defeated peoples to adopt Islam.

*   *   *

Roman power had been based on the naval command of the Mediterranean. After the collapse of the Western Roman Empire, Byzantium had continued the same naval tradition. Although the Arabs had conquered Palestine and Syria on land, the Byzantine fleet continued to cruise in the Mediterranean off the coasts of these provinces. For this purpose, it possessed land bases at Alexandria in Egypt and in Cyprus.

At the beginning of December 639, a force of about 3,500 Arab tribesmen crossed the Egyptian frontier at Al Arish and set off westwards across the Sinai Peninsula. Its commander, Amr ibn al Aasi, had previously been in command of a column in Palestine. Egypt, at the time, was an extremely wealthy country, the principal supplier of grain to the imperial capital of Byzantium. It contained many rich and ancient walled cities, and a strong Byzantine garrison, while the imperial fleet lay in the harbour of Alexandria. To attempt the conquest of so great a country with 3,500 ragged bedouins appeared insane. The khalif, however, raised an army of 12,000 men in Medina and despatched it under Zubair ibn Awwam to reinforce the invaders. With some 15,000 men, Amr ibn al Aasi in July 640 fought a battle against the Byzantines at Heliopolis, now a suburb of Cairo, and inflicted upon them a heavy defeat.

Cyrus, the Orthodox Patriarch of Alexandria, was also the governor of Egypt. He adopted a completely defeatist attitude and concluded with Amr ibn al Aasi a draft agreement to surrender Egypt to the Arabs, subject only to ratification by the emperor. Soon afterwards, on 11th February, 641, the old Emperor Heraclius died. Cyrus took advantage of the ensuing confusion to push through his policy of surrender and the Arabs finally occupied Alexandria in September 642.

*   *   *

After the occupation of Medain, the Persian capital, in April 638, the Khalif Umar had forbidden the Arab armies in Iraq to cross the mountains into Persia. The valleys of the Tigris and Euphrates were enough for the Arabs, he said, and the Persians were welcome to keep the mountains to the east. Three years of peace followed, during which the young King Yezdegird was raising new forces. The Arabs, alarmed by these reports of military activity,

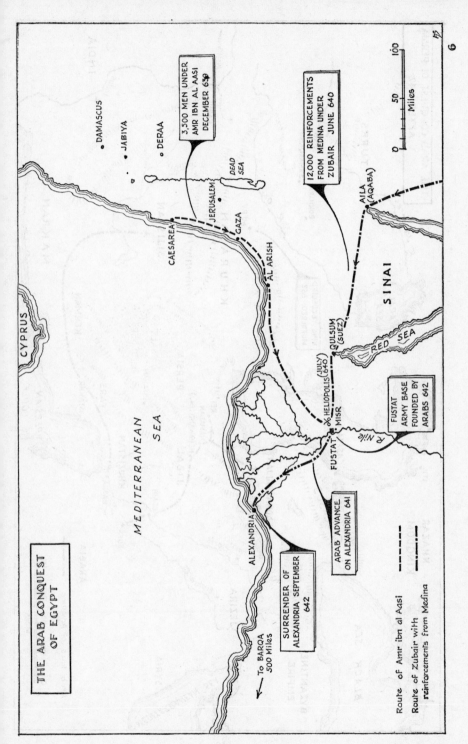

THE ARAB CONQUEST OF EGYPT

3,500 MEN UNDER AMR IBN AL AASI DECEMBER 639

12,000 REINFORCEMENTS FROM MEDINA UNDER ZUBAIR JUNE 640

FUSTAT ARMY BASE FOUNDED BY ARABS 642

ARAB ADVANCE ON ALEXANDRIA 641

SURRENDER OF ALEXANDRIA SEPTEMBER 642

CYPRUS

MEDITERRANEAN SEA

DAMASCUS
JABIYA
DERAA
DEAD SEA
JERUSALEM
CAESAREA
GAZA
AL ARISH

SINAI

AILA (AQABA)

RED SEA

QULSUM (SUEZ)

HELIOPOLIS (JULY) 640
MISR
FUSTAT

R. Nile

ALEXANDRIA

To BARQA 500 Miles

Miles
0   50   100

Route of Amr ibn al Aasi
Route of Zubair with reinforcements from Medina

29

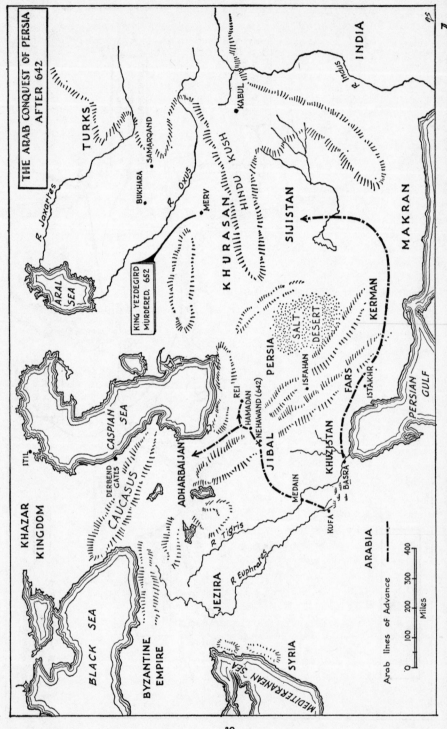

THE ARAB CONQUEST OF PERSIA
AFTER 642

TURKS

ARAL SEA

R. Jaxartes

R. Oxus

SAMARQAND

BUKHARA

MERV

KHURASAN

HINDU KUSH

KABUL

INDIA

R. Indus

KING YEZDEGIRD
MURDERED. 652

SALT DESERT

PERSIA

ISFAHAN

SIJISTAN

MAKRAN

KHAZAR KINGDOM

ITIL

CASPIAN SEA

DERBEND GATES

CAUCASUS

ADHARBAIJAN

REI

HAMADAN

NEHAWAND (642)

JIBAL

KERMAN

FARS

ISTĀKHR

PERSIAN GULF

BLACK SEA

BYZANTINE EMPIRE

R. Tigris

JEZIRA

R. Euphrates

MEDAIN

KUFA

KHUZISTAN

BASRA

ARABIA

MEDITERRANEAN SEA

SYRIA

Arab lines of Advance

0   100   200   300   400
Miles

appealed to the khalif for permission to destroy the new Persian army before it invaded Iraq. In 642, they crossed the Zagros mountains and defeated Yezdegird's army in a great battle at Nehawand. Never again was the King of Kings to put an army in the field against the Arabs. Abandoning the cautious policy to which he had hitherto adhered, the khalif ordered his armies to pursue the defeated Persians wherever they fled. A year later, the Arabs reached the shores of the Caspian, while in the south they pushed steadily forward, taking Isfahan, Fars, Kerman and advancing towards Khurasan. King Yezdegird fled from place to place before them, being finally assassinated in 652 at Merv in Khurasan. Eight centuries were to pass before Persia was able once more to crown a king of her own.

* * *

On 3rd November, 644, the Khalif Umar ibn al Khattab was assassinated by a Persian slave in Medina. As he lay dying, he nominated five leading Muslims as an electoral committee to choose his successor.

It will be remembered that, for several generations before Muhammad, the leadership of Quraish had been in dispute between the clans of Beni Umaiya and Beni Hashim, the Prophet himself belonging to the latter. When he began to preach, he was in general supported by Beni Hashim, while the principal opposition was provided by Beni Umaiya, under their chief, Abu Sofian. When Muhammad captured Mecca and became the virtual ruler of Arabia, Beni Umaiya accepted Islam and secured a number of lucrative posts in the government. In the general atmosphere of religious fervour the old parochial rivalries seemed to have been forgotten.

Abu Bekr and Umar, the Prophet's two immediate successors, were men utterly devoted to religion and belonged to minor clans of the tribe of Quraish. The five men chosen by the dying Umar to elect his successor were of course all of Quraish but unfortunately the only two serious candidates were one of Beni Umaiya and one of Beni Hashim. Othman ibn Affan of Beni Umaiya had been one of Muhammad's first converts and had successively married two of his daughters. Ali ibn abi Talib was a cousin of the Apostle but, being much younger than he was, had been brought up almost as his own son in Muhammad's house, for the Prophet had no son of his own. He also had married one of Muhammad's daughters. Consequently both Othman and Ali possessed many qualifications to succeed him, both being among his first converts and both having married daughters of his. After long and heated debates, Othman was eventually acclaimed as the new khalif.

During the twelve years of Othman's reign (644–656), the Arab conquests continued, though in a manner slightly less sensational than in the reign of Umar. In Africa, the Muslims carried their arms as far as Tripoli in North Africa but failing to consolidate their hold on that area, established a firm frontier at Barqa. In the north, they reached the snow-covered barrier of the Caucasus. On the east, the whole of Persia was occupied as far as Samarqand and Bukhara beyond the Oxus and up to the Hindu Kush and the Indus, on the frontiers of ancient India. On the west—an even more startling develop-

GENEALOGICAL TREE OF QURAISH

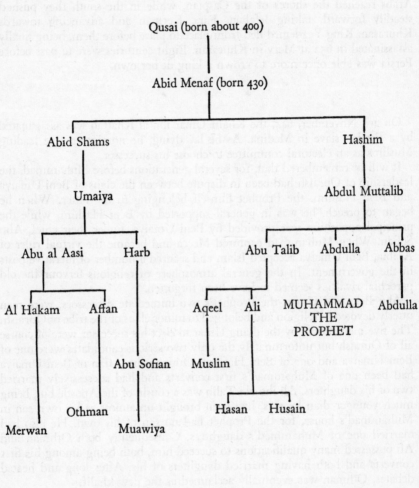

Qusai (born about 400)

Abid Menaf (born 430)

Abid Shams   Hashim

Umaiya   Abdul Muttalib

Abu al Aasi   Harb   Abu Talib   Abdulla   Abbas

Al Hakam   Affan   Aqeel   Ali   MUHAMMAD   Abdulla
                                  THE
                            PROPHET

Abu Sofian   Muslim

Othman   Hasan   Husain

Merwan   Muawiya

BENI UMAIYA   BENI HASHIM

ment—they took to the sea. Building fleets in Egypt and in Syria, they captured Cyprus and defeated the Byzantine fleet in a succession of naval engagements. As has already been stated, Roman, and later Byzantine, supremacy had been built up on sea power in the Mediterranean. The loss of the command of that sea was perhaps the heaviest blow which Byzantium had hitherto received from the Arabs.

While, however, during the khalifate of Othman, the Arabs continued victorious, internal rivalries commenced to divide the new empire at home. It will be remembered that the Khalif Umar had decided that the conquering Arabs were not to acquire land or engage in trade in the occupied provinces but were to remain as a separate imperial race, living on pensions in military cities established for the purpose at Jabiya in Syria, at Kufa and Basra in Iraq, and at Fustat in Egypt. With the gradual slowing down of the pace of conquest, the soldiers lay idle and unemployed in their cantonments. Muhammad had permitted the use of captured women as the wives or concubines of the victorious Muslims, whom the plunder of their amazing victories had made rich. Living thus in luxurious idleness, the formerly lean and hardy tribesmen became haughty, undisciplined praetorians, constantly engaged in intrigues and disorders. When several garrisons complained against their commanders, the weak Othman hastened to dismiss the generals in order to gain the favour of the troops, thus only adding to the spirit of arrogance and discontent. Religious fervour, moreover, which had supplied the driving force of the early conquests, was already beginning to cool. The chief complaint made against Othman, however, was to the effect that he placed his relatives of Beni Umaiya in all the most important and lucrative appointments.

In 654, the old khalif reached the age of eighty. The cantonments at Kufa, Basra and Fustat were seething with discontent. The troops in Syria alone were well disciplined and loyal. Muawiya, the son of Abu Sofian, once Muhammad's principal opponent, was governor of that province, to which he had been appointed by Umar ibn al Khattab fourteen years earlier. During this long period of office, he had won the enthusiastic loyalty of the people as well as of the army. He had not adhered to Umar's policy of isolating the Arab garrison from the native inhabitants. He had established his capital in Damascus, not in the military cantonment of Jabiya, and had thereby integrated his administration and the army with the population of Syria.

Early in 656, the spirit of mutiny in the camps of Fustat, Kufa and Basra came to a head, and detachments from each of the three garrisons marched on Medina. Entering the city, they established themselves in the great mosque in the centre of the town and besieged the khalif in his house. Four members of the electoral committee which had chosen Othman were present at the time in Medina. Ali ibn abi Talib, the cousin and virtually the adopted son of the Prophet, was the most prominent of them. But while these elders were lavish in their advice to the bewildered old khalif, they made no attempt to rescue him from the mutineers.

As soon as Muawiya in Damascus heard that Othman was besieged in his house, he sent a relief column to his rescue. When this force was one hundred and fifty miles from Medina, the mutineers decided to make an end. Breaking into the house, they slashed the old man to death with their swords, as he sat quietly reading the Qoran.

The murder of Othman by Arab troops changed everything in the Muslim world. For twenty-five years the Arabs had lived in an enthusiastic dream. They were God's chosen people, destined to conquer the whole world and subject it to the divine rule. The Prophet and his two successors were divinely appointed instruments of God's will, fervid, dedicated, indifferent to wealth or comfort. But with the murder of Othman, the religious dream was shattered, and the greedy, raiding days before Islam had returned once more.

*   *   *

Six days after the murder of Othman, Ali ibn abi Talib was acclaimed khalif in Medina. Everybody had criticized Othman during his lifetime but now that he had been brutally done to death, a reaction set in. Demands were heard everywhere for the punishment of the murderers. One of the chief complaints against Othman had been to the effect that all the provincial governors chosen by him had been his near relatives from Beni Umaiya. But Ali was from Beni Hashim. He could not have been accused of nepotism if he had left Othman's governors in office, at least for a time. Instead of doing so, however, he immediately dismissed them all. Muawiya, however, refused to resign his post. His province of Syria stood solidly behind him and his army was loyal and well disciplined. Ali was unable to evict him.

Muawiya was of Beni Umaiya and Ali was of Beni Hashim. Thus between the new khalif and his insubordinate governor the old feud between the two clans seemed about to revive. Muawiya, however, did not at first openly rebel. He merely demanded that the murderers of Othman be punished. Ali's neglect to avenge the blood of his predecessor soon led to accusations of collusion with the murderers. Two other members of the electoral committee which had chosen Othman, namely Zubair and Talha, disappeared from Medina, and raising some three thousand men in Mecca, marched across the Arabian peninsula to Basra, where they raised the standard of revolt. Ostensibly their complaint was that Ali refused to punish the murderers of Othman, but actually both were doubtless inspired by private ambition. Ali, after some difficulty in raising the necessary troops, followed them. A battle, known in Arab history as the Battle of the Camel, was fought outside Basra in December 656, the rebels were defeated and Zubair and Talha were killed.

Having disposed of Zubair and Talha, Ali marched to Kufa, where he established his headquarters, and summoned Muawiya once more to swear allegiance to him. The governor of Syria again declared his readiness to do so, as soon as the murderers of Othman had been punished. Seeing that negotiation was vain, Ali marched on Syria with 50,000 men. At Siffeen, he met Muawiya at the head of an army of equal strength. In the middle of July 657, all attempts to find a compromise having failed, the two armies joined battle.

For two days the carnage continued without reaching a decisive result, but on the third day victory seemed to be within Ali's grasp. Then Muawiya made use of a stratagem. A detachment of cavalry rode out from the Syrian

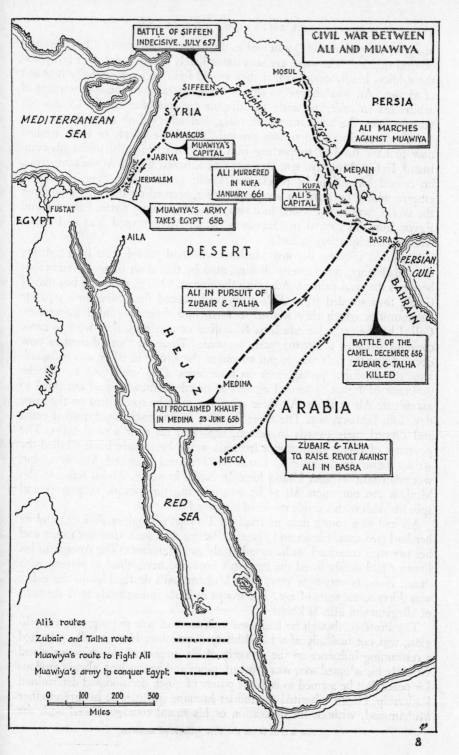

CIVIL WAR BETWEEN
ALI AND MUAWIYA

BATTLE OF SIFFEEN
INDECISIVE. JULY 657

MEDITERRANEAN
SEA

PERSIA

SYRIA

MOSUL

SIFFEEN

R. Euphrates

R. Tigris

ALI MARCHES
AGAINST MUAWIYA

DAMASCUS

MUAWIYA'S
CAPITAL

JABIYA

PALESTINE

JERUSALEM

MEDAIN

ALI MURDERED
IN KUFA
JANUARY 661

KUFA

ALI'S
CAPITAL

I R A Q

FUSTAT

EGYPT

MUAWIYA'S ARMY
TAKES EGYPT 658

AILA

BASRA

DESERT

PERSIAN
GULF

BAHRAIN

ALI IN PURSUIT OF
ZUBAIR & TALHA

H E J A Z

R. Nile

BATTLE OF THE
CAMEL. DECEMBER 656
ZUBAIR & TALHA
KILLED

MEDINA

A R A B I A

ALI PROCLAIMED KHALIF
IN MEDINA 23 JUNE 656

ZUBAIR & TALHA
TO RAISE REVOLT AGAINST
ALI IN BASRA

MECCA

RED
SEA

Ali's routes
Zubair and Talha route
Muawiya's route to fight Ali
Muawiya's army to conquer Egypt

0   100   200   300
Miles

8

35

army with copies of the Qoran tied to their lances, and crying, "Let the word of God decide." The same cry was immediately taken up by Ali's army and the soldiers loudly declared that they would fight no longer. At the moment of victory, Ali was obliged to sign a truce, agreeing to the appointment of arbitrators in order to settle the dispute by reference to the Qoran. Six months later, the arbitration took place, but achieved no decisive result.

Ali's cause continued to lose ground. The fickle people of Kufa seemed now to have tired of supporting him and refused to enlist under his command. In 658, Muawiya sent an army and annexed Egypt. At the same time, he caused himself to be proclaimed khalif in Jerusalem. The new Arab empire which, only five or six years earlier, seemed on the way to conquer the world, was now divided into two, Muawiya ruling Syria, Palestine and Egypt from his capital in Damascus, while Ali governed Iraq and Persia from his headquarters in Kufa.

Many old soldiers, devoted Muslims who had passed their lives fighting the unbelievers, were utterly disillusioned by this clash of world ambitions between the rival princes. Adopting the slogan, "No government but that of God", they seceded from Ali's army and banded themselves into separate communities which they wished to form into divinely guided theocracies. Called by the orthodox Muslims Kharijites or outsiders, they were to cause constant troubles for many years to come. Three of these dissenters now decided that the only way to put an end to the schism in Islam was to assassinate the principal protagonists on both sides. One undertook to kill the governor of Egypt, a second agreed to murder Muawiya and the third to assassinate Ali in Kufa. All three crimes were to be committed on the same day, 20th January, 661. The three fanatics, having exchanged mutual oaths and dipped their swords in poison, separated on their several tasks. The governor of Egypt escaped scot free, his would-be assassin having killed the wrong man. In Damascus, Burak al Temeemi attacked Muawiya, but wounded him without killing him. In Kufa, however, Abdul Rahman ibn Muljam ran out upon Ali as he was entering the mosque to prayers and split his skull with a single stroke of his sword.

Ali had as a young man married the Prophet's daughter Fatima,[4] and by her had two sons, Hasan and Husain. Fatima died soon after her father and her two sons remained Muhammad's only two grandsons. The Apostle in his lifetime had dearly loved the two little boys and never tired of playing with them. Now, twenty-nine years after Muhammad's death, Hasan, the elder, was thirty-seven years of age. The troops in Kufa immediately took the oath of allegiance to him as khalif.

The Prophet, though he had used violence and war to propagate his religion, was not basically of a bloodthirsty disposition. He normally exercised a restraining influence on the savagery of his supporters. Ali, his cousin and virtually his adopted son, was prudent, pious and benevolent, always anxious for peace, but he seemed to lack the power of quick decision and determined leadership. Hasan inherited the milder humane qualities of his grandfather Muhammad, without his dedication or his moral courage. Faced with the

4. The accent is on the first syllable—Faatimma.

prospect of civil war against Muawiya, he decided to abdicate and retired with his younger brother Husain to a life of seclusion in Medina. There he died, eight years later.

* * *

Muhammad had died in 632, the acknowledged ruler of the Arabian peninsula. In the twenty-five years following his death, the hitherto backward Arabians burst out of their native deserts to overthrow simultaneously the two greatest military empires of their world, Byzantium and Persia. They deprived the Byzantines of two-thirds of their territories, while they annihilated the kingdom of Persia.

The Arab tribesman was bred to raiding and war, while the hardship of life in the desert had inured him to privation and exhaustion. But before Islam his military virtues had been expended in unending internal wars of tribe against tribe. Muhammad not only united the people of Arabia but he also fired them with a passionate and devoted enthusiasm which made them unconquerable. This fervid spirit seems to have been imbibed by his companions directly from the Apostle himself. Thirty years after his death, few survived of those who had known him in person. In the second generation of Muslims the pristine fervour of the companions had cooled. The enjoyment of great wealth, the indulgence in luxury, wives and concubines, had introduced a worldly atmosphere. Old tribal feuds came to life again and the pre-Islamic life of murder and robbery seemed to be about to return.

Apart from this general cooling off of pious devotion, the new empire faced a number of peculiar problems. Muhammad had left no instructions in regard to the succession. Abu Bekr, the first successor, had been elected by the acclamation of a number of people who happened to be present at the critical moment in Medina. On his deathbed, Abu Bekr had nominated Umar ibn al Khattab. When the latter was murdered, he succeeded before dying in naming the members of an electoral committee to choose his successor. The electors, not without considerable and heated discussion, chose Othman to the exclusion of Ali. Thus, of the three first khalifs, no two had been appointed in the same manner.

The assassination of Ali caused the whole empire to fall under the control of Muawiya, but it did so *de facto* rather than *de jure*. The strongest precedent which existed for the selection of a khalif was that of acclamation by the people of Medina. Both Abu Bekr and Ali had been chosen in this manner, but half the empire had subsequently rejected Ali. In any case, Muawiya moved the capital to Damascus and Medina thereafter became merely a provincial town, with the result that acclamation by the people of Medina was no longer a practicable manner of selection. This difficulty of ensuring a peaceful method of succession was to haunt the Arab Empire throughout the whole of its existence.

A second problem which confronted the Arabs in 661 was that of the insubordinate soldiery whom the Khalif Umar had collected in great military cantonments, isolated from the civil population. This difficulty was ultimately overcome by abandoning the policy of Umar and by allowing the Arabs to engage in commerce, to acquire land and to mix with the populations of the conquered countries. Such a development was doubtless an improvement on a situation in which armies of arrogant soldiers terrorized the empire or engaged in civil wars against one another, but it led in other directions to the disadvantages which Umar had perhaps foreseen when he decided to keep the Arabs as a race apart.

The almost miraculous early Arab conquests had been carried out purely by the people of the Arabian peninsula. These had a certain affinity with the populations living along the Euphrates and east of the Jordan, areas into which Central Arabians had infiltrated for many centuries. But the peoples of the Arabian peninsula bore virtually no racial relationship to the populations of Egypt and of the coastal districts of Palestine and Lebanon. Indeed their qualities often appeared diametrically opposed to one another. The Central Arabians were extremely hardy and warlike, mentally straightforward, simple-minded and direct. The coastal populations of the Eastern Mediterranean were, on the contrary, intellectual, refined, subtle, flexible but with little inclination to military service. The free intermixture and intermarriage of the two inevitably led to the loss of the supreme military virtues of the Central Arabians, whose numbers were extremely small in proportion to the populations of the conquered territories.

The third problem which confronted the new Arab empire in 661 was that of the weakening of religious enthusiasm. The extraordinary conquests of the first twenty-five years after Muhammad's death had been made possible by intense religious fervour and the simple minded belief that those killed in wars against the unbelievers were immediately transported to Paradise. The intensity of this religious fervour was due almost entirely to the personality of the Prophet himself. Thirty years after his death, a new generation had grown up, which had obtained its religious inspiration second-hand. Moreover, whereas the Prophet's Companions had won their way to victory through many dangers, the younger generation had grown up in wealth and luxury. Intermixture with the sophisticated populations of the Byzantine and Persian empires had also done much to introduce that more worldly outlook, which the Khalif Umar had dreaded when he decreed the continued segregation of the Arab race.

We may thus perhaps divide the period with which we are dealing into three stages. Firstly the years of religious enthusiasm and miraculous conquests, extending from the death of Muhammad in 632 for twenty-four years until 656, when Othman was murdered. Then the period of the civil wars, which marked the transition from the fervour of a theocracy to the routine of an ordinary civil state. Finally, in stage three, the Arab Empire became a worldly Great Power, similar to the Roman and Persian Empires before it or to the Turkish, Spanish or British which followed its decline and collapse.

NOTABLE DATES

Flight of Muhammad to Medina	622
Muhammad's conquest of Mecca	630

Death of the Prophet Muhammad	632
Year of the Apostasy	632–633
Battle of the Yarmouk and final conquest of Syria	636
Battle of Nehawand and final defeat of Persia	642
Occupation of Alexandria and final conquest of Egypt	642
Assassination of the Khalif Othman	656
Civil war between Ali and Muawiya	656–661
Assassination of Ali, leaving Muawiya sole khalif	661

PERSONALITIES

The Prophet Muhammad
His first four successors

Abu Bekr	632–634
Umar ibn al Khattab	634–644
Othman ibn Affan	644–656
Ali ibn abi Talib	656–661

Muawiya ibn abi Sofian, first khalif of Beni Umaiya
Abu Sofian, head of the Beni Umaiya clan and the strongest
    opponent of Muhammad
Yezdegird III, the last Sassanid King of Persia
Heraclius, Emperor of Byzantium

For a general chronology of the whole period of this book see Appendix
II, page 367.

II

The Tragedy of Kerbela

In a distant age and climate, the tragic scene of the death of Husain will awaken the sympathy of the coldest reader.

GIBBON, *Decline and Fall of the Roman Empire*

One by one the defenders fell, until at last there remained but the grandson of the Prophet. Faint with loss of blood, he soon sank to the ground and the murderous crew rushed upon the dying hero.

AMEER ALI, *A Short History of the Saracens*

Those who would slay the prophets unjustly and kill those among men who enjoin justice, announce to them a painful chastisement. *Qoran* III, 20

II

THE TRAGEDY OF KERBELA

THE assassination of Ali and the subsequent abdication of his eldest son Hasan removed all opposition to Muawiya. Beni Hashim had no other serious candidate available and Beni Umaiya exercised undisputed sovereignty from their capital in Damascus. In Medina the tradition of religious fervour and devotion to the memory of the Apostle still persisted but without the military power to assert a claim to the khalifate. The situation was not without irony, for Beni Umaiya, under the leadership of Abu Sofian, had been the bitterest opponents of the Prophet and of Islam. The empire had been conquered by the religious fervour of the Muslims, but now the former enemies of religion had become the rulers of that empire.

No sooner was Muawiya firmly established in the khalifate than military activity was resumed. In North Africa, the Arabs under Uqba ibn Nafi pushed westwards as far as modern Tunis, and in 670 founded a great military base at Qairawan, on lines similar to Fustat, Kufa and Basra. At sea there was even greater activity, for Muawiya had conceived the idea of capturing Byzantium itself and thereby finally destroying the Byzantine empire, as that of Persia had been destroyed. In the year 670, an Arab fleet sailed through the Dardanelles unopposed and laid siege to the city of Constantinople [1] itself. In 672, an Arab fleet captured Rhodes, doubtless as an advanced base for the operations against Byzantium. Further west, Arab fleets twice raided Sicily. After a seven years' siege, however, the Arabs in 677 abandoned their fruitless attacks on the walls of Byzantium.

In the East, the Muslims had, in the khalifate of Othman, borne their triumphant banners across the Hindu Kush and had taken Kabul.[2] During the five years of civil war between Muawiya and Ali, however, Kabul had successfully revolted and several frontier fortresses had been lost. During Muawiya's reign the frontier position in the east was fully re-established. This was largely the result of the genius of one great man. Zayyad was the son of Sumaiya, a notoriously promiscuous slave girl of Mecca. His paternity being unknown, he was commonly called Zayyad the son-of-his-father. Having learnt to read and write as a boy—a rare accomplishment at the time in Arabia—he went as a clerk to the army of Basra at the time of the conquests, taking the trouble also to master Persian. By capability and diligence he worked his way to the top and was appointed by Ali to be governor of South Persia with his capital at the ancient Persepolis, called by the Arabs, Istakhr.[2]

After the murder of Ali, Muawiya won over Zayyad to the Umaiyid cause

1. Byzantium and Constantinople are alternative names for the same city. The Turks now call it Istanbul.
2. Map 7, page 30.

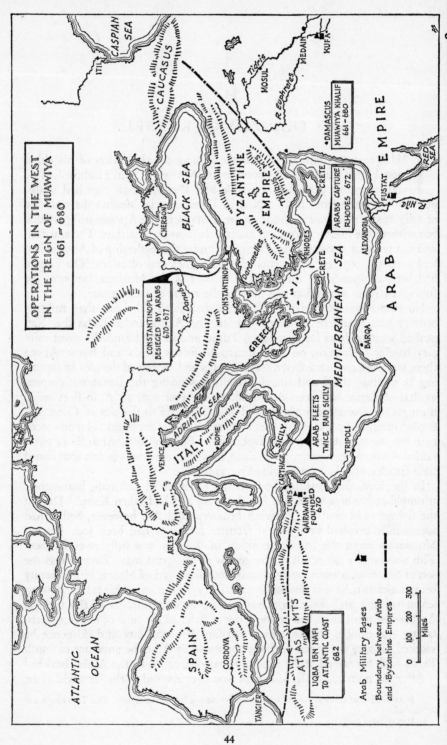

OPERATIONS IN THE WEST
IN THE REIGN OF MUAWIYA
661 – 680

CASPIAN SEA

ITIL

CAUCASUS

CHERSON

BLACK SEA

R. Tigris
R. Euphrates
MOSUL
MEDAIN
KUFA

DAMASCUS
MUAWIYA KHALIF
661 – 680

BYZANTINE EMPIRE

Taurus

Cardanelles
CONSTANTINOPLE

R. Danube

CONSTANTINOPLE
BESIEGED BY ARABS
670 – 677

GREECE

CRETE
RHODES

ARABS CAPTURE
RHODES 672

ADRIATIC SEA

VENICE

ITALY

ROME

MEDITERRANEAN SEA

ALEXANDRIA

FUSTAT

RED SEA

R. Nile

ARAB EMPIRE

BÁRQA

TRIPOLI

Sicily

ARAB FLEETS
TWICE RAID SICILY

CARTHAGE
TUNIS
QAIRAWAN
FOUNDED
670

ATLANTIC OCEAN

SPAIN

CORDOVA

TANGIER

ATLAS MTS

UQBA IBN NAFI
TO ATLANTIC COAST
682

ARLES

Arab Military Bases
Boundary between Arab
and Byzantine Empires

0   100   200   300
Miles

44

by the remarkable device of recognizing him as his brother. Claiming that his old father Abu Sofian, Muhammad's bitter enemy, had patronized the immoral Sumaiya, he admitted the governor of South Persia to the patronymic of Zayyad ibn abi Sofian, and confirmed him in his appointment and later made him governor of Kufa, Basra and the whole of Persia, half the total area of the empire. A man of quite extraordinary capabilities, Zayyad ruled Iraq and Persia with a rod of iron. Discipline was restored in the armies, successful campaigns were fought on the frontiers of India and Turkestan and law and order were maintained. In spite, however, of Muawiya's un-opposed accession to the khalifate, the supporters of Ali and of Beni Hashim continued to work against the Umaiyid domination, though their activities were driven underground by the persecution inflicted upon them. Zayyad the-son-of-his-father died in 673, but in 676 his twenty-eight year old son Ubaidullah ibn Zayyad was appointed governor of Basra. We shall hear more of this young man shortly.

* * *

As Muawiya grew old, the vexed question of the succession once more assumed importance. The khalif decided to appoint as heir-apparent his own son Yezeed. The hereditary principle had never been recognized by the Arabs and Yezeed was, moreover, an obviously unsuitable candidate. Irreli-gious and frivolous, he had lived nearly all his life in the gay and luxurious city of Damascus, the majority of the inhabitants of which were still Christians. Such, however, was the prestige of Muawiya that, with the assist-ance of a certain amount of bribery and intrigue, he succeeded in securing an oath of allegiance to Yezeed from nearly all the provinces.

The principal exception was the city of Medina which had been the capital of the empire during the years of the great conquests, which still felt itself to be the Prophet's own city and where some of the surviving companions of Muhammad kept alive the memory of the days of idealism and fervour. Muawiya decided to visit Medina himself and endeavour to win popular sup-port for the succession of Yezeed. His efforts met with little success.

The principal opposition came from the sons of former khalifs. Most prominent of these was Husain, the eldest surviving son of Ali. He and his brother Hasan had been very dear to their grandfather, the Prophet. Now in middle age, Husain was a man of high character, sincerely religious, rever-enced and loved by the people of Medina. After him came the sons of the first two khalifs, Abdul Rahman the son of Abu Bekr and Abdulla the son of Umar. These took the view that, if the khalifate were hereditary, they had more right to the succession than the frivolous Yezeed. If it were by selection of the best available candidate, then Yezeed had none of the necessary qualities. But the most formidable opponent of Muawiya's policy was Abdulla the son of that Zubair who had rebelled against Ali and been killed in the Battle of the Camel outside Basra. Abdulla ibn Zubair was a young man of restless energy, commanding personality and unquenchable courage. In no measured terms he told the khalif to his face that nothing would persuade him to swear allegiance to Yezeed. Muawiya accepted from the citizens of Medina their oaths of allegiance to his son, but failed to persuade Husain or Abdulla ibn Zubair to fall into line. Returning to Damascus, Muawiya died in 680 at the age of seventy-seven years. He had reigned for twenty years over the vast Arab Empire, to which, after the civil disturbances of Othman and Ali, he had restored internal peace and external victory. His failure to secure the succession was to plunge the Arabs once more into bloodshed and schism.

* * *

Yezeed was aware of the opposition to his succession on the part of the people in Medina. No sooner did he succeed his father in April 680 than he sent orders to the governor of Medina, to summon Abdulla ibn Zubair and Abdulla ibn Umar ibn al Khattab to take the oath of allegiance. The governor first summoned Husain, the grandson of the Prophet, and invited him to take the oath. Husain, however, procrastinated and left the governor's house without swearing but without bidding defiance. The governor thereupon summoned Abdulla ibn Zubair, who replied that he would come shortly. Then, as night closed in, he slipped out of Medina and rode in haste to Mecca. Abdulla ibn Umar, however, the son of the second khalif, answered the governor's summons and swore the oath required of him. The following night Husain himself escaped from Medina and proceeded to Mecca also. Thus Yezeed's two most dangerous opponents had slipped through the governor's fingers.

Incensed at such bungling, Yezeed sent a new governor who proceeded to arrest and flog those known to be opposed to Yezeed's succession. Bitter indeed was it to the people of Medina and Mecca to remember the last days of the Prophet in their midst fifty years before, and after his death, the years of passionate devotion and faith, the exaltation of the warriors leaving for the wars, bent only on securing victory for the cause of God or on falling as martyrs in His service. Such as fell, they believed, had been instantly welcomed into the gardens of Paradise by the houris, those black-eyed smiling virgins, immortally beautiful and ever young. Then all true Muslims were brothers and none claimed precedence over his fellow, unless it were in his ardour to attain the glory of martyrdom. Now all the glory had sunk to a sordid struggle for worldly wealth and power. Husain, however, appears to have been surrounded by an odour of sanctity, due to the fact that he was actually the Prophet's grandson and perhaps also to his hitherto blameless life, but Abdulla ibn Zubair was merely a political opponent of the régime.

It was while these events were taking place that messengers arrived in Mecca from Kufa bearing letters for Husain inviting him to come and assume the leadership in Iraq. The wording was perhaps equivocal but there can scarcely have been any doubt that the proposal involved rebellion against Yezeed's government in Damascus, especially in view of the fact that Ali, Husain's father, had held court in Kufa while Muawiya, Yezeed's father, was ruler of Damascus. In other words, it must have been obvious that the proposal would in all probability lead to a recrudescence of civil war.

Husain was undecided. He had kept clear of politics since the assassination of his father twenty years before. It was obvious that he was more worthy of elevation to the khalifate than was Yezeed. Pious, courteous, dignified, he was the grandson of the Prophet himself, whereas Yezeed was the grandson of Abu Sofian, the bitterest opponent of Muhammad. Meanwhile letters continued to pour into Mecca from Kufa and from Basra, urging the need for swift action and pledging military support. Husain ibn Ali and Abdulla ibn Zubair were the only two serious rivals to Yezeed, but of the two Husain's prestige was infinitely the higher, both by reason of his lineage and of his character. As long as Husain was alive, there was no hope of advancement to the khalifate for Abdulla. Seeing the vacilliation of Husain, Abdulla urged him strongly to go to Iraq, perhaps, the Arab historians suggest, in the hope of thereby removing his most serious competitor.

Husain's well-wishers in Mecca urged him on no account to go to Kufa, where the fickle citizens had refused to fight for his father Ali under similar circumstances. So great was the reverence entertained for him by all Muslims, they pointed out, that his best course was to remain praying in the mosque in Mecca. Under such circumstances, the khalif's minions would not dare to touch him. Abdulla ibn Abbas[3] suggested to Husain that the Kufans should first rise and drive out their governor, thereby committing themselves to action. If, however, he prophesied, Husain left Medina while the governor of Kufa was still in his office, his troops patrolling the streets and his officials collecting taxes, then at the last moment the Kufans would lose their nerve and Husain would be betrayed. If, he added, Husain felt unsafe in Mecca, he would do better to seek asylum in the mountains of the Yemen, rather than brave the open plains of Iraq. Abdulla ibn Abbas is represented as giving wise and sincere advice, while Abdulla ibn Zubair urged Husain to go, hoping for his ruin.

Eventually Husain sent his cousin Muslim, the son of Aqeel[3] the son of Abu Talib, with orders to proceed to Kufa, to investigate the situation and to report back. Muslim was received enthusiastically by the secret supporters of Beni Hashim, no less than twelve thousand of whom are alleged to have secretly pledged their devotion to Husain between the hands of Muslim. Exhilarated at finding so much enthusiasm, Muslim wrote urgently to Husain, begging him to come to Kufa immediately. Informers had meanwhile hastened to the governor of Kufa to warn him of what was afoot. The governor, however, was a native of Medina, not a member of the Beni Umaiya clan. When supporters of Yezeed in Kufa charged him with weakness and urged him to take drastic action to stamp out the potential sedition, he replied that weakness was preferable to rebellion against God, feeling doubtless, like many earnest Muslims, unable to contemplate violence against the very family and descendants of the Prophet. Seeing his hesitation, Yezeed's supporters sent a message post haste to Damascus.

Only one man was ruthless enough to deal with sedition in Kufa, Yezeed's advisers told him, and he was the then governor of Basra, Ubaidullah the son of Zayyad the son-of-his-father. A trusted old freedman of Muawiya, in support of this advice, produced a letter ostensibly written by

3. Quraish genealogical tree, page 32.

his former master, appointing Ubaidullah governor of Kufa, but which, it was alleged, Muawiya died before he could sign. Convinced by these arguments, Yezeed signed the letter. Receiving the khalif's orders, Ubaidullah left Basra secretly and reached Kufa before anyone was aware of his appointment.

Meanwhile, Husain, acting on the letter which he had received from his cousin Muslim, set out in August or September 680 to cross the eight hundred miles of desert which separated Mecca from Kufa. He made no attempt to raise forces or enlist armed supporters. He was accompanied by the whole of his family, chiefly women and children, and by a small number of retainers and intimate friends. "The hearts of the people were with him," said al Farazdaq the poet, "but their swords were with Beni Umaiya and the result was in the hands of God."

In the interval, Ubaidullah had not been idle. Before entering Kufa, he had given three thousand dinars[4] to a faithful freedman, whom he instructed to enter Kufa from the north, to seek out the supporters of Husain and to inform them that he had been sent by sympathizers in Syria to contribute the money to their funds. The conspirators were deceived, admitted the freedman to their councils and accepted the sum offered. Scarcely had Ubaidullah taken up his residence in the governor's castle than his freedman informed him of the details of the plot and the names of the principal conspirators. Acting upon this report, Ubaidullah gave orders for the immediate arrest of the host in whose house Muslim lay concealed. He then sent for the leaders of the town and warned them, to their alarm, that each of them would be held personally responsible for any of his followers who joined any conspiracy.

No sooner did Muslim hear of his host's arrest, than he rightly presumed that the governor had received information of the conspiracy and that the time for action had come. Calling upon his supporters to fulfil their pledges, he surrounded the governor's castle with four thousand men. The garrison, a mere fifty men, hastily closed the gates and manned the walls, but could scarcely have withstood a serious assault.

At this crisis, Ubaidullah showed himself to be a real leader of men. He did not lose his head. No arrows were discharged from the walls. Instead of resorting to violence, the governor sent some trusted retainers to mingle with the crowd, to whisper to the people the danger of engaging in hostilities with the government and to warn them that an army was coming from Damascus. He had taken the precaution of keeping the leaders of the town in the castle, after giving them his lecture in the morning. Now he ordered them to stand on the castle walls and call out to the people to disperse. One by one, the members of the crowd stole away to their homes. By the evening the streets surrounding the castle were deserted.

Muslim, Husain's cousin, found himself abandoned. He could not return to his former hiding place, the owner of which had been arrested. He accepted hospitality in another house, but no sooner had he lain down to rest than an informer went to the castle and at midnight, the police broke into the

4. The dinar was the gold coin of the period.

building. Muslim, sword in hand, held them at bay in the doorway until the officer in charge secured his surrender under a guarantee of his personal safety. When he was brought before the governor, however, the latter repudiated the guarantee and ordered his instant decapitation. His headless trunk was thrown from the castle walls into the town square below.

At dawn, Muslim's former host was taken out and publicly beheaded in the sheep market in the centre of the town. His headless corpse was then crucified on top of the town garbage heap. The brutal Ubaidullah had a knack of adding such minor disgusting touches to his severities. The two severed heads were laid before the governor in council in his castle.

By these ruthless measures, Ubaidullah the son of Zayyad cowed the people of Kufa in twenty-four hours. On the following day, not a murmur was to be heard in the city. It was 9th September, 680.

While Muslim was being led away through the streets under arrest, he had called out loudly, "Will no one send to meet Husain and tell him not to come here, for the people of Kufa have betrayed him as they betrayed his father." Some well-wisher heard the cry and, stealing from the town, set out to meet Husain in the desert.

* * *

Before leaving Mecca, Husain had sent a foster-brother of his on to Kufa to announce his early arrival. Meanwhile, however, Ubaidullah had terrorized the Kufans into subjection, and the messenger was arrested before he even reached the city. Ubaidullah told him that if he mounted the battlements of the castle and called out to the crowd in the market place below, invoking curses on Husain, he would consider sparing his life. But when Husain's messenger stood up upon the wall, he cried out blessings on Husain and urged the Kufans to support him, until Ubaidullah called out angrily to cast him down. The devoted messenger was thrown from the battlements into the square below. All his bones are said to have been broken but he was still alive, until some compassionate bystander put him out of his agony.

Meanwhile Husain, with his convoy of women and children, was trekking slowly across the deserts of Arabia. As he travelled through the grazing grounds of the nomads, many tribesmen volunteered to join him, until he had acquired a considerable force. When the whole party arrived at Zibala, however, they encountered the messenger who had set out to meet them as the result of Muslim's last appeal. In one devastatingly clear moment of insight Husain knew that all was lost. Gathering together all the bedouins who had joined him en route, he told them of the execution of Muslim and of his messengers and explained that he no longer had any supporters in Kufa. He then ordered them all to disperse to their tribes. Many begged him to return to Mecca, but he only replied that his fate was in the hands of God. Next morning the camels were loaded and he moved northwards once more with only his little family convoy.

Four bedouins of the tribe of Tai encountered him and begged him to take refuge with the tribes in the mountain of Ajja, in the deserts of northern Nejed. Their tribe would protect him, they exclaimed, with twenty thousand

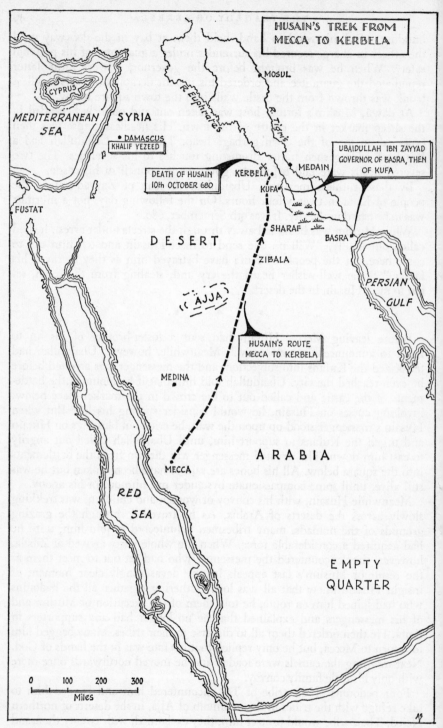

HUSAIN'S TREK FROM
MECCA TO KERBELA

CYPRUS

MEDITERRANEAN
SEA

SYRIA

R. Euphrates

R. Tigris

MOSUL

DAMASCUS
KHALIF YEZEED

DEATH OF HUSAIN
10th OCTOBER 680

KERBELA

MEDAIN

UBAIDULLAH IBN ZAYYAD
GOVERNOR OF BASRA, THEN
OF KUFA

FUSTAT

KUFA

DESERT

SHARAF

BASRA

PERSIAN
GULF

ZIBALA

AJJA

MEDINA

HUSAIN'S ROUTE
MECCA TO KERBELA

ARABIA

MECCA

RED
SEA

EMPTY
QUARTER

0   100   200   300
Miles

10

sabres and no government could seize him there, but Husain only thanked them and travelled on. After watering at Sharaf, the little party moved on across a stony rolling plain, when suddenly someone called that they could see palm trees. All pulled up, sitting on their camels and straining their eyes to see through the shimmering mirage. The palm trees seemed to be moving and, as they drew nearer, revealed themselves to be a detachment of cavalry sent out by Ubaidullah ibn Zayyad to scout for the convoy. Their horses were thirsty, so Husain caused them to be watered from water skins which he was carrying on his camels. It chanced to be the hour of prayer, and the "enemy" cavalry lined up behind the grandson of the Prophet to join in the service. The commander of the cavalry then informed Husain that he had orders to escort him into Kufa. Thereafter the little convoy kept trying to edge away to the west, while the cavalry endeavoured, though with a reasonable degree of consideration, to shepherd them eastwards into Kufa.

It is impossible, at this distance of time, to know what was in Husain's mind, after he heard at Zibala the news of the disappointment of his hopes. There was then still time to turn back. Did he believe that, if he did so, he would be arrested and executed in Mecca? If so, the only course left to him was, as the bedouins had suggested to him, to become a fugitive in some wild mountain range. Perhaps, as the grandson of the Prophet, he felt that such a course would be beneath his dignity. Perhaps he did not believe that even Beni Umaiya would venture to kill him.

Eventually the little convoy, constantly trailed by its cavalry escort, passed up the desert some twenty miles west of Kufa, to the vicinity of the modern town of Kerbela. Meanwhile the cavalry had received fresh orders from Ubaidullah instructing them to bully and bluster, to exhaust the personnel and the camels alike by compelling them to camp without grazing and above all by denying them water. The party were now within sight of the Euphrates with its palm gardens and villages but the cavalry threw a cordon round their camp, refusing to allow them to obtain water. Some of the men with Husain urged him to attack the cavalry, as it was obvious that the enemy would soon receive reinforcements. But Husain refused to be the first to use violence. "If we die trusting in God, father," said his young son Ali, "we shall have done nothing wrong," "God reward you, my son," replied Husain quietly, "he is a good son who strengthens his father with such words." It was 2nd October, 680. The whole party spent the night without water.

* * *

Meanwhile in Kufa, Umar ibn Saad ibn Abi Waqqas had arrived with four thousand men. His father—a cousin of Muhammad himself and one of his first converts—had been the conqueror of Iraq from the Persians forty-four years earlier. Ubaidullah informed him that he must take his troops and kill Husain. Umar protested strongly and begged to be excused the task but Ubaidullah was inexorable. On 3rd October Umar accordingly moved out with his four thousand troops and bivouacked a short distance from the little convoy, which consisted of seventy-two men, thirty-two being horsemen and forty on foot.

Umar then sent a messenger to Husain to ask him why he had come. Husain replied that he had come at the invitation of the people of Kufa, but that if they did not now want him, he would go away. On receiving this message, Umar is alleged to have exclaimed, "God grant that we may not have to fight him." A further message then arrived from Ubaidullah, saying that Husain must swear allegiance to Yezeed. At night, Husain's brother, Abbas, took with him a party of men with some empty water skins and crept down to the Euphrates. They were discovered, a skirmish ensued, one of Husain's men was killed, but nevertheless some water was got back to the camp, where the children were faint from thirst.

On the morning of 4th October, Husain asked for an interview with Umar, at which he proffered three solutions. He asked either to be allowed to return to Medina, or to go to Damascus and place his case before Yezeed himself, or to be allowed to go to some distant frontier to fight against the infidels. Umar hastened to transmit these proposals to Ubaidullah, adding on his own behalf, "Thank God here is a way to a peaceful solution."

Ubaidullah at first seemed to agree, but there was present another military commander, second only to Umar in seniority. This man, Shemmer ibn dhi al Joshan,[5] strongly urged the governor to insist on Husain's unconditional surrender, hinting at the same time that Umar was in collusion with Husain. Ubaidullah was persuaded, if he needed persuasion, and sent Shemmer himself with a letter to Umar, ordering him to demand Husain's unconditional surrender. Should he refuse, Umar was to attack and kill him. As soon as he was dead, the cavalry were to trample his body under the feet of their horses, until it was completely mangled. His head was to be cut off and sent to Ubaidullah. Once again, the governor was not content to kill his enemies, but must needs then savage their dead bodies. The letter ended with a threat. "If you execute my orders," wrote the son of Zayyad, "you will receive benefits and rewards. If not, consider yourself dismissed, and hand over your command to Shemmer."

The same afternoon Umar gave orders to the cavalry to mount and advance. Husain was sitting in front of his tent and had fallen into a doze when his sister Zeinab ran up to him, calling out that the enemy was coming. Husain looked up and said to her, "I was asleep and in my dream I saw the Apostle of God, and he said to me, 'You are coming to me now.'" Husain then sent his brother Abbas forward to Umar, asking him to postpone the attack until the next morning that he might prepare for death, a request to which Umar courteously consented.

Husain spent the night in prayer and in comforting the women and children, telling them of the vanity of this life and that all men must die. Then he ordered that the tents be pitched close together, so that the tent ropes overlapped. He told the men and boys to scatter under cover of darkness and make their way to safety. "It is I alone whom they wish to kill," he said. "It is not necessary for you all to die." But all elected to remain with him until the last.

At dawn, Husain drew up his seventy-two men for battle. In the centre,

5. Joshan was a coat of chainmail. The name therefore means Shemmer of the coat of mail.

his brother Abbas carried his banner. As the long line of cavalry approached, he mounted his mare and, raising his hands, exclaimed, "Oh God, Thou art our trust in every danger, our hope in every extremity." Then, as they drew nearer, he called to the advancing troops, "I am the son of the daughter of your Prophet." "Is not the son of Fatima better than the son of Sumaiya?"[6] called one of the men from behind him. The commander of the cavalry, who had first met Husain's party at Sharaf and escorted him to Kerbela, had spoken to him often and had been influenced by his personality. Dashing out of the ranks of the army, he placed himself beside Husain, crying that he preferred death and paradise to a longer life and hell-fire.

The cavalry pulled up a short distance from the little party and its tents, but showers of arrows began to come over. Several of the little group were killed and wounded. As was the custom in Arab battles of those days, individual champions then stepped forward challenging those on the other side to single combat, thereby prolonging the agony of the day. At noon, in spite of the battle, Husain and his men said their prayers, half of them praying at a time while the others fought.

By the early afternoon, the numbers of Husain's men were greatly reduced, though he himself was still unhurt, the archers presumably directing their aim elsewhere. Two brothers from among his following came to him and asked if they could die between him and the enemy. Walking together towards the Umaiyid line, they stopped, looked round and called, "Peace be upon thee, O son of God's Apostle." Then running straight into the enemy's ranks, they fell covered with wounds.

A little son of Husain was killed by an arrow, and soon afterwards another son called Qasim. Husain himself picked up the little body and laid it in the tent beside his dead brother. There were now scarcely any men left with Husain, though nobody seemed to dare to kill him. Then Malik ibn Nusair, of the tribe of Kinda, charged at him and struck him a blow on the head, so that the blood flowed down and soaked his clothes.[7]

This tragic and brutal incident was to rend Islam apart and the schism which resulted has still not been healed today. There has perhaps been a tendency to idealize the character of Husain against which it is wise to guard, if we wish to adhere to historical accuracy. It is necessary in this connection to mention that, during these last poignant moments, he is reported to have called frequently upon God to revenge his death on his attackers. "O God, slay them all. Let not one escape. Let them all be for hell-fire." To pray for the forgiveness of his tormentors may be incumbent on the Christian martyr, but the principle of retaliation is too deeply engrained in the Arab mentality.

Husain, wounded and bleeding, was now left almost alone, surrounded by several thousand of his assailants, yet none seemed to have the courage to give him the *coup de grâce*. At some stage he seems to have mounted his

6. Sumaiya was the prostitute who had been the mother of Zayyad, Ubaidullah's father.

7. If the battle in reality lasted several hours, it is obvious that it cannot have been pressed. Perhaps the archers were told to snipe Husain's supporters in the hope of taking him alive. An Umaiyid report says the battle was short.

mare but his persecutors, thinking perhaps that he meant to break away, shot the mare and she fell. An arrow struck Husain in the face and became embedded in his jaw but he wrenched it out by force. By this time he was probably only half conscious and kept calling feebly for water, as he stood in front of the tent. The enemy meanwhile had broken into the tents behind him, though Husain called to them to spare the women. A little boy ran out of the tents and up to Husain, crying that he would die with father. At the same moment, a soldier ran at Husain with his sword, but the little boy raised his arm to protect himself, and the sword slashed off his hand above the wrist. His father snatched him up in his arms, saying "You and I will now soon be with the Apostle of God."

Husain now stood at bay alone, when the voice of Shemmer suddenly called on the troops to kill him. Some rushed in, one striking him with his sword on his shoulder, another slashing his left arm, until he staggered forward and backward like a drunken man. Then a soldier ran him through with a lance and he finally fell to the ground. A man called Siran ibn Aris leapt upon the fallen body and cut off his head. The spell of reverence was broken. A horde of soldiers ran forward and in a few seconds the corpse was stripped naked. One tore off his cloak, another his shirt, a third grabbed his sword, a fourth his sandals. Then the brutal troops, drunk with blood and greed, turned on the tents, scrambling for the remaining horses and camels, the food and the bedding, and even tearing the clothes off the women.

At this moment, the commander Umar ibn Saad ibn abi Waqqas, arrived on the scene, and rescued the women. He ordered the troops to give back the property they had looted but none took any notice. He then called for volunteers to trample the body of Husain underfoot, as Ubaidullah had ordered. Ten horsemen volunteered and rode their horses back and forth over the body until it was mangled and unrecognizable. Husain's head was sent by special messenger to Ubaidullah ibn Zayyad in Kufa. All seventy-two men with Husain had been killed. Eighty-eight men of the Kufa army were dead, not counting the wounded. The savage Shemmer spent the last hours of the day cutting off the seventy-two heads of Husain's dead relatives and retainers. It was 10th October, 680.

*   *   *

Next morning Ubaidullah was sitting in the governor's hall of public audience receiving the congratulations of the citizens. Before him lay the severed head of Muhammad's grandson. As he talked airily to his visitors, the sadistic Ubaidullah kept toying with the bloody head with the end of his sword. At length an old man burst out, "Stop playing with that head with your sword, for by God I have seen the lips of the Apostle of God pressed in kisses on those lips," then he broke down into wild sobs. "May God make your eyes to weep," said the son of Zayyad savagely, "if you were not so old as to be senile, I would have your head cut off this minute." The old man rose and hastened sobbing from the hall. As he pushed his way through the crowds jostling one another outside, he cried, "Today the Arabs have become slaves. After so much glory, they have become servile slaves."

The women of Husain's family were then led into the audience hall, barely covered in a few rags which the soldiers had left them. Then the seventy-two severed heads were carried before Ubaidullah. "Well," asked the latter brightly, addressing the wretched and bedraggled women, "what do you think of what God has inflicted on your family now?" "God will judge between you and them on the Day of Resurrection," replied Husain's sister bravely.

*   *   *

The heads of Husain and his seventy-two supporters were sent by special messengers to Yezeed in Damascus. When they were laid out before him, the young man is said to have wept and exclaimed, "May God curse the son of Sumaiya. If I had been there I should have spared Husain, may God have mercy on him." The convoy of half-naked and shivering women travelled to Damascus more slowly. When they arrived, Yezeed is said again to have cursed Ubaidullah. Then he ordered that the women be given clothing and food and sent with all respect and under escort to Medina. In the Holy City they were received with universal wailing and lamentation, and, as we shall see, were to lead to endless troubles for Beni Umaiya and for Islam.

Yezeed's show of weeping and his public imprecations on Ubaidullah the son of Zayyad can scarcely be accepted at their face value. His father, the Khalif Muawiya, had had a working arrangement with Zayyad, according to which the latter kept the people of Iraq in subjection by extreme severity, while Muawiya gained popularity by assuming a patriarchal and compassionate manner. Their two sons cannot have been ignorant of the system. A few months after the massacre at Kerbela, Ubaidullah was promoted to be governor of Kufa, Basra and all Persia, the eastern half of the whole empire, which his father Zayyad had also governed for the Khalif Muawiya.

*   *   *

In the seventh century, the word shia signified merely a party. The Arab historians speak of the shia of Yezeed and the shia of Husain in describing their respective supporters. But the massacre of Kerbela gave the word a new significance. Those who had followed Ali ibn abi Talib, Muhammad's son-in-law, and his son Husain conceived a passionate devotion to their memory. This closely knit group gradually became *the* party, the Shia *par excellence*. The brutalities of Kerbela can never be expunged, and the Shia, the devotees of Ali and Husain, remain to this day a separate branch of Islam.

*   *   *

The peoples of Lower Iraq and Persia are still almost entirely Shiites. Every year, on the first of the Arabic month of Muharram, the day on which Husain's little convoy pitched its camp without water on the plain of Kerbela, begins their annual ten day period of fasting and lamentation. Every day, in every camp, town and village, the pathetic story is read aloud, with every emotional detail, to weeping congregations. Every night for thirteen centuries men have paraded the streets, stripped to the waist, flogging their backs with whips and chains and chanting dirges to Husain. On 10th Muharram, the day of Husain's death, the battle would be enacted on a piece of open ground outside every town. A group of persons with a small tent would represent the devoted little band, a larger group of horsemen the Umaiyid army. One, particularly prominent, would play the part of the infamous Shemmer.

After the battle, a procession would form up to return to the town, with camel-litters carrying the dead Husain and a number of pathetic little children, their shirts tied over their heads to give them the appearance of headless corpses. The severed heads, made of wood and painted a ghastly pale green to simulate death, would lie beside the corpses. The square of the town and the flat roofs of the houses would be packed with women and children, who would set up a heartrending weeping and wailing as the grisly caravan passed by. The whole effect was passionately emotional and beyond words pathetic, one which I could myself never witness with dry eyes. Whatever Husain suffered in his lifetime has won for him at least the fervid and tragic devotion of millions of simple Muslim hearts.

NOTABLE DATES

Foundation of Qairawan	670
Siege of Constantinople	670–677
Capture of Rhodes	672
Death of Zayyad, the-son-of-his-father	673
Death of Muawiya ⎫	
Acclamation of Yezeed ⎭	April 680
Massacre of Kerbela	10th October 680

PERSONALITIES

The Khalif Muawiya ibn abi Sofian   661–680
The Khalif Yezeed, son of Muawiya   680–683
Uqba ibn Nafi, commander in North Africa,
    founder of Qairawan
Zayyad the-son-of-his-father,
    viceroy of Iraq and Persia.
Husain son of Ali ibn abi Talib,
    and grandson of the Prophet.
Abdulla ibn Zubair, opponent of the
    Khalif Yezeed.
Ubaidullah, the son of Zayyad,
    governor of Kufa.
Shemmer, the villain of the
    massacre of Kerbela.

III

Arab Anarchy

Freedom and not servitude is the cure of anarchy; as religion, and not atheism, is the true remedy for superstition.   EDMUND BURKE

Government and co-operation are in all things the laws of life; anarchy and competition the laws of death.   JOHN RUSKIN

Do they provoke me to anger? saith the Lord.
Do they not provoke themselves to the confusion of their own faces?
Jeremiah VII, 19

When in the thick of the combat heroes unflinchingly
Cry in men's ears their defiance, danger forgot by them,
There where the horsemen rode strongest I rode out in front of them,
Hurled forth my war-shout and charged them: no man thought blame of me.
Deep through the sand-drifts charged horsemen, teeth grimly set,
Urging their war-steeds, the strong-limbed, weight bearers all of them,
Swiftly the camels too urged by me, spurred by my eagerness
Forward to deeds of high daring, deeds of audacity.   ANTAR IBN SHEDDAD

III

ARAB ANARCHY

WHETHER or not Yezeed was genuinely outraged by the savagery of Ubaidullah, the khalif was soon made aware that the political consequences were likely to be serious. The return of the women and children of Husain's family provoked, as already related, passionate mourning and intense indignation in Medina, the city which for fifty years had cherished the Apostle himself and his descendants. In Mecca, Abdulla ibn Zubair found his position immensely enhanced. On the one hand, Husain, whose claims to the khalifate had been so much stronger than his own, was now out of the way. On the other, the brutality of the day of Kerbela had caused an intense reaction against Yezeed all over the Arab world. Encouraged by these factors, Abdulla ibn Zubair began openly to denounce the Beni Umaiya dynasty. Soon it was rumoured that he was secretly receiving oaths of allegiance to himself.

Alarmed at the rising sedition in the Hejaz, the governor of Medina succeeded in persuading a deputation of the notables of the town to pay a visit to Yezeed in Damascus, hoping that the khalif would be able to win them over to his side, whether by persuasion or by lavish gifts. But the attempt was a failure, and the pious delegates, on their return, only made matters worse by reporting with horror that Yezeed drank wine and that the city of Damascus was given over to frivolity.

Nearly all the Arab historians whose works are still extant wrote in the days of the Abbasid dynasty, which overthrew and succeeded the Umaiyids. As a result, all have striven to discredit the memory of Beni Umaiya to such an extent that the historian finds it difficult to form a reliable estimate of their characters. Yezeed was thirty-five years old when he was proclaimed khalif, and had lived all his life in Syria. The people of Medina had preserved, to a considerable extent, the puritan tradition of the Prophet, who had disapproved alike of wine, music, silk clothing and other amenities of ordinary civilized life. To them, Damascus was a sink of every iniquity, if only because these luxuries were there in frequent use. Yezeed's mother, Maysun, came of the bedouin tribe of Kelb and had become famous as a poetess in her own right. Living in a palace in Damascus had no attractions for her, and she lamented her longing for the desert in a famous poem, beginning:

> "A tent with rustling breezes cool
> Delights me more than palace high,
> And more the cloak of simple wool
> Than robes in which I learned to sigh." [1]

1. Nicholson, *A Literary History of the Arabs.*

Muawiya is said to have divorced her when he heard this poem, with the result that Yezeed spent more time than would otherwise have been the case with the nomads of the Syrian desert. The bedouins were deeply steeped in the old Arab traditions of war, hospitality and poetry, traditions dating from many centuries before Islam. Although they had formed the bulk of the Arab armies during the great conquests, the tribes were not in general very religious. Thus we see that Yezeed had been brought up partly among the cheerful, luxury-loving Damascenes and partly among the warlike and poetic, though still half-pagan, bedouins. We might not consider wine, music or silk to be deadly sins, but to the strict traditionists of Mecca and Medina, they were anathema.

On the whole we may perhaps conclude that Yezeed was a man of the world, enjoying his pleasures, perhaps to excess, for he was very fat even at thirty-five. Some Arab historians allege that he was constantly drunk, which may have been true. I have myself, however, noticed that nowadays, Arabs who do not drink believe that anyone who takes alcohol at all must be always drunk. It does not appear that Yezeed completely neglected the affairs of state.

*   *   *

In the autumn of 682, religious fervour, combined with the bitterness caused by the massacre of Husain and his companions, resulted in open revolt in Medina. Members of the Beni Umaiya clan and their retainers, totalling some one thousand men, were besieged in their houses in the town by the excited citizens. The siege was perhaps not closely pressed and the insurgents, though bitter and indignant, were ill-disciplined and unorganized. Nevertheless the authority of the khalif had been defied, his governor driven from office and his relatives insulted and besieged.

Yezeed could not overlook such a revolt and an army was summoned to the colours in Damascus. Twelve thousand men were soon under arms, the command being given to Muslim ibn Uqba ibn Nafi. (His father had led the invasion of North Africa and had, a year before, been killed in the Atlas mountains by the Berbers.[2]).

In August 683, Muslim ibn Uqba reached Medina. As Yezeed had ordered, he gave the people of the town three days' grace to return to their allegiance. Boiling with rage at the indignity thus offered to the Prophet's City and filled with the haughty obstinacy of the morally self-satisfied, the insurgents rejected the offer with contempt.

On the expiry of the ultimatum, the Damascus army moved in towards the city by the Kufa track, which emerged from the lava slopes east of the town. The indignant citizens did not await attack but pouring out of the city they charged the advancing troops with desperate courage. For a short time the Umaiyid army was thrown into disorder, the standard-bearer was cut down, the banner fell to the ground and the frantic Medinis nearly cut their way to the commander himself. But brave as were the citizens, they were not an organized army. The army of Damascus had become trained and disciplined. The attack was held until the propitious moment and then

2. Page 43.

Muslim ibn Uqba launched his counter-attack, having already sent a column to make an outflanking movement and attack Medina. The citizens were slowly forced back, until they suddenly heard shouts of victory behind them. Looking round, they saw the flank column already in occupation of the town, whereupon they broke and fled.

For three days the Prophet's City was subjected to fear and humiliation. Many leaders were executed for refusing to swear allegiance to Yezeed. The remaining citizens were obliged to take the oath of obedience, though Muslim ibn Uqba informed them that their ultimate fate would depend solely on the clemency of the khalif. A small son of Husain called Ali had, as if by a miracle, survived the massacre of Kerbela and had returned to Medina with the women. But Yezeed had given special orders that no harm was to come to the child. Later, with the title of Zain al Abdeen—the Ornament of the Worshippers—he was to be one of the Shiite imams.

This battle has come down in history by the name of the Battle of the Lava. It took place on 26th August, 683. Muslim ibn Uqba then moved on south-wards to attack Mecca, but two or three days later he died. The historians give no reason for his sudden decease.

To the religious, the storming of the Prophet's City was one more act of impiety and sacrilege to be laid at the door of the infamous Beni Umaiya. For Medina had given refuge to the Prophet Muhammad when he had been obliged to flee from Mecca, and he had passed the rest of his life there. In Medina he had carried out his ministry till all Arabia was reduced to submission and there he lay buried with his two successors Abu Bekr and Umar ibn al Khattab. It was more than fifty years since the Prophet had died, yet there were still men in the town who had been his Companions. The puritan religious enthusiasm which the Apostle of God had aroused was still, in this isolated desert oasis, a living tradition.

When Muslim lay dying, his last words were that two things in his life had given him joy—the repetition of the Muslim creed and the punishment of the people of Medina. The recorded last words of famous men are often apocryphal, yet we can in a way appreciate the indignation of the followers of Yezeed. For the people of Medina and Mecca, in their narrow self-righteousness, were only stirring up civil war. It was no longer possible, as they demanded, to govern the vast Arab empire from a desert town cut off from the active world of commerce and politics.

With the death of Muslim ibn Uqba, the command passed to Husain ibn Numair al Sakooni, who marched southwards to reduce Mecca also to obedience. Unlike the citizens of Medina, the Meccans obeyed the voice of a single leader, Abdulla the son of Zubair, himself a claimant to the khalifate. The Holy City lay in a narrow valley surrounded by mountains, which offered no open space adequate for a pitched battle. On the 26th September, 683, the Syrian army occupied all the surrounding heights and opened a bombardment of the town below them with their mangonels. The siege was closely pressed and the town suffered much damage from the bombardment, even the Kaaba, the holy temple itself, being struck by the rocks from the mangonels until it was half in ruins. On 1st November, 683, the Kaaba was accidentally set

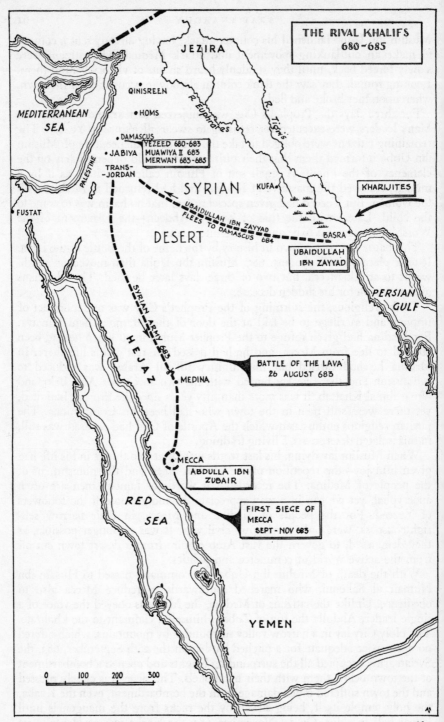

THE RIVAL KHALIFS
680~685

JEZIRA

MEDITERRANEAN
SEA

QINISREEN

HOMS

R. Euphrates

R. Tigris

DAMASCUS

YEZEED 680-683
MUAWIYA II 683
MERWAN 683-685

JABIYA

TRANS-
JORDAN

PALESTINE

SYRIAN

KUFA

KHARIJITES

FUSTAT

UBAIDULLAH IBN ZAYYAD
FLEES TO DAMASCUS
684

DESERT

BASRA

UBAIDULLAH
IBN ZAYYAD

PERSIAN
GULF

SYRIAN ARMY 683

H E J A Z

MEDINA

BATTLE OF THE LAVA
26 AUGUST 683

MECCA

ABDULLA IBN
ZUBAIR

RED
SEA

FIRST SIEGE OF
MECCA
SEPT - NOV 683

YEMEN

0   100   200   300

11

on fire by one of the defenders and the roof burnt.

The siege had lasted sixty-four days, when, on 27th November, 683, Abdulla ibn Zubair called out across no-man's-land, "O men of Syria, your tyrant is dead." Soon afterwards a messenger reached the besieging army also with the news that the Khalif Yezeed had died in Syria. He was thirty-eight years old and had ruled for three years and six months, leaving behind him as heir a sickly youth of thirteen, who was acclaimed in Damascus as Muawiya II.

When news reached Mecca of the death of Yezeed, both armies ceased fighting and Husain ibn Numair invited Abdulla ibn Zubair to meet him between the lines. Perhaps the commander of the Damascus army feared that anarchy would result from the succession of a child to the khalifate. Whatever was his motive, Husain ibn Numair told Abdulla ibn Zubair that he was the man most fitted to be khalif and invited him to accompany the Syrian army back to Damascus to assume control of the empire. But the son of Zubair, for reasons which we can only guess, refused. The Damascus commander was taken aback and could only remark with some contempt that Abdulla did not seem to be the man which his reputation had depicted him to be. After further thought, Abdulla modified his refusal. If, he said, the army would march back to Damascus and there proclaim him khalif, he would proceed to Syria to take up his duties. Husain rejected such a proposal with some scorn. If Abdulla were not man enough to march in person, he could scarcely expect the army to do all the work for him. The army thereupon raised the siege of Mecca and marched back to Damascus. The chance offered to Abdulla ibn Zubair to save the empire from civil war was never to return. Meanwhile the thirteen-year-old Muawiya the Second was proclaimed khalif in Damascus while Abdulla ibn Zubair was at the same time acclaimed khalif in Medina, and once more the empire was divided between two rival claimants.

We can only conjecture the reasons which caused Abdulla ibn Zubair to refuse the offer made to him by the Damascus army. Perhaps the fate of Husain at Kerbela was paramount in his mind. He too had been invited and had taken the invitation at its face value only to be betrayed and killed. Yet if this had been the sole reason, Abdulla could have raised an army in Arabia, where his cause commanded considerable support, and could have marched on Damascus protected by a force of his own. He was to continue for several years to press his claim to the khalifate, while himself remaining in Mecca. Although as a young man he had taken part in the great conquests, he had now lived for many years in the Holy City. In this atmosphere of religion, constantly surrounded by the surviving Companions of the Apostle of God and by the memories of the past, he never grasped the fact that the Arab Empire had now become a great, worldly power, basing its strength on commerce, finance, administration and trained armed forces, and that the old theocracy centred on the holy places and the Companions of the Prophet could no longer control it. Inevitably the capital had been transferred to a wealthy, prosperous and advanced country in close contact with the up-to-date civilized world.

*   *   *

GENEALOGY OF BENI UMAIYA

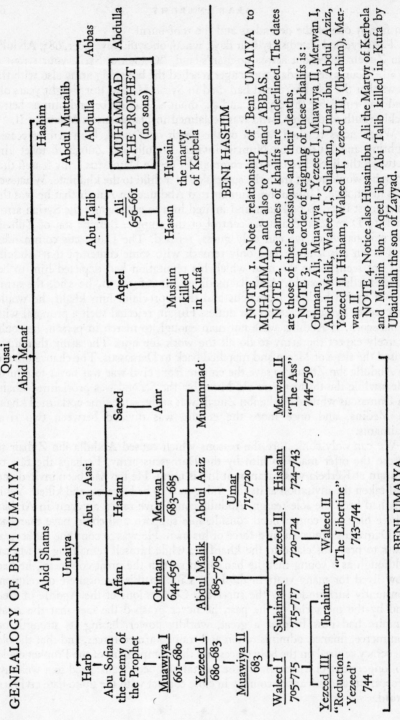

NOTE 1. Note relationship of Beni UMAIYA to MUHAMMAD and also to ALI and ABBAS.

NOTE 2. The names of khalifs are underlined. The dates are those of their accessions and their deaths.

NOTE 3. The order of reigning of these khalifs is: Othman, Ali, Muawiya I, Yezeed I, Muawiya II, Merwan I, Abdul Malik, Waleed I, Sulaiman, Umar ibn Abdul Aziz, Yezeed II, Hisham, Waleed II, Yezeed III, (Ibrahim), Merwan II.

NOTE 4. Notice also Husain ibn Ali the Martyr of Kerbela and Muslim ibn Aqeel killed in Kufa by Ubaidullah the son of Zayyad.

We have already seen that Ubaidullah ibn Zayyad, after the massacre of Husain and his followers at Kerbela, had been made viceroy over the eastern half of the empire, including Basra, Kufa and Persia. His father, Zayyad the-son-of-his-father, had held the same post a few years before. When news reached Basra of the death of Yezeed, Ubaidullah ascended the pulpit of the great mosque and invited the people of Basra to proclaim him as khalif (for politics as well as worship were conducted in the mosque). He had, he explained, been examining the census of fighting men and had found 80,000 men registered in the district of Basra alone and 140,000 in the eastern half of the empire. Consequently the men of Basra had nothing to fear from any rivals and could safely elect a khalif of their own choice. The speech produced the desired effect and those present acclaimed the son of Zayyad as their new ruler.

When, however, a delegation was sent to secure the adherence of Kufa, the people of that town emphatically rejected the candidacy of Ubaidullah and elected one of themselves as their leader until it should be seen who would succeed to the khalifate.

Three aspirants to be Prince of the Faithful were thus in the field in December 683. The child Muawiya II had been acclaimed in Damascus, Abdulla ibn Zubair was recognized in the Hejaz and Ubaidullah ibn Zayyad in Basra.

Meanwhile an emissary had arrived in Basra from Mecca, stating that Abdulla ibn Zubair had been acclaimed as khalif in the holy cities and inviting the people of Basra to swear allegiance to him. Differences of opinion soon appeared in the town. The first civil war between Muslims had broken out twenty-six years earlier, when Ali ibn abi Talib, the Prophet's son-in-law, was khalif in Kufa while Muawiya I was proclaimed in Damascus. Many deeply religious veterans of the great conquests had, as already mentioned, been sickened by these contests between ambitious rivals and had proclaimed their devotion to a pure theocracy. "No rule but that of God" had been their slogan, an objective difficult to attain in a workaday world. Zayyad the-son-of-his-father and his son Ubaidullah had acted with extreme rigour against these Kharijites. Now in December 683, when Ubaidullah pressed his claim to the khalifate in Basra, a considerable body of these puritan sectaries appeared in the city, vowing that their persecutor should not longer continue in power.

Thus, with true Arabian anarchy, Basra now split into three parties, partly on tribal lines. The armies which had conquered Iraq for Islam forty years before had consisted of contingents from the tribes of Central Arabia, each tribe constituting what we should call a unit. When Basra became a great military base, the different tribal contingents camped each in its own cantonment. Thus tribal loyalties had been perpetuated in the army.

The tribe of Azd now proclaimed its adherence to the cause of Ubaidullah, and engaged in a battle with his enemies, the theocratic puritan Kharijites. Azd were joined by Beni Bekr, while Qais and Beni Temeem joined in against them. Early in 684, the province of Basra was plunged into bloody civil strife. At this stage, however, Ubaidullah lost his nerve and took to flight. Accompanied by an escort of his supporters of the Azd and Beni Bekr tribes, he escaped into the desert and made his way safely to Damascus, taking with him the contents of the Basra treasury.[3]

Ubaidullah had become an object of hatred in Iraq for four reasons. Of these the first, and the most important, was the brutal massacre of Husain and his party at Kerbela, but, in addition, his severity, and especially the great number of people whom he had put to death, had made him enemies. His arrogance and the vast sums of money which he had spent in building himself a palace had further angered the equalitarian Arab tribesmen. The fourth reason sheds an interesting light on the internal administration of the empire.

Forty-five years earlier, the Arabs had conquered Iraq from the Persians. In general, however, they had not then settled down to work the land but had carried on their military campaigns beyond Iraq far into Persia. Such Persian notables as had submitted and professed Islam were allowed to remain on their land. One of the complaints against Ubaidullah was that he had farmed out the taxes to these Persian landowners (most of them now in the second generation since the conquest). To such complaints, the son of Zayyad replied that it was not feasible to farm the taxes to Arab notables, because if he endeavoured to call one of them to account he would summon his tribe and armed disturbances would immediately threaten. The Persian land-owners, however, had no armed support on which to lean and were thus obliged to render faithful service, or, if they failed to do so, they could be summarily dismissed.

After the flight of Ubaidullah from Basra, the tribes continued to fight one another for a short time. Then tiring of the constant insecurity and bloodshed, they concluded a truce, blood money was paid for the men killed, and a local leader was elected as temporary governor, until the situation in the whole empire should become clearer. Kufa had likewise chosen a ruler of its own, but none of these governors enjoyed the support of any central government, for none existed. As a result administration virtually broke down, violence and robbery reigned supreme and every man—or at least every tribe—pursued only its own advantage.

The eastern half of the Arab empire included the countries now known to us as Persia and Afghanistan and a part of Pakistan. North Persia was governed from Kufa, south and east Persia from Basra. With Kufa and Basra themselves in anarchy, chaos soon spread to the Persian provinces also. The Turks, profiting by this Arab anarchy, crossed the Oxus to invade Persia. Yet so dynamic was still the fighting power of the Arabs that the local contingent of Beni Temeem was sufficient alone to rout the formidable Turks and drive them out of the empire, though the other tribal forces in Persia were engaged in killing one another.

*   *   *

In December 683, as already explained, three rival khalifs were in the field, the child Muawiya in Damascus, Abdulla ibn Zubair in Mecca and Ubaidullah

3. We have seen such *coups d'état* and counter-coups in our own times in the Middle East.

ibn Zayyad in Basra. Two months later, however, Muawiya had died and Ubaidullah had fled. For the moment, Abdulla ibn Zubair remained the only candidate in the field. Both Kufa and Basra sent deputations to Mecca to tender their allegiance, while delegations even arrived from Qinisreen and Homs in Syria and from Egypt. If Abdulla even now had marched on Damascus, the empire might have been united, but he remained obstinately in Mecca, far from the centres of life, commerce and wealth.

In the spring of 684, the empire seemed to be ready to fall like a ripe apple into the lap of Abdulla ibn Zubair. Beni Umaiya were all gathered in Damascus and Merwan ibn al Hakam, the oldest and most respected member of the family, was about to ride to Mecca to offer their submission to the son of Zubair and thereby to reunite the empire. One man was to prevent that union—Ubaidullah ibn Zayyad, who at this moment arrived in Damascus, having fled from his post in Basra.

With all his violence and cruelty, there must have been something about this young man, for he was still in his twenties, many years younger than Merwan. Hearing of the latter's intention to submit to Abdulla ibn Zubair, Ubaidullah denounced such craven defeatism in no measured terms. Merwan himself was the rightful chief of the Arabs, he claimed. Beni Umaiya had already supplied four khalifs. They were the natural leaders. Merwan himself must seize the throne of the empire. Electrified by such energy, Beni Umaiya collected their supporters at Jabiya, the military base south of Damascus. Palestine, Homs and Qinisreen had declared their allegiance to Abdulla ibn Zubair. Trans-Jordan and Damascus acknowledged Merwan and another civil war had begun.

Of all the many reasons which the Arabs found for fighting one another, one of the most inexplicable was their division into northern and southern groups. According to ancient tradition, the inhabitants of the Arabian peninsula consisted of two races. The northern division were the progeny of Adnan, a descendant of Ishmael, the son of Abraham, and their home was in the northern Hejaz. The southern group were the descendants of Qahtan, sometimes identified with Joktan, a descendant of Shem.[4] These fabulous pedigrees need not concern us. The home of the southern race was alleged to have been Yemen, though at the time of which we are writing the two groups were geographically intermixed, many so-called southern tribes having been for centuries established in the Syrian desert.

It may well be that so ancient a tradition was based on some racial conflict in the remote past, and that this early hostility resulted in a whole system of alliances which embraced all the tribes of the peninsula, rather than a division between the descendants of two ancestors. Such alliances between tribes have been observable in our own time (and even among the nations of the world). Tribes A and B are in conflict. Three hundred miles away, tribes C and D start a dispute over some local affair, in no way connected with A and B, but each of them feels the need of an ally. C approaches A with the result that D makes a treaty with B. Soon other tribes, each of them with its individual fears or ambitions, join one or other group, the respective alliances eventually

4. Genesis X, 25.

becoming so strong that no individual tribe has the courage to remain in isolation. Whether by a genuine kinship of blood or by some such process of alliances, the fact remains that, in the seventh and eighth centuries, all the tribes of Arabia claimed descent either from the northern or the southern race.

In Syria, the two principal tribes were Kelb, who were southerners and Qais, who were of the northern group. It will be remembered that the mother of the Khalif Yezeed was Maysun the poetess and came of the tribe of Kelb, which thereby achieved a privileged position with the Umaiyids, a fact much resented by Qais. The chief of the Kelb tribe was governor of Jordan, which province therefore supported the Umaiyids. It was for this reason, rather than from any religious motive, that Qais in Syria declared their adherence to Abdulla ibn Zubair as the legitimate khalif.

Meanwhile the party of Abdulla ibn Zubair had concentrated at Marj Rahit, on the edge of the desert east of Damascus. Merwan marched against them with 6,000 men. The operations lasted only twenty days, ending, in July 684, in the Battle of Marj Rahit in which the supporters of Abdulla ibn Zubair were defeated. The remnant fled to Kirkisiya, the ancient Circesium, on the Euphrates, and Merwan was recognized as khalif by all Syria and Palestine. Marching into Egypt, he drove out the governor appointed by the son of Zubair, and annexed the country to his Syrian provinces. Once again the empire was divided between two rival khalifs from different branches of Quraish.

* * *

During the governorship of Ubaidullah ibn Zayyad, the former supporters of Husain had remained quiet in Iraq, but with the anarchy which followed the death of Yezeed and the flight of Ubaidullah from Basra, they began to communicate with one another with a view to concerting a plan to avenge the blood of Husain. It will be remembered that, after the death of Muawiya I, the people of Kufa had invited Husain to come to Iraq. Ubaidullah the son of Zayyad had crushed the dissidents in the town and had killed Husain with extreme brutality while the people of Kufa were still cowed.

But when the shock was over and Husain and his party had been exterminated, his supporters in Iraq bitterly regretted their failure to defend him. Passionately acknowledging their fault, they could think only of how to atone for their cowardice and their betrayal of the grandson of God's Apostle. "How," they asked one another, "shall we be able to meet God on the day of judgement? How can we face the Prophet himself in Paradise, when on earth we have been guilty of such abject treachery? The only manner in which we can atone for our dastardly guilt would be by dying as martyrs in the attempt to avenge his blood." At first they exchanged these sentiments secretly but the flight of Ubaidullah emboldened them to come into the open. Under the leadership of one Sulaiman ibn Surad, they began to hold meetings publicly in Kufa to consider their course of action.

At the beginning of October 685, the Shiites of Kufa gathered under arms outside the city. The nominal governor was a man sent by Abdulla ibn Zubair from Mecca, but he appears to have been too weak to intervene. Moreover

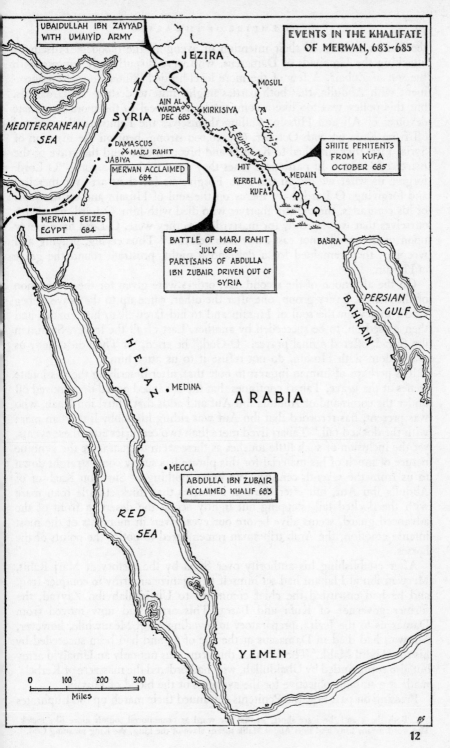

EVENTS IN THE KHALIFATE
OF MERWAN, 683–685

UBAIDULLAH IBN ZAYYAD
WITH UMAIYID ARMY

JEZIRA

MOSUL

AIN AL
WARDA
DEC 685

KIRKISIYA

R. Tigris

SYRIA

R. Euphrates

SHIITE PENITENTS
FROM KUFA
OCTOBER 685

DAMASCUS
MARJ RAHIT

HIT

JABIYA

KERBELA
KUFA

MEDAIN

MERWAN ACCLAIMED
684

IRAQ

MEDITERRANEAN
SEA

MERWAN SEIZES
EGYPT 684

BATTLE OF MARJ RAHIT
JULY 684
PARTISANS OF ABDULLA
IBN ZUBAIR DRIVEN OUT OF
SYRIA

BASRA

PERSIAN
GULF

BAHRAIN

HEJAZ

MEDINA

ARABIA

MECCA

ABDULLA IBN ZUBAIR
ACCLAIMED KHALIF 683

RED
SEA

YEMEN

0   100   200   300
Miles

12

the Shiites announced their intention of avenging the blood of Husain by attacking the Umaiyids of Damascus, who were disputing the empire with the son of Zubair. A few of the more level-headed Shiites desired an agreement with Abdulla, that both parties might unite to destroy the Umaiyids, but this policy was too like a compromise to appeal to the more passionate devotees of Ali and Husain. Calling themselves the Penitents, they moved off from Kufa on 20th October, 685, 16,000 strong, bent on the invasion of Syria. First they marched to Kerbela and bivouacked round the grave of the martyred Husain. In passionate tones they cried with one accord, "O Lord, forgive us what we did in the past. Forgive us for thou art ever merciful and forgiving. O Lord, have mercy on the soul of Husain and on the souls of his comrades, the faithful martyrs who died with him. O Lord, we pledge ourselves that we are ready for martyrdom as they were. O Lord have mercy upon us that we be not cast away into hell-fire." Thus crying, praying and weeping, they remained for a day and a night, prostrate round the grave of Husain.

On the afternoon of the second day, orders were given for the resumption of the march. Every group, one after the other, came up to the grave to beg God's mercy on the soul of Husain and to bid farewell to his remains and then passed on, to be succeeded by another. Last of all the leader, Sulaiman ibn Surad, offered a final prayer. "O God," he cried, "if Thou didst deny us martyrdom with Husain, do not refuse it to us after him."

It is perhaps of human interest to note that, after describing the passionate scenes at the grave, Tabari continues that the advanced guard then moved off under the command of Abdulla ibn Auf and adds that "Sirri ibn Kaab, who was present, has recorded that ibn Auf was riding his cobby little roan mare with the docked tail." Tabari lived more than two centuries after these events, yet the inclusion of such little touches as these seem to guarantee the genuine nature of much of his material for this phrase has surely come straight down to us from the seventh century. We know nothing of Sirri ibn Kaab or of Abdulla ibn Auf, but after thirteen centuries that thickset little roan mare with the docked tail, stepping out lightly across the desert in front of the advanced guard, seems alive before our eyes. Even in moments of the most intense emotion, the Arab tribesman remembered to notice the points of the horses.

After establishing his authority over Syria by the victory at Marj Rahit, Merwan ibn al Hakam had set himself to organize an army to conquer Iraq, and he had entrusted the chief command to Ubaidullah ibn Zayyad, the former governor of Kufa and Basra. This army had now moved from Damascus to the Jezira, preparatory to invading Iraq. Meanwhile, however, Merwan had died in Damascus at the age of 63 and had been succeeded by his son Abdul Malik.[5] The fact that this army was not only an Umaiyid army but also commanded by Ubaidullah, who had ordered the massacre of Kerbela, made it a suitable objective for the avengers of the blood of Husain.

Pressing on past Hit, the Penitents continued their march up the Euphrates

5. Both the a and the i are short, so that the word as pronounced sounds more like melek. The word means king and thus Abdul Malik means slave of the king, the King meaning God.

until they reached Kirkisiya. This place was the last outpost of the territories which had accorded at least nominal recognition to Abdulla ibn Zubair. After the Battle of Marj Rahit, Abdulla's last supporters in Syria had taken refuge within its walls. The governor of Kirkisiya welcomed the Shiites with enthusiasm as comrades in arms against the common Umaiyid enemy and proposed to them the pooling of their resources with those of Ibn Zubair. But the Penitents excused themselves. "Abdulla ibn Zubair is fighting for wordly dominion," they said, "but our object is different. We have given up our homes, our wives, our children and our possessions. We seek only martyrdom, to expiate our guilt and to avenge the blood of Husain." After replenishing supplies at Kirkisiya, they continued their march to Ain al Warda, not many miles further up the Euphrates. Next day, the advanced guard drove in the outposts of the Syrian army.

Ubaidullah ordered Husain ibn Numair al Sakooni to advance (the same who had besieged Abdulla ibn Zubair in Mecca in the reign of Yezeed), and the following morning the battle began in earnest. The Penitents charged the Syrian army with such impetuosity that, in spite of their inferior numbers, they forced it back steadily at the price of heavy fighting. But during the night, a further 8,000 reinforcements were sent up by Ubaidullah and a desperate struggle was maintained throughout the second day of the battle, without leading to a decisive result. The Penitents were about 16,000 strong. It is unlikely that the Umaiyid army, which had mobilized for the conquest of Iraq, can have had less than 30,000 or 40,000 men, but it was probably not concentrated when the Shiites arrived, so that perhaps only one column of the Damascus army was engaged on the first day.

During the second night, a further 10,000 men reached the Umaiyid army with the result that on the third morning of battle, the Shiites found themselves hopelessly outnumbered. Relentlessly the Syrian army closed around the devoted remnant. So desperate were the Penitents in hand-to-hand battle that the enemy adopted the device of holding back from close quarters and pouring arrows in on the survivors from every direction. Seeing his men falling fast, Sulaiman ibn Surad, the Shiite commander, dismounted from his horse, drew his sword and broke his scabbard. Others followed his example. In a compact company, they fought their way desperately with slashing swords into the Umaiyid ranks. Fighting in the van, Sulaiman ibn Surad soon earned his crown of martyrdom. Another leader instantly stepped forward, crying, "Whoever wants the life after which there is no death, let him draw near to his Lord by killing the deceivers, that his soul may fly to Paradise," and the little remaining band closed its ranks and fought on. In a brief lull in the fighting, a man of the tribe of Kinda, who was accompanied by his small son, stepped from the Shiite ranks and called to the Syrian army to ask if any men of Kinda were among them. Four men stepped forward from the enemy. "I am Abdulla the son of Aziz the Kindi," the Penitent shouted, "take this boy and care for him and send him back to his people in Kufa." "You are my cousin," cried a man from the Umaiyid ranks, "come over, you and the boy, and your lives will be saved." "I cannot do that," answered the boy's father. "My comrades, whose piety was a light to all the country, have but now preceded me to Paradise and I am in haste to join them." Pushing his son, who clung to him weeping, into the hands of the enemy, he drew back a few paces, then sword in hand dashed forward into the Syrian ranks and fought until he fell.

This incident reminds us that this was not a battle between Syrians and Iraqis, as today we know them. Both countries had been conquered fifty years earlier by the warlike tribes of Central Arabia and the armies which fought one another in the cause of one or other claimant to the khalifate, were still armies of Central Arabian tribesmen, who had not yet become lost in the native populations of the conquered countries.

Towards the evening of the third day of battle, it was obvious that the dwindling numbers of the Shia would soon be completely exterminated. One of the leaders, Rifaa ibn Shaddad, passed round the word for a gradual fighting withdrawal. Some of the Penitents refused to obey and one group of a hundred and another of thirty, forming up shoulder to shoulder, and preceded by their tribal banners, fought their way into the Umaiyid ranks till all were killed. The remainder, a small remnant, withdrew under cover of darkness, and marching all night, had vanished from the battle area when morning dawned. The Syrian army made no attempt to pursue.

But when daylight returned, many of the Penitents regretted their own survival and wished to go back. Only with great trouble did their leaders persuade them to continue their retreat. One man alone insisted on returning. Next day, a solitary figure, he came in sight of the Damascus army. Adjusting his equipment and drawing his sword, he charged straight at the enemy many thousand strong. His longing for martyrdom was not to be denied.

The Battle of Ain al Warda seems to have taken place in December 685. As the remnant of the army marched disconsolately back to Kufa, it encountered the contingents from the Shiites of Medain and Basra, coming up to join in the campaign. Like typical Arab tribesmen, their efforts had not been co-ordinated and the Kufans had been virtually exterminated before the men of Basra and Medain took the field. On hearing of the tragic battle of Ain al Warda, the columns dispersed sorrowfully to their homes.

It is impossible not to feel both amazement and compassion at the devotion and gallantry shown by the Penitents of Kufa. Yet it is to be noticed that their repentance for their betrayal of Husain could only take the form of revenge on his murderers. The ethics of revenge have played so profound a part in the history of the Arabs and of Islam that it is worthwhile to consider them for a moment.

Central Arabia had, before the birth of Muhammad, possessed no government, for the poverty and sparsity of the population scarcely sufficed to support one. Where there were no laws, no police and no public authority, a man who was wronged could obtain no redress except as a result of his own action. If his property had been stolen, his only hope of recouping his losses was to steal the property of the thief. If he could not do this alone, his relatives were obliged to assist him. If a man were killed, the damage could not be repaired, but his relatives would at least endeavour to balance the account by killing the murderer. This system of an eye for an eye and a tooth for a tooth was everywhere in force in Arabia when Muhammad preached. The Prophet was, on the whole, a man who preferred persuasion to violence, but he was also a man of his age. He advocated forgiveness and reconciliation, where these were possible, but he did not deny the right of revenge.

With the establishment of regular governments, however, private revenge became not only unnecessary but a menace to society. Yet, unfortunately, it had become difficult to denounce it, for it had been sanctioned by the Apostle of God himself. As a result, this terrible theme of revenge has continued to haunt Arab society down even to our own times. In the same manner, the Shiite penitents did not use their devotion to Husain as an incentive to imitate his virtues but rather sought to show their passionate loyalty by killing all those connected with his death or by themselves dying in the attempt.

NOTABLE DATES

Revolt in Medina against the Khalif Yezeed	682
Battle of the Lava	August 683
First Siege of Mecca	Sept. to Nov. 683
Death of Yezeed	
Muawiya II acclaimed khalif in Damascus	November 683
Abdulla ibn Zubair proclaimed in Mecca	
Death of Muawiya II	February 684
Battle of Marj Rahit	
Merwan acclaimed khalif in Damascus	July 684
Battle of Ain al Warda	December 685

PERSONALITIES

Khalifs

Yezeed ibn Muawiya I	680–683
Muawiya II ibn Yezeed	683–684
Adbulla ibn Zubair proclaimed khalif in Mecca	684
Merwan ibn al Hakam	684–685
(Syria and Egypt only)	
Abdul Malik ibn Merwan	685

Ubaidullah ibn Zayyad, attempted to proclaim himself khalif in Basra but was driven out

IV

Vengeance for Husain

If ye avenge not him, the son of the best of you,
Then fling, fling the sword away, and naught but the spindle ply.

HAMMAM IBN GHALIB AL FARAZDAQ[1]

It will have blood they say; blood will have blood.   SHAKESPEARE, *Macbeth*

Revenge is a kind of wild justice, which the more man's nature runs to, the more ought law to weed it out.   FRANCIS BACON

1. Nicholson, *Literary History of the Arabs.*

I V

VENGEANCE FOR HUSAIN

WHEN he was acclaimed in Damascus in the year 685, the new Umaiyid khalif, Abdul Malik ibn Merwan, was confronted with a situation which might well have daunted the most courageous. Apart from inter-tribal rivalries, such as a local war in Khurasan, there were four groups of combatants engaged in civil war. The Umaiyids controlling Syria and Egypt and Abdulla ibn Zubair ruling Arabia and Iraq were occupied in a dynastic struggle for the throne. Shortly before his death, Merwan had sent an army to the Hejaz to take Medina, but it had been repulsed and its commander killed. When, therefore, Merwan's son, Abdul Malik, was acclaimed in Damascus, he found himself firmly in control of only Syria, Palestine and Egypt.

The second khalif, Umar ibn al Khattab, was alleged to have ruled that, in order to become legally khalif, a man had to be recognized as such by all the Muslims. There had been a short interval, before Merwan had set up his standard in Damascus, when Abdulla ibn Zubair had been recognized in all the provinces. According to the purists, therefore, he had become khalif and, as there was no machinery for deposition, he must remain the only legal khalif until his death. In actual fact, however, there were now two rivals in the field contesting the khalifate.

In addition to the two rival khalifs, there were two religious groups in arms, particularly in Iraq. The Shia, or adherents of Ali ibn abi Talib and his martyred son Husain, were strongest in central Iraq, the area from Kufa to Medain. They admitted the need for a khalif who should also be a temporal ruler, but they rejected the claims of the Beni Umaiya family and of Abdulla ibn Zubair, insisting that the khalifate should be hereditary in the descendants of the Prophet through his daughter Fatima, the wife of Ali. Their fanaticism was immensely intensified by their feeling of guilt in that it was they themselves who had betrayed the legitimate heirs to the throne, Ali [2] and Husain.

The other religious armies in the field were those of the Kharijites, the outsiders, who may be compared to the Levellers of Cromwell's time. Disgusted with the endless civil wars provoked by rival claimants to the khalifate, they pursued the ideal of a theocracy. Some of the less extreme Kharijites, however, admitted the need of a human ruler, but claimed that he should be the Muslim best qualified for the post, not necessarily of Quraish, possibly not even an Arab.

When Abdul Malik was acclaimed khalif in Damascus in 685, a Kharijite

---

2. Ali had been assassinated in Kufa on 20th January, 661.

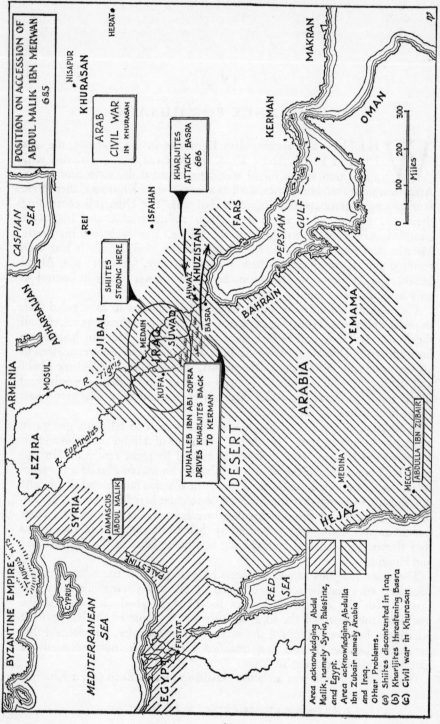

POSITION ON ACCESSION OF
ABDUL MALIK IBN MERWAN
685

ARAB CIVIL WAR
IN KHURASAN

KHARIJITES ATTACK BASRA
686

SHIITES STRONG HERE

MUHALLEB IBN ABI SOFRA
DRIVES KHARIJITES BACK
TO KERMAN

ABDUL MALIK

ABDULLA IBN ZUBAIR

Area acknowledging Abdul
Malik, namely Syria, Palestine,
and Egypt.

Area acknowledging Abdulla
ibn Zubair namely Arabia
and Iraq.

Other Problems.
(a) Shiites discontented in Iraq.
(b) Kharijites threatening Basra.
(c) Civil war in Khurasan.

BYZANTINE EMPIRE
TAURUS MTS.

MEDITERRANEAN SEA

CYPRUS

FUSTAT

EGYPT

RED SEA

HEJAZ

MECCA

MEDINA

PALESTINE

DAMASCUS

SYRIA

JEZIRA

R. Euphrates

MOSUL

ARMENIA

ADHARBAIJAN

CASPIAN SEA

REI

ISFAHAN

NISAPUR

KHURASAN

HERAT

JIBAL

R. Tigris

MEDAIN

KUFA

IRAQ

SUWAD

BASRA

AHWAZ

KHUZISTAN

FARS

PERSIAN GULF

BAHRAIN

KERMAN

MAKRAN

OMAN

ARABIA

YEMAMA

DESERT

0   100   200   300
Miles

78

army 10,000 strong was operating in Khuzistan and was even threatening to capture Basra. The governor of that city (appointed by Abdulla ibn Zubair) twice led out the army of Basra against them but on both occasions was heavily defeated, until at length the Levellers appeared on the banks of the river opposite the city. In this crisis, a new commander, Muhallab ibn abi Sofra, was appointed to lead the army of Basra and, by his own generalship, succeeded near Ahwaz in inflicting a defeat on the fanatics, who withdrew eastwards into Kerman. We shall hear of Muhallab again. Meanwhile, however, a more pressing danger arose in northern Iraq.

* * *

In the year 634, during the khalifate of Umar ibn al Khattab, a certain Abu Ubaid ibn Masud had been appointed to command the army which was about to invade Persia.[3] Rashly crossing the Euphrates in face of the Persian army, the Arabs had been attacked by the enemy, whose onslaught was led by elephants. Though a bad general, Abu Ubaid was a brave man. Attacking the leading elephant sword in hand, he was trampled to death, and his army suffered a disastrous defeat.

A son of this gallant but rash commander, by the name of Mukhtar, was now living in Kufa. When the arrival of Husain had been expected in that town, Ubaidullah ibn Zayyad had thrown Mukhtar into prison, as a suspected sympathizer with the family of Ali ibn abi Talib. He had remained in custody until after the death of Husain. He had eventually been released, but not until after Ubaidullah, while cross-questioning him, had struck him in the face with the hilt of his sword, causing a horrible injury. Ubaidullah's habit of personally striking those brought into his presence earned him many bitter enemies, of whom Mukhtar was henceforward one. Swearing vengeance on Ubaidullah ibn Zayyad, Mukhtar left Kufa for Mecca and joined the Kharijites for a time. Returning to Kufa after the flight of Ubaidullah, he was again imprisoned, this time by the governor appointed by Abdulla ibn Zubair. Eventually released once again, he placed himself in touch with the Shia in Kufa, though he refused to accompany Sulaiman ibn Surad on the expedition which ended in the disastrous battle at Ain al Warda. The death of so many Shia leaders in that battle enabled Mukhtar in 685 to make himself the acknowledged leader of the surviving Shiites of Kufa. Then suddenly they rose in revolt. Pouring out of their houses and gathering in bands in the narrow streets and open spaces, they collected soon after dark, rallying to their battle cry, "O Victorious! Vengeance for Husain." The governor (on behalf of Abdulla ibn Zubair) summoned the leaders of the town to arms and a confused night of fighting in the dark streets ensued. By dawn, the Shiites, though in a minority, were in possession of the town, and Mukhtar seated himself in the audience hall of the governor's castle.

Mounting the pulpit at public prayers, he announced his programme to the assembled people. He would be guided, he said, by the Qoran and the Traditions of the Prophet, would seek revenge for the blood of the martyred decendants of Muhammad, and would fight against those who had usurped

3. *The Great Arab Conquests.*

the khalifate. He promised also especially to protect the poor and the oppressed. Following on this announcement, the people of Kufa were called to
swear allegiance to their new master. This done, he despatched governors in
his name to assume control of the provinces of Armenia, Adharbaijan, Mosul
and Jibal, the Persian province north-east of Kufa.

As a result of Mukhtar's *coup d'état* in Kufa, the situation had therefore
changed in the autumn of 685. The Kharijites had been driven away from
Basra and retired from the scene but there were now three candidates for
imperial rule. Abdul Malik ibn Merwan in Damascus controlled Syria and
Egypt. Abdulla ibn Zubair now held only Arabia and Basra, while Mukhtar
ibn abi Ubaid was established in Kufa, and the provinces of northern Persia.
All semblance of imperial control had vanished from Khurasan, where rival
Arab tribes were still enjoying a free-for-all civil war.

It will be remembered that Ubaidullah ibn Zayyad, after Ain al Warda,
had moved into the northern Jezira, where he was occupied for a year in
suppressing the Qais tribes, which had espoused the cause of Abdulla ibn
Zubair. Soon after the arrival of Mukhtar's governor in Mosul, Ubaidullah
approached that town at the head of the Umaiyid army. The Shia, hopelessly
outnumbered, evacuated Mosul and withdrew to Tikrit. The position of
Mukhtar had suddenly become precarious. With the supporters of Abdulla
ibn Zubair in control of Basra and the Umaiyid army under Ubaidullah in
Mosul, he seemed likely to be crushed between the upper and the nether
millstone.

The majority of the Arabs of Kufa were not Shiites. Mukhtar had seized
power by a determined *coup-de-main*, the Shia forming a small but dedicated
party, who had taken the majority by surprise. News of the withdrawal of
Mukhtar's governor from Mosul encouraged the leading citizens, who began
to gather secretly in one another's houses to plot the overthrow of the Shia.
The principal complaints of the Kufans against Mukhtar were that he had
claimed to be acting on behalf of the surviving descendants of Ali in Mecca
and had produced letters to this effect, but that these documents had now
been proved to be forged. Secondly, his promise to assist the poor and the
oppressed had taken the form of freeing the slaves and seducing the freedmen
of the Arab leaders and enlisting them in his army. His action in enlisting
slaves and freedmen was presumably mere short-term opportunism. The
majority of Arab Kufans being against him, he was obliged to turn for
recruits to the subject races. The majority of the slaves were doubtless Persians,
who (or whose fathers) had been captured by the Arabs during the great
conquests fifty years earlier. Many of these slaves had since been freed by
their masters but had remained in their service as armed retainers.

On 21st July, 686, the town rose against Mukhtar and his followers and
another day of bitter and confused street fighting resulted. The Arab
historians rarely present us with a continuous narrative. They preferred to
record a succession of fragments of information, received by them allegedly
through a long chain of intermediaries, from some person present at the
incident reported. Often these various items contradict one another, but
occasionally they appear to record a really first hand narrative, the vividness

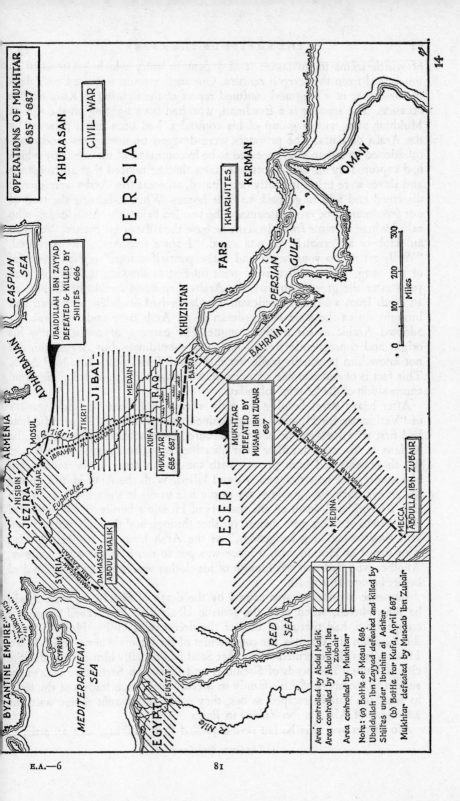

OPERATIONS OF MUKHTAR
685 ~ 687

CIVIL WAR

KHURASAN

PERSIA

KHARIJITES

FARS

KERMAN

OMAN

BAHRAIN

PERSIAN GULF

KHUZISTAN

UBAIDULLAH IBN ZIYAD
DEFEATED & KILLED BY
SHIITES 686

CASPIAN SEA

ADHARBAIJAN

ARMENIA

JIBAL

MEDAIN

IRAQ

BASRA

KUFA

MUKHTAR
685-687

MUKHTAR DEFEATED BY
MUSAAB IBN ZUBAIR
687

MOSUL

TIKRIT

NISIBIN

SINJAR

JEZIRA

R. Tigris

IBRAHIM AL ASHTAR

R. Euphrates

SYRIA

DAMASCUS

ABDUL MALIK

BYZANTINE EMPIRE

TAURUS MTS

CYPRUS

MEDITERRANEAN SEA

EGYPT

FUSTAT

RED SEA

R. NILE

DESERT

MUSAAB IBN ZUBAIR 686

MEDINA

MECCA

ABDULLA IBN ZUBAIR

Miles
0   100   200   300

Area controlled by Abdul Malik
Area controlled by Abdullah ibn Zubair
Area controlled by Mukhtar

Note: (a) Battle of Mosul 686
Ubaidullah ibn Zayyad defeated and killed by
Shiites under Ibrahim al Ashtar
(b) Battle for Kufa, April 687
Mukhtar defeated by Musaab ibn Zubair

of which seems to guarantee it as a genuine story which has reached us untouched from the seventh century. One such account is quoted by Tabari in the course of a long and confused report of the fighting in Kufa on this occasion. The speaker is a freedman, who had been fighting on the side of Mukhtar and, with a group of his comrades, had been taken prisoner by the Arabs of Kufa. The prisoners were dragged up one by one and cross-questioned by a man who appeared to be in command of the company which had captured them. Our informant states that he noticed that all freedmen and slaves were being instantly decapitated, whereas free Arabs were merely disarmed and told to go back to their homes. When it became the turn of our freedman to be cross-questioned, he was led before the Arab leader, who asked where he came from. In reply he gave the tribe of his master. "Are you an Arab or a Persian?" he was asked. "I am a free Arab," he answered. "Well, get off to your home and make yourself scarce," replied the chief of the gang. This incident is of great interest as showing that in 686, fifty years after the great conquests, the Arabs themselves could not distinguish an Arab from a Persian freedman. The latter had doubtless been born and brought up as the slave or freedman of an Arab tribe and had probably adopted Arabic as his mother tongue. His masters, of course, knew his origin and consequently treated him as a subordinate, but Arabs who did not know him personally could not distinguish him from a pure-bred Arab. This fact is of considerable significance when we come to consider the racial composition of the "Arabs" of today.

After heavy street fighting the Shia, stirred to a frenzy by their war-cry of "Vengeance for Husain", at last gained the upper hand. When Mukhtar had first seized power, he had endeavoured by conciliation to win over the Kufans to his side, but after their abortive rising, he changed his attitude. All those who had been present with the Kufan army at the martyrdom of Husain were now dragged out and killed. With the Arab idea of an eye for an eye, they were made as far as possible to die in the manner in which they had inflicted death on the martyrs of Husain's family. Those who had shot arrows at them were themselves shot through and through with arrows, "till they looked like hedgehogs," as the Arab historian records. A man who thrust at Husain with a lance was put to death in the same manner. Another who had stripped Husain of his clothes was himself stripped naked before being put to death.

Immense satisfaction was caused by the death of Shemmer, who, it will be remembered, when even the sadistic Ubaidullah had leaned towards a compromise, had persuaded him of the necessity of killing Husain. Umar ibn Saad ibn abi Waqqas, the commander of the Umaiyid army which killed Husain, was also executed. His father Saad had actually himself founded the city of Kufa.[4] The heads of Shemmer and Umar ibn Saad were sent to the surviving members of Ali's family in Mecca. Such Arab leaders of the town as were not caught escaped as best they could and sought refuge with the adherents of Abdulla ibn Zubair in Basra.

No sooner was this Kufan revolt quelled than Mukhtar sent an army to

4. *The Great Arab Conquests.*

Mosul to oppose the advance of Ubaidullah ibn Zayyad. He entrusted the command to Ibrahim ibn Malik al Ashtar,[5] whose father had been a famous and fanatical fighter in the armies of Ali ibn abi Talib, twenty-five years earlier. It is noticeable how many prominent men of the 680's were sons of the chief commanders in the earlier conquests. Obviously the fame of their fathers had helped them also to reach distinction, but instead of remaining together as a ruling military caste, we now find them exterminating one another in suicidal civil wars.

Ibrahim ibn Malik al Ashtar advanced by forced marches to Mosul, and found Ubaidullah ibn Zayyad with the Umaiyid army camped outside the town. The following day at dawn the two armies drew up opposite one another. Ibrahim rode down the Shiite line, stopping by each tribal war banner and calling out: "O police of God, O defenders of religion, O party of justice. In front of you is Ubaidullah, who killed Husain, the son of Fatima, the daughter of God's Apostle. It was he who prevented him, his women and his children from drinking the water of the Euphrates. Pharaoh himself did not persecute the Children of Israel as he persecuted the family of the Apostle of God."

The Umaiyid army was by far the more numerous, but its left wing consisted of Qais, whose loyalty to the Damascus dynasty was more than doubtful. When the Shiites launched their attack, the Qaisites gave way and, after bitter fighting, the Syrian army collapsed. Three hundred Shiites, who had bound themselves with an oath to kill Ubaidullah, fought their way side by side through rank after rank of the enemy until they came up with the son of Zayyad and fulfilled their vow. Husain ibn Numair al Sakooni, who, in the reign of Yezeed had bombarded Mecca, was also killed.[6] Ibrahim ibn Malik al Ashtar then occupied Mosul and sent out columns which captured Nisibin and Sinjar.

In a striking example of poetic justice, the severed head of Ubaidullah was placed before Mukhtar in the audience hall of the castle of Kufa, in which, only four years before, Ubaidullah had himself toyed with the bloodstained head of the martyred Husain.

*   *   *

While these stirring events had been taking place in the Mosul area, Musaab, the brother of Abdulla ibn Zubair, had arrived in Basra to assume command. The sudden rise of Mukhtar had injured the cause of the son of Zubair more than that of the Damascus khalif. Abdulla had insisted on establishing his capital in Mecca, in the desert peninsula of Arabia, an area which produced fine fighting men but no revenue. He was therefore entirely dependent on the revenues of Iraq and Persia. The establishment of Mukhtar in Kufa had deprived the Meccan khalif of the revenues of Iraq, except for the province of Basra, and had cut off his access to most of Persia. Abdul Malik ibn Merwan was financially and geographically far better placed. Syria and Egypt were adjacent to one another and were the two richest provinces of the empire. The Umaiyids were therefore able, if

5. *The Great Arab Conquests.*   6. Page 61.

necessary, to continue to govern Syria and Egypt indefinitely as a separate kingdom. But Abdulla ibn Zubair must recover the revenues of Iraq immediately or his régime would collapse. As a result, it was the forces of Ibn Zubair which now advanced from Basra against Kufa.

Before leaving Basra, Musaab called to his aid Muhallab ibn abi Sofra, whom we last encountered driving the Kharijite Levellers from Basra. Muhallab, after his victory, had been appointed governor of South Persia by Abdulla ibn Zubair. Now, summoned by Musaab to join in the campaign against Mukhtar, he took his time in answering the summons. When at length he reached Basra "with an immense army", he went to see Musaab. Asked by the orderly at the door to give his name, he struck him in the face causing his nose to bleed and pushed his way in. Ubaidullah may or may not have been a sadist, but here we find another example of an arrogant Arab chieftain striking people in the face. It is ironical to remember that when, in the lifetime of Muhammad, an Arab chief showed signs of arrogance, the Prophet described his action as a remnant of heathenism. Muslims, in the opinion of the Apostle of God, should not be boastful or arrogant. Yet perhaps few, if any, races could have achieved the amazing conquests which the Arabs had made in fifty years, without losing their heads. There is a tradition to the effect that the Prophet himself once remarked that, if all the arrogance in the world were collected together, nine-tenths of it would be found to belong to the Byzantines. Little can he have foreseen that his own Arab compatriots within fifty years would have inherited the same quality from their defeated enemies. Suffice it for us to notice that the Arabs had now become a haughty aristocracy, for their very arrogance was to lead before long to their loss of power.

Another interesting point in the matter of Muhallab ibn abi Sofra is that, for the first time, we see the governor of a Persian province called to assist one side in an Arab civil war. His force, the historians allege, was a large one but it is not possible to ascertain its composition in terms of Persians or Arabs. Undoubtedly, however, it must have included Persian Muslims and freedmen. The commanders were still, of course, all of the Arab race.

Reinforced by the army of South Persia, Musaab ibn Zubair marched on Kufa. Mukhtar himself remained in Kufa but his army moved out to meet the invaders. It will be remembered that a large proportion of Mukhtar's troops had been recruited from the Persian slaves and freedmen of the Arab aristocrats of Kufa, while many of the latter had escaped to Basra and were now advancing with the army of Musaab. Thus in this campaign we see Persians on both sides. The suicidal mutual carnage between the Arab chiefs and tribes had made it necessary to recruit Persians, a process which was gradually to change the composition of the Arab empire.

When the two armies met, the Shia first charged with their usual vigour and the struggle for some time was undecided. Then Muhallab advanced for the decisive attack, the Kufa infantry gave way and Mukhtar's army dissolved in flight. When news of the disaster reached Mukhtar in the castle of Kufa, one of his supporters asked him what was now to be done. "There is nothing to do but to die," he replied quietly. Collecting the remnants of his adherents, he formed them up in line of battle at Harura, a village a few miles from Kufa. In a second battle, which lasted a day and a night, the Shia army was finally dispersed, Musaab ordering that all prisoners be put to death. Eventually Mukhtar, with a handful of followers, shut himself up in the castle of Kufa.

But the position was now hopeless, and the besiegers blockaded the castle so closely that those within could obtain neither food nor water. Eventually Mukhtar addressed his comrades. "When I saw the confusion of the empire," he said, "one claimant in Damascus, one in Mecca, with Yemama in revolt and Arabia in confusion, I too set myself up as one of them. I did no more than the others, except that I exacted vengeance for the blood of Ali and Husain, which the people of Muhammad had neglected to do. But now it is better to die honourably sword in hand, than to drag on the siege in this castle in fear and humiliation." Followed by nineteen of his devoted adherents, Mukhtar then drew his sword and, emerging from the castle into the streets of the town, met death with his face to the enemy. Those who remained in the castle surrendered soon afterwards and were executed in cold blood. Mukhtar's death occurred in April 687. He was sixty-seven years old.

These terrible Arabs, whose conquests in fifty years had struck terror into all the nations around them, seemed now, through their narrow and jealous quarrels, intent on the commission of race suicide. Yet, with all their folly, it is impossible not to be impressed by the impassive courage with which, at any moment, they were prepared to face death. That the first Muslim conquerors should have done so seems less remarkable, for they were inspired by passionate religious enthusiasm and believed that death in battle against infidels meant instant admission to the eternal delights of Paradise. Yet, surprising as it may seem, they continued to display, in their jealous worldly rivalries, an indifference to death little short of that of the earlier conquerors.

*   *   *

The elimination of Mukhtar left the rival khalifs of Damascus and Mecca to fight it out between them, though the Kharijites in southern Persia continued to raid the lower Tigris area from Medain to Basra. Before, however, Abdul Malik ibn Merwan could devote all his energies to the war against his competitor, he was obliged to deal with a rival nearer home. Amr ibn Saeed ibn al Aasi was his own cousin.[7] He claimed that Merwan had promised to leave the throne to him but had subsequently broken his pledge and appointed his own son Abdul Malik as the heir. As a result, Amr ibn Saeed claimed openly that he, not Abdul Malik, was the rightful khalif. The two cousins became increasingly hostile to one another, although they still appeared together in public in apparent amity. Abdul Malik, however, lived in constant fear of assassination, or of a *coup d'état* in favour of Amr. At last one day the khalif invited his cousin to visit him the same evening in his private apartments. He was at first cordially welcomed, though he noticed

7. Genealogical tree, page 64.

that Abdul Malik was surrounded by his brothers and intimate retainers. Shortly after his entry, however, the doors closed behind him. After an exchange of recriminations, the khalif signed to a retainer. The man struck at Amr but failed to kill him, for the victim had taken the precaution of wearing a coat of chain mail underneath his robes. The sons of Merwan hesitated, an unseemly struggle ensued. Amr was eventually thrown to the ground when the khalif himself, kneeling upon his chest, cut his cousin's throat with his own hands. A crowd had meanwhile collected outside the palace and the adherents of Amr ibn Saeed threatened disorders. The head of Amr was hastily severed from his body and thrown to the people, to convince them that the cause was lost. The crowd thereupon dispersed.

It may seem curious to us that the public should thereafter continue loyally to serve a ruler who had murdered his cousin with his own hands. Perhaps a people so inured to war and so ready to face death themselves, could consider that it was only natural that a man should dispose of a rival in this manner. Actually the Apostle of God had himself caused a number of his opponents to be removed by assassination but these had been unbelievers, who were opposing the spread of Islam. He had strongly condemned the murder of other Muslims.

* * *

In 689, the Byzantine Empire had threatened a more active policy on the Arab frontiers, and Abdul Malik, anxious before all else to re-unite the empire, had agreed to pay to Byzantium a tribute of a thousand dinars every week. Considering himself thereby made secure from Byzantine attack and no longer afraid to leave Damascus lest his cousin seize the khalifate in his absence, Abdul Malik ibn Merwan early in 691 prepared in earnest for a military campaign. The nearest enemy was not Abdulla ibn Zubair in Mecca but his brother Musaab in Iraq. The fickle Kufans had already tired of the rule of Musaab and Abdul Malik had been in correspondence with many of their leaders, who had promised him their support. He now advanced with his army to the upper Euphrates, while Musaab moved northwards from Kufa to meet him. In the summer of 691, the two armies confronted one another at Deir al Jailiq in the Jezirah. The gallant Ibrahim ibn Malik al Ashtar, who had, in the interests of Mukhtar, defeated and killed Ubaidullah ibn Zayyad at Mosul, was commanding Musaab's advanced guard and charged the leading formation of the Damascus army putting it quickly to flight, but in the ensuing action Ibrahim himself was killed.

Musaab then ordered various leaders to advance but each one began to make excuses. "I do not wish my men to suffer unnecessary casualties," said one. "I must ask you to excuse me," said another. "Why should I advance, when no one else seems to be advancing?" replied a third. Musaab's heart sank as he suddenly realized that, unknown to him, all this had been arranged beforehand in secret correspondence with Abdul Malik. "O Ibrahim," he exclaimed, "but Ibrahim is no longer with me today." Indeed Ibrahim ibn al Ashtar seems to have been the only loyal commander that day. While the armies still faced one another, Muhammad ibn Merwan, the brother of

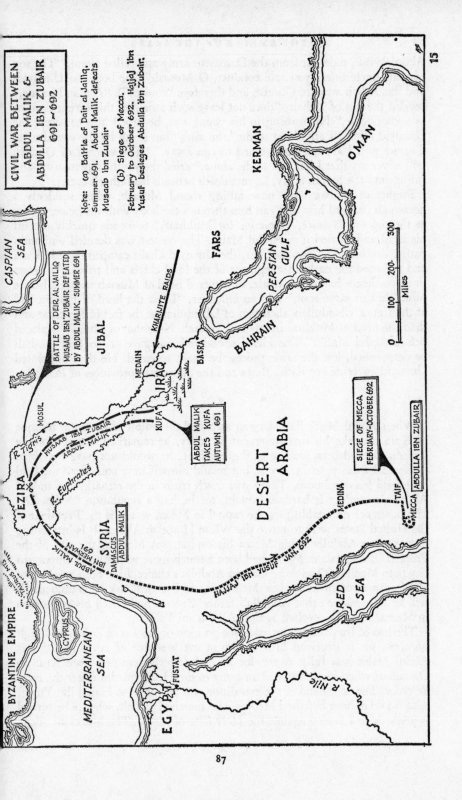

CIVIL WAR BETWEEN
ABDUL MALIK &
ABDULLA IBN ZUBAIR
691 - 692

Note: (a) Battle of Dair al Jailiq.
Summer 691. Abdul Malik defeats
Musaab ibn Zubair

(b) Siege of Mecca.
February to October 692. Hajjaj ibn
Yusuf besieges Abdulla ibn Zubair.

CASPIAN
SEA

BATTLE OF DEIR AL JAILIQ
MUSAAB IBN ZUBAIR DEFEATED
BY ABDUL MALIK. SUMMER 691

JIBAL

KHARIJITE RAIDS

MEDAIN

IRAQ

KUFA

BASRA

BAHRAIN

FARS

PERSIAN
GULF

KERMAN

OMAN

300

200

100

0

Miles

R. Tigris

MOSUL

MUSAAB IBN ZUBAIR

ABDUL MALIK

R. Euphrates

JEZIRA

ABDUL MALIK
TAKES KUFA
AUTUMN 691

DESERT
ARABIA

SYRIA

DAMASCUS

ABDUL MALIK

IBN MEKRAN
691

ABDUL MALIK

HAJJAJ IBN YUSUF JAN. 692

MEDINA

TAIF

SIEGE OF MECCA
FEBRUARY-OCTOBER 692

MECCA   ABDULLA IBN ZUBAIR

RED
SEA

BYZANTINE
EMPIRE

MEDITERRANEAN
SEA

CYPRUS

Taurus Mts

FUSTAT

EGYPT

R. Nile

15

Abdul Malik, rode out from the Damascus army and called aloud, "The son of your uncle offers you safe conduct, O Musaab" (for both the Umaiyids and ibn Zubair were of Quraish and therefore "cousins"). "A man like me," replied the son of Zubair, "does not leave such a field as this except dead or as a conqueror," but turning to his young son, he urged him to accept the Umaiyid offer. "I am about to die", he said, "but death by the sword is no disgrace and I am not accustomed to run away." "The women of Quraish will never say that I left you to die alone," cried the youth impetuously, and riding into the Syrian army, he met death beneath his father's eyes.

Flights of arrows were now falling round Musaab, when suddenly a horseman charged him and ran him through the body with his lance, crying at the top of his voice, "Revenge for Mukhtar." Someone quickly cut off his head and carried it to Abdul Malik. The contest was decided without a battle. Probably in December 691, the Umaiyid khalif camped outside Kufa and accepted the oaths of allegiance of the local chiefs and tribes. As he sat in the audience hall of the castle, the severed head of Musaab was laid before him. "In this same spot," said an onlooker, "I saw the head of Husain laid at the feet of Ubaidullah, then that of Ubaidullah at the feet of Mukhtar and then the head of Mukhtar in front of Musaab. Now that of Musaab is placed before Abdul Malik." The khalif shuddered and gave orders that the hall be demolished, lest the same process be again repeated. He then appointed Umaiyid governors to Kufa, Basra and the dependent provinces of Persia.

* * *

When Abdul Malik ibn Merwan ascended the pulpit of the great mosque of Kufa to make his first statement of policy, he remarked that if Abdulla ibn Zubair had been worthy of the khalifate, he would not have remained passive all these years in Mecca, but would himself have come into the field to defend his dominions. There was much truth in the remark, and indeed Abdulla's conduct is hard to explain, for he had a reputation for bravery. His insistence on establishing the capital in Mecca was as if the President of the United States were to move the White House to Alaska. It is interesting to note that Abdulla made Mecca his capital, not Medina, the city of the Prophet. Before Islam, Mecca had been a much more wealthy and important city than Medina. Thus there may, in Abdulla's choice, have been an element of Meccan resentment against Medina, as well as jealousy of Damascus. It will be remembered that Abdulla's father, Zubair, had raised his supporters in Mecca, when he revolted against Ali ibn abi Talib.[8]

The loss of Iraq and Persia made the position of the son of Zubair wellnigh hopeless, for it deprived him of almost every source of revenue. Of this Abdul Malik was fully aware, for he had scarcely returned from Kufa to Damascus when he despatched an army to the Hejaz to administer the *coup de grâce*. The command of the expedition was entrusted to Hajjaj ibn Yusuf, who is said to have bypassed Medina, and marched to Taif, whence he turned westwards and moved against the Holy City of Mecca. The historians allege

8. Page 34.

that the siege of Mecca began in February 692, but that would scarcely allow
sufficient time, if Abdul Malik had been in Kufa in December 691. Perhaps
the campaign in Iraq was earlier in 691.

The siege of Mecca lasted eight months and seventeen days. Though
Abdulla ibn Zubair may have shown little initiative during the previous ten
years, he displayed inexhaustible courage and determination when his cause
was already lost. Hajjaj had planted mangonels on the mountains which from
every side dominated the town. The ammunition used in these great catapults consisted of pieces of rock, of which the mountains themselves were
composed and thus an unending bombardment could be maintained. While
the Meccans were closely besieged, supplies were ample in the Umaiyid
camp, even the cakes and sweetmeats of Damascus being in good supply.

Hajjaj made use of diplomacy as successfully as he directed the operations
of war. By offering safe conduct to all who deserted the cause of Abdulla, he
gradually reduced the strength of the garrison. No less than ten thousand
men are said to have deserted to the Syrian army during the course of the
siege. Sorties by the defenders, which had at first been frequent, became
impossible as the garrison weakened. Finally scarcely a handful of men
remained with Abdulla, even two of his sons deserting at night to surrender
to the enemy.

The mother of Abdulla ibn Zubair was Asma, daughter of Abu Bekr, the
closest friend and first successor of the Prophet Muhammad himself. Seventy
years before, after preaching in Mecca, the Apostle had been persecuted and
his life threatened by the people of the town. Stealing out of the city at dusk,
he had lain concealed with Abu Bekr in a cave of those same mountains,
whence the Umaiyid missiles were now raining down upon the Holy City.
For three nights, while the hue and cry persisted, Asma had carried food to
the two fugitives under cover of darkness.[9] On the fourth night, the Prophet
and his companion decided to escape to Medina. Asma as usual had brought
them a parcel of food. Uniting two belts which she was wearing round her
dress, she used them to tie the bag of provisions to the saddle of one of the
camels. As "she of the two belts", she had been for seventy years one of the
heroines of Islam, and was still alive at the time of the siege. Abandoned by
nearly all his followers, including even his near relatives, Abdulla went to
consult his aged mother, who must have been over eighty years old. "Mother,"
he is alleged to have said, "everyone has deserted me, even my son and my
own family. Only a handful are left, scarcely capable of holding out for
another hour. The enemy is offering to spare my life and to give me all that
I need to live. Tell me, Mother, what you think." "You know better than I
do, my son," replied the old lady. "If you believe your cause to be right, you
should be ready to die for it. Free men do not surrender merely because
they are deserted by their cowardly comrades. If, on the other hand, your
object in this war has been mere worldly gain, then it is only reasonable
now to accept a worldly compromise." Abdulla stooped over the frail figure
and kissed her hair. "That too is my opinion," he said. "From the day on
which I claimed the khalifate, I have sought religion, not the world, nor

9. *The Great Arab Conquests.*

have I pursued the pleasures of life. But I wanted to hear your view. I shall be killed today, Mother, but do not mourn for me."

Emerging alone, sword in hand, from one of the gates of the Kaaba enclosure, he chased the enemy up the narrow lanes at the foot of the mountains which hemmed in the city. Soon a missile struck him in the face and his blood flowed down his beard and clothes. Pausing for a second, he cried in stentorian tones:

"No craven wounds our backs shall stain with shame,
But down our breasts our glorious blood shall flow."[10]

Then other missiles struck him and he fell prostrate. Word was soon carried to Hajjaj, who, with one companion, hastened to where the body lay. "No woman ever bore a better man than this," said Hajjaj's comrade. "What," cried the latter, "are you praising a man who rebelled against the Prince of the Faithful?" "Yes," replied the first. "We have besieged him here for eight months, though the town is fortified by neither wall nor ditch, and, in every sortie he made, he drove us back." It was 3rd October, 692, when Abdulla ibn Zubair thus met his death.

*   *   *

Over-simplification is one of the greatest pitfalls to the political observer. It is all too easy to denounce the wicked Beni Umaiya and to praise the martyrs whom they defeated or killed. But the result is not entirely satisfactory, for we also find worthy and religious men fighting on their side and denouncing with bitterness the captious opposition of their rivals. Nor do we appear to be entirely justified in condemning all those concerned as a lot of quarrelsome Arabs squabbling over the loot. The passionate devotion of the Shiite penitents at the grave of Husain exonerates them of materialistic objectives. The Kharijites, who demanded a theocratic republic and were governed by a council of godly men, seem to have provoked the most unqualified condemnation of the historians. Yet though the various governors of Kufa and Basra put many thousands of these people to death, they persisted in their beliefs, showing extraordinary powers of endurance.

In the same manner, there must have been more in the quarrel of the Umaiyids and Abdulla ibn Zubair than the mere jealous rivalry of princes. As has already been suggested, Mecca and Medina were remote desert caravan stations far from the centre of gravity of the brilliant and wealthy empire which the enthusiasm of the first Muslims had built up. Beni Umaiya had now virtually become natives of Damascus and had grown up in the cosmopolitan atmosphere of Syria, with its thousand year old Greek and Roman culture and a history extending back long before that. The greater part of the people of Syria, including most of the better educated, were still Christians, who also supplied the majority of the government officials with whom the khalif was obliged to work. To abandon the centre of this active world and carry back the seat of imperial government to a remote desert oasis must to the Umaiyids have appeared completely unpractical. More-

10. The quotation is from a classical Arab poem.

over, Syria faced the Byzantine Empire, the only world power which could
in any way compete with the Arabs. If the government returned to the Hejaz,
would not the Byzantines attempt to reconquer Syria? We can imagine even
wise and pious supporters of Beni Umaiya saying, "We deeply venerate the
holy cities of Mecca and Medina, but it is no longer practical politics to
continue civil government from there. Those who rebel against the Damascus
khalif will simply destroy the empire and the Muslim community."

Abdulla ibn Zubair is said to have justified his rebellion by saying that
he had been carried away by pious indignation when he saw those things
openly practised which God had forbidden. Perhaps therefore we are justified
in concluding that he saw in himself the defender of the true faith preached
by the Apostle of God. His mother, as we have mentioned, was the heroine
of the Prophet's escape from Mecca, almost the Arab Flora Macdonald, if
such a comparison be admissible. His father Zubair had been one of the
Apostle's closest companions. His father's mother had been Muhammad's
aunt. There is a curious story that when Abdulla ibn Zubair was a boy, the
Prophet had one day been bled for some indisposition. Seeing the young
Abdulla, Muhammad had called to him and said, "Abdulla, take this bowl of
blood and pour it away where no one will see it." But when the boy left the
room, he drank the blood. "Many people," writes the Arab historian, "used
to think that he derived his strength and courage from that blood." Perhaps
he thought so himself.

The historians in general bear witness to the piety of Abdulla, his immensely long devotions and his attachment to the House of God, the Kaaba
temple of Mecca. Some allege that he spent whole nights kneeling or pros-
trated in prayer. The Damascus party were to attribute his piety to hypocrisy.
There is another factor, however, which may at times be traced in the conduct of the early Muslims, namely the fear of hell. The Prophet had described
in the most terrifying terms the excruciating tortures to which the wicked
would be subjected. Many believers resorted to fasting, weeping and all-night
prayers in the anxious hope of avoiding so terrible an ultimate fate.

Ibn Zubair, it was said, excelled in three things, bravery, piety and eloquence. He had a voice which, when he preached, resounded in the hills
around the town. On only one fault were his friends and his foes agreed and
that was his avarice. He was not a generous giver, a serious shortcoming in
the opinion of the people of Arabia. But he was alleged to have been a just
judge.

"Thou didst remind us of Abu Bekr[11] when thou didst rule us,
Of Othman and ibn al Khattab, and the poor were glad.
Unfailing justice didst thou deal out to the people,
But in the morning came dark clouds to make us sad."

The dark clouds which followed the death of Abdulla were the final
establishment of the dynasty in Damascus and the sinking of Mecca into
political insignificance, an old "cathedral city" far removed from the bustle
of modern life.

11. Abu Bekr, Umar ibn al Khattab and Othman were the first three successors of Muhammad.

The civil war had lasted twelve years from the rebellion of Husain and then that of Abdulla ibn Zubair to the final establishment of Abdul Malik as sole khalif. Yet we may see in these apparently wasteful and bloody struggles not merely the petty rivalries of a lot of squabbling Arabs but the travail necessary for the emergence of a new social order, in which both the innovators of Damascus and the religious conservatives of Medina, the supporters of the divine right of the family of Ali and the Kharijite theocrats, all conscientiously believed in the rightness of their respective causes.

The bellicose nature of the primitive Arab race doubtless resulted in the attempt to settle every difference by war.

> "On the back of my mare
> With my lance by my side,
> That's the way I would live,
> All the rest I deride,"

the bedouin poet had sung. But this warlike frame of mind did not produce the conscientious differences of opinion which divided the faithful—it merely meant that every such difference of opinion was settled by battle.

NOTABLE DATES

Abdul Malik ibn Merwan acclaimed in Damascus	685
Mukhtar's *coup d'état* in Kufa	Autumn 685
Battle of Mosul. Ubaidullah ibn Zayyad killed by Shia	686
Defeat and death of Mukhtar	April 687
Battle of Deir al Jailiq. Defeat and death of Musaab ibn Zubair	Summer 691
Kufa submits to Abdul Malik	Autumn 691
Siege of Mecca by Hajjaj	February–October 692
Death of Abdulla ibn Zubair Abdul Malik sole khalif	} 3rd October 692

PERSONALITIES

Abdulla ibn Zubair, khalif in Mecca
Abdul Malik ibn Merwan, khalif in Damascus
Muhallab ibn abi Sofra, military commander, defeated the Kharijites.
Mukhtar ibn abi Ubaid, leader of the Shiite revolt in Iraq.
Ubaidullah ibn Zayyad, the man who ordered the death of Husain, now killed by the Shia at Mosul.
Musaab ibn Zubair, brother of Abdulla, defeated Mukhtar, and was himself killed by Abdul Malik.
Hajjaj ibn Yusuf, besieged Mecca and killed Abdulla ibn Zubair.

V

The Great Abdul Malik

While Egypt was won almost without a blow, Latin Africa took sixty years to conquer. It was first invaded in 647 but Carthage was not subdued till 698, nor was the whole province finally reduced for eleven years longer.

E. A. FREEMAN, *History of the Saracens*

Abdul Malik's . . . problem now was to devise a new organization. The inevitable answer was a greater degree of centralization, concentrating authority in the ruler and basing it on the military power of the army of Syria. The Caliphate of Abdul Malik was still not an autocracy of the old oriental type, but rather a centralized monarchy, modified by Arab tradition and by the remnants of the theocratic idea. PROFESSOR BERNARD LEWIS, *The Arabs in History*

V

THE GREAT ABDUL MALIK

THE death of Abdulla ibn Zubair seemed to leave Abdul Malik ibn Merwan in undisputed control of the empire. Only in Khuzistan, east of Baasra, the Kharijites continued their reign of terror. Muhallab ibn abi Sofra had established the reputation of being the only man who could deal with them, and the khalif now ordered a levy of troops from Kufa and Basra to operate under his command and stamp out these obstinate fanatics. With considerable difficulty 10,000 troops were levied in Kufa and despatched to join Muhallab in Ram Hormuz, but almost all of them deserted and returned to their homes before reaching their destination. Constantly in rebellion, repeatedly refusing to serve when called upon by legitimate authority, the Kufans had exhausted the patience of every government. In January 695, the khalif wrote to Medina to Hajjaj ibn Yusuf, the man who had defeated Ibn Zubair, to proceed immediately as governor of Kufa and Basra.

Hajjaj was not the man to let the grass grow under his feet. With an escort of only twelve men on swift camels, he crossed the Arabian desert, and arrived in Kufa before anyone knew that he had left Medina. Entering the great mosque with his kerchief [1] drawn across his face, he mounted the pulpit and called the people to assemble. Then suddenly removing the covering from his face, he began, "I see heads in front of me ripe to be cut off. Methinks I see the blood spurting between the kerchiefs and the beards. If any man of the levy ordered to join Muhallab is found in Kufa in three days' time, his blood will flow and his property will be confiscated." He then retired to the governor's quarters and said no more.

On the third day, Hajjaj mounted the pulpit once again and called for the levies to join Muhallab. A man of Beni Temeem stood up and began to argue, but the new governor signed to the guard, a soldier stepped forward and cut off the heckler's head. The town crier was then sent through the streets to announce, "Umair ibn Dhabi came after the expiry of the three days and admitted that he had heard the call-up. He was executed. Any more of Muhallab's levies still here this evening will be put to death in the same manner." The historian adds solemnly that an hour later there was a traffic jam on the Euphrates bridge, caused by troopers setting out to join the army. Thus reinforced, Muhallab engaged the fanatics and drove them in flight into the recesses of the Persian mountains.

The Kharijites had developed their own system of tactics, based on extreme mobility and the retention of the initiative. If the situation turned against

---

1. Arab headgear always consisted of a cloth, either wound round the head or kept in place by a rope. I have used kerchief as perhaps preferable to headcloth.

them, they would fade away, but a few days later would suddenly appear unexpectedly elsewhere, surprise and exterminate some isolated column or detachment and disappear once more. They were especially skilful at night attacks and many a column had been suddenly surprised at night to find a horde of wild tribesmen slashing right and left with their swords in the very midst of the sleeping soldiers. Muhallab, to counter such tactics, was in the habit of surrounding his camp every night by a ditch. The undisciplined Kufan units who, even after joining the army, refused to dig after a day's march, were duly surprised by the fanatic swordsmen and suffered heavy casualties.

But while Muhallab was making steady if unspectacular progress in Khuzistan, a Kharijite revolt suddenly began in May 695 in the Jezira, west of Mosul. Under the leadership of a certain Shabeeb, a small but extremely mobile force of the fanatics swept across the country from Mosul to Kufa, Medain, Khaniqin and back. Successive columns sent in pursuit were ambushed or surprised and routed. In September 695, they were threatening Kufa itself. For more than a year, Shabeeb spread terror and devastation up and down Iraq. The hard core of the Kharijites were stern republicans, desperate fighters whose motto was "no rule but that of God". Their long and undefeated career in Iraq, however, resulted in their being joined by many with less worthy motives, murderers, debtors, malcontents and criminals. Far more interesting, however, from a social point of view, are the relations of the Kharijite rebels with the country people, for the farmers and agricultural workers, especially on the Tigris, were still Persians. Sixty years had elapsed since the first Arab conquest of Iraq. When the occupation of the country was completed, the Arab armies had been concentrated in two main cantonments at Kufa and Basra and the troops had been forbidden to acquire land or engage in cultivation. The original farmers were to remain on the land, paying tribute to their conquerors. We have already seen that Ubaidullah ibn Zayyad had even allowed the Persian landowners to farm the taxes.

The original Arab conquerors had been mostly nomadic tribesmen from the desert, who had settled in the two cantonments, now become cities. It is a remarkable fact that nomadic bedouins become transformed into city-dwellers more easily than into farm-workers, for the nomad, like the citizen, lives by his wits. To him the solid and monotonous labour of the farm-worker is infinitely wearisome.

As a result, both owing to policy and to inclination, the agricultural work of Iraq was still in the hands of Persians, who, once the citizens of the mighty Sassanid empire, were now reduced to the position of a subject race, toiling to supply their Arab masters, but without voice in the government and without any possibility of power or advancement. Such persons might well sympathize with a daring band of rebels against the established government, and the ancient records speak of many occasions on which the Kharijites were entertained by the villagers to a meal, while the Persian landowner kept a watch for any government forces which might be approaching. The leaders of the fanatics and of the government troops were, of course, all alike Arabs, whose insane mutual hostilities were to give hope once more to the conquered

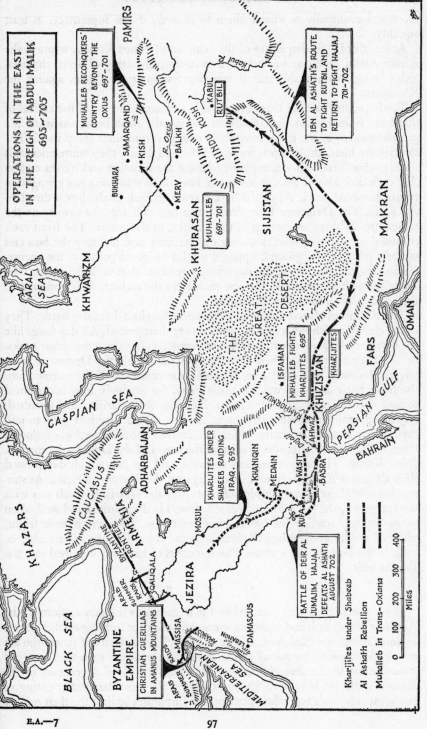

OPERATIONS IN THE EAST
IN THE REIGN OF ABDUL MALIK
695-705

MUHALLEB RECONQUERS'
COUNTRY BEYOND THE
OXUS 697-701

IBN AL ASHATH'S ROUTE
TO FIGHT RUTBIL AND
RETURN TO FIGHT HAJAJ
701-702

MUHALLEB
697-701

MUHALLEB FIGHTS
KHARIJITES 695

KHARIJITES

KHARIJITES UNDER
SHABEEB RAIDING
IRAQ. 695

BATTLE OF DEIR AL
JUMAJIM, HAJJAJ
DEFEATS AL ASHATH
AUGUST 702

PAMIRS

Kabul R.

KABUL

RUTBIL

HINDU KUSH

SAMARQAND

BUKHARA

KISH

R. Oxus

BALKH

MERV

KHWARIZM

ARAL SEA

KHURASAN

SIJISTAN

MAKRAN

THE GREAT DESERT

OMAN

CASPIAN SEA

ISFAHAN

RAMHORMUZ

Dujail

AHWAZ

KHUZISTAN

FARS

PERSIAN GULF

BAHRAIN

ADHARBAIJAN

KHANIQIN

MEDAIN

WASIT

BASRA

KUFA

ARMENIA

BYZANTINE FRONTIER

CAUCASUS

KHAZARS

MOSUL

JEZIRA

Arab
summer
raids

QALIQALA

BLACK SEA

BYZANTINE
EMPIRE

CHRISTIAN GUERILLAS
IN AMANUS MOUNTAINS

MASSISA

MAMISTRA

Arabs
summer
raids

LEBANON

DAMASCUS

MEDITERRANEAN SEA

Kharijites under Shabeeb
Al Ashath Rebellion
Muhalleb in Trans-Oxiana

0   100   200   300   400
Miles

races and eventually to enable them to recover, if not supremacy, at least equality.

At length Hajjaj, despairing of the fickle and factious Kufans, wrote to the Khalif Abdul Malik and asked for a force from the army of Syria, the local levies being so unreliable that it was hopeless to employ them against the Kharijites.

Twelve centuries after these events, it is a pleasure to read of the arrival of this force from Damascus. Unmilitary though the Arab historians were, the professionalism of the army from Syria emerges from their every word. The sentries are alert, the camp is fortified before nightfall, the commander calls up his subordinate officers, explains to them the situation and makes certain that each unit knows what it has to do. How little soldiering has changed in twelve hundred years. When the Syrian army arrived, Shabeeb was threatening Kufa. The Damascus force drew up in line of battle, the cavalry on the wings, the infantry, drawn up in three ranks, in the centre. The front rank consisted of pikemen who, kneeling on one knee and planting the butt-end of their pikes in the ground, opposed a solid hedge of points to the enemy. Behind the pikemen stood the swordsmen, ready to deal with the enemy who broke through the pikes. In the rear rank were the archers, their bows ready, their quivers well stocked with arrows.

The Kharijites always attacked. They never fought a defensive battle. They either charged with desperate bravery or they disappeared. All day long, like the dervishes at Omdurman, they threw themselves in vain at the steady ranks. In the later afternoon, when their charges slackened, the Damascus army advanced slowly in a solid line, sweeping the remnants of the enemy from the field. Such an army was too professional for Shabeeb, long accustomed to easy victories over the Kufan levies. Next day the Kharijites had vanished, appearing again soon afterwards near Ahwaz, where they had gone to join their fellow sectaries in south Persia. The Syrian expeditionary force followed them and another battle was fought on the banks of the Dujail—the modern River Karun. The same story was repeated, and the fanatics all day pressed their desperate charges without success against the disciplined ranks. At sunset they withdrew across a bridge of boats over the Dujail. Shabeeb was with the rearguard, the last man to cross the river. He dismounted and walked on to the bridge, leading his horse. Halfway across, however, it took fright, plunged wildly and pushed Shabeeb into the river. Clad in his armour, he sank to the bottom like a stone. The remnants of his army vanished into the Persian hills.

*   *   *

Many people today are puzzled by the tremendous military exploits of the Arabs in the seventh and eighth centuries and the poor fighting quality shown by some of the so-called Arab armies of today. The majority of those who are now called Arabs have racially little connection with the men who emerged from Arabia in the seventh century. However, the rapid degeneracy of the Kufans is also of interest. Sixty years before, the most desperate fighting of the great conquests had taken place on the Euphrates against the then mighty

Persian empire. The decisive battle of Qadasiya, a gruelling struggle lasting four days with very heavy casualties, was fought only a few miles from Kufa. When victory over Persia was won, the victorious Arabs established their main base at Kufa. In 695, the Kufans who fled before Shabeeb were the grandsons—in a few cases the sons—of the heroes of Qadasiya.

Three causes for this extraordinarily rapid degeneracy may be traced. Firstly, the Prophet himself had recognized as legitimate the use as concubines of women captured in war with unbelievers. The conquest of the ancient, wealthy and luxurious Persian Empire had brought fantastic rewards. Every Arab soldier was able to secure great numbers of wives and concubines and ample wealth with which to support them. Thus the once lean and hardy warriors of the desert quickly became physically enervated by idleness and luxury.

The second cause of the military deterioration of the Kufans arose indirectly from the same source, namely the multiplication of wives and concubines. But it was a weakening of loyalty and conviction rather than a physical deterioration. It seems only natural to suppose that many of these Greek, Persian or Armenian concubines were neither enthusiastic Arabs nor even genuinely convinced Muslims. Their upbringing of their children might well, therefore, be liable to sow in the minds of the infants ideas calculated to weaken alike their warlike Arab spirit and their unquestioning Muslim devotion. The mere knowledge that a child's mother and her relatives were Greeks or Persians would unconsciously produce a broader outlook and weaken the readiness to die unquestioningly for the victory of the Arabs.

The third reason for the new unwillingness of the Kufans to fight probably lay in their many divided loyalties. Some favoured the Shia, others had supported Abdulla ibn Zubair, yet another group sympathized with the Kharijites. Moreover, many of the people of the city were now ex-slaves of varied racial origins, to whom their Arab masters had given their freedom.

It is especially noteworthy that the smaller dissenting sects were still able to engender the extraordinary fighting quality of sixty years before. The Shiites and the Kharijites alike produced the passionate enthusiasm which sought martyrdom in battle and which had been responsible for the great conquests. The fact, already emphasized, that the khalifate combined political and religious rule, resulted in a damping down of spiritual fervour. The khalifs of Damascus were often capable rulers but no saints. Men of the world, who believed in the need for stable government, were thus fain to adopt a religious compromise. Even if the successor of the Apostle of God drank wine, wore silk and kept a private orchestra, it was necessary in the public interest to swear loyalty to him. Like all state-established churches, the orthodox Muslims tended to be lukewarm and their religion was modified by political expediency. The uncompromising adhered to the more closely-knit dissenting sects.

* * *

In the east, Hajjaj ibn Yusuf was promoted by the khalif to be viceroy of all Iraq and Persia. The destruction of the Kharijites had released Muhallab ibn Abi Sofra, who was appointed governor of Khurasan and the north-east frontiers. For the first time for fourteen years, peace was established at home and the Arab war-banners moved forward once more against the Turks of the eastern borderlands. Crossing the Oxus, Muhallab occupied Kish, where he remained for a year collecting tribute and inflicting punishment on the rebellious. The Arabs had invaded the country beyond the Oxus many years before, but control had been lost during the years of civil war.

To the Arabs, everything beyond the Oxus was simply called Beyond-the-River. Geologically, however, the mountainous plateau of Iran ended at the Murghab River, two hundred miles south-west of the Oxus, which lay in the centre of a vast plain extending as far as the Jaxartes. In the days of Cyrus and Darius, the Persian Empire had extended to the Jaxartes, but subsequently waves of Mongol invaders had driven the Persians back to the Murghab, where the frontier lay at the time of the Arab invasion. The population of the area between the Murghab and the Jaxartes, however, was still basically Iranian, though it had for several centuries been to varying degrees tributary to the Turks, who lived east of the Jaxartes.

Consequently the land Beyond-the-River had long been the cockpit of Central Asia, constantly disputed between the Turks and the Persians. Thus pulled this way and that, the populations between the Murghab and the Jaxartes had failed to unite politically. When the Arabs arrived, the area was a patchwork of small principalities, a situation greatly facilitating its conquest.

In spite of political insecurity, however, Trans-Oxiana was extremely wealthy, civilized and sophisticated. Its prosperity was due to the fact that the main trade route between the Chinese and Persian Empires passed through it, and its merchants came and went regularly to China. The cities of Samarqand, Bukhara and Baykand were wealthy depots of this commerce.[2]

The campaigns of Muhallab beyond the Oxus did not enable the Arabs to establish a regular administration and the local rulers were left in their principalities subject to the payment of tribute. At least, however, Arab prestige was successfully restored. Hajjaj then turned his attention to Rutbil, the ruler of Kabul, a city which had also been taken before the civil wars but had meanwhile been lost again. The governor of Sijistan was ordered to advance against Rutbil and bring him to submission, but the operation miscarried. Hajjaj determined to organize a new expedition strong enough to ensure success. For this purpose he raised ten thousand men each from Kufa and Basra, and confided the command to Abdul Rahman ibn al Ashath,[3] one of the principal Arab chiefs in Kufa, who advanced into Sijistan. So lavishly had Hajjaj provided for this army, which cost two million dirhems to equip, that it was nicknamed by the Arabs the army of peacocks. Abdul Rahman ibn al Ashath advanced somewhat languidly into the territory of Kabul, plundering cows and sheep, but failing to press the campaign to a decision. When Hajjaj wrote him a reprimand, Abdul Rahman read it out indignantly to his subordinate commanders; shouts of anger rose and soon the cry of "Down

2. H. A. R. Gibb, *The Arab Conquests in Central Asia.*
3. Al Ashath had been one of the great warriors of Islam in the first conquests. *The Great Arab Conquests.*

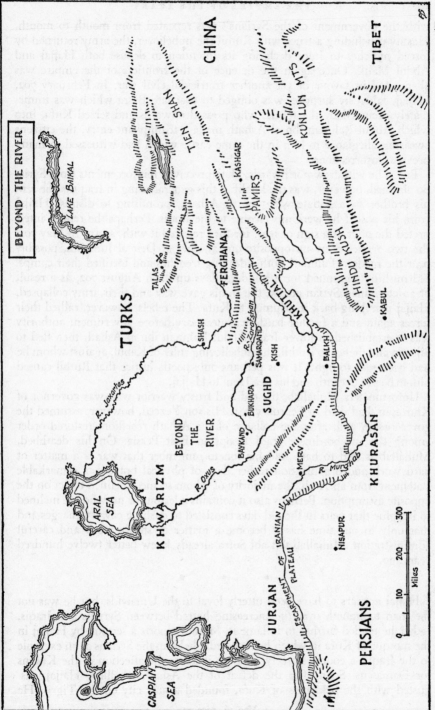

with the government of the Syrians" was repeated from mouth to mouth. Hastily concluding a truce with Rutbil the unbeliever, the army returned by forced marches to Iraq, declaring its intention to depose both Hajjaj and Abdul Malik. Once again the defence of the frontiers of the empire was abandoned in favour of yet another fratricidal civil war. In February 702, Hajjaj, taken by surprise, was obliged to evacuate Basra which was immediately occupied by the rebels, who pressed onwards and seized Kufa, into which Abdul Rahman ibn al Ashath made a triumphant entry, the citizens swearing allegiance to him in the same castle which had witnessed so many previous insurrections.

But as he withdrew northwards, Hajjaj received reinforcements from Syria. So alarmed, however, was the khalif at this general rising in Iraq that he sent his brother to negotiate with Ibn al Ashath, promising to dismiss Hajjaj from his post if he were unwelcome to the Iraqis. Perhaps the rebels interpreted the offer as a sign of fear, for they rejected it with scorn. In May 702, the two armies drew up opposite one another at Deir al Jumajim, possibly near the modern Falluja.[4] Both sides dug trenches and fortified their camps. Skirmishing continued for a hundred days until, in August 702, as a result of a determined Syrian attack, the Iraqis gave way and their army collapsed, Hajjaj marching back in triumph to Kufa. The rebels, however, rallied their forces again and a further battle was necessary before government authority was re-established in lower Iraq. Abdul Rahman ibn al Ashath then fled to Sijistan and thence to Rutbil, the unbelieving ruler of Kabul, against whom he had been sent to fight. It was perhaps only poetic justice that Rutbil caused him to be put to death and his head sent to Hajjaj.

Unfortunately Muhallab, the old and trusty warrior who was governor of Khurasan, had died in February 701. His son Yezeed, however, assumed the governorship and, after the collapse of the Ashath rebellion, restored order among the insubordinate Iraqi troops in East Persia. On his deathbed, Muhallab is said to have told his son to remember that war is a matter of hard work and organization rather than of physical bravery, a remarkable statement from an Arab, the majority of whom seemed inclined to act on the opposite assumption. Perhaps also it contains a lesson for us, who are inclined to imagine that wars in the old days consisted of dashing cavalry charges and that only in our time has it become a matter of steady work and careful administration. Muhallab ibn abi Sofra already knew better twelve hundred years ago.

*   *   *

Hajjaj appears to have been utterly loyal to the Umaiyids, but he was not the man to smooth over the increasing hatred between Syrians and Iraqis, rather he tended further to inflame it. Masudi reports a sermon by Hajjaj in the mosque of Kufa in which he repeatedly held up the Syrians as an example to the Iraqis, a course scarcely likely to increase the affection of the Kufans for Damascus. Soon after the defeat of the Ashath rebellion, Hajjaj, disgusted with the fickleness of Kufa, founded a new city on the Tigris. He

4. Map 16, page 97.

called it Wasit, or Central, because it was equidistant between Kufa, Basra and Ahwaz.

Sixty years earlier, the Arabs had emerged as conquerors from Central Arabia. One Central Arabian army had invaded Syria, while another simultaneously attacked Iraq. Yet sixty years later, we find the army of Iraq demanding furiously to be led against the army of Syria. In some respects, the rivalry was due to geography. Syria and Iraq were each self-contained countries, separated from one another by several hundred miles of desert. If the imperial capital were in Damascus, Kufa and Basra became remote provinces, deprived of favour or advancement. If, on the other hand, the capital were at Kufa, Damascus would sink into distant neglect. Thus the geographical separation between Syria and Iraq created a situation which led to increasing jealousy between the two armies, even if the men of both were of the same nation.

But were they still both of the same nation? The second generation of conquerors, though still calling themselves by Arab names, were of mixed descent. Moreover—a point extremely interesting to consider—before the Arab conquests, Syria had been part of the Roman Empire and Iraq of that of Persia. The frontier between Europe and Asia before the conquests had not been (as we now regard it) at the Bosphorus but along the Perso–Byzantine border on the Upper Euphrates. Thus the Arab conquerors who had settled in Syria found themselves in an atmosphere of classical Roman civilization, whereas those in Iraq lived in oriental surroundings.

Another noteworthy feature of the Ashath rebellion is the fact that this man, a Muslim Arab chief, could confide in Rutbil of Kabul, a non-Arab and non-Muslim, against the Prince of the Faithful in Damascus. Ibn al Ashath had previously been sent by Hajjaj against Shabeeb and the Kharijites and had been defeated. He had indeed been accused of cowardice and had been publicly blamed by Hajjaj. It seems probable that this incident had rankled and, as has so often occurred with Arabs, personal pique outweighed his sense of duty to the nation and to his religion. We must not, however, judge him by modern standards of patriotism. In mediaeval Europe, great nobles frequently rebelled for a matter of personal honour. Nevertheless this matter of individual Arab pride is something of a feature of that nation and cannot pass completely unnoticed.

* * *

But while so many disturbances were plaguing the eastern half of the empire, in the west the Arabs were everywhere on the offensive once again. Every summer one or other of the sons of the khalif led an inroad into Byzantine territory. In 700, Waleed ibn Abdul Malik raided Asia Minor. In 701, it was the turn of Ubaidullah ibn Abdul Malik, who attacked the Qaliqala area near the sources of the Euphrates. In 702 it was Abdulla ibn Abdul Malik. None of these summer raids produced any permanent accession of territory, but they proved at least that the Arabs had recovered their morale and something of their former aggressiveness.

An interesting factor in the operations against the Byzantine Empire was provided by the activities of the Jarajima in the Amanus mountains.[5] These people were Christians, left behind by the retreat of the Byzantines across the Taurus, sixty years earlier. From their mountain fastnesses, they sturdily defended their independence against the Muslims, even at times penetrating southwards into the mountains of the Lebanon, inhabited by their Maronite fellow-Christians. So troublesome were they to the Arabs that both Muawiya and Abdul Malik paid them a subsidy to keep quiet. It is fascinating to notice that nearly all the problems of our own times—the jealousy between the Iraqis and the Syrians, the rivalry between the Shiites and orthodox Muslims and the obstinate resistance of the Christians of Lebanon to Muslim domination—all were already in evidence in the seventh century.

The Arab failure to subject Lebanon completely to their rule, or at least to their religion and culture, is also another example of their dislike of mountains. It is inconceivable that, with their imperial capital in Damascus, they were unable to stamp out hostility in the Lebanon. When obliged to do so, as in Persia, they fought successfully in mountains. But again and again, where a range of mountains lay within their territory, they omitted completely to mop it up. The result was that the peoples of the mountainous enclaves remained quiet when the Arabs were strong. But as soon as the government became pre-occupied or weak, nuclei of resistance appeared all over the empire. Such were to be Leon and Galicia in Spain, the Atlas Mountains in North Africa, and the Dailamite country at the southern end of the Caspian.

*   *   *

Meanwhile, however, great events were taking place in North Africa. Before these can be narrated in detail, it will be useful to make a short digression to describe the country and its people.

In Roman times, the name of Africa was applied only to the territory in the vicinity of Carthage, that is to say approximately the modern Tunisia. The Arabs transformed the name into Ifriqiya, and applied it to the central portion of the coast, extending approximately from Tripoli to the centre of what is now called Algeria. Western Algeria and Morocco—to use their modern names—were known to the Arabs as the Maghrib, or the land of the sunset. In no case, however, were the names of Africa or Ifriqiya applied to the continent south of the Sahara.[6]

The Maghrib and Ifriqiya form a single geographical unit. The Atlas Mountains commence near the southern boundary of Morocco and peter out a few miles south of the city of Tunis. They are separated from the sea on the north by a coastal plain averaging about one hundred miles wide. South of the coastal plain the Atlas Mountains cover an area some one thousand two hundred and fifty miles long (about as far as from London to Bucharest), and a hundred miles wide. So formidable a wall of mountains naturally shuts off most of the rain from the interior and the country south of the mountains quickly shades off, through a belt of grazing alfalfa grass and scattered oases, into the great Sahara Desert.

These three belts of country—coastal plain, mountains and semi-desert steppe —have throughout history given rise to three contrasting ways of life. The coastal plains have been intensively cultivated, covered with towns and villages and dotted here and there with rich and ancient cities, which have played a significant rôle in the history of the commerce and the art of the Mediterranean. Connected by sea with the then most civilized nations of the world [7] —Egypt, Greece, Rome, Byzantium, France and Spain—the population of the coastal plains was a mixture of every race which lived in the Mediterranean basin.

Few, however, of the many races which had settled on the coastal plains had attempted seriously to control, much less to colonize, the tangled mountain chains of the Atlas. Here, from time immemorial, had dwelt a race of hardy mountaineers, some living as sedentary cultivators—for there were fertile plains between the mountain chains—others as semi-nomadic tribes, partly engaged in agriculture, partly in wandering with their sheep and goats. The area south of the mountains, down into the great Sahara, was the territory of the entirely nomadic grazing tribes, who wandered incessantly across desert and steppe with their herds of camels.

The original inhabitants of the whole area were—and still are—known as the Berbers. The coastal plain was populated by a mixture of Berber blood with Phoenician, Greek, Italian, Vandal, Spanish and other Mediterranean strains, but the mountain and desert people were still almost entirely Berbers, who had only mingled to a small extent with other races.

In historical times, the city of Carthage was founded about 814 years before Christ, by Phoenicians from Tyre and Sidon, whom we would call Lebanese. The Phoenicians were sailors and traders, and established colonies all along the coasts of North Africa, Spain and Sicily. They made no attempt to conquer the Berbers of the interior. After long wars, Carthage was destroyed by the Romans in 146 B.C., and her territory annexed by Rome. In 14 B.C. the Roman proconsul of North Africa made Carthage once more the capital of the province. With the collapse of the Western Roman Empire, Carthage was conquered in A.D. 439 by the Vandals, a barbarian tribe from northern Europe. It remained under Vandal rule until it was recaptured in A.D. 553 by the Byzantines under the famous Belisarius, during the reign of the Emperor Justinian. It remained the capital of the Byzantine provinces in Africa until it was destroyed by the Arabs, as will shortly appear.

In general, the wars of Carthage, Rome and Byzantium were waged in the coastal plains and the Berbers of the Atlas had remained virtually independent. Themselves a martial race, however, they had served as mercenaries in the armies of the empires which had successively occupied the coast. Many Berbers, doubtless, had been educated in the cities on the seashore and had adopted the manners and the civilization of the Mediterranean but the tribes of the Atlas and the Sahara had remained unchanged, offering a savage resistance to all attempts to subdue them.

*   *   *

7. Omitting China which was outside the area with which we are dealing.

No sooner had the Arabs conquered Egypt than, in the autumn of 642, they had sallied out to the west and occupied Barqa.[8] In 643 they had seized Tripoli but, having plundered the city, withdrew once more to Barqa. In 647, they returned once again and defeated Gregory, the Byzantine governor of Carthage, at Sufetula in Southern Tunisia.[9] Unable to besiege the Byzantine coastal fortresses, however, the Arab commander, who was already one thousand seven hundred miles from his main base in Egypt, was unable to hold the country. He returned to Barqa with his plunder and the Byzantines resumed control from their capital at Carthage.

Nevertheless the prestige of Byzantium had been badly shaken, a large part of the province of Africa having been overrun by the Arabs, the cities plundered and the inhabitants driven off as slaves. The Muslims had eventually retired of their own accord but the empire had been proved to be too weak to protect its subject.

Further raids would doubtless have followed, had not the civil war between Ali and Muawiya put an end, for the time being, to Arab expansion. Indeed it was not until 665, eighteen years after the Arab victory at Sufetula, Muawiya being now firmly established as khalif, that another Arab army reached the area. It defeated a Byzantine force near Sousse but thereupon once again withdrew with its plunder to Egypt.

In 670, the Arabs had made a more serious attempt at permanent conquest. Uqba ibn Nafi, realizing that a forward base was necessary if serious military operations were to be undertaken in Ifriqiya, founded the city of Qairawan as an advanced military depot. The site was carefully chosen in the midst of an extensive and slightly undulating plain, covered with the low scrub on which camels grazed with relish. The Arabs in Ifriqiya confronted two enemies, the Byzantines in their coastal fortresses and the Berber tribes in the Atlas. Each of these enemies moved in an element uncongenial to the Arabs —the Byzantines on the sea, the Berbers in the mountains. If Uqba had established his base on the coast, it would have been exposed to Byzantine naval attack; if he had sited it near the mountains, the Berbers could have approached it unseen. But the site selected was thirty-five miles from the seashore, while twenty-five miles to the west, the lower slopes of the Atlas showed pale blue across the open plain. Whoever wished to attack Qairawan would have to do so across rolling steppe country, similar to that in which the Arabs had gained nearly all their greatest victories.

In 682 Uqba set out to conquer the West. Without pausing to besiege the Byzantine fortresses on the coast, he pushed forward a thousand miles westward to Tangier, defeating various forces of Byzantines and Berbers who attempted to bar the way. From Tangier he is alleged to have followed the Atlantic coast for a further five hundred miles to the vicinity of the modern town of Aqadir, where tradition depicts him as calling God to witness that the Atlantic alone prevented him from riding on for ever to the West, to fight against and slay all those who worshipped other than the one God.

In 683, returning eastwards apparently right through the Atlas Mountains, he rashly divided his army into several independent columns, proceeding

8. Map 19, page 109.   9. *The Great Arab Conquests*.

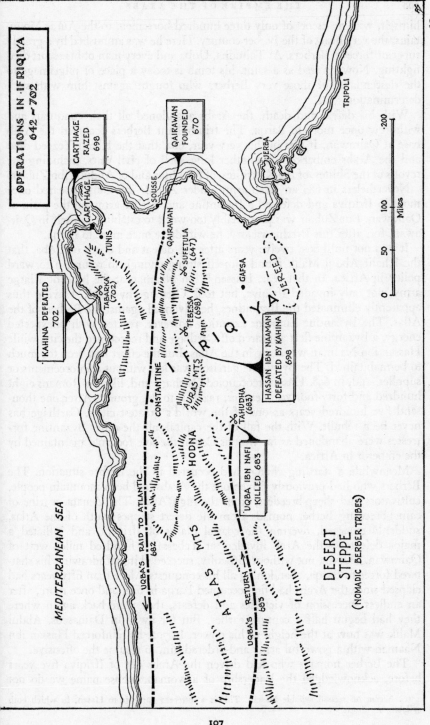

OPERATIONS IN IFRIQIYA
642 ~ 702

CARTHAGE RAZED 698

QAIRAWAN FOUNDED 670

TRIPOLI

JERBA

200

100

50

Miles

0

KAHINA DEFEATED 702

TABARKA (702)

TUNIS

CARTHAGE

SOUSSE

QAIRAWAN

SUFETULA (647)

TEBESSA (698)

GAFSA

JEREED

I F R I Q I Y A

CONSTANTINE

AURAS MTS.

HODNA MTS.

HASSAN IBN NAMAN DEFEATED BY KAHINA 698

TAHUDHA (683)

UQBA'S RAID TO ATLANTIC 682

UQBA IBN NAFI KILLED 685

UQBA'S RETURN 683

ATLAS MTS.

MEDITERRANEAN SEA

DESERT STEPPE
(NOMADIC BERBER TRIBES)

himself, with an escort of only three hundred horsemen, to the Auras Mountains, the very heart of the Berber country. Here he was ambushed by a greatly superior force of Berbers. At Tahudha, Uqba and every man of his escort died fighting. Now revered as a saint, his tomb is today a place of pilgrimage to the descendants of those very Berbers who fought against him with such determination.

With his defeat and death, the Arabs abandoned all their conquests and withdrew once more to Barqa. The triumphant Berbers occupied the Arab base at Qairawan. It was in this very year, 683, that the Khalif Yezeed died and the Arabs embarked on another long spell of civil wars, including the revolts of the Shiites, of the Kharijites, of Mukhtar and of Abdulla ibn Zubair.

Nevertheless in 686 an Arab army under Zuhair ibn Qais appeared once more in Ifriqiya and defeated a Byzantine and Berber army on the plain of Qairawan. But Zuhair was presumably too weak to establish himself in Qairawan, for, after this Pyrrhic victory, he withdrew once more to Barqa.

It was not until 695, twelve years after the defeat and death of Uqba, that the Khalif Abdul Malik found himself strong enough to resume a forward policy in Africa. In that year, Hassan [10] ibn Naaman at the head of a large army, not only invaded Ifriqiya, but took Carthage by asault. Having thus apparently eliminated the Byzantines, he advanced against the Berbers of the Atlas. The Byzantine Emperor Leontios, however, reacted with unexpected energy, a Byzantine fleet appeared off Carthage and reoccupied the city, while Hassan ibn Naaman was away in the Atlas. But the effort had been too much to be maintained. The Byzantine garrison was left without reinforcements or supplies, and, in 698, Hassan reoccupied Carthage and, like the Romans eight hundred and forty-four years earlier, razed it to the ground. After one thousand five hundred years as one of the world's greatest cities, Carthage has never been rebuilt. With the fall of the capital, all the other Byzantine fortresses were abandoned as far west as Ceuta, the sole foothold maintained by the emperor in Africa.

Meanwhile a startling change had occurred in the Berber situation. The Berbers who had previously driven out the Arabs had been mountain people, cultivators and sheep-breeders, from the high Atlas. The Zenata, a tribe of camel-breeding Berber nomads from the desert steppes south of the Atlas, suddenly emerged, overran the coastal plains of Ifriqiya, and inflicted a major defeat on the Arab invaders at Tebessa, a hundred miles west of Qairawan. Hassan, not without difficulty, succeeded in withdrawing his shattered forces to Barqa, abandoning all his conquests. More than fifty years had elapsed since the Arabs had first occupied Barqa in 642, and once more, after an endless succession of victories and defeats, they were back again where they had begun half a century earlier. But far away in Damascus, Abdul Malik was now at the height of his power. In 702, he reinforced Hassan ibn Naaman with a powerful army and ordered him to resume the offensive.

The Berber nomads who had driven the Arabs out of Ifriqiya five years before, acknowledged the leadership of a woman, whose name we do not

10. Accent on second syllable Hassán. This is a different name from Hasan, in which both syllables are short.

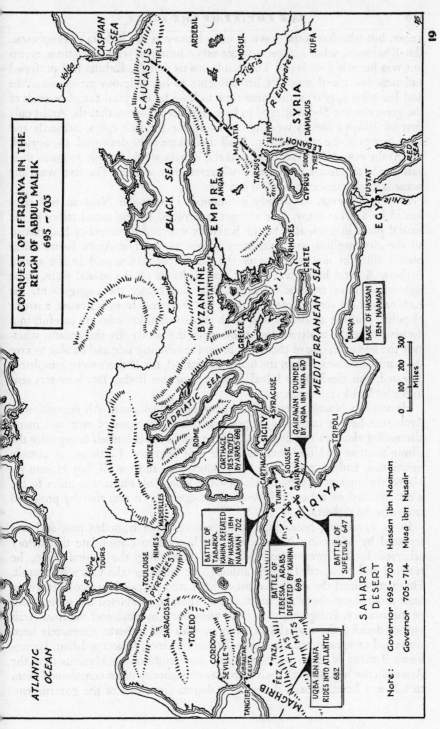

CONQUEST OF IFRIQIYA IN THE
REIGN OF ABDUL MALIK
695 - 705

BATTLE OF
TABARKA.
KAHINA DEFEATED
BY HASSAN IBN
NAAMAN 702

CARTHAGE
DESTROYED
BY ARABS 698

QAIRAWAN FOUNDED
BY UQBA IBN NAFA 670

BATTLE OF
TEBESSA. ARABS
DEFEATED BY KAHINA
698

BATTLE OF
SUFETULA 647

UQBA IBN NAFA
RIDES INTO ATLANTIC
682

BASE OF HASSAN
IBN NAAMAN

Note: Governor 695-705 Hassan ibn Naaman
Governor 705-714 Musa ibn Nusair

Miles
0 100 200 300

know, but who has come down to us in history as the Kahina or prophetess. Ibn Khaldoun, who, however, wrote seven hundred years after these events but was himself a native of Tunis, informs us that the Kahina had professed Judaism. She owed much of her influence to her religious pretensions. She and her tribe appear at the same time to have been typical camel-nomads of the great deserts. She is alleged to have told her followers that the Arabs only coveted Ifriqiya for its wealthy cities and for the rich crops, orchards and olive groves of the coastal plain. If all these were to be destroyed, she argued, the Arabs would come no more and the Zenata would be able to graze their vast herds of camels unmolested wherever they wished. For five years the nomads made a desert and called it peace.

In 702, however, as already mentioned, Hassan ibn Naaman was reinforced by a great army. The ravages committed by the camel tribes in the coastal plain in pursuance of the Kahina's scorched earth policy had turned all the city-dwellers and cultivators against them. The Arabs found unexpected allies in the remnants of the Greek population and in the settled Berbers. A great battle was fought near Tabarka on the coastal plain, some eighty-five miles west of Carthage. The day before the engagement, the Kahina sent her sons to join the enemy as "deserters" from her cause, a stroke of policy familiar to Berber and Arab tribesmen alike, who are careful, in a decisive struggle, to divide the members of the family. By this means, whatever the outcome, one of them will be on the winning side and be able to save the family fortunes. When the battle was joined, the Berbers were completely defeated, and the Kahina killed. The head of this Berber Boadicea was sent to Abdul Malik in Damascus.

Hassan ibn Naaman returned in triumph to Qairawan. All opposition to Arab rule had at last been suppressed, after sixty years of war and many alternating victories and disasters, and the governor set himself to organize the administration and the finances of his vast province. Carthage, as already mentioned, had been razed to the ground once and for all, but Hassan replaced the ancient city by developing the village of Tunis, ten miles to the west. Situated on a lagoon instead of the open sea, it was thereby protected from direct naval attack.

In or about 705, however, Hassan was removed from his post and was replaced by Musa ibn Nusair, who set himself to consolidate the victory achieved by his predecessor. Marching first along the coastal plain, he reached and occupied Tangier, although he failed to take Ceuta by assault. He then pacified the Atlantic coast of what we now call Morocco. Returning once more across the plains south of the Atlas, he completed the subjugation of the country. Religion and politics went hand in hand and the final Arab victory decided the majority of Berbers, who had hitherto alternately been converted or apostatized after each defeat or victory, to accept Islam. Henceforward many of them were to appear more enthusiastic Muslims than the Arabs themselves, though their rejection of authority often constrained them to follow a heretical sect, differing in dogma from that of the government.

*   *   *

Ever since the first Arab conquests in the 630's, Byzantine officials had continued to conduct the civil administration in Syria and Palestine, while in Persia the same task was still entrusted to Persian officers. In former Byzantine territories, the public accounts had hitherto been kept in Greek, in the eastern half of the empire in Persian. It was only during the reign of Abdul Malik that orders were enforced that all accounts be kept in Arabic. He also was the first khalif to mint his own coins, Byzantine and Persian money having hitherto been legal tender. The Byzantines had used a gold coin, the solidus, as the basis of their currency. The gold dinar was the Arab equivalent of the solidus. The Persians, however, had employed the silver dirhem and the Arabs struck silver dirhems on the same model. Thus the Arabs had two principal coins, the gold dinar and the silver dirhem. In the time of Abdul Malik, the dinar was equivalent to ten silver dirhems. Later the dirhem fell to twelve or even fifteen to the dinar. It is almost impossible to compare the purchasing power of these coins to anything in our own modern world—very roughly we assume the dinar to correspond to the pound sterling, the dirhem to something approaching two shillings.

The taxes collected by Abdul Malik's government were based on the system originated by the Prophet himself and systematized by Umar ibn al Khattab. The principal taxes consisted of:—

(a) The Poor Tax. This tax instituted by Muhammad himself, bore a socialistic complexion. It was collected, often in kind, on domestic animals and agricultural products, and was then distributed to the poor. To pay this tax was an essential duty of the Muslim faith.

(b) The poll-tax, collected from tolerated non-Muslims. Every adult male paid an annual tribute, varying from one to four dinars per head.

(c) Land tax. This also was heavier for non-Muslims than for Muslims.

(d) Payments made under special agreements which had been concluded when certain towns or districts had capitulated to the original Arab conquerors.

(e) One-fifth of all booty taken in war.

Under the extremely simple and democratic system inaugurated by the Prophet himself, all the income of the state belonged to the whole community of the Muslims and was equally divided among them, leaving nothing in the treasury and providing for no government expenditure. It was obviously impossible to rule an empire without money in the treasury, but the first charge on the state was still that of the annual salaries paid to Arabs, on the principles introduced by Umar ibn Al Khattab.

In Abdul Malik's reign, the government had assumed an aspect not unlike that of a modern state. Under the title *diwans*, various departments handled the business of government. There was a finance department, for example, and an army department and archives were kept with copies of all state papers. Each department retained copies of all the correspondence which it issued.

A highly organized postal system based on Damascus maintained communications with the remotest outposts of the empire. Relays of horses were held in readiness all along the main roads which radiated from Damascus to the four corners of the khalif's dominions. Carrier pigeons were also used for urgent messages.

The principal task of the post office, however, was not to carry private but government mail. It is doubtful whether it handled private letters at all and, if it did so, (as Masudi says it did) whether it was a part of its official duty, a favour to oblige friends or a private enterprise on the part of the postmen. In the provinces, the Postmaster was one of the most important officials, for he combined supervision of the posts with intelligence duties. An important part of his work was the submission of secret reports to Damascus on everything that happened in his province. He thus constituted a valuable check on the activities of the governor and the other senior officials. Whether it were an increase in Shiite propaganda, embezzlement of funds by the collectors of the land tax or the purchase of a new concubine by the governor, everything formed the subject of a secret report by the Postmaster. A modern touch is supplied by the fact that Postmasters were instructed to submit a separate report on each subject, so that each, on its receipt in Damascus, could be minuted to the appropriate department.[11]

Abdul Malik took a personal interest in the administration of the empire. On one occasion he received a report to the effect that a certain provincial governor was in the habit of accepting gifts. The khalif summoned him to Damascus and, when he was brought in, asked him bluntly, "Have you ever accepted a present since you became a governor?" "O Prince of the Faithful," replied the official, "your dominions are prosperous, the taxes are pouring in, your subjects are living in ease and comfort." "Answer my question," interrupted the khalif sternly, "have you ever accepted a present since you became a governor?" "Well, yes," admitted the unhappy man. "You have betrayed your trust," interposed Abdul Malik, cutting short any further argument. He then gave orders for the man's immediate dismissal.

The intermixture of the conquering Arab race with the original inhabitants of Iraq has already been mentioned. In Syria the same process was taking place. The structure of society envisaged by the first conquerors was one in which the Muslim Arabs would remain segregated as an imperial aristocracy, living in the great military cities. Their sole duties would be war and government and they would all receive state salaries. Compared with the native populations of these teeming provinces, the number of these pure Arabians was extremely small. About the year 700 for example, the number of Arabian Muslims receiving state salaries in the province of Damascus was 45,000, while in the province of Homs there were only 20,000.[12] In the reign of Abdul Malik, the majority of the people of Syria were still Christians. Moreover, the Arabs were almost entirely settled in the great cities or were alternatively still nomadic desert tribes. As in Iraq, the villagers and agricultural workers consisted principally of the original natives and the rural areas had scarcely been changed by the Arab conquests.

The most profound social changes of the period of Beni Umaiya in Damascus resulted from the immense scale on which slavery was practised.

11. Von Kremer, *The Orient under the Caliphs*.
12. Hitti, *History of the Arabs*.

The chief source of slaves was the prisoners of war. After every campaign many thousands, sometimes tens of thousands, of prisoners were sold as slaves. Soon prominent Arab chiefs would possess several hundred slaves. Zubair, the father of Abdulla ibn Zubair, bequeathed on his death a thousand male and female slaves. The Prophet himself had stated the freeing of a slave to be a meritorious action, with the result that thousands of these captured foreign slaves became freedmen. During the period of Beni Umaiya rule in Damascus, we find increasingly frequent mention of freedmen as carrying out confidential missions for their masters or fighting in their retinue in battle. We have seen that one of the complaints made against Mukhtar by the Arab chiefs of Kufa was that he enlisted their freedmen and slaves in his army, thereby removing them from the control of their masters. Normally, however, the freedman remained in the service of his original owner as his bodyguard, or in some cases as his confidential secretary. The majority of them had become Muslims.

Little or no attempt was made during the reigns of the early Beni Umaiya to convert the native populations to Islam, and that for two reasons. Firstly, since the original conquests, it had been laid down that non-Muslims were to pay a different and higher scale of taxes than Muslims. Thus any wholesale conversion to Islam was liable to involve the state treasury in a considerable loss of income. The revenue of Egypt, where the people were more ready than in any other conquered country to adopt Islam, fell to less than one half its former figure in the first twenty years after the conquest. The second reason why the Arabs made few efforts to convert the conquered peoples was that theoretically all Muslims were equal. The Arabs, however, were a conquering race, who preferred to regard the Egyptians, the Syrians and the Persians as their social inferiors.

But although the Arabs did not seek proselytes to Islam, the numbers of the conquered peoples converted continued to increase, both in the persons of freedmen and slaves, and also among the ordinary population who saw in conversion a way to attain social equality with the conquerors. In practice, however, the original Arab conquerors were by no means anxious to accept converts as their equals. The new converts, therefore, became an increasingly discontented social class, endeavouring in vain to climb to equality with their masters.

* * *

Abdul Malik died on 8th October, 705, at the age of sixty. He had ruled in Damascus for nearly twenty-one years, but during the first seven years, his khalifate had been disputed by Abdulla ibn Zubair. As a young man, when his father Merwan had been governor of Medina under Muawiya I, he had devoted himself to religious studies and was able to hold his own with the most learned doctors in the holy cities, in the interpretation of the Qoran and the Traditions of the Prophet. When he became khalif in Damascus, worldly business doubtless occupied most of his time to the exclusion of religious studies. He was a master of eloquence and was said never to make a grammatical error in Arabic. Like almost every Umaiyid, and most Arabs, he was a poet. In his old age, he is said to have written the following verses, lamenting the vanity of life.

> Long have I lived in this sad world of sighs,
> A blood-drenched world which compassed me with strife:
> Where fleeting happiness so quickly flies
> And fades like memories of some former life.
> Would that I'd never risen to a throne
> Nor with vain pleasures filled my wanton mind,
> But like a hermit lived, in want, alone,
> Till for the tomb I left this world behind.

The Arab historians have loaded Abdul Malik with reproaches because he supported Hajjaj. The Umaiyids appointed three successive viceroys in Iraq, all of them violent, cruel and vigorous. The first was Zayyad-the-son-of-his-father, the second Ubaidullah the son of Zayyad, who caused the death of Husain, and the third Hajjaj ibn Yusuf. In defence of their methods, it was easy to plead the fickleness, sedition and treachery of the Kufans, who had first supported and then murdered Ali ibn abi Talib and his son Husain. Yet we cannot avoid the impression that, while severity may have been essential, such wholesale repression merely defeated its own object and drove the people of Kufa and Basra to fresh rebellions, which were ultimately to culminate in the ruin of the Umaiyid family. While a deep vein of compassion for the poor and the weak leavened the Arab mentality, yet, in so far as government was concerned, there was also a certain cynicism which assumed that men could really only be ruled by force and fear.

Yet so conflicting and prejudiced are the accounts of the Arab historians that it is extremely difficult to reach final conclusions. A distinguished European orientalist has given us a much more favourable estimate of Hajjaj. "Zayyad-the-son-of-his-father and Hajjaj", he writes, "were the two great viceroys of the Umaiyids in Iraq. Both looked upon themselves as upholders of ordered government and they repaid the confidence reposed in them by conscientiously discharging their duties, without troubling themselves about public opinion. Hajjaj was not behind his predecessor. His administrative measures regarding taxation and the encouragement of agriculture were epoch-making. His word had the force of law. In no circumstance did his courage fail him. In adversity it rose to its highest pitch. He was harsh and occasionally severe but never cruel or miserly. In life and death he had a clear conscience. Other crimes imputed to him were pure inventions and the result of malice."[13] In the field of administration, Hajjaj re-dug many irrigation canals on which the life of Iraq depended. He also made state loans to farmers as is done nowadays by agricultural banks. When he died, he left nothing behind him but his Qoran, his arms and a few pieces of silver.

In spite of his early devotion to religious studies, Abdul Malik used to drink wine after he became khalif in Damascus. He was also not indifferent to the fair sex and was said to be much under the influence of his wife Atiqa.

13. Professor Wellhausen. I have shortened the original.

Discussing women, he is alleged to have said that the man "who desired to take a female slave for his amusement, let him take a native of Barbary, and he who needs one in order to have children should choose a Persian, but if he required one for service, then it would be best to select a Greek." The incident illustrates the variety of girl slaves which seems to have been easily available.

In spite of the practice of concubinage, however, the position of Arab women was still influential. According to a modern historian, the introduction of eunuchs did not take place until the reign of Waleed II, grandson of Abdul Malik, in 743. They were brought to Damascus from Byzantium. The seclusion of women does not appear to have come into force until the Abbasid period, in accordance with the general trend towards orientalization, to which reference will be made in a later chapter.

In spite of his interest in women, Abdul Malik was no playboy. Asked who was the best of men, he is alleged to have replied, "he who is humble in a lofty station, devout though in authority and just though in power." He was blamed for parsimony, perhaps only because he kept watch on the treasury instead of throwing away money by handfuls, which was the traditional ideal of an Arab prince.

In brief, Abdul Malik ibn Merwan was an exceptionally capable man, sometimes appearing to be religious, well educated, with literary tastes and socially pleasant but at times ruthless, when the safety of the state appeared to be threatened. On the whole, it is impossible to deny him the title of greatness as a ruler, even if we tend to refuse him any claim to moral grandeur.

A year before his death, Abdul Malik caused the oath of allegiance to be taken to his son Waleed as heir apparent. His second son Sulaiman was nominated as the successor of Waleed. The latter assumed the khalifate unopposed on 8th October, 705, on the death of his father.

NOTABLE DATES

Hajjaj appointed governor of Kufa	January 695
Khariji revolt in Iraq under Shabeeb	May 695
Hassan ibn Naaman captures Carthage	695
Rebellion of the Kahina in Ifriqiya	} 700
Hassan ibn Naaman withdraws to Barqa	
Ashath rebellion in Iraq	February 702
Ashath rebels defeated at Battle of Deir al Jumajim	August 702
Kahina defeated at the Battle of Tabarka	702
Musa ibn Nusair succeeds Hassan ibn Naaman as governor of Ifriqiya	705
Death of Abdul Malik	8th October, 705

PERSONALITIES

Abdul Malik ibn Merwan, khalif	685–705
Muhallab ibn abi Sofra, great Arab military commander in Persia	

Hajjaj ibn Yusuf, governor of Iraq
Abdul Rahman ibn al Ashath, chosen by Hajjaj to
    command against Kabul. Rebelled against Hajjaj
Hassan ibn Naaman, Arab commander in the conquest
    of Ifriqiya
Kahina, the priestess, leader of the Berber revolt
Musa ibn Nusair, new governor of Africa
Waleed ibn Abdul Malik, khalif   8th October, 705

VI

Andalus

Gentle river, gentle river,
Lo, thy streams are stained with gore.
Many a brave and noble captain
Floats along thy willowed shore.

All beside thy limpid waters,
All beside thy sands so bright,
Moorish chiefs and Christian warriors
Joined in fierce and mortal fight.

THOMAS PERCY, from an Old Spanish Ballad

Tarik had advanced as far as the Laguna de Janda when he heard that King Roderic was marching against him at the head of a large army. Tarik never thought of retreat; ambition, cupidity and fanaticism urged him on . . . He found himself in command of a force of twelve thousand men. This was small in comparison with Roderic's host, but treachery came to the aid of the Moslems.

DOZY, *The Moslems in Spain*

VI

ANDALUS

IN spite of the many civil wars in the first part of his reign, Abdul Malik had done an immense work for the empire. Internal peace had been established, the administration reformed, the accounts and records had all been compiled in Arabic and the whole government machine consolidated. It is true that this increased efficiency had been to some extent achieved by an increase of despotism. Muawiya, the first Umaiyid khalif, had been in his manners little more than the Arab chief of tradition, sitting in public with the citizens who openly criticized the actions of the government to his face. Abdul Malik was the first khalif who forbade criticism of the government. When he gave audience, guards with drawn swords stood behind him.

The second khalif after the Prophet, Umar ibn al Khattab, when he heard that the governor of Iraq normally closed the door of his house, sent him a message to leave the door open, as the public should have access to their ruler at all times. Now in Damascus the khalifs lived in a palace, guarded by soldiers, chamberlains and court officials. It must be admitted that the democratic methods of the first khalifs were no longer practicable in a great and civilized empire. Yet Umar ibn al Khattab had died only forty-one years before Abdul Malik became khalif. The change—nothing less than a social revolution—had therefore been extremely rapid. Both the Byzantine and the Persian Empires had long been accustomed to despotic personal rule and their traditions were rapidly gaining influence over the Arabs.

It is worthy of note also that three of the first four khalifs of the democratic days had been assassinated, a fact justifying some security precautions. But the aspect of the khalifate which must appear the most open to criticism was the extreme severity with which every dissident movement was suppressed. Racial, religious and social problems were inevitable, especially in an empire conquered so rapidly and consisting of so many different races. Yet, as we have seen, every revolt was put down with relentless severity.

To some extent this savagery may be attributed to the fact that nearly all the rebellions took place in support of some rival claimant to the khalifate, rather than in furtherance of a political objective. Indeed the scope for purely political reforms was to a great extent limited by the belief that all that was needed for the guidance of men, as individuals or as communities, was contained in the Qoran and the Traditions. Yet there were many discontented persons and classes. Unable openly to oppose a system of government ostensibly based on orders issued by God Himself, the dissatisfied tended to express their resentment by supporting a rival claimant to the khalifate, for the Qoran and Traditions had omitted to lay down rules regarding the selection of the successors of the Prophet. Consequently all expressions of political unrest were channelled into the one form of opposing the khalif in person, a fact which may have inclined the khalifs to the use of harsh repressive measures.

Such methods, however, naturally produced bitterness and gave rise to feuds and hatreds which still survive today. Indeed the student of Arab history can scarcely avoid the conclusion that the ever-recurring mistake all through their history has been their too hasty and too violent use of force. Apart, moreover, from any question of policy, these methods resulted in the deaths in battle of tens of thousands of the bravest and noblest Arabs, just at the moment when they were most needed in the service of their still expanding empire. In 705, however, when Waleed ibn Abdul Malik succeeded unopposed to the khalifate, internal peace was established and the Arab banners were advancing once more on all the frontiers.

When the great Muhallab ibn abi Sofra had died in Khurasan, the governorship of the province had been assumed by his son Yezeed. Hajjaj now removed Yezeed from his post and imprisoned him, accusing him of extravagance and of the misuse of public funds. It appears also that he had caused a revival of Qais-Yemen party strife, whereas Muhallab had held the balance even. Muhallab, it is true, had been a great lord, who distributed hospitality and patronage with a free hand. In these early days, the absence of a regular system of accounts and audit inevitably resulted in considerable confusion between the public and personal funds administered by provincial governors. This financial vagueness enabled these magnates to build up vast systems of patronage and personal loyalty to themselves by the generous distribution of money which, according to our ideas, really belonged to the government. It is true that, by thus reinforcing their own prestige, they were able to keep internal order and extend the imperial frontiers, for the distant khalif was too far away to inspire personal loyalty. Yet to prevent such great lords establishing their own dynasties—as indeed they did two centuries later when the khalifs grew weak—it was doubtless advisable to transfer them at times from one post to another.

Thus the removal of Yezeed from the governorship held by his father Muhallab may well have been a wise step on the part of Hajjaj. Yet, as usual, the action taken was too violent, for Yezeed was thrown into prison without trial—an action which was to lead to yet another rebellion.

In place of Yezeed ibn Muhallab, Hajjaj appointed Qutaiba ibn Muslim to be governor of Khurasan. The new nominee amply justified his selection for he proved himself an extremely successful commander. No sooner had he been appointed than he crossed the Oxus at the head of an army and in a series of successful campaigns he inflicted summary punishment on all who, during the years of civil war, had shown hostility to Arab rule. From the Oxus he passed on to the Jaxartes as will be told in the next chapter. In southern Persia, Muhammad ibn Qasim, a relative of Hajjaj, led an army across Mekran and in 708 engaged in hostilities with the King of Sind.

On the Byzantine frontier the same aggressive pattern was maintained. Several fortresses were captured in the annual summer raids, including the southern Heraclea and Tuwana, places of some importance beyond the Taurus. Maslama ibn Abdul Malik, Waleed's brother and a remarkable

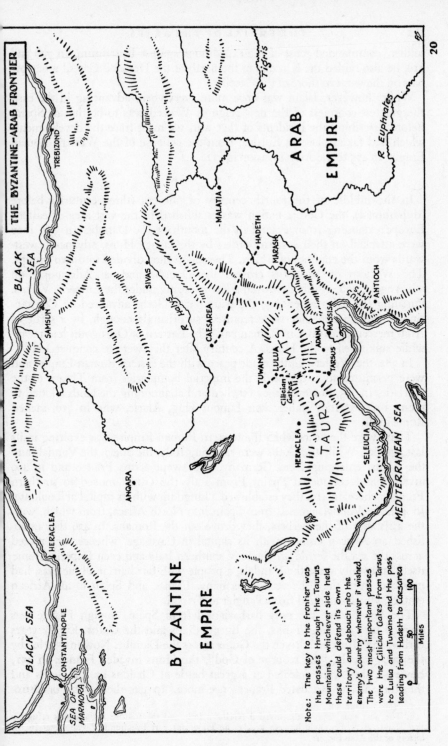

THE BYZANTINE-ARAB FRONTIER

BLACK SEA

TREBIZOND

ARAB EMPIRE

R. Tigris

R. Euphrates

SAMSUN

MALATIA

SIVAS

HADETH

MARASH

R. Halys

CAESAREA

AMANUS MTS

ANTIOCH

BLACK SEA

ANGARA

TUWANA

LULUA

Cilician Gates

TAURUS MTS

ADANA

MASSIS

TARSUS

HERACLEA

BYZANTINE EMPIRE

HERACLEA

TAURUS

SELEUCIA

MEDITERRANEAN SEA

CONSTANTINOPLE

SEA OF MARMORA

Note: The key to the frontier was
the passes through the Taurus
Mountains, whichever side held
these could defend its own
territory and debouch into the
enemy's country whenever it wished.
The two most important passes
were the Cilician Gates from Tarsus
to Lulua and Tuwana and the pass
leading from Hadeth to Caesarea

0   50   100
|————————|————————|
        Miles

20

soldier, commanded most of the expeditions against Byzantium. In 708 and 710, he also raided the Khazars to the north of the Derbend Gates,[1] a narrow pass on the western shore of the Caspian.

While, however, Islam was once more everywhere advancing in the east, the greatest conquest of the new reign of Waleed was to be that of Spain. Before describing the incidents of that war, we must trace the developments which had taken place in Europe, from the collapse of the Western Roman Empire in 475 to the Arab invasion in 711.

*   *   *

In the middle of the fourth century of our era (three centuries before Muhammad), the Gothic nation was established in the vast area of eastern Europe extending from Poland to the mouth of the Danube. In 377, they were attacked on their eastern borders by the savage Huns, advancing westwards from the confines of China. Thereupon they divided into two groups. The Western or Visigoths crossed the Danube and, at Adrianople on 9th August, 378, utterly destroyed a Roman army under the Emperor Valens. Pursuing the defeated enemy, the triumphant Goths advanced on Constantinople from which they were repulsed, surprisingly enough, by a sortie of Arab mercenary cavalry in Roman pay. The Eastern or Ostrogoths had meanwhile submitted to the Huns. A century later they were to conquer Italy.

In 382, the Western Goths made peace with the eastern Roman Empire and were permitted to settle inside the imperial boundaries from Thrace to the Adriatic. In 395, however, they rebelled and abandoning the lands allotted to them, invaded Italy under their famous king, Alaric, who in 410, sacked Rome itself.

These were the years when the western Roman Empire was expiring in its last agonies. While the Goths were ravaging Italy, the Suevi, the Vandals and the Alans, emerging from Germany, had swept across France and in 409 invaded and conquered Spain. From Italy the Goths moved to southern France, where, in 419, they established a kingdom with its capital at Toulouse. In 429, the Vandals crossed from Spain into North Africa, from which, with the assistance of the Berbers, they drove out the Romans. In 439 they established an African empire with its capital in Carthage, whence they raided across the sea the fertile provinces of southern Italy and even Imperial Rome itself. In twenty years the Vandals, a people with fair hair and blue eyes, had marched from the Elbe across Germany, France and Spain to an African empire, which extended from Tangier to Tripoli.

The Suevi were the only barbarians left in Spain, though France was divided between the Franks, the Burgundians and the Goths. Eighty years earlier, the Huns had driven the Goths across the Danube. Now in 450, led by the savage Atila, "the scourge of God", the Huns invaded France. In 451, however, they were defeated at a great battle at Chalons by the Goths and the Romans and evacuated France once more.[2] In 488, the Eastern or Ostro-

1. Map 7, page 30.
2. The next year, 452, Attila invaded Northern Italy and the fugitive Italians took refuge in the islands of Venice, which were to play an important part five hundred years later in the history of the Arab Empire.

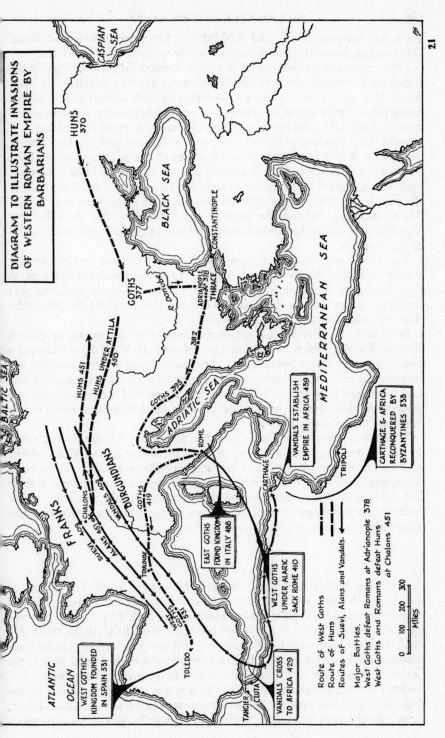

goths had conquered Italy and established a kingdom of their own there. Our concern, however, is henceforward solely with the Western Goths.

These, once more resuming their travels, crossed the Pyrenees, easily defeated the Suevi and conquered Spain, where in 531 they established a kingdom which was to endure for two somewhat unstable centuries. The Gothic monarchy of Spain was in theory elective, and not hereditary, a system which provoked periodic disturbances and was ultimately to prove its undoing.

Spain had previously for seven centuries formed part of the Roman dominions. When the Gothic conquest occurred, the social condition of the country was deplorable. A small number of ancient senatorial families owned vast estates, worked by thousands of serfs and slaves, who formed the bulk of the population, while gangs of bandits and outlaws roamed the countryside. Then, as already related, the country was invaded by the Suevi and the Vandals, who carried fire, sword and plunder through the length and breadth of the peninsula.

The Goths who conquered Spain were few in number and constituted merely an aristocratic ruling class, who lorded it over the slaves and serfs, as their Roman predecessors had done. In 587, Reccared, King of the Goths, was converted to the Catholic faith, and in 616 began to persecute the Jews, who were extremely numerous and prosperous in Spain.

In France, the Franks had weakened, while the Byzantine, or eastern Roman, Empire, which had meanwhile defeated the Vandals, maintained a precarious control over North Africa. As a result, Spain was free from foreign invasion for more than a century. The once warlike Goths, who under Alaric had terrorized Italy and sacked Rome, had abandoned the use of arms and passed their idle lives in luxury and pleasure on their estates, waited upon hand and foot by slaves and serfs.

Witiza was King of the Goths from 697 to 710, but it is not clear whether he died or was murdered at the end of his reign. Suffice it to say that Roderic, a Gothic nobleman, whose father had apparently been killed by the previous king, was raised to the throne in his place. In theory the monarchy was elective but the sons of Witiza were thrown into opposition to the new ruler, either because they had themselves hoped to secure the succession, or perhaps because their father had been removed by foul methods.

*   *   *

Musa ibn Nusair had been, earlier in his career, involved in a case of peculation in Basra and had been dismissed from his employment. He had apparently owed his appointment as governor of North Africa to the influence of Abdul Aziz, Viceroy of Egypt and brother of the Khalif Abdul Malik. He had, however, proved himself a capable and energetic officer. Under him, effective Arab control had for the first time been established as far west as the Atlantic. The town of Ceuta alone, under its governor Count Julian, had resisted all his attempts to capture it. Ceuta was in theory a Byzantine colony but the empire was too weak and too remote to afford it any assistance. Julian, who owned estates in southern Spain, had apparently been on intimate terms with the former king, Witiza, to whose daughter he may have been married. Both he and the sons of Witiza, however, appear to have concealed their resentment against Roderic. According to tradition, Count Julian's daughter (who may have been the niece of Witiza's sons if Julian's wife was indeed the late king's daughter) was at the court of King Roderic, who, struck by her beauty, had seduced her innocence.

For whatever reason, Julian, having first energetically repulsed the Arab attack on Ceuta, subsequently opened a correspondence with Musa ibn Nusair, to whom he proposed a joint invasion of Spain, offering to supply the ships to transport the Muslims across the straits. Musa reported these advances to Waleed, but the khalif replied dubiously that the enterprise appeared too dangerous. He, however, authorized a reconnaissance.

Accordingly in July 710, Musa despatched a force of four hundred men and one hundred horses, in ships provided by Julian. The party landed at Algeciras, plundered the neighbouring country and returned to Africa. Encouraged by the success of this raid, Musa ibn Nusair in April 711 sent seven thousand men under the command of Tariq ibn Zayyad, a Berber freedman of his own. The majority of the force consisted of Berbers. It had taken the Arabs sixty years to conquer North Africa and now, for the first time, all the Berbers had submitted and professed Islam. But how long would so warlike a race remain submissive? Is it possible that Musa ibn Nusair regarded the raiding of Spain merely as a useful outlet for the warlike energies of the Berbers, rather than as an opportunity to add a vast new territory to the empire? The theory would at least explain the reason why the expedition consisted so largely of Berbers and, which is more remarkable, was entrusted to a Berber commander.

Tariq established his base on the rock of Gibraltar, ever since called after his name, Jebel Tariq, or the mountain of Tariq. Musa followed up the first expedition by sending a further five thousand men, bringing the total to twelve thousand. Meanwhile King Roderic had summoned his army to his banner and was advancing southwards to repel the invaders. The two armies met at the Wadi al Bekka, a few miles east of Cadiz.[3]

Roderic is alleged to have been in command of 25,000 men to Tariq's 12,000, but little reliance can be placed on such numbers. Apparently unaware of their treachery, the king had placed the two wings of his army under the command of the two sons of Witiza. No sooner was the battle joined than both Gothic wings withdrew from the field. The centre, which was commanded by Roderic himself, offered a more prolonged resistance but was eventually overwhelmed. Roderic was never seen again and was presumably killed, though his body was never identified among the great numbers of dead. The Gothic army was virtually exterminated.

The most plausible explanation of the treachery of Julian and of the sons of Witiza is that they visualized Tariq's expedition as a mere raid. Indeed, as will appear, it seems possible that Musa's orders to Tariq were indeed to this effect, and that he may well have told Julian that only a raid was contemplated. But on that July day in 711, Tariq was the man of destiny. Seeing the utter destruction of the Gothic army, he took the fateful decision to go on.

3. Dozy. *The Moslems in Spain.*

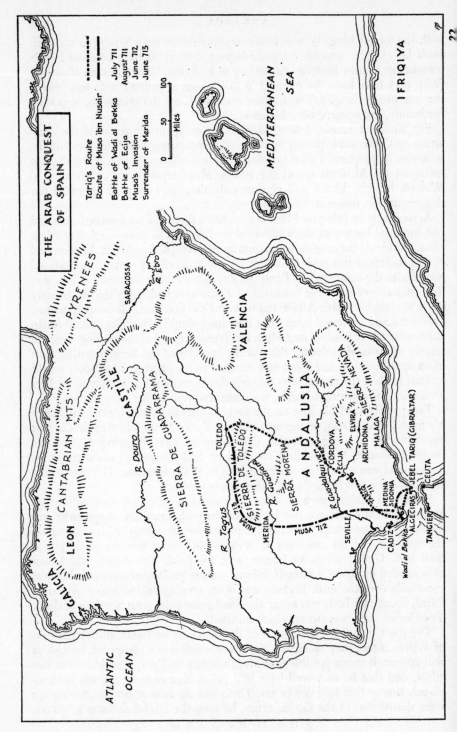

THE ARAB CONQUEST
OF SPAIN

Tariq's Route ......
Route of Musa ibn Nusair ———

Battle of Wadi al Bekka   July 711
Battle of Ecija   August 711
Musa's Invasion   June 712
Surrender of Merida   June 713

0   50   100
Miles

PYRENEES

SARAGOSSA

R. Ebro

CANTABRIAN MTS.

LEON

GALICIA

CASTILE

R. Douro

SIERRA DE GUADARRAMA

VALENCIA

TOLEDO

R. Tagus

SIERRA DE TOLEDO   713

MUSA

MERIDA

R. Guadiana

SIERRA MORENA

ANDALUSIA

R. Guadalquivir

CORDOVA

ECIJA

ELVIRA   SIERRA NEVADA

ARCHIDONA

MALAGA

TARIQ

SEVILLE

MUSA 712

CADIZ

MEDINA
SIDONIA

ALGECIRAS   JEBEL TARIQ (GIBRALTAR)

CEUTA

TANGIER

Wadi al Bekka

MEDITERRANEAN
SEA

IFRIQIYA

ATLANTIC
OCEAN

22

Not only so, but after detaching columns to capture Cordova, Archidona and Elvira, he decided to march straight on Toledo, the Gothic capital.

If Tariq in reality had originally only 12,000 men, the columns which he detached to capture the three cities can scarcely have amounted to less than 2,000 troops, while we may assume at least 1,000 casualties in the battle. This would leave him at the most some 9,000 men in his main body. With this small force, he marched straight for the heart of the Gothic kingdom, two hundred and fifty miles away across ranges of unknown mountains.

The terrifying uncertainty which assails a commander about to march into unknown enemy country can perhaps only be appreciated by those who have actually found themselves in such a situation. To us, who know what ultimately happened, Tariq's decision may not appear dramatic but if we imagine ourselves in his position, we may find ourselves obliged to confess that it was an act of outstanding courage. But Tariq was a man who, like the German General Staff in 1940, understood the paralyzing effect of the blitzkreig (for in such matters war never changes). He realized that immense results could be obtained if he could instantly exploit his victory, while the Goths were still in panic and without a leader. A few days' delay would give the enemy time to recover psychologically, to appoint a new commander and to adopt further measures. Their panic must be kept at its hysterical maximum. After fighting another action at Ecija, he made for Toledo at full speed. His daring was fully justified, for when he arrived, he found the capital half-deserted, government and nobles alike having fled in panic. The invaders were everywhere assisted with information by the Jews, who had been persecuted by the Goths.

Dashing, front-line soldiers like Tariq often, in the heat of battle, forget to report their situation to their commanders-in-chief, pacing anxiously up and down at headquarters. We can sympathize with Musa ibn Nusair in Tangier when he was informed that his freedman, after winning a great victory, had disappeared into the heart of Spain with only 9,000 men.

Having obtained possession of Toledo, Tariq behaved with exemplary moderation. Those who wished to go into exile were permitted to do so, taking their movable property with them. The brothers of Witiza were rewarded for their treachery with the grant of the Gothic crown lands, which included more than three thousand farms. A number of churches were appointed for Christian worship and the bishops and priests were allowed to continue their ministry. Basing himself on Toledo, Tariq then set about the task of pacifying the northern provinces of Castile and Leon.

The following summer, June 712, Musa ibn Nusair himself crossed the straits, leaving his eldest son Abdulla as viceroy of North Africa. His army consisted of 18,000 men, most of whom were Arabs, including many noble Quraish and descendants of the Companions of the Prophet. Musa accepted the easy surrender of Medina Sidonia, but Seville resisted with more determination. The palm must, however, be awarded to Merida, the siege of which was prolonged for several months and cost the Muslim army the lives of many martyrs. Seven centuries earlier, the veteran legionaries of Augustus had been settled in this Roman colony.

Sixty years before, during the great Arab conquests, the Arabs had been invincible in the field but the least city wall had sufficed to repulse them. Now, however, they had acquired the more scientific skills of warfare. Wooden towers were built to overlook the city walls and were laboriously pushed forward on rollers until they could shoot into the town at close range. Mangonels threw their great rocks into the city and a close watch prevented the entry of provisions or reinforcements from the country. The gallant resistance of Merida emphasizes the immense value of Tariq's decision to exploit his victory, while the initial panic of the Goths still paralyzed their resistance. If he had indeed waited to report back to Musa, the defenders would have had time to recover their balance and every town might have been a Merida.

The city, faced with starvation, eventually negotiated an honourable capitulation. The inhabitants were allowed the alternatives of voluntary exile or the payment of tribute. The churches were divided between the Muslims and the Christians and the lands and wealth of those killed or who had left the district, were seized as a reward for the believers. Merida capitulated on 1st June, 713, a year after Musa's landing in Spain. It is not clear why Tariq, whose headquarters were at Toledo only a hundred and fifty miles from Merida, did not report to his chief during the course of this year.

After accepting the surrender of Merida, Musa marched to Toledo. Tariq came to meet him but was greeted roughly by his master, who took him severely to task, ordered his arrest and possibly also caused him to be flogged. The majority of Western historians seem to have passed over this incident with the remark that Musa was obviously jealous of his subordinate's success. The methods of thought of the early Arabs were, however, in some ways so different from our own that it may be worth our while to pause to consider it. Tariq appears to have been a Berber client of Musa, possibly a former slave liberated by him.

According to the thinking of the time, the freedman was bound to remain the devoted client of the man who had set him at liberty. In innumerable accounts of contemporary battles, we find Arab nobles escorted in action by young Turkish, Persian or Berber freedmen, who on a stricken field again and again gave their lives in defence of their masters. Musa therefore probably regarded Tariq as a man who owed everything to him and whose duty it was to die in self-effacing sacrifice for his master. Indeed this confusion between personal service and official office runs through all the history of the Arab countries. The great man promoted those whom he trusted and whom should he trust more than his own household servants? This interpretation, moreover, explains the equally surprising fact that after inflicting such punishment, Musa once more placed Tariq in command of important operations. For Musa doubtless considered the Berber to be, not an army officer under his command, but a domestic who needed putting in his place but who, having taken his punishment, was still an inalienable member of his household.

The point leads us on to the whole question of nepotism, which has formed so common a cause of misunderstanding. It is noticeable that, whenever a prominent Arab was appointed by the khalifs to an independent command, he immediately nominated his sons, his brothers or his freedmen to the principal posts beneath him. When Ubaidullah ibn Zayyad was Viceroy of Iraq and Persia, his brothers were made governors of Persian provinces. When Muhallab was governor of Khurasan, his sons held commands under their father. When Musa himself crossed into Spain, he left his eldest son as his Viceroy of North Africa. The examples could be multiplied indefinitely.

This system was so general and so open, that it cannot have been regarded as in any way discreditable. Indeed in a state of society in which dishonesty was not uncommon and rebellion comparatively frequent, the system presented certain advantages. The distant governor in Khurasan or North Africa was inevitably obliged to fend for himself. The time required to receive orders, still more reinforcements, from Damascus was prohibitive. When, therefore, the khalif entrusted the care of a distant province to a reliable governor, he expected the latter to provide his own staff from persons upon whom he could completely rely. Naturally with the strong family feeling existing among the Arabs, such persons often consisted of the governor's closest relatives, freedmen and slaves, for the maintenance of discipline among whom he, as head of their family, not the government, was solely responsible.

While Musa and Tariq were engaged in the subjugation of northern Spain, the governor's eldest son, Abdul Aziz ibn Musa, was employed in regularizing the situation in the south. Here, in April 713 (while Musa was still besieging Merida), he concluded an agreement with Theodemir, the Gothic noble who held sway in this part of the country, and whose name the Arabs had simplified to Tadmir. The terms of the treaty laid down that Tadmir would remain in control of his principality, and that no injury would be offered to the lives, the property, the women or the children, the religion or the churches of the Christians. Tadmir further undertook to surrender seven cities to Arab garrisons, and not to assist the enemies of the khalif but on the contrary to give information of their intentions. He was bound to pay a poll tax of one gold piece per head for every noble and half a gold piece for every commoner, adult men only being liable. Contributions of wheat, barley, honey and oil were also to be made for the support of the Muslim garrisons. These terms closely resemble those granted fifty or sixty years earlier, during the first Arab conquests in Syria, Iraq and Persia.

The remainder of Spain surrendered without any great show of resistance. This result was facilitated by another condition which had everywhere distinguished Arab policy. Those who voluntarily negotiated their surrender, as in the case of Tadmir, received generous terms, but those who were conquered by force retained no rights at all, they themselves, their wives and children were sold as slaves and their property was distributed among the Muslims. Unless, therefore, there were a strong prospect of ultimate victory —and no such hope seemed to remain in Spain—it was far wiser to negotiate a capitulation rather than to fight on to the end. Excepting, therefore, the mountain districts of Galicia, the remainder of what is now Spain and Portugal was successfully pacified within a year of the surrender of Merida.

It is the frequent practice of European writers to state that the Arabians had no idea of politics except tribal rivalry and it must be admitted that much of their history in Umaiyid times seems to justify such strictures. Yet we are bound also to recognize the extraordinary breadth and wisdom of their policy as conquerors, a wisdom exceeding that shown by the Great Powers of our own times in their insistence on unconditional surrender after both World Wars. Indeed it is as conquerors that the early Arabs show up best. Their extraordinary hardihood and bravery in the field, the generous terms which they offered to those who surrendered and the faithfulness with which the terms were observed, offer an example to many more modern states. It was only after the completion of their conquests, in the enjoyment of wealth, luxury and security, that their morals suffered a rapid decline.

Musa was pressing hard on the remaining Christians who were still in arms in the wild mountains of Galicia, when, in the summer of 714, he received from the Khalif Waleed a peremptory order to report immediately to Damascus. Tariq apparently received a similar summons.

Musa had committed a crime far worse than cruelty or injustice—he had been too successful and had grown too powerful. As Governor of Africa from Tripoli to Morocco, and conqueror of Andalus—the name the Arabs gave to all their territory in Spain—he controlled an area almost as great as that ruled by his master from Egypt to India. Had he so wished, he could quite possibly have made himself independent of the Damascus khalifate. No Arab historian seems to have suggested that Musa harboured any such idea, though several of them allege that he seriously considered the conquest of France and Italy and a return to Syria by way of Greece, capturing Byzantium en route. Had the Arabs not already wasted so many lives and years in fratricidal civil wars, such a programme might not have been beyond their powers, for there were at the time no powerful states in Europe to oppose them. Moreover they had recently acquired the enormous additional manpower of the converted Berbers, a hardy, warlike and partly nomadic race like themselves. But the Arabs missed these opportunities. Soon after the conquest of Spain, they were to resume their internecine battles and their racial pride prevented them from according equality to the Berbers, in enthusiastic partnership with whom they might well have conquered Europe.

If the jealousy of the Khalif Waleed had in reality been the reason for Musa's recall, the latter seems to have adopted the wrong policy to allay the suspicions of his master. His progress from Ceuta through Africa and Egypt to Palestine was one immense triumphal procession. He was followed, if the report be true, by four hundred Gothic nobles wearing golden coronets, a train of some eighteen thousand slaves, and immense riches gathered in the ancient cities of Andalus.

When Musa reached Tiberias with this splendid retinue, he heard for the first time that the Khalif Waleed was dangerously ill. At the same time he received a message from the khalif's brother, Sulaiman ibn Abdul Malik, ordering him to await further orders in Tiberias. Abdul Malik, it will be remembered, had before his death caused the people to swear loyalty to Sulaiman as the successor to Waleed, should the elder brother die first.

The brothers, Waleed and Sulaiman, were not on cordial terms. Now, anticipating the early death of the khalif, Sulaiman wished the Spanish triumphal entry to take place after his accession. Musa was faced with an awkward decision. If he delayed his arrival in Damascus at Sulaiman's request and Waleed recovered, then the latter would obviously be indignant. He decided to disregard Sulaiman's message and to proceed. The Khalif Waleed was well enough to receive him but, shortly afterwards, suffered a relapse and died. No sooner did Sulaiman assume the khalifate than Musa, instead of being a triumphant hero, found himself regarded as a criminal. He was flogged, abused, insulted and condemned to pay a fine of two hundred thousand gold pieces, presumably the amount of wealth which he was thought to have accumulated. Already an old man, he was eventually permitted to retire and end his days in poverty and obscurity in the oasis of Wadi al Qura, a hundred miles north of Medina.

Tariq ibn Zayyad, to whose lightning march on Toledo the easy conquest of Spain was principally due, was more fortunate than his master. He was not punished for his services. A Berber client, he presumably was not considered dangerous to the supremacy of the khalif, and was accordingly released and permitted to return to his original avocation of a domestic servant.

The elimination of Musa and Tariq did not entirely allay the khalif's fears, for, before leaving Spain, Musa had appointed his second son Abdul Aziz to act as governor. When information reached the son of the reception accorded to his old father, he might well renounce his allegiance to Damascus. A party of assassins was accordingly despatched with all speed by the khalif from Syria to Andalus, where they were successful in murdering Abdul Aziz in Cordova. His severed head, carried back to Damascus, was, by a peculiar refinement of cruelty and hate, despatched by the khalif to the aged Musa in his desert retreat.

*   *   *

The conquest of Andalus by the Arabs was not an unmitigated catastrophe for many of the inhabitants, a great part of whom had been serfs or slaves in the times of the Goths. The aristocratic Arabs were not, on the whole, deeply religious but were both tolerant and broadminded. No attempt was made to convert Christians to Islam, a process which, as already explained, resulted in a loss of revenue to the government.

In some areas, the previous landlords were allowed to retain their lands, as we have seen in the case of Tadmir. The land confiscated by the Arabs, the property of landlords who had fled or been killed and the lands belonging to the Church, were divided up between the believers. The Arabs, as we have seen, were, at this stage, contemptuous of agriculture and despised farmers. As a result, the original cultivators were left on the land, on condition of paying a share of the crop to their new landlords.

Islam, however, did offer a new alternative to the serfs and the slaves of non-Muslim masters, for by pronouncing the formula "I bear witness that there is no god but God and that Muhammad is the Apostle of God," they could obtain their freedom from their Christian or Jewish owners. The

Prophet had laid down the principle that Jews and Christians were to be tolerated, but on condition of their behaving with humility. In other words, they were to become a socially inferior class. In accordance with this rule, Christians could not own Muslim slaves, who were automatically freed on professing Islam. Muslims, however, could own Muslim slaves. Thus a Gothic noble who professed Islam was able to retain his slaves, but one who remained a Christian could not do so, unless the slaves themselves remained Christians also.

The decision that the mere pronunciation of the Islamic formula of faith made a man a Muslim was perhaps one of the most far-seeing of the Prophet's policies. Even Muhammad's closest disciples often complained of the insincerity of such conversions which were so easy that, in a moment of danger or depression, non-Muslims were strongly tempted to recite a few words and thereby apparently to save themselves. But whereas the Apostle of God accepted such conversions without question, he was merciless to apostates who afterwards renounced Islam and whose punishment was normally death. The entrance into Islam was deceptively easy but no recantation was possible. Moreover the children of such converts could be brought up as genuine Muslims.

Thus many serfs and slaves hastened to secure their freedom by pronouncing the Muslim formula. A few were subsequently afflicted by qualms of conscience, so that a community of secret Christians came into existence. To renounce Islam openly meant death, so these people remained professing Muslims, who practised the Christian rites in secret. To the great majority of members of the depressed classes, however, Christianity had never meant much.

Socially the Arab conquest had some highly beneficial results. The confiscation of the properties of many of the Gothic nobles, of the Crown and of the Church, had, on the whole, greatly increased the number of small farmer landowners. Even where the land was acquired by some Arab noble, the latter's contempt for agriculture often gave the tenants a free hand to develop the land as they wished, provided that they paid their rent. Thus the bedouin scorn of farmers was in some ways a blessing in disguise.

But although the serfs and slaves could become free men by repeating the Muslim formula, they did not in practice achieve social equality thereby. In theory all Muslims were equal. In practice, the Arabs were a ruling aristocracy who had no intention of admitting non-Arab Muslims to equality. It was this very anomaly which, as we have seen, was already arousing discontent in Persia, Iraq and Syria. Soon, all over the empire, the non-Arab Muslims were to rise in their wrath against the haughty domination of the Arabs. In Spain the Arabs were more contemptuous of the renegade Christian who had become a Muslim, than of those who had adhered to their original faith.

One community above all others profited by the Arab conquest, namely the Jews. Having been previously persecuted by the Christians, they now enjoyed the same toleration as their former masters. Moreover, resentful as they were against their former persecutors, they acted continually as the spies, informers and advisers of the Muslims against the Christians.

NOTABLE DATES

Gothic conquest of Spain	509
Accession of the Khalif Waleed	8th October, 705
Roderic becomes King of the Goths	710
First Muslim raid on Spain	Summer 710
Tariq's invasion	April 711
Battle of Wadi al Bekka	July 711
Musa's invasion of Spain	June 712
Surrender of Merida	June 713
Recall of Musa	714
Arrival of Musa in Damascus	February 715
Death of the Khalif Waleed	23rd February, 715

PERSONALITIES

Waleed ibn Abdul Malik, the khalif
Musa ibn Nusair, governor of North Africa and conqueror of Spain
Roderic, King of the Goths
Count Julian, governor of Ceuta, who suggested to Musa the conquest of Spain
Tariq ibn Zayyad, the real conqueror of Spain
Abdul Aziz, son of Musa ibn Nusair, assassinated in Cordova
Sulaiman ibn Abdul Malik, the successor of Waleed as khalif.

VII

The End of Mare Nostrum

Once did she hold the gorgeous East in fee
And was the safeguard of the West.
And when she took unto herself a mate
She must espouse the everlasting sea.   WORDSWORTH

After the conquest of Spain, the Western Mediterranean became a Musulman lake . . . Islam had shattered the Mediterranean unity which the Germanic invasions had left intact. This was the most essential event of European history which had occurred since the Punic Wars. It was the end of the classic tradition. It was the beginning of the Middle Ages.

HENRI PIRENNE, *Muhammad and Charlemagne*

Thus much is certain; that he that commands the sea is at great liberty, and may take as much and as little of the war as he will.   FRANCIS BACON

VII

THE END OF MARE NOSTRUM

HAVING completed our description of the conquest of North Africa and Spain, we must digress from the strictly chronological account of the Arab Empire to consider one of the most important results of the Arab conquests—the Dark Ages of Europe. Our intentional neglect of Arab history, to which I have already referred[1] has resulted in an important misapprehension—the illusion that the Dark Ages were due to the conquest of Europe by the northern barbarians.

We, who live in Western Europe, are too much inclined to think that England and France played an important part in the Roman Empire. In fact, however, the Roman Community was basically a "lakeside" population, living round the shores of the Mediterranean. For several centuries the Middle Sea was entirely a Roman sea—"Our sea" they called it. No other Power possessed any part of its shores. In considering antiquity, it is essential to divest our minds of the idea of Europe, Asia and Africa as three different continents. Neither the Romans nor the Arabs had any such conception. To both the Romans and the Byzantines, all the shores of the Mediterranean constituted a single geographical unit, a classification much nearer to the real facts than the modern tendency to group, for example, Algeria and Tunis with Central Africa, as parts of the same continent.

As a result of its being a lakeside community, the frontiers of the Roman Empire were all land frontiers, running generally parallel to the shores of the Mediterranean at a distance of between two hundred and four hundred miles inland from that sea. For this reason, the wars of Rome—at least after the elimination of Carthage—were all land wars. This was due to the fact that there was no other Power on the Mediterranean to wage a naval war against her. As a result, we are inclined to think of Rome as a military rather than a naval power. In reality her whole dominion was based on sea power. Roman colonization of Northern France, Belgium, Holland and Britain (to give them their modern names) was merely in the nature of an imperial outpost to keep the northern barbarians from achieving access to the shores of the Mediterranean.

It is true that at the beginning of the fifth century, the barbarians began to invade the empire on a large scale and even to reach the Mediterranean, but the invasion of the northern barbarians differed in a remarkable manner from the Arab conquests. The Goths, the Vandals, the Lombards and the Franks were deeply impressed by the magnificence and the civilization of Rome. No moral force drove them forward to attack the empire, for most of them were still heathen. As soon as they forced themselves into Roman

1. See Preface.

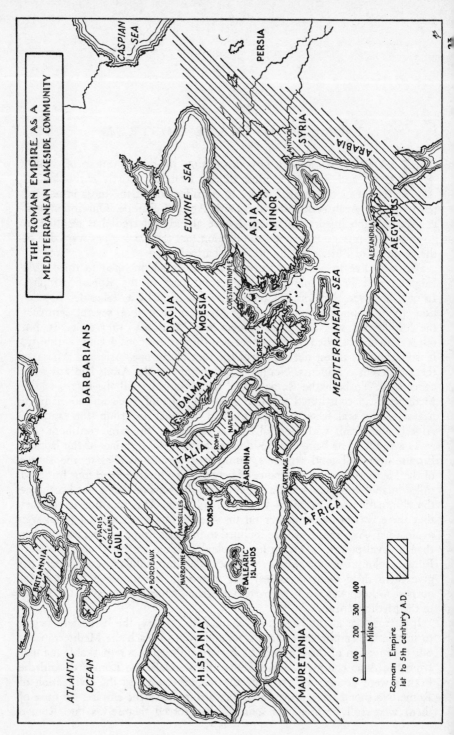

THE ROMAN EMPIRE AS A
MEDITERRANEAN LAKESIDE COMMUNITY

CASPIAN SEA

PERSIA

BARBARIANS

ATLANTIC OCEAN

EUXINE SEA

ASIA MINOR

ANTIOCH

SYRIA

ARABIA

ALEXANDRIA

AEGYPTUS

MEDITERRANEAN SEA

CONSTANTINOPLE

DACIA

MOESIA

GREECE

DALMATIA

ITALIA

ROME

NAPLES

SARDINIA

CORSICA

CARTHAGE

AFRICA

BRITANNIA

PARIS
ORLEANS
GAUL

BORDEAUX

MARSEILLES

NARBONNE

BALEARIC ISLANDS

HISPANIA

MAURETANIA

0 100 200 300 400
Miles

Roman Empire
1st to 5th century A.D.

territory, they took Latin names, imitated the manners of those whom they had conquered, were converted to Christianity, and sought titles and honours from the imperial court. The Arabs, on the contrary, claimed, in their first religious enthusiasm, to possess a faith higher than Christianity and affected to despise the populations of the empire. Thus the barbarian invasions from Northern Europe did not destroy the fact that the Mediterranean was still a Roman lake. The barbarians wished to join the Roman world as it was, not to change it.

After the disappearance of the western emperor in 475, Byzantium became the only surviving representative of the empire but Byzantium was even more sea-minded than Rome. Constantinople was the world's greatest seaport, and the city contained many industries, which produced manufactured goods for export. Moreover the site of Constantinople made it a great commercial centre. The Eastern trade converged to it from Syria and Persia, Russian[2] products came from the Black Sea, and those of Europe and North Africa from the Mediterranean.

The first serious blow to Roman sea power occurred in 427, when the Vandals crossed from Spain to Africa, capturing Carthage, Byzantium's great naval base at the junction of the eastern and western Mediterranean, in 439. The Vandals, basing themselves on Carthage, captured Sardinia, Corsica and the Balearics. A new sea power had appeared in the Mediterranean and the very existence of the empire was threatened. Byzantium was aware of the fact that Vandal sea power threatened her survival, but, for the moment, the arrival of the Huns on the frontier of the Danube made it impossible for her to react.

When Justinian became emperor of Byzantium in 527, he fully appreciated the situation. He made a humiliating treaty with Persia in order to be free from commitments. Persia was a danger to Byzantium but the navigation of the Mediterranean was her very life blood. In 533, Justinian concentrated all his strength against the Vandals. Within the course of a year, they had been defeated and the whole of North Africa returned to Byzantine rule. The Goths in Spain had grown idle and luxurious. The Franks, who were establishing themselves in France, had not taken to the sea. Italy had also been re-conquered by Justinian. The Mediterranean was once again a Roman lake.

From 533 onwards, the Mediterranean shores became once more populous through trade. The products of India, and even of Indonesia, Malaya and China were available all round its shores. Much of the sea-borne trade was handled by Syrians—in modern language we should call them Lebanese—the descendants of the ancient Phoenicians. Syrian merchants were to be found in all ports of the Mediterranean, Constantinople, Antioch, Alexandria, Carthage and Marseilles. We even hear of them in Naples, Bordeaux, Orleans and Paris. The population of Narbonne in 589 consisted of Goths, Romans, Jews, Greeks and Syrians.[3]

The safe navigation of the Mediterranean re-established a wealthy, com-

2. I use Russia in the modern geographical sense. The word was not invented in the fifth century.
3. Henri Pirenne, *Muhammad and Charlemagne*.

mercial and urban population. There was intense activity in the harbours all round the shores of the Middle Sea. Gold, silver, and eastern textiles were available everywhere in Italy, France and Spain. Silk was imported in great quantities and the fashions of Constantinople were copied in the West as those of Paris were in the eighteenth and nineteenth centuries. It is surprising to read that Syrian wines were imported into France. Perfumes, incense, and spices as condiments with food played a much greater part in the life of those times than in our own. They had been imported by Rome from China, India and Arabia. Pepper, cummin, cloves, cinnamon, nard, dates, figs, almonds, pistachios, olives and rice all reached Western Europe by way of the Eastern Mediterranean. Much olive oil was also imported from the same source and was used both for cooking and in lamps.

Another import of immense value was papyrus, which was made solely in Egypt. It was the material in common use for writing and thus the very survival of civilization might almost be said to have depended on it. Whole cargoes of papyrus were unloaded at the harbours of the Western Mediterranean. One of the chief cargoes carried in the ships on their return to the East was fair-haired slaves from Britain and Northern Europe. Timber was also exported from Western Europe to the East.

Another great advantage enjoyed by Mediterranean commerce at the time was the fact that the Byzantine gold solidus was everywhere legal tender, in the Gothic and Frankish kingdoms of Spain and France, as much as in Africa, Egypt, Syria and Greece. Thus merchants were free from the trammels of exchange and currency problems. There appears to have been a great quantity of currency in circulation, and many rich merchants and capitalists regularly lent money at interest.

Thus from the defeat of the Vandals in 533 until the Arab conquests a little more than a century later the pattern of trade which had existed throughout the five hundred years of Roman rule was resumed. The Eastern or Greek half of the Mediterranean had always been the richer and the more civilized, and during this century of commerce the great merchants and the commercial ships were nearly all Greek or Syrian. It was an economy very similar to our own, characterized by far-reaching overseas commerce, great harbours, wealthy merchants and capitalists, free circulation of money, busy cities and money-lending at interest. From the political angle, the Western half of the Roman Empire had been divided into a number of barbarian states, but the Goths, Lombards and Franks had no basic reason for hostility to Byzantium. On the contrary, the emperor still enjoyed great prestige, and many of these kings acknowledged his suzerainty and even asked him to confirm their accession to the throne, though they would of course have resisted any attempt by Byzantium to re-impose political control—a situation not unlike that of the British Commonwealth since the First World War.

Thus the political disintegration of the Western Empire had not destroyed the commercial trade routes of Roman imperial days, nor had the barbarian invasions produced a feudal system or an agricultural economy, such as was to be established later in Western Europe. The barbarian kings had no desire whatever to change the lucrative Roman commercial system; indeed they derived immense profits from the prosperity of this commerce, as a result of which they were able to collect large sums of cash in customs and taxes. Byzantium was impoverished by the wars with Persia but the Mediterranean as a whole was wealthy and prosperous. Nobody, moreover, foresaw a catastrophe. The Arabs had never been a menace to their neighbours. In the past, it had been from Russia and Central Asia that conquerors had always emerged, but now the barbarians had come and had been integrated into the Roman commercial scene.

*　　*　　*

If the Arabs had burst out of the Arabian Peninsula to conquer the Byzantine empire merely because they were tempted by its wealth, the result would have been utterly different. It was for this reason that the northern barbarians had come, who, as we have seen, had adopted Roman manners and the imperial religion, as soon as they had established themselves. Had the Arabs come for the same reason, they too would have become Romanized and Christianized and the life, at least the commercial life, of the Mediterranean would have gone on as before. But the Arabs came convinced that their new religion made them superior to others. They did not, therefore, become Romanized, as the northern barbarians had done. On the contrary, the inhabitants of the former Roman provinces became Arabicized.

The Arab historians represent Musa ibn Nusair as considering the conquest of France and Italy and proposing to return to Syria through Greece to take Byzantium from the West. Had such a plan succeeded, the unity of the Mediterranean would have been restored, but as an Arab instead of a Roman lake. Instead, the khalifs turned to luxury and despotism and the conquests petered out, leaving the Mediterranean bisected. In general, however, sea power in the Mediterranean had passed to the Muslims.

Although the Byzantine Emperor continued to maintain a fleet, it was normally cooped up in one quarter of the Mediterranean, that along the coasts of Asia Minor and Greece, as far as Sicily.

In the second half of the ninth century, as we shall see, the Muslims took Sicily, Corsica and Sardinia, and again it seemed possible that they might conquer all the shores of the Mediterranean, but, once again, they just failed.

If Islam had not included an obligation to holy war, the Arab conquest of North Africa and Spain would not have destroyed the commerce of the Mediterranean. The conquest would have been followed by peace and a resumption of world trade. In fact, however, the Mediterranean, for centuries past the highway of commerce, was to become, for six hundred years, a no-man's land, navigated principally by war-fleets and pirates.

Even before the conquest of Spain, the trade between Western Europe and the East must have virtually ceased. Syria had been conquered by the Arabs in 636, and, as we have seen, most of the merchants and the trading ships had been Syrian. Egypt was conquered in 642, and the greater part of the Eastern trade had previously come through that country. In 648, the Arabs began themselves to organize battle fleets in Egypt and Syria, and for this purpose

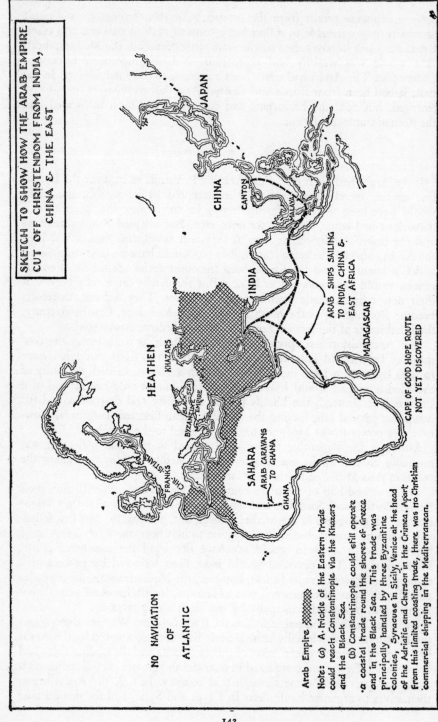

SKETCH TO SHOW HOW THE ARAB EMPIRE
CUT OFF CHRISTENDOM FROM INDIA,
CHINA & THE EAST

JAPAN

CHINA

CANTON

MALAYA

INDIA

ARAB SHIPS SAILING
TO INDIA, CHINA &
EAST AFRICA

MADAGASCAR

CAPE OF GOOD HOPE ROUTE
NOT YET DISCOVERED

HEATHEN

KHAZARS

BLACK SEA

BYZANTINE
EMPIRE

CHR.
FRANKS

SAHARA

ARAB CARAVANS
TO GHANA

GHANA

NO NAVIGATION
OF
ATLANTIC

Arab Empire ▩

Note: (a) A trickle of the Eastern Trade
could reach Constantinople via the Khazars
and the Black Sea.
    (b) Constantinople could still operate
a coastal trade round the shores of Greece
and in the Black Sea. This trade was
principally handled by three Byzantine
colonies, Syracuse in Sicily, Venice at the head
of the Adriatic and Cherson in the Crimea. Apart
from this limited coasting trade, there was no Christian
commercial shipping in the Mediterranean.

doubtless commandeered most of the ships. Thereafter the hitherto peaceful and prosperous North African provinces were torn by alternate Arab invasions and Berber rebellions, until, in 698, Carthage, the great harbour and naval base, was captured by the Arabs and razed to the ground.

Thereafter Europe was completely cut off from world trade—China, India, Malaya and the continent of Africa down to Madagascar and Ghana were open to Arab trade, but Christendom was entirely isolated. The Byzantine fleet was able still to protect coastal trade between Constantinople, Greece and the Adriatic but no more. France and Italy suddenly found the whole of their wealthy eastern trade cut off. In the words of Ibn Khaldoun, "The Christians could no longer float a plank upon the sea."

A complete revolution in the life of Western Europe resulted. Papyrus, hitherto the common everyday writing material, was the first to vanish. All the archives of the Frankish Merovingian court had been kept on papyrus. Suddenly the supply ceased and was replaced by parchment locally made from animal skins. The first royal document of the Frankish government produced on parchment was dated 12th September, 677. Soon afterwards, spices, previously in common daily use, disappeared likewise. Pepper, cloves, nard, cinnamon, dates and pistachios soon vanished. Henceforward the lists of food-stuffs contain no imported articles, but only bread, pork, fowls, eggs, vegetables, fish, cheese and other obviously locally grown produce. Olive oil, in the same manner, was soon in extremely short supply. Some could be grown in southern France or Italy, but the amount thus obtained could only supply a fraction of the demand. It could no longer be spared for lamps and we find the churches going over to candles. Silk ceased to be worn, though in earlier times both men and women had used it at the Merovingian court.[4]

In the same manner, the supply of gold was cut off. The Merovingians at first alloyed their gold coins with an increasing admixture of silver, but eventually even this became impossible. In Charlemagne's time, only silver coins were in use. When Charlemagne became the ruler of France and Germany in 771, he found himself at the head of an inland state with no external commerce.

Another important result of the Arab control of the Mediterranean was that it destroyed the influence of Byzantium in Western Europe. After the collapse of the Western Roman Empire in 475 until the Arab conquests two centuries later, Byzantine influence had been slowly growing in the West, whether owing to its commerce and its merchants, its scholars or its artists. The infestation of the Mediterranean with Arab fleets and pirates not only severed Western Europe from Egypt and India, but also cut it off from Byzantium. Consequently Charlemagne and his successors were obliged to build up a new civilization, almost entirely independent of Byzantine, and even of Roman, tradition. Had the Arab conquests never taken place, Western Europe would have developed on Eastern Roman lines, an urban civilization, with wealthy merchants and powerful cities. Such a civilization was to return to the West but not until six or seven centuries had elapsed and Europe was again able to trade freely with the world.

4. Henri Pirenne. Op. cit.

For the present, Charlemagne's empire had no external commerce and consequently no great merchants, and very little cash. The countries which he ruled had to live on local produce and, as a result, land and not cash became the source of wealth. The great men of the state were not now the urban business men and the capitalists but the landed barons, a system which remained in existence, to some extent at least, up to the nineteenth century. Moreover the absence of commerce and thus of liquid money in the hands of the government, led to the feudal system itself. For the emperor, or the local rulers, having their wealth in the form of land and not of money, were unable to pay regular armies. To atone for their poverty in cash, they gave land in return for military service. Moreover where there was no commerce the cities dwindled and the baron's castle, not the city council chamber, became the centre of power and influence.

Soon education suffered, from the poverty of the towns and from the lack of materials on which to write. A community of farmers saw little need for literacy or, at any rate, could not achieve it. Before long, only the Church produced men who could read and write. The Dark Ages of Europe had arrived. This relapse into ignorance has been erroneously attributed to the barbarian conquests, whereas in reality it appears to have been principally due to the Arab encirclement of Europe. The Dark Ages did not begin with the barbarian invasions in the fifth century but with the Arab closure of the Mediterranean in the seventh. They slowly came to an end after the year 1000, as the Arab Empire weakened.

But while France and Germany became entirely feudal, agricultural and self-sufficient, certain places in Italy maintained a precarious commerce with Constantinople. The first and the greatest of these was Venice. In the fifth century, the first inhabitants of these inhospitable little islands at the head of the Adriatic had been some unfortunate fugitives from the mainland, fleeing in panic from the massacring hordes of Attila and the Huns. At the beginning, these wretched refugees barely kept body and soul together by fishing. Naturally they took to the sea for a living, while the privations which they endured made them hardy and adventurous. Soon they developed their navigation and in the eighth century, when the ports of Italy and France had been killed by Arab command of the sea, Venetian ships were sailing regularly round Greece to Constantinople. The city placed itself under Byzantine protection, a convenient system, for the emperor was too far away to interfere in their affairs. During the ninth century, Venice extended her authority over part of the Dalmation coast and enjoyed, more or less, the naval command of the Adriatic. A few lesser Italian ports on the south-west coast competed with Venice for the eastern trade though on a smaller scale. All these Italian ports were purely commercial, though their fleets at times assisted the emperors and engaged the Arab fleets at sea. At other times, however, they were not above trading with the Muslims on the quiet, even exporting white slaves to the Arab countries.

As a result of the continuance of this trade, even though it were only a trickle, spices, perfumes, precious fabrics, gold and papyrus continued to arrive in Venice and in Southern Italy. There were even gold coins in circulation in Southern Italy, when the Emperor Charlemagne was obliged to use only a silver currency.

*   *   *

From our point of view, however, by far the most exciting aspect of the centuries during which the Arabs had command of the sea in the Mediterranean, was that of the social results. We have seen that the cessation of overseas commerce entirely changed the social structure of Western Europe. The class of merchants and capitalists disappeared, the cities dwindled and France and Germany became agricultural countries, ruled by landowners. As the emperors and the princes had no money to pay regular armies, the feudal system of military service came into existence. It is interesting to notice that the Arabs, as they grew richer and richer from their vast world commerce, moved in the other direction. Whereas their original military conquests had been carried out on a tribal basis under chiefs (the Arab equivalent of the feudal system), the khalifs, as we shall see below, gradually went over to paid mercenary armies.

A civilization based on agriculture and aristocracy produces a mentality entirely different from that of a commercial and industrial state. The leaders of the people under such a dispensation take their chief pride in military exploits, in heroic deeds, noble hospitality and romantic love. These were the very ideals which the ancient Arabs had pursued, at the time when Rome and Byzantium were basing their power on wealth, commerce, navigation and great cities. When the Arabs seized the trade, Western Europe turned to the "Arab" virtues of war, hospitality and romance, while the Arab empire, with its immense wealth, turned to materialism, as we shall see later when discussing the khalifate of Baghdad.

But there is another aspect even more fascinating still. The Arabs in Spain, far from the corrupting materialism of Baghdad, were to retain their admiration for war, hospitality and love. Their continued devotion to these "Arab virtues" struck a sympathetic chord in the minds of the feudal aristocracy of Western Europe who, deprived of their commerce by the Arabs, had fallen back on these same virtues. Although their religious differences caused them to be often at war, yet the Christian knights of France and the Muslim cavaliers of Andalusia conceived a respect, even an admiration, for one another.

While, therefore, from about 700 onwards, the pattern was one of agriculture in Western Europe and commerce and industry in the Arab Empire,[5] Spain constituted to some extent an exception in the West. In the East, however, the Byzantine area from the Adriatic to Constantinople just succeeded in retaining the old commercial background. In the eighth and the ninth centuries, trade barely survived, owing to the dangers to navigation from Arab piracy. Constantinople could still trade with Russia across the Black Sea and a trickle of the eastern trade remained, either through the heathen Khazars north of the Caucasus, or through smugglers or by means of Jewish merchants who had the entry to both sides. For the two hostile camps which

5. The exact reverse of today's situation.

faced one another across the Mediterranean were Christendom and Islam. Both sides were ready to trade with Jews or heathen, who were neutral.

The survival of this trade perpetuated the merchant class and the power of cities in this limited area. In Byzantium and in Southern Italy, the merchants were often in conflict, or at least in political rivalry, with the landowners and the aristocracy, but the continuance of overseas commerce prevented the establishment of a complete feudal system. In Southern Italy, the ports of Salerno, Naples and Amalfi engaged in periodical disputes with the Duke of Benevento, who, however, through their commerce, had succeeded in retaining a gold currency in his dominions. Venice, safe on her islands, maintained her own plutocratic system of government. From the tenth century onwards, the weakening of the Arab Empire allowed to Europe a gradual resumption of trade with the East, which was followed by the Renaissance and the return of the spirit of commercialism, with its accompaniments of city life and capitalism. Nevertheless the feeling that landowners were superior to business men survived in Western Europe well into the nineteenth century.

Perhaps the full flowering of any culture requires a combination of the romantic and martial spirit of rural society with the wealth, learning and enlightenment of a commercial community. The reason why Europe attained such a cultural florescence in the eighteenth and the nineteenth centuries cannot be understood by us unless we are willing to take into account the influence of the Arab imperial period on the development of the West.

VIII

The Years of Victory

The Lord have mercy on Waleed and where is the like of Waleed, who conquered India and Spain and built the mosque of Damascus and who used to
give plates of silver to be divided among the poor.

Suyuti, History of the Khalifs

Pierced have we with our spear-points their backs the fleers,
Smitten low with our swords and pruned their proud ones.
Yea, the heads of their mighty have rolled before us,
Like loads let loose on a road from beasts unburdened.
Still with might we assailed, we pushed, we pressed them,
Lopped their heads at the neck, laid bare their shoulders ...
Bite we sharp with our swords, nor apportion mercy,
Swift, ere these shall have seen the hand that smites them.
Reckless we in the mêlée, our swords and their swords;
Wooden swords you had deemed theirs in the hands of children ...
Lo, the lands we o'errun till the plains grow narrow,
Lo, the seas will we sack with our war-galleys.
Not a weanling of ours but shall win to manhood,
Find the world at his knees, its great ones kneeling.

Amr ibn Kulthum (trans. by Wilfrid Blunt)

VIII

THE YEARS OF VICTORY

BEFORE recounting the story of the Arab conquest of Spain, we left the Khalif Waleed in Damascus in 710. We must now go back a few years to consider the state of the Byzantine Empire, in the territory of which great events were soon to take place. The Eastern Roman Empire appeared to be once again on the verge of extinction. In fact—incredible as it would have seemed then to be—it still had seven centuries of existence before it, a period longer than the complete lives of most of the empires of history.

In 685, the year in which Abdul Malik ibn Merwan had been acclaimed khalif in Damascus, the Emperor Justinian II had ascended the throne at the age of sixteen. The Byzantine Empire seemed to be at its last gasp. On the European shore, Constantinople was threatened by the Slavs and Bulgars, on the Asian by the Arabs. At first Justinian II met with some success, for the Arabs were preoccupied with the civil war between Abdul Malik and Abdulla ibn Zubair. The emperor conquered Armenia but, having done so, he could not resist the temptation to coerce the Armenian church to conform with the Greek Orthodox dogma. The Armenians rose against him and drove out his armies.

At the same time, the civil war between the Arabs had come to an end and the Muslims, denouncing the truce they had previously made, invaded Asia Minor. In the hope of staving off a new war with the Arabs, Justinian withdrew from the Amanus mountains the Christian mountaineers, who had hitherto greatly hampered the military operations of the Arabs.

In 695, however, Justinian II, who had proved a cruel tyrant, was dethroned by a military *coup d'état* in Constantinople. His nose was cut off and he was exiled to the Crimea. Refusing to give up, however, he established relations with the Khazars and married Theodora, sister of the Khan of that nation. The Byzantine government protested and the Khazars seem to have tired of him and sent a man to murder him. Justinian strangled the would-be assassin, made a hairbreadth escape, was nearly shipwrecked in a storm in the Black Sea, sailed up the Danube and made friends with Terbelis, King of the Bulgars. Eventually, an almost miraculous feat, he recaptured the throne of the empire in 705, the year of Waleed's accession to the khalifate.

Not only was Constantinople threatened by the Bulgars from the west and by the Arabs from Asia Minor, but the greater part of Italy was in the occupation of barbarians, although the cities of Rome and Ravenna still acknowledged their allegiance to the Eastern Empire. In this desperate situation Justinian, now nicknamed Slitnose, decided to issue a theological statement. In Rome the Pope immediately protested. Justinian ordered his arrest but the troops took the side of the Pontiff and refused to carry out the emperor's orders. In 710, the troops in Ravenna also mutinied and killed the imperial governor. Again and again, in the stormy history of Byzantium, when the situation was peculiarly precarious, the emperors issued theological statements which immediately alienated the few subjects who still acknowledged their supremacy.

After a stormy reign filled with adventures worthy of a Hollywood film story, Justinian Slitnose was assassinated in 711. If his reign had been chaotic, his death led to complete anarchy. It was at this moment that the Umaiyid Empire of Damascus reached the highest pinnacle of its power. On the west, its victorious armies were overrunning Spain. On the east, as will be shortly related, they were pressing on to the frontiers of China.

The apparent disintegration of the Byzantine Empire offered an irresistible temptation to the Arabs, now once again embarked on campaigns of conquest on all fronts. In 711, the year of the death of Slitnose, three major Muslim expeditions penetrated Byzantine territory, two under the command of sons of the Khalif Waleed and one under his brother, the seasoned veteran, Maslama ibn Abdul Malik. In the following year, 712, Abbas ibn Waleed captured Antioch in Pisidia, halfway between the former frontier and Constantinople.

Arab strategy had changed as a result of the apparent collapse of the Byzantine state. The annual summer raids into imperial territory had previously been virtually a matter of routine, from which no decisive results had been expected. Now, however, the Arab advance was a regular planned invasion. The khalif's armies were pushing steadily onwards with the deliberate intention of reaching and capturing Constantinople and of destroying the Byzantine Empire once and for all.

At the time of the great Arab conquests seventy years earlier, the first enthusiastic Muslims had poured out of Central Arabia and attacked their neighbours in every direction at the same time. Although the first passionate enthusiasm had now cooled, the same tradition was still maintained. The garrisons of every province attacked the enemies immediately opposed to them. If the whole strength of the empire could have been concentrated on one front, the subsequent history of the world might have been very different. If the main forces of the Arab Empire had been sent to Spain, they might from there have conquered France, and Italy and Musa's dream of attacking Constantinople through Italy and Greece might have come true. Alternatively if the khalif's armies had been concentrated in Asia Minor, Constantinople might have been taken and the Byzantine Empire destroyed from the east. The Arab armies could then have marched on to the conquest of Greece and Italy. Such strategy never appears to have been considered; perhaps it would in any case have been impossible. The different territories of the empire tended to become increasingly parochial. The Persian frontiers had, from the first, been the responsibility of the garrisons of Kufa and Basra. The Syrian army operated on the Tarsus border. Spain was a world of its own, maintaining its local armies. Not only so, but, as we have seen, an ever-widening breach separated the armies of Iraq and Syria, who at times appeared readier to fight one another than a foreign enemy.

The slowness of communications in those days might well be accepted as sufficient explanation for this tendency to parochialism but it may be noticed that the Roman Empire in its prime controlled almost as large an area without permitting these local limitations in its defensive measures. Two explanations may be put forward to explain the greater success achieved by the Romans in this field. Of these the more important seems to be the speed with which the Arab Empire was built. Rome expanded slowly for centuries and thus had many generations of experience behind her by the time that her empire reached its fullest extent. The Arab Empire reached its greatest dimensions in seventy years, a period quite inadequate to produce, out of an ignorant and illiterate tribal society, an imperial ruling class, with minds wide enough to consider world policies.

The second reason, probably the result of the first, was that, in the early years, no one foresaw these problems. The Iraqis were employed in Persia and the Syrians against Byzantium, because in the heat of action this seemed the easiest way. Later on, it was too late to organize a regular system of reliefs, Iraqi units being sent to Spain and vice versa. Yet Rome had used these methods five centuries earlier. It may be noted, however, that while the Roman Empire was nearly as large as that of the Arabs it was more compactly sited round the shores of the Mediterranean. Its greatest length was 2,600 miles, that of the khalif's dominions 4,250 miles. The fact that the Arab armies of the provinces operated only on their own frontiers made it impossible to concentrate a major military enterprise against one enemy at a time.

Leaving the Arab armies fighting their way across Asia Minor in the year 712, we must turn to consider the progress of events on the eastern frontier. Having suppressed the rebellions in Iraq and Persia, Hajjaj was now on the offensive beyond the borders of the empire. In 711, he had appointed Muhammad ibn Qasim al Thaqafi, a cousin of his own, to invade India. In 712—the wonderful year of victories in which Musa ibn Nusair crossed into Spain and Abbas ibn Waleed was halfway to Constantinople—Muhammad ibn Qasim defeated and killed Dahir, the Brahman King of Sind, in a pitched battle. In 713, he took Multan and extended his control over most of what is now West Pakistan.

Meanwhile in a succession of victorious campaigns based on Merv in Khurasan, Qutaiba ibn Muslim crossed the Oxus and took Khiva and Bukhara. In 712 he laid siege to Samarqand. When closely pressed, the besieged sent a secret appeal to the people of Ferghana, asking them to surprise the Arab camp by a night attack. Qutaiba's spies, however, immediately reported the plan to him with the date of its proposed execution. After dark on the night in question, he sent four hundred cavalry silently out of his camp, up the track which came from Ferghana. Some of these took up a position across the road, while two detachments were concealed near the track a little further on. In the small hours of the morning, the Ferghana relief column rode down the track, fondly imagining that they were about

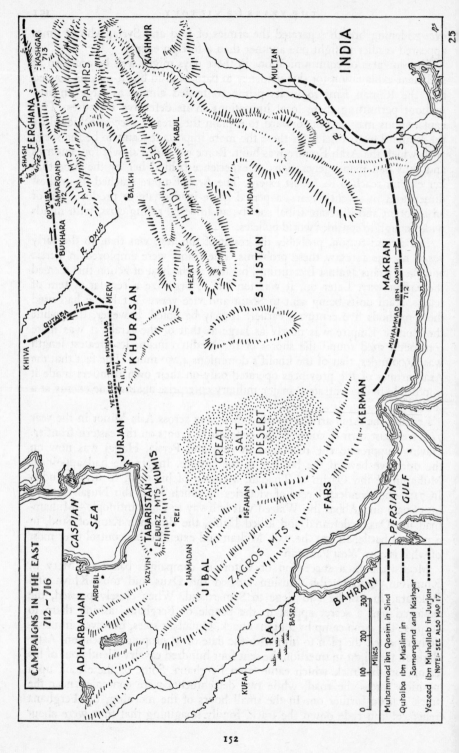

CAMPAIGNS IN THE EAST
712 ~ 716

KASHGAR
713

FERGHANA
R. SHASH
R. JAXARTES
PAMIRS
ALAI MTS
SAMARQAND
712
BUKHARA
QUTAIBA
KASHMIR
INDIA
KABUL
HINDU KUSH
MULTAN
R. INDUS
R. OXUS
BALKH
QUTAIBA 711
MERV
HERAT
SIND
KANDAHAR
YEZEED IBN MUHALLAB
714
SIJISTAN
MAKRAN
MUHAMMAD IBN QASIM
712
KHIVA
KHURASAN
JURJAN
TABARISTAN
ELBURZ MTS.
KUMIS
REI
GREAT
SALT
DESERT
KERMAN
CASPIAN
SEA
KAZVIN
HAMADAN
ISFAHAN
JIBAL
FARS
PERSIAN
GULF
ZAGROS MTS
ADHARBAIJAN
ARDEBIL
BAHRAIN
IRAQ
BASRA
KUFA

Muhammad ibn Qasim in Sind ▬ ▬ ▬
Qutaiba ibn Muslim in
Samarqand and Kashgar ▬ ‧ ▬ ‧ ▬
Yezeed ibn Muhallab in Jurjan ▪▪▪▪▪▪▪▪
NOTE:– SEE ALSO MAP 17

Miles
0   100   200   300

25

152

to surprise the Arab camp. Suddenly they ran into the block which the Arabs had set up across the road and immediately attacked it with vigour. Just, however, when the two sides were fully engaged, the two ambushes charged the enemy in the rear. The relief column was almost exterminated. At sunrise, the four hundred Arab horsemen rode back into camp, every man with the head of an enemy champion dangling from his saddle. Unlike the easy conquest of Spain, fifty years of fighting on the Oxus had resulted in a ruthless warfare in which few prisoners were taken. It is in these sieges also that we first read of the Muslims driving mineshafts beneath the walls of an enemy city. Obviously the Arabs had by now become competent professional soldiers.

Samarqand was taken in 712. Buddhism seems to have been here the prevalent faith. There were also Majians, or fire-worshippers, whose temples, together with the sacred fire burning in them, were destroyed. Qutaiba ordered the destruction of all idols in the city. The inhabitants, however, warned the Muslims that such a sacrilegious attempt would inevitably result in their extermination, but Qutaiba thereupon threw them down and set fire to them with his own hand.

But there was one result of the capture of Samarqand far more important than the burning of temples or the decapitation of the prisoners. The city contained a factory for making paper, an industry first invented in China and which had been brought to Samarqand by a group of Chinese artisans. The industry was carried by the Arabs to Baghdad, Damascus, Cairo, North Africa, Sicily and Spain. Arab manuscripts on paper, written in the ninth century, still exist. The manufacture of paper did not spread to Europe until four hundred years after the Arabs began to use it. It reached the West in the twelfth century through the factories established by the Arabs in Sicily and Spain. Their fortunate acquisition of the process of paper-making from the Chinese played a considerable part in the great flowering of science and culture among the Arabs in the ninth and tenth centuries, as will be seen in subsequent chapters.

In spite of the severity of this long drawn-out warfare in Central Asia, the Arabs made steady progress under Qutaiba. An increasing number of conversions to Islam took place among the Persian and Turkish inhabitants and the Arab armies were accompanied by more and more locally raised levies of Muslim converts. This development was partly due to the wise policy of Qutaiba himself. He realized that the Arabs could not hope to rule these remote territories in Central Asia unless they could secure the friendship and co-operation of the inhabitants. He made frequent use of Persians as agents, officials and even as local governors, until some of the Arabs complained that the governor was "going native". It is noticeable that all the great Arab viceroys of Persia, Zayyad the-son-of-his-father, Muhallab and Qutaiba, were careful to conciliate the Persians but their efforts were insufficient to overcome the ill-effects of the arrogance of many of the Arab chiefs.

In 712, Qutaiba advanced to the Jaxartes, occupying Shash and Ferghana. In 713, he even raided Kashgar in Chinese territory. Crossing the mountains east of Ferghana, an Arab army occupied the town, taking prisoners and loot. According to Ibn al Athir, the force advanced beyond Kashgar "almost to China". It is unfortunate that no detailed account of this expedition has come down to us, involving, as it did, the crossing of some of the highest mountains in the world.

Subsequently a messenger reached Qutaiba from the Emperor of China, with an invitation to a delegation of Arabs to visit the Imperial Court. For this purpose, Qutaiba selected a party of twelve men, remarkable both for their fine physique and their eloquence. He caused them to be lavishly equipped and after giving them his personal instructions, sent them off from Kashgar. When summoned to their first audience with the Emperor of China, the Arabs bathed, donned their softest and richest clothing and perfumed themselves generously. The audience was brief and no conversation took place, but after their withdrawal, the emperor asked his courtiers what they thought of the strangers. They replied that they appeared completely effeminate with their soft clothing and their sensuous perfumes.

For the second audience, the Arabs dressed in good but simple attire. Again the emperor consulted his subordinates who expressed the opinion that this time they looked more like men. For a third interview, the Muslims donned their armour and helmets, their swords hung by their sides, their bows were slung from their shoulders, and they mounted their horses, with their long lances in their right hands. When they approached the imperial presence, they struck their lances into the ground, dismounted and advanced to the throne in full armour, their garments girt up as if for battle. At the end of the audience, they remounted their horses and engaged in a mimic battle with sword and lance at full gallop. The emperor again consulted his courtiers who replied, doubtless truthfully, that they had never before seen people like these.

Eventually the emperor is said to have summoned the leader of the Arab delegation to a personal interview, the only occasion on which the Arab historian reports any conversation as having taken place. "You have now seen the extent of my dominions," the emperor began (it was about two thousand miles from Kashgar), "your lives are in the hollow of my hand. I want to ask you a question. If you lie to me, you will be put to death. Why did you change your clothes at every audience?" "Our dress the first day," replied the Arab leader, "was that which we wear among our wives or in the midst of our families. On the second day, we put on the clothing which we use to visit our own rulers. On the third day we bore the appearance we show to our enemies."

"That seems reasonable enough," said the emperor benignly, "and now you have leave to return to your master. Tell him that I am aware of his greed but also of his lack of manpower. He had better not fall foul of me or I shall send against him people who will destroy both him and you."

"How can he be short of men," replied the Arab boldly, "when the advanced guard of his cavalry is in China and its rearguard in the land of olive groves?[1] And how can he be greedy for this world, which is worth

1. Spain.

nothing? And as for your threats to kill us, the day of our death is fixed in advance and we look forward to that day without fear or repulsion."

"What then does your master want?" enquired the emperor.

"He has sworn," answered the gallant Hubaira, "that he will not turn back until he has trodden the soil of your country, until he has placed his seal on the necks of your kings and collected your tribute."

"We will extricate him from his oath," replied the emperor blandly, apparently by no means incensed at the suggestion of tribute. "We will send him some of the soil of our country that he may tread it, and some of our sons will go with you that he may seal their necks, and, as for tribute, we will send him what will suffice him."

A golden dish was accordingly brought, in which were placed a few handfuls of Chinese soil. Four young men were detailed to accompany the Arabs that Qutaiba might set his seal upon their necks and return them. Then the members of the delegation were loaded with gifts and a rich present of gold and silk was given to them for their master, to release him from his oath to take tribute from the Emperor of China.

Such is the picturesque account given by Tabari. It is not improbable, however, that the mission had in reality a commercial objective. The peoples of Trans-Oxiana derived their wealth from the trade with China. Perhaps the Arab raids on Kashgar had alarmed them. A state of war between the Arabs and the Chinese Empire would put an end to trade and might prove their financial ruin. Qutaiba, we have seen, was anxious to conciliate the inhabitants, and may well have sent the delegation at their request to ensure the uninterrupted continuance of their commerce. Many other embassies were to visit the Chinese court in the years to come. Chinese records confirm 713 as the date of Qutaiba's mission and record that the Arabs refused to perform the customary kow-tow to the emperor.[2]

* * *

While the triumphant Arab war-banners were being borne forward to victory in Spain, in Asia Minor, in Sind and in Central Asia, Waleed in 705 had appointed as governor of Medina a young man who, unlike the men of his race and generation, was not interested in war. Umar ibn Abdul Aziz was the cousin of Waleed, his father Abdul Aziz having been the brother of Abdul Malik.[3] No sooner did he arrive in Medina to take up his office than he summoned the religious leaders and the qadhis to his house. He informed them that he wished to govern solely according to God's law and begged them to give him frequently the benefit of their advice, by which he promised always to be guided. So modest a ruler filled the people of Medina and Mecca with delight, after the various sieges and choppings-off of heads to which they had grown accustomed in the previous twenty-five years.

Meanwhile, however, Hajjaj ibn Yusuf was still governing the eastern half of the empire with his iron rod. It is true that rebellion and resistance had ceased and that the troops, once more disciplined and victorious, were

2. H. A. R. Gibb. Op. cit.   3. Genealogical tree, page 64.

invading China and India. But the blood which the dictator had shed could not so easily be forgotten. Many Iraqis no longer desired to live in a country of which Hajjaj was the ruler but preferred to move to Medina or Mecca, where the pious young governor had apparently discovered the secret of maintaining order without bloodshed. Umar remained for six years governor of Medina, devoting most of his time to religious studies, though he lived in comfort and was not insensible to worldly pleasures. During these years, the migration of Iraqis to Medina had annoyed Hajjaj, who eventually wrote to Waleed, complaining that under Umar ibn Abdul Aziz the holy cities had become centres of intrigue against himself on the part of dissident Iraqis. On his deathbed, his father Abdul Malik had begged the young Waleed always to be guided by the advice of Hajjaj, the one completely loyal servant of the dynasty. "My son, you need him more than he needs you," the old khalif had said.

Waleed had taken to heart his father's advice and invariably complied with every request made to him by the governor of Iraq and Persia. Not only did he decide immediately to dismiss Umar but he nominated to the vacancy the candidate put forward by Hajjaj. The new governor on arrival in Medina gave orders for all Iraqis to return to their country forthwith, or to face the usual penalty of decapitation. Umar ibn Abdul Aziz returned without protest to Damascus in 712. The Iraqi discontent, however, was soon to end, for Hajjaj died in August 713, after governing the eastern provinces of the empire for twenty years. He was only fifty-four years old at his death.

An amusing story of Hajjaj is told by Masudi. While he was governor of Iraq, a young cousin of his, a fellow-tribesman of Thaqeef, visited him and asked him why he did not appoint free Arabs like himself to govern "these town fellows." Hajjaj was himself well educated, spoke excellent Arabic, composed verses and quoted the classics. This rough tribal lad was obviously quite ignorant. "The townsmen you speak of can read and write and have learnt arithmetic," explained the governor. "You are illiterate and I do not suppose you can even add."

"I daresay I can add and write as well as they can," said the bedouin angrily.

"Well, let us see," replied Hajjaj, doubtless with a twinkle. "How would you divide three dirhems between four applicants?"

For a moment the tribesman appeared nonplussed. Then he answered cheerfully: "Certainly, O Ameer. I would give a dirhem each to the first three and then," opening a dirty bag tied to his belt, "I would give the fourth man a dirhem from my own purse. You cannot catch me out with these townsman's tricks.

The governor and his companions roared with laughter at this sally. "By God"[4] said Hajjaj, "the people of Isfahan are three years in arrears with their taxes. None of the governors I have sent have succeeded in making them pay anything—you are just the man for the job."

The sophisticated Isfahanis were delighted when an illiterate bedouin arrived as their governor. Such a simpleton, they were sure, would easily be

4. Among Muslims, to swear by God is not considered blasphemous.

outwitted. So they greeted him with extravagant respect, kissing his hands and his feet.

"Why haven't you paid your taxes?" asked the new governor bluntly.

"Our former governors have all oppressed us," whined the citizens, immensely amused at so simple-minded a rustic.

"Well, what are you going to do about it now?" asked the governor.

"Give us eight months and we will collect the money," they replied, with their tongues in their cheeks.

"Take ten months," said the tribesman, "but give me the names of ten guarantors who will stand security."

When the ten months were over he sent for the sureties and asked for the money. "The season had been a bad one—business was at a standstill—the winter rains had failed," all the old excuses were produced. "Cut off the head of the first guarantor," said the Arab, "and nail it up on the door of the office."

A few hours later, a second head joined the first, but before a third could be decapitated, four years' arrears of taxes had been paid in. Our tribesman proved a successful governor of Isfahan for many years to come.

The name of Hajjaj ibn Yusuf has been passed down to history as the very prototype of the ruthless tyrant. Some accuse him of cruelty and sadism. Apart from the many whom he put to death, he is said to have left the prisons full, of women as well as of men. Others, who dislike the Iraqis, exclaim in admiration that he was the only man who ever really handled the people of that country as they deserved. It is true indeed that the people of Kufa had become notorious for fickleness and sedition. To deal with their faults, three successive autocratic governors had risen to office, Zayyad the-son-of-his-father, Ubaidullah the son of Zayyad and Hajjaj ibn Yusuf. Each of these had given Iraq and Persia many years of peace and security, whereas, when more moderate governors took office, chaos had returned. They had thus given rise to a tradition that the Iraqis could not be governed except by force—a tradition which still to some extent haunts Arab politics. Yet it was disproved, not only by the early Muslims but by Muawiya I, founder of the Beni Umaiya dynasty, who allowed a considerable degree of free speech and who was the only khalif against whom there was never a rebellion.

Abdul Malik, it may be remembered, had named Waleed as his successor and after him his second son Sulaiman. The people had sworn an oath of allegiance to both. Some two years before his death, Waleed had attempted to exclude his brother Sulaiman with whom, as we have seen, he was not on cordial terms, and to secure oaths of allegiance to his own son as heir-apparent. Sulaiman, however, refused to abandon his right. Waleed had written to the provincial governors to obtain oaths of allegiance to his son but only Hajjaj, and Qutaiba ibn Muslim in Khurasan, had complied. In Damascus the young Umar ibn Abdul Aziz, the pious former governor of Medina, stated that he had taken the oath of allegiance to Sulaiman in Abdul Malik's time and that he could not go back on it. Waleed ordered his imprisonment.

Waleed died at the end of February 715, at the age of forty-six. He had ruled for ten years, and left behind him nineteen sons. His reign had been one endless succession of military victories. In the ten years of his khalifate the empire had expanded more rapidly than in any other equal period before or since, except the reign of Umar ibn al Khattab from 634 to 644. Waleed did not lead his armies in person in battle, though his sons and especially his brother, Maslama ibn Abdul Malik, were constantly engaged in the war against Byzantium. But though Waleed did not himself command his armies, his wise and firm control was largely responsible for internal peace and consequently for external expansion. His enemies accused him of being obstinate, autocratic and tyrannical, his friends claimed for him the credit for firmness and strength. Financially he was generous and expended great sums on buildings and public works.

His memory is particularly connected with the extension and embellishment of the great mosque of Damascus. Nearly all the Umaiyids carried out improvements to their capital but Waleed probably more than any other. The waters of the river Barada, which flows through the city, were by them so controlled and canalized that almost every house of any consideration had a fountain or a marble cistern in its courtyard. "The palace," writes an old Arab chronicler, "was completely paved with green marble. In the midst of the court-yard was a great basin of water, which irrigated a garden, where stood all kinds of the most beautiful plants and trees; while countless singing-birds, whose songs were equal to the sweetest melodies, enlivened and animated it."

"The palace of the Caliphs," writes Von Kremer, "shone with gold and marble, fine mosaics adorned the walls and the floor, ever-flowing fountains and cascades diffused a fragrant coolness and their sweet murmur conduced to a refreshing slumber. The ceilings of the rooms glistened with gold. In the inner apartments dwelt the fairest women in the world."[5]

Waleed was particularly popular in Syria, where he instituted charitable measures to care for the poor, the lepers and the blind. He was especially interested in the encouragement of industry but architecture was perhaps his chief hobby.

His Arabic was ungrammatical, because he had refused to pay any attention to his lessons when he was a boy. His indulgent father had eventually told his tutors to leave him alone. But his uneducated way of speaking had nevertheless caused anxiety to Abdul Malik, who was a purist in speech. It was related that, when Umar ibn Abdul Aziz had been governor of Medina, Waleed performed the pilgrimage and preached in the Prophet's mosque. During the course of his sermon, he quoted a verse from the Qoran, "O that death had made an end of me",[6] making a wrong case ending. Umar ibn Abdul Aziz and Sulaiman ibn Abdul Malik, Waleed's brother, were standing beneath the pulpit, whereupon Sulaiman exclaimed, "By God, I would that it had." It is interesting to notice that the extraordinary tyranny of the Arabic language already existed.[7]

5. Von Kremer. Op. cit. I have slightly abridged the original.
6. Qoran. Chap. LXIX.
7. The Arabic language enjoyed immense religious prestige because God Himself was believed to have used it to dictate the Qoran. It was thus the language of Heaven.

On the whole, Waleed seems to have been a serious and capable ruler, under whom the empire achieved the high water mark of its military glory. The criticism since directed against him has been largely due to the severities of Hajjaj, whose every action Waleed supported unreservedly.

* * *

Sulaiman ibn Abdul Malik was acclaimed khalif at Ramla in Palestine on the day on which Waleed died in Damascus in February 715. Immediately those who had supported Waleed were dismissed, while those who had made trouble in Waleed's reign were promoted. Hajjaj had been fortunate enough to die before Waleed. It will be remembered that Yezeed, the son of the great Muhallab, had been imprisoned by Hajjaj. He had, however, escaped from confinement and had taken refuge with Sulaiman, where those discontented with the rule of Waleed were presumably always welcome. Waleed had immediately ordered Sulaiman to hand over the fugitive. But, according to the ancient customs of the Arabs, a host was bound to defend his guest and Sulaiman refused. The tension between the khalif and his brother threatened to explode into violence but Yezeed ibn Muhallab offered to give himself up rather than be the cause of civil war. Eventually Yezeed surrendered himself but Sulaiman sent his own son with him, chained with the same chain as Yezeed, to beg the khalif not to besmirch his honour as an Arab by inflicting any injury on his guest. Waleed recognized the justice of the appeal and released Yezeed.

(In 1929, a man entered my camp in the deserts of Iraq who was wanted by Ibn Saud for a serious crime. The king demanded his surrender, but when I pleaded that he was my guest, he immediately abandoned his claim.) [8]

It will be remembered that Waleed had attempted to secure oaths of allegiance to his own son as heir apparent, but that only Hajjaj and Qutaiba ibn Muslim had expressed willingness to comply. Hajjaj was dead but Qutaiba was still at the head of his army on the frontiers of China. When news reached him of the death of Waleed and the accession of Sulaiman, he foresaw his own ruin and probable death. He consulted his brothers and his intimates, several of whom advised instant rebellion. In distant Khurasan, with a triumphant army at his back, he would be beyond the power of the Damascus khalif.

In an evil moment, Qutaiba accepted their advice and collecting the troops he delivered a speech in which he denounced the new khalif and appealed to the army to support him in announcing his deposition. "You will find me," he cried, "an Iraqi in every respect. An Iraqi by my father and my mother, an Iraqi by birth, an Iraqi in my emotions, in my thinking and in my loyalty. Do not allow the Syrians to come and destroy your country. See how prosperous you are here in Khurasan. Public security is established, the roads are safe, business is active. Where war formerly raged, you can now travel without fear or hindrance to Balkh, to Bukhara and to Samarqand. Stand by me and we will not allow the Syrians to interfere."

When the army commander terminated his speech, there were no cheers.

8. *The Story of the Arab Legion.*

Many soldiers looked upon one another and said doubtfully, "What he is advocating is civil war, and that has brought untold misfortunes on the country in the past." It is interesting to notice that townsmen of Kufa and Basra only formed a minority of the army, the greater numbers being members of nomadic tribes. Tabari gives the composition of the army in Khurasan at this time as follows:

People of Basra	9,000
People of Kufa	7,000
Beni Bekr	7,000
Beni Temeem	10,000
Azd	10,000
Abdul Qais	4,000
Freedmen and local converts	7,000
	54,000

Out of fifty-four thousand men, only a total of sixteen thousand came from Kufa and Basra. Qutaiba's unscrupulous attempt to stir up schism between Syrians and Iraqis might have appealed to them, but probably provoked less response from the tribesmen. Seeing that his appeal was not meeting with success, Qutaiba lost his temper and broke out in abuse of Beni Bekr, Beni Temeem, Abdul Qais and Azd, mentioning each tribe by name. Nothing could have been more disastrous, for these fierce, passionate men could be roused to a frenzy on a point of honour. The commander whom they had followed to victory for years had abused them in the most opprobrious terms. All was over between them. Nothing remained but to wipe out these insults in blood.

The camp was in confusion, men everywhere were running to arm, others were arguing, others shouting. Qutaiba seems to have realized that he had sealed his own death warrant. He retired and sat down in his tent. At first he called for his horse but then decided that it would be useless to mount. He carefully put on a kerchief which his mother had once sent to him and which he always wore in battle. (It is curious to find so ruthless a fighter so sentimental.) The roaring of the mutinous troops grew louder. Qutaiba sat quietly on his couch—these men always knew how to die. Soon the rioters surrounded the tent. Some of the commander's own staff slipped away and deserted him. He stood up and faced his own soldiers, and recited:

"Every day I trained him at shooting,
And, when he became proficient, it was I whom he shot."[9]

Then the angry troops rushed the tent and in a few moments all was over. Qutaiba seems to have been a capable commander. He had won all his battles over people who had always been splendid fighters. Moreover his campaigns were conducted in remote and difficult country near the roof of

9. The quotation is from a pre-Islamic poem. When I was dismissed from command of the Arab Legion, one of my former soldiers sent me these same two lines on a piece of paper.

the world, where he was obliged to rely entirely on his own resourcefulness. We do not know why he behaved in the way he did, but it is possible that he had information to the effect that Sulaiman proposed to have him executed and consequently that his only chance of survival was to carry his army into rebellion.

With the deaths of Hajjaj and Qutaiba, the advance into Central Asia was halted for twenty-five years. Two such outstanding leaders could not easily be replaced.

* * *

No sooner had Sulaiman been acclaimed as khalif than he appointed Yezeed ibn Muhallab to be governor of Iraq. Thinking that to be the successor of Hajjaj would be no easy task, however, Yezeed persuaded the khalif to excuse him from that post and to select him as governor of Khurasan in succession to Qutaiba. It will be remembered that his father, the famous Muhallab ibn Abi Sofra, had occupied the same position. The people of Jurjan were Turks and had for a long time made things difficult for the Arabs by raiding into Kumis and Tabaristan.[10] It will be seen that the centre of Persia was occupied by the great Salt Desert, which approached to within a hundred miles of the southern shores of the Caspian. This defile a hundred miles wide was filled by the Elburz Mountains. By raiding into this area, the people of Jurjan were frequently able to cut communications between Rei and Khurasan. As a result of the difficulties of this passage, the Arab communications with Khurasan had hitherto run from Basra through Fars and Kerman.

Yezeed ibn Muhallab decided to deal with the Turks of Jurjan. In a hard-fought campaign, he defeated them with great slaughter, killing large numbers of them in battle and cold blood, for all prisoners seem to have been beheaded. The women and children were sold as slaves. Plunder worth forty millions or more of dirhems was sent to the khalif in Damascus in the form of the statutory fifth. In his despatch reporting the success of the campaign, Yezeed boasted that neither Sapor nor Chosroes, pre-Islamic emperors of Persia, nor Umar ibn al Khattab or Othman, the early Muslim conquering khalifs, had ever succeeded in inflicting such a defeat on the Turks. All along the eastern frontiers, from the Caspian to the Indus, the Arabs had now left behind them the frontiers of Persia and were everywhere engaged with Turks, Mongols, Chinese and Indians. Yezeed's campaign in Jurjan took place in 716 and 717.

NOTABLE DATES

Justinian "Slitnose" proclaimed Byzantine Emperor	} 685
Abdul Malik ibn Merwan proclaimed khalif	
Death of Abdul Malik	} 705
Waleed proclaimed khalif	
Death of Justinian Slitnose	711
Anastasius II proclaimed emperor	713
Umar ibn Abdul Aziz, governor of Medina	705–710

10. Map 25, page 152.

PERSONALITIES

Khalifs
Abdul Malik ibn Merwan
Waleed ibn Abdul Malik
Sulaiman ibn Abdul Malik

Maslama ibn Abdul Malik, Arab commander on the
    Byzantine front
Musa ibn Nusair, Arab commander in Spain
Qutaiba ibn Muslim, Arab commander on the Chinese frontier
Muhammad ibn Qasim, Arab commander on the Indian front
Hajjaj ibn Yusuf, governor of Iraq and Persia
Yezeed ibn Muhallab, imprisoned by Hajjaj, made governor
    of Khurasan by Sulaiman
Umar ibn Abdul Aziz, governor of Medina

Justinian II Slitnose, Byzantine Emperor

IX

The Good Khalif

The deliverance of Constantinople may be chiefly ascribed to the . . . efficacy of the Greek fire . . . This improvement of the military art was fortunately reserved for the distressful period, when the degenerate Romans of the East were incapable of contending with the warlike enthusiasm and youthful vigour of the Saracens.   GIBBON, *Decline and Fall of the Roman Empire*

He was uniformly of opinion which, though not a popular one, he was ready to aver, that the right of governing was not property, but a trust.
                                                        CHARLES JAMES FOX

Magnanimity in politics is not seldom the truest wisdom; and a great empire and little minds go ill together.   EDMUND BURKE

Are there some understanding men among you? If your heart is full of rivalry and jealousy, then do not boast of your wisdom . . . For wherever you find jealousy and rivalry you also find disharmony and all other kinds of evil. The wisdom that comes from God is . . peace-loving, gentle, approachable, full of tolerant thoughts.
                                    James XIII, 13 to 17 (Trans. J. B. Phillips)

When a king is said to be a kind man, the reign is a failure.
                                                        NAPOLEON BONAPARTE

THE GOOD KHALIF

B Y far the greatest enterprise undertaken in the reign of Sulaiman ibn Abdul Malik was the siege of Constantinople. In this he was encouraged by an alleged prophecy that the capital of the Byzantine empire would be captured by the Muslims in the reign of a ruler who bore the name of a prophet.[1] We have already seen that the Arab armies had fought their way across Asia Minor to within a hundred and fifty miles of Constantinople in the reign of Waleed, their progress having been greatly facilitated by the chaotic conditions prevalent in the Byzantine empire during the reign of Justinian II Slitnose. But after the death of the latter, confusion became even worse confounded.

He had been succeeded in the purple by the commander who had led the revolt which had dethroned him. After a reign of only eighteen months, however, the usurper Philippicus was himself assassinated and a new emperor, amid popular acclamations, assumed the title of Anastasius II. During his brief reign, information reached Constantinople of the vast preparations which were going forward in Syria with a view to the final capture of Byzantium. Sufficient warning was obtained to enable the Byzantine government to lay in great quantities of supplies within the walls and to order the weak and the incapable to leave the city. The vast towers and battlements were repaired and heightened, large reserves of weapons, projectiles and warlike stores were assembled, and the fleet was enlarged by the hasty construction of additional ships.

In 716, however, Anastasius was degraded, while the troops acclaimed as emperor an unknown government official by the name of Theodosius. As Maslama ibn Abdul Malik, at the head of the Arab army, drew nearer to Constantinople, the capital relapsed into increasing chaos. Yet at the moment of supreme crisis, the imminence of danger produced the man who was to save the state.

Leo, surnamed the Isaurian, was of humble extraction, and had been born in the year 680, on the borders of Syria near Marash.[2] He is alleged to have been able to speak Arabic fluently. He had achieved a distinguished military career in the Byzantine forces and had been appointed by Anastasius II to command the eastern army, that which was charged with the defence of the frontier of Armenia. When, however, the usurper Theodosius seized the throne from Anastasius, Leo marched on Constantinople, Theodosius was thrust from the throne into a monastery and the Isaurian was acclaimed

---

1. Sulaiman was of course the Arabic equivalent of Solomon. The prophecy was fulfilled seven centuries later when Constantinople was captured by the Ottoman Turks under a Muhammad.
2. Isauria was a small province on the Northern slopes of the Taurus Mountains.

THE ARAB ATTACK ON CONSTANTINOPLE
712 ~ 717

Advance of the Arab Army.

emperor with the title of Leo III. There was not an instant to be lost, for
Maslama, with 80,000 men, had crossed unopposed at Abydos on the Dardanelles and was marching up through Thrace to attack the city from the
west. He had been instructed by the khalif to continue the siege until the
city was taken, no matter what the cost. To prove his determination, he had
ordered every horseman in the army to load two sacks of grain on his horse.
No sooner was the army established before the walls of the city, than the
besiegers ploughed up the soil outside their camps and sowed the seed which
they had brought with them, resolved patiently to await seed time and harvest
until victory crowned their arms. They rapidly dug their trenches opposite
the walls, erected wooden huts to accommodate those out of range of the
enemy missiles and prepared their movable towers and mangonels in readiness for an assault.

So desperate did the situation appear that Leo decided first to try diplomacy,
whether in the hope of reaching an understanding or merely in order to gain
time. A message was sent to Maslama asking for the despatch of a pleni-
potentiary, to whom was offered a tribute of one gold piece per head for every
inhabitant of the city, if the Arabs consented to raise the siege. "We fight for
religion," Ibn Hubaira had replied, "not for worldly gain." "It is true that,
in the past, you and we fought for religion," replied Leo, "but it is no longer
true. Now we are fighting for power and empire," a statement probably
true as far as Beni Umaiya were concerned. In any case, the offer of a cash
ransom was rejected and the siege began in earnest. The city of Byzantium
was built on a narrow promontory surrounded on three sides by water. The
fourth side was defended by immense walls and towers and, although repeatedly attacked for a thousand years, was never captured by assault until
its final fall to the Ottoman Turks in 1453. Indeed it was probably impregnable
to the armies of the eighth century.

Soon after the arrival of the Arab army, the fleet sailed through the Dardanelles and across the sea of Marmora to maintain the blockade of the city
from the sea as the army was doing on the land side. The Byzantines had
drawn a chain across the entrance to the Golden Horn. When the Arab fleet
had taken up its station opposite the city, the chain was apparently relaxed
and a fleet of ships, belching forth the famous Greek fire, suddenly bore
down upon the Arab fleet which suffered a complete naval disaster. Arab
tactics at sea consisted almost entirely of charging and grappling with the
enemy's ships and thereby transforming the engagement into the kind of
desperate hand-to-hand mêlée with which they were familiar on land. Such
tactics were rendered impossible against ships fitted with flame-throwers.
The Greek galleys were equipped with a nozzle in their bows from which a
jet of flame emerged, presumably under pressure, and set fire to enemy ships
before they could grapple. The same inflammable liquid was used on projectiles, which were wrapped in some material like tow, previously saturated
in the oil. The missile was fired from a catapult, when the tow had been
ignited, and came flying through the air wrapped in flame and making a
peculiar and alarming noise. The flaming liquid could also be poured from
the battlements of the city on troops attempting to scale the walls.

PLAN OF CONSTANTINOPLE
IN 716

BOSPHORUS

ASIAN SHORE

CHRYSOPOLIS

PERA
GALATA

PEGAE

PICRIDION

Golden Horn

Chain closing entrance
to the Golden Horn

KALIGARIA

FORUM OF
THEODOSIUS

STA. SOPHIA

HIPPODROME

Porta
Leonis

FORUM
OF CONSTANTINE

HARBOUR

ADRIANOPLE
GATE

HARBOUR

GATE OF
S. ROMANUS

GATE OF RHEGIUM

SEA OF MARMORA

GATE OF
PSAMATHIA

Ditch

CITY WALL

GOLDEN GATE

N

0   ½   1
Mile

Note: Constantinople was impregnable because
it was surrounded by water on three sides. The
Byzantine Fleet sallied out of the Golden Horn
and destroyed the Arab Fleet with flame-throwers.
Thereafter the city could be replenished and
reinforced by ships from the Bosphorus.

168

By an extraordinary triumph of security, the secret of the liquid which made Greek fire was kept inviolate by the Byzantine authorities for four hundred years until it was eventually obtained by the Muslims in time to enable them to employ it against the crusaders. The subsequent discovery of gunpowder in the fourteenth century has served to diminish in our eyes the importance of the Greek fire which preceded it by seven centuries, yet, if it had not been available to the Byzantines, our own world today might have been very different. For many historians believe that without it Byzantium could not have held out against the Arabs, who, having once captured the capital of the east, could have flooded onwards into Europe. The barbarian governments of Greece, Italy and Gaul would scarcely have been able to resist the relentless advance of the Muslims, especially as, at the same moment, the Arabs and the Berbers from Spain were invading the south of France.

Such speculations are of purely academic interest today. Suffice it to say that Leo the Isaurian, by the destruction of the Arab fleet, had won the first battle of the siege. The second was won by General Winter. By a piece of singular ill fortune for the Arabs, the winter of 716–717 was peculiarly severe and deep snow covered their camp for more than three months. Food and forage were desperately scarce and the clothing of the men, most of whom had come from warm climates, was doubtless quite inadequate. The Arabs, one of their historians [3] reports, were obliged to eat their animals, their skins as well as their flesh, the roots and the leaves of trees and indeed everything they could lay hands on except the earth. The hardships which they endured, shivering in their wooden huts, remind us forcibly of the privations suffered more than eleven centuries later by the British army in the Crimea. Moreover the loss of their fleet made it impossible for them to expect the arrival of additional supplies or equipment from Syria or Egypt.

With the spring the condition of the besiegers improved, and reinforcements, weapons and food arrived in new fleets equipped in Africa and Egypt. But, while these ships were able to land their cargoes at a distance from Constantinople, it was no longer possible to blockade the city, for fear of another fire attack on the Arab ships. Thus ample supplies could reach Byzantium from the Bosphorus while the besiegers continued half-starved outside the walls. At the same time the morale of the Byzantines was constantly revived by the energy and courage of Leo.

Undoubtedly, however, the emperor's greatest triumph was his success in persuading the Bulgars on the Danube to attack the Arabs from the west. Soon the besiegers found that they were themselves besieged between the city walls on the one hand and the hordes of the barbarians advancing against them through Thrace on the other. It is even alleged that the Byzantines succeeded in disseminating in the Arab camps a rumour that the Franks and other unknown nations of the West were marching to defend the Christian cause against the invaders. Thus the summer, which should have given the Arabs the opportunity of pressing the siege more vigorously, was spent in desperate fighting on two fronts against the Bulgars and the Byzantines, while both food and equipment remained lacking, for the advance of the

3. Ibn al Athir.

barbarians had made it impossible for the Arabs to forage in the countryside of Thrace.

*   *   *

While the struggle beneath the walls of Constantinople was deciding the history of the world, the young Khalif Sulaiman had been acclaimed by the whole Arab Empire. The Arab historians have been kinder to his memory than to that of the majority of the Umaiyids. Their preference may have been due, at least in part, to the fact that Abdul Malik and Waleed had supported Hajjaj, whereas Sulaiman was believed to have disapproved of his methods. Hajjaj, Qutaiba and Muhammad ibn Qasim, the commander in the Indian campaign, had been Qaisites, while Sulaiman favoured the Yemenite party.

It will be remembered that, when Waleed had attempted to exclude Sulaiman from the succession, his first cousin, Umar ibn Abdul Aziz, had refused to change the oath of allegiance to Sulaiman which he had sworn by the deathbed of Abdul Malik. As a result, Waleed had thrown Umar into prison. Sulaiman had retained a deep sense of gratitude to Umar ibn Abdul Aziz for this display of moral courage, with the result that, as soon as he became khalif, he listened much to Umar's advice. The two men were profoundly different in character, for Sulaiman was vain and worldly, while Umar was pious and serious. Yet the new khalif admired his cousin and trusted him completely. One of Sulaiman's first actions had been to remove certain irregularities which had crept into the procedure followed at public prayers, a measure which we can probably justly attribute to the advice of Umar. A prohibition against singing—the Prophet had disapproved of music—may also probably be ascribed to the same source.

Being still in his thirties, Sulaiman was perhaps excusably fond of pleasure. We read of him dressed in a green silk costume sent from Persia, admiring his own good looks in a mirror, and exclaiming aloud, "I am indeed the young king." The very words used, if correctly reported, are significant of the changing times, for the early khalifs regarded themselves as the leaders of a religious community, and indignantly rejected any accusation that they were kings.

Sulaiman, however, was perhaps chiefly distinguished for the voracity of his appetite, a quality indeed which led to his early death. He is alleged, for example, at a single meal to have eaten a whole lamb, six chickens, seventy pomegranates and a basket of currants. Even when he was asleep at night, baskets of sweetmeats were placed beside his bed, so that, if he woke, he had merely to stretch out his hand to find some delicious morsel. It is scarcely surprising that he died of a digestive complaint. In spite of this gluttony, however, he took an active interest in military affairs, was determined to capture Constantinople and died in camp with the army.

When he lay ill of the complaint from which he died, he consulted one of his confidants regarding the succession. His eldest son Daood was with the army before Constantinople. Were he appointed to succeed him, a long interregnum would take place before he could return to Damascus, and civil war might break out again in the interval. His second son was too young. "What about Umar ibn Abdul Aziz?" suggested his adviser.

"Neither my sons nor those of Abdul Malik would accept him," replied the khalif.

"Appoint him to succeed you directly," retorted Raja, "and your brother, Yezeed ibn Abdul Malik, to follow him. When they see that the khalifate will return to the sons of Abdul Malik, they will accept Umar in the interval."

This tactful plan was adopted. Sulaiman wrote out a will naming Umar ibn Abdul Aziz to succeed him, but stipulating that, on his death, the khalifate would return to Yezeed ibn Abdul Malik. This will was then placed in a sealed envelope. Sulaiman was nevertheless anxious regarding the reception which the document was likely to receive. He accordingly ordered Raja to summon the princes of the Umaiyid family to swear allegiance to the person, whoever he might be, who was named in the khalif's sealed will. A few days later Sulaiman died.

When the seal of the letter was broken and it was revealed that Umar ibn Abdul Aziz had been nominated, the sons of Abdul Malik (of whom he had left seventeen) were at first disposed to object. But when they heard that one of them, Yezeed, would succeed Umar, they acquiesced. Preparations were then hastily made for the ceremony of the public swearing of allegiance. There was a trampling of horses' hoofs at the door, a groom led forward a magnificent charger and the princes and nobles, all splendidly mounted, prepared to join in the procession.

"What is all this?" enquired the new khalif.

"It is the charger for the Prince of the Faithful to ride in the procession," replied a courtier.

"I have no need of it," answered Umar quietly. "Bring me round my old mule."

This little incident was to set the tone for the whole reign.

*　　*　　*

Meanwhile a desperate battle was still being fought beneath the walls and ramparts of Constantinople and in the fields of Thrace. What might have been the ultimate result is now pure conjecture, for the Khalif Sulaiman, up to the time of his death, appeared to be as determined as ever, and was busily collecting men and supplies to reinforce the army. Umar ibn Abdul Aziz, however, was a man with a strikingly different outlook on life, for he was guided by conscience and religion, rather than by warlike ambition or sensual enjoyment. One of his first acts was to write to Maslama ibn Abdul Malik ordering him to abandon the siege and to return to Syria.

*　　*　　*

In the early days of Islam, eighty or ninety years before the time of which we are writing, the first two of Muhammad's successors had lived like simple peasants in Medina, while their armies were already defeating the great empires of Persia and Byzantium. Umar ibn Abdul Aziz was, through his mother, the great-grandson of Umar ibn al Khattab, the Prophet's second successor, a man notorious for his ascetic life, which, however, formed no great contrast to the way of life of his supporters, all of whom were religious enthusiasts. But since those early days, the Arabs had built up the greatest empire of their age, the khalifs lived in palaces, surrounded by a crowd of courtiers and preceded and followed by guards and household troops.

In the gay, worldly city of Damascus, amid these brilliant surroundings, Umar ibn Abdul Aziz endeavoured to imitate the austerities of his great-grandfather. He was said to possess only one shirt, dirty and patched, and to live almost entirely on lentil soup. So scrupulous was he to differentiate between his private property and the public purse, that he would use a government candle while dealing with his official correspondence, but as soon as the task was over, he would light a private lamp of his own and extinguish the government candles.

Many such stories related of him are doubtless exaggerated, while others may appear to us frankly absurd. Yet at times, in spite of the historians, we are led to suspect that the Khalif Umar ibn Abdul Aziz was the possessor of an acute insight into public affairs. The empire had for sixty years been divided into bitterly hostile camps by the feud between the Beni Hashim and Beni Umaiya clans of Quraish—a rivalry which had led to the murder of Husain and the formation of the Shia. Ever since the days of Muawiya I, the mosques of Syria had called down curses on the family of Ali ibn abi Talib at public prayers. During the khalifate of Umar ibn Abdul Aziz alone, the practice was discontinued. Its prohibition was perhaps rightly attributed to the piety of the khalif but it was also undoubtedly wise policy to attempt to heal those feuds which had already so often plunged the empire into civil war.

In place of the cursings hitherto pronounced against the rivals of Beni Umaiya, he ordered the following prayer to be read from the pulpits at Friday prayers:

"O Lord, pardon us and our brethren who have preceded us in the faith. Do not leave in our hearts any bitterness against our fellow believers. O Lord, Thou art always ready to pardon and to spare us."

A certain Yahya al Ghassani was appointed by Umar to be governor of Mosul. When he took up his appointment, he found theft and burglary rife in the town. He accordingly wrote to the khalif to inform him of the state of the city and to ask him, "Whether I should take men up on suspicion and chastise them on mere accusation, or arrest them on clear proof and according as the law directed." Umar ibn Abdul Aziz wrote in reply that men should only be arrested on clear proof and as the law directed, "for if justice will not make them honest, then may God not reform them."

This brief excerpt from an eighth-century correspondence throws a vivid light not only on the views held by the pious khalif but also on the methods of government hitherto in force. To chastise men, and even to cut off their heads, on mere suspicion was perhaps the method employed by Ubaidullah ibn Zayyad and Hajjaj, and it is significant that the new governor of Mosul thought it necessary for him to seek the khalif's orders regarding the method to be followed. In his subsequent account of his period of office the governor wrote, with reference to Umar's letter, "I therefore acted accordingly and

I did not leave Mosul until it had become one of the most orderly of cities and least frequent in theft and house-breaking."

We may perhaps be tempted to condemn Arab justice for the fact that a question such as that put by the governor of Mosul should have been necessary. It is well, therefore, to remember that haphazard methods of justice were universal in the world of those days. Even the often-vaunted Roman justice made use of an equally rough and ready system. In Acts XXII, 24, for example, we read of a Roman captain who, with his troops, rescued Paul from a crowd of rioting Jews. When he had taken him into the castle, the captain "bade that he should be examined by scourging, that he might know wherefore they cried so against him." Even in British history, to be "put to the question" meant to be tortured with the object of extorting a confession. Umar's ideas on justice seem to have been in advance of his time.

The Arab historians ascribe Umar's administrative regulations to his piety alone and love to enlarge upon his asceticism, his charity and the manner in which he passed a great part of every night in prayer, the tears streaming down his face. The sarcastic Gibbon, following in their footsteps, has dismissed the reign of Umar ibn Abdul Aziz in one sentence. "The throne," he writes, "was degraded by the useless and pernicious virtues of a bigot." Are we to accept these estimates at their face value or was Umar in reality a ruler and administrator in advance of his contemporaries? Was he not acting as a wise statesman in endeavouring to heal the bitter hatreds which divided Beni Umaiya from Beni Hashim? Were the careful separation of public from private expenditure, and the punishment of accused persons only after they had been proved guilty according to law, the pernicious virtues of a bigot?

The student of the early Arab empire is constantly amazed by the suddenness of the change from the idealistic theocracy of the rule of the first two khalifs from 632 to 644, to the tyranny, greed and bitter civil wars which had become the rule rather than the exception only fifty years later. It is true that arbitrary rule and internal disturbances were common also in Christian Byzantium at the same time, as for example in the reign of Justinian Slitnose. Rebellion, intrigue and personal ambition were the characteristics of public affairs in every country in the eighth century and murder, torture and imprisonment without trial were the methods employed by all parties. It is the idealism of Abu Bekr, Umar ibn al Khattab and Umar ibn Abdul Aziz which are exceptional.

Reference has already been made to the fact that the Prophet had laid down the policy that Christians and Jews were not to be forcibly converted to Islam but were to pay heavier taxes than Muslims. Thus the conversion to Islam of men professing other religions meant that the converts paid lighter taxes and the treasury suffered a loss in revenue. In fact, however, these provisions had often not been carried out and converts had been obliged to continue the payment of taxes on the old scale. Umar ibn Abdul Aziz ruled that the original policy must be punctually observed. The decision resulted in a great increase in conversions to Islam all over the empire. Obviously these changes of religion were inspired by financial rather than conscientious motives, but nevertheless a great gain to Islam resulted. The converts may indeed have been insincere but their children were brought up as Muslims. After two or three generations, the motives which had inspired the original conversions were forgotten.

Umar ibn Abdul Aziz was doubtless right in insisting that non-Arab Muslims should be treated as the equals of Arabs. The latter were a small minority ruling-class in the empire and the non-Arab majority was becoming increasingly restive. Integration was the only alternative to revolution. Moreover the equality of all Muslims was a basic article of Islam, which took no cognisance of race.

Financially, however, Umar was faced with a dilemma which he failed to overcome. To admit non-Arab Muslims to equality would produce two consequences. Of these the first was that the treasury would suffer a heavy loss of income. The second was that non-Arabs would be entitled to state annuities, which, ever since the second khalif, Umar ibn al Khattab, had been paid only to persons registered in the census as Arabs. Thus the state revenue would fall at the same moment as the government would undertake a heavy new commitment for salaries. The Khalif Umar ibn Abdul Aziz doubtless regarded the question from a religious rather than from a financial point of view. When told that if all members of the subject races were converted, the treasury would be bankrupt, he replied, "God sent His Prophet to do the work of an apostle, not that of a tax-collector." His first object was to enforce the system which had originated under the Prophet and the first two khalifs. It is easy enough to say that conditions were changed and that the khalif was a fool, but this is to ignore the fact that an almost insuperable problem did in fact exist.

Umar ibn Abdul Aziz, who had the courage of his convictions, ordered that non-Arab Muslims should pay only the same taxes as Arabs and should also be entitled to annuities. As a result the treasury was soon in difficulties, and it is impossible to know what would have happened to the state finances if the khalif had not died soon afterwards. His successors cancelled his measures and returned to the previous system of taxing non-Arab converts as if they had been non-Muslims. This naturally produced heightened resentment among the subject races, resulting in revolution thirty years later.

When we look back now, we can see the dilemma more clearly than was possible to Umar and his contemporaries, but even now it is not easy to see what solution, if any, was practicable. If, as was sooner or later inevitable, non-Arabs were to pay the same taxes as Arabs, then the whole tax system would have to be reformed and Arabs would have to pay more, so that the same total of state revenue could be maintained. In other words, the financial measures introduced nearly a century earlier in the primitive community in Medina were no longer adequate for the world's greatest empire. Complete fiscal reform was essential.

Neither Umar ibn Abdul Aziz nor his contemporaries could see this. For them the issue was limited to the narrow question—should non-Arab Muslims pay at the same rates as Arabs or not? But even if Umar had realized the need for financial reforms, it is unlikely that he or anyone else would have had the power to introduce them. Two insuperable obstacles stood in the way. Firstly the Arabs, who were still the ruling class, might well have resisted and caused another civil war—secondly the existing methods and rates of taxation had originated with the Prophet and the first two khalifs, and thus enjoyed a religious authority, which it would probably have been impossible to surmount.

No great military campaigns took place in the reign of Umar ibn Abdul Aziz. A slight revival of Kharijite activity in the Jezira was suppressed. The Khalif Umar handled the incident in a manner which differed widely from the methods of his predecessors, who had employed the chopping off of heads, hands and feet against the Kharijites more even than against other rebels. Umar ibn Abdul Aziz, on the other hand, invited them to send a delegation to Damascus to put forward their grievances.

On the arrival of two Kharijite representatives, the khalif was at pains to refute their arguments and to explain that Muhammad himself had forbidden one Muslim to kill another, though the Kharijites held it right to put to death all professing Muslims who did not belong to their own narrow sect. Although the heretics continued in their mistaken beliefs, they made no more trouble in Umar's lifetime.

The reign of the good khalif was remarkably free from sedition and civil strife, yet it may be argued that it was in his time that the seeds were sown of that revolution which was utterly to destroy the dynasty. This was not surprising but rather in accordance with normal political development. For it has often occurred that a country has remained quiet throughout periods of arbitrary and autocratic rule but that sedition has broken out as soon as a more just and liberal administration has been established. Thus the benevolent khalifate of Umar inaugurated the movement which was to lead to the ruin of his family.

Umar ibn Abdul Aziz died on 10th February, 720, at the age of thirty-nine, after reigning for only two years and five months. Some reports allege that he was poisoned by his Beni Umaiya cousins, whose pensions he had reduced, or who were anxious that the khalifate should pass to one who would enable them to enjoy themselves at court as they had done formerly. So much political propaganda was subsequently directed against the Umaiyids, however, that such charges cannot be unreservedly accepted.

*   *   *

While Beni Umaiya had migrated almost entirely to Syria, whence they ruled an empire extending from the Pyrenees to the Indus, their Quraish rivals, Beni Hashim, had remained in Mecca and Medina, where they continued to live in obscurity, taking no part in public affairs. Beni Hashim themselves were now divided into two branches, the descendants of Ali ibn abi Talib and those of Abbas.[4] The two branches were equally closely related to the Prophet on the male side, for both Abu Talib and Abbas had been uncles of Muhammad. But the descendants of Ali had the advantage in that the latter had married Fatima, the Prophet's daughter. Through her, therefore,

4. Genealogical tree, page 32.

the children of Ali ibn abi Talib were the direct descendants of the Apostle of God. Moreover they had played a prominent rôle in the rise of Islam. Ali had been khalif and his son Husain, as we have seen, had been martyred at Kerbela, thereby giving birth to the Shia sect.

The descendants of Abbas had played no political rôle until the reign of Umar ibn Abdul Aziz. In the year 718, however, the principal member of the Abbasid family was a certain Muhammad ibn Ali ibn Abdulla ibn Abbas,[5] who lived in the Shera, the area west of Maan, now in the kingdom of Jordan. Syria was happy, and loyal to Beni Umaiya. Consequently Muhammad ibn Ali ibn Abbas sent secret emissaries to Iraq and to Khurasan, always jealous and resentful of Damascus, to engage in political propaganda in favour of the house of Abbas. The movement soon spread, especially in Khurasan, an area which had gained a reputation for lawlessness, turbulence and military qualities.

In the year 722, in what is now southern Jordan, a son was born to Muhammad ibn Ali ibn Abdulla ibn Abbas, the head of the Abbasid clan of Quraish, the organizer of this network of underground propaganda against Beni Umaiya. The infant was named Abdulla. It so happened that, a few days later, a secret delegation of conspirators from Khurasan came to discuss their plans with Muhammad ibn Ali. Sedition, they reported, was spreading rapidly and the provincial governors had been unable to identify any of the workers, who in general posed as merchants in order to justify their movements from place to place. The proud father brought out his tiny son in his arms and showed him to these secret supporters. The baby was one day to be the first of a long line of emperors, and to gain the well-earned title of the Bloodshedder.

*   *   *

No sooner was Umar dead than Yezeed ibn Abdul Malik was acclaimed khalif, according to the succession appointed by his elder brother, the Khalif Sulaiman. A somewhat colourless character, he reigned for four years, dying at Irbid, in what is now northern Jordan, on 28th January, 724. He was under the influence of Umar ibn Abdul Aziz while the latter was alive and is said to have imitated his example for forty days after becoming khalif. Then the power and the temptations of office were too strong for him and he devoted himself to pleasure.

Yezeed ibn Abdul Malik had two singing girls, whose names have come down to us in history, Hababa and Sallama. He had bought Hababa for four thousand dinars when on a pilgrimage to Mecca in the train of his elder brother, the Khalif Sulaiman. The latter, however, had for some reason unstated (for Sulaiman himself was no prude) prohibited the purchase and Hababa was sold to a man from Egypt. Four years later, Yezeed himself became khalif. On this auspicious occasion, his wife Suada asked him if there was anything in the world which he still desired or if every ambition had now been gratified. "I still want Hababa," replied the tactless husband. Suada sent to Egypt in search of the slave girl, bought her back for four

5. Genealogical tree, page 222.

thousand dinars and arranged for her to be smuggled into the palace. Bathed, perfumed and marvellously clad, Hababa was seated in a room behind a curtain. When her husband entered, Suada artlessly repeated her former question, "Is there anything in the world, my dear, which you still desire?" "You've asked me that before," replied Yezeed testily, "and I told you I still wanted Hababa." "Well, here is Hababa, my dear," replied the perfect wife, drawing back the curtain with a sweeping gesture and retiring tactfully from the apartment.

But the course of true love was destined to be but brief, for Hababa died not long afterwards. Overwhelmed with grief, the khalif remained closeted in his room for seven days, refusing to see anyone, to the consternation of his soldier brother Maslama, who had no patience with such unrestrained emotion. Alarmed lest Yezeed make the very khalifate a laughing stock, he persuaded him once more to appear in public.

Yezeed II leaves us with the impression of a weak and shallow character. He was influenced in the direction of piety while Umar ibn Abdul Aziz was alive, but quickly became worldly when that influence was removed. It is perhaps sufficient to say that we remember him chiefly as the owner of the two lovely girl-slaves, Hababa and Sallama.

NOTABLE DATES

Accession of Sulaiman ibn Abdul Malik	715
Siege of Constantinople	716–717
Death of Sulaiman	}717
Accession of Umar ibn Abdul Aziz	
Death of Umar ibn Abdul Aziz	720
Accession of Yezeed II ibn Abdul Malik	720
Birth of Abdulla ibn Muhammad ibn Ali the Abbasid	722
Death of Yezeed ibn Abdul Malik	724

PERSONALITIES

Khalifs
Sulaiman ibn Abdul Malik
Umar ibn Abdul Aziz
Yezeed ibn Abdul Malik

Byzantine Emperors

Justinian II Slitnose	705–711
Philippicus	711–713
Anastasius II	713–716
Theodosius III	716
Leo III the Isaurian	716–741

Maslama ibn Malik, army commander-in-chief
Muhammad ibn Ali the Abbasid, organizer of revolutionary
        propaganda for Beni Abbas

X

Farmer George

I have enjoyed every pleasure in the world, save one. I have never had the companionship of a real friend, in whose company I could relax my vigilance concerning what passed between us.   THE KHALIF HISHAM

On the plain of Tours the Arabs lost the empire of the world when almost in their grasp. Insubordination and inter-tribal jealousies, which have ever been the curse of Moslem communities, led to that disastrous issue.
                              AMEER ALI, *A Short History of the Saracens*

The conquest of Spain marks the nearest approach that the Arabs ever made to World-Empire.
                              R. A. NICHOLSON, *A Literary History of the Arabs*

X

FARMER GEORGE

HISHAM ibn Abdul Malik was acclaimed khalif in succession to his brother Yezeed, at the age of thirty-four. Whereas Yezeed had preferred the northern or Qaisite tribal faction, Hisham leaned rather to the Yemenites. The year after his accession, there was actually a battle in Khurasan between the two tribal groups, although the frontier was threatened at the time by the Turks.

The usual raids into Byzantine territory continued but were limited to summer forays only. There was no longer any attempt to invade the empire and besiege Constantinople. Indeed the energetic character of the Emperor Leo the Isaurian seemed to have injected new life into the ancient and somewhat jaded empire of Byzantium. In spite of this revival, however, Maslama ibn Abdul Malik again took Caesarea in 726 and the Arabs retained possession of the Taurus passes. An innovation at this time was the despatch of the fleet each year to carry out its own summer raid in the Mediterranean.

In 728, the problem of the taxation of converts to Islam suddenly assumed an acute form in Khurasan. A new governor of the province, appointed by Hisham, formed a delegation to tour the country beyond the Oxus and to urge the people to become Muslims. Before embarking on their mission, the would-be proselytizers enquired of the governor whether such heathen as professed Islam would thereby be freed from paying the poll-tax. It will be remembered that the Prophet himself and the Qoran had stated that the tax must be paid by non-Muslims with humility. The governor confirmed that converts to Islam would be immune from poll-tax, an answer undoubtedly theoretically correct.

Armed with this promise, the mission set out to tour the towns of the Oxus and the Jaxartes. They met with a response beyond all their, or the governor's, expectations. The public flocked to be admitted to Islam and to secure immunity from the tax. But soon messages reached the governor from the provincial tax-collectors. "Everyone is being converted and the people are all building mosques," the reports said. "There will be virtually no poll-tax henceforward. How will the administration be carried on without the money?" In passing, it is interesting to notice the words attributed by Tabari to the revenue officials. "*Sar al nas kulhum arab*," he writes, "All the people have become Arabs." This artless sentence explains in five words much of the confusion which exists today in the use of the word Arab. The earliest conquerors had been Arabs and Muslims, and the two designations had at the first appeared to be synonymous. When the Turks of central Asia or the Goths of Spain became Muslims, they were as often as not said to have become Arabs.

Presumably the governor had not foreseen a financial crisis. Suddenly faced with so awkward a situation, he told the tax-collectors that they could continue to collect poll-tax from all who had paid it formerly, whether they had now been converted or not. But the attempt to collect it from the new converts produced an extremely violent reaction. Many of them recanted. Some wrote to the Khaqan of the Turks inviting him to come and take the country. The situation of the converts who recanted was precarious, for death was the penalty of apostasy. Eventually the public indignation boiled over and, in the summer of 728, Trans-Oxiana rose in revolt.

The situation had changed materially since the victories of Qutaiba fifteen years earlier. His campaigns had been directed against the native rulers of Trans-Oxiana. The Turkish tribes beyond the Jaxartes were preoccupied fighting one another. Commencing in 716, however, within a year of the death of Qutaiba, the Türgesh tribe under a new chief—called by the Chinese Su-Lu—had established a Turkish kingdom in the Ili valley.[1] The Chinese probably disliked the existence of a powerful Turkish confederation but as they could not at the moment prevent its formation, they may well have encouraged the new Khaqan to attack the Arabs. The first Türgesh appeared in Trans-Oxiana in 720. When, therefore, revolt broke out in 728 against the exorbitant Arab taxation, a powerful Turkish army from beyond the Jaxartes was ready to join in. The Arabs found themselves in desperate straits—isolated garrisons were besieged and the whole territory beyond the Oxus was in the hands of the rebels and their Turkish allies.

In 729, the governor was removed and a certain Junaid ibn Abdul Rahman was sent from Damascus to take command. The new governor was rumoured to have been selected because he had presented two magnificent collars set with jewels to Hisham and to his wife. Junaid had no previous experience of warfare against the Turks on these wild mountain frontiers. He made all the mistakes which the inexperienced have made time and again from that day to this. He marched a column up a mountain valley without first taking the precaution of picketing the heights, with the result that the force was attacked with a rain of missiles from the high ground on both sides of the valley. The old hands who had spent their lives fighting on the frontier were angry and contemptuous at the ignorance of the new palace general. One of them seized his horse by the bridle and cried, "If you are going to act like this, you will not only lose this army but all Khurasan."

To do him justice, Junaid does not seem to have been arrogant, or perhaps he had come to realize that desperate battles with Mongol tribesmen in the snow-covered ranges of Central Asia were not as easy as presenting jewelled necklaces to queens in the palaces of Damascus. At any rate, he sought the advice of his more experienced subordinates, and, after a long and critical campaign and many casualties, the Khaqan of the Turks was obliged to withdraw to his own country and Junaid ibn Abdul Rahman in the summer of 730 reoccupied Samarqand and Bukhara.

The Khazars, on the other side of the Caucasus, had doubtless been encouraged by the Arab reverses beyond the Oxus, for, in the summer of 730,

1. See Map 17, page 101.

they emerged from their country, invaded Adharbaijan, defeated the Arab forces, killing their commander, and occupied Ardebil. It was found necessary to send the khalif's brother, the inexhaustible Maslama ibn Abdul Malik, before they could be driven out once more and forced back through the defile of the Derbend Gates into the country north of the Caucasus. Before returning to Syria, the stern Maslama invaded their territory, stormed many towns, took prisoners, drove off the women and children as slaves and burned the countryside, killing the son of the Khan of the Khazars in the process. He then spent a year building defences in the Derbend defile to prevent any further Khazar invasions. On the withdrawal of Maslama ibn Abdul Malik, Merwan ibn Muhammad ibn Merwan [2] was made governor of the Jezira and Adharbaijan in 732.

It is of interest to note in passing that the Roman Empire had battled for more than three centuries to hold the barbarians on the line of the Rhine and the Danube, while the Arabs, for an approximately equal period, fought back the pressure of the Turks and the Mongols in the Central Asian gap between the Caucasus and the Hindu Kush. Both empires, as they weakened, gradually sold the pass by engaging barbarians in their own forces as mercenaries. Finally both empires were over-run and destroyed by the barbarians against whom they had struggled for so long, but whom, meanwhile, they had admitted into their own armies.

A certain Asad ibn Abdulla had been made governor of Khurasan. In the summer of 737, he undertook a punitive expedition against Khuttal, in which great quantities of sheep, plunder and prisoners were collected. Many of the inhabitants even fled across the border into Chinese territory. In October the Arab column withdrew and was bivouacked on the north bank of the Oxus, resting and sorting the plunder. The Khaqan of the Turks, who had given so much trouble on the frontier in recent years that the Arab soldiers had nicknamed him "old bothers", seemed for the moment to be quiet.

Unexpectedly a local notable informed Asad ibn Abdulla, the army commander, that the Khaqan was coming. But the general disbelieved the story —"probably only the usual panic" was doubtless his reaction. Then, all of a sudden, the Turks were there, only a mile or two away. Their scouts, scattered horsemen here and there, could be seen approaching. The first idea of the Arabs, surprised, dispersed and disorganized, was to put the river between them and the enemy. There was very nearly a panic. Asad, even in these circumstances unwilling to leave all the loot, called out for every man to carry a sheep with him. All plunged, helter-skelter, into the river, which, however, was in some places too deep to ford. Some, struggling with the kicking sheep, were swept from their horses, until Asad called out to them to leave the sheep. The troops were still crossing when the Turks appeared on the bank, seizing much equipment, the plundered sheep, the camp followers and many Arab prisoners. Then, almost without pausing, they too splashed into the stream at the heels of the Arabs, who just succeeded in forming camp and getting into position. They were only saved from a disaster by the fall of night.

2. Genealogical tree, page 64.

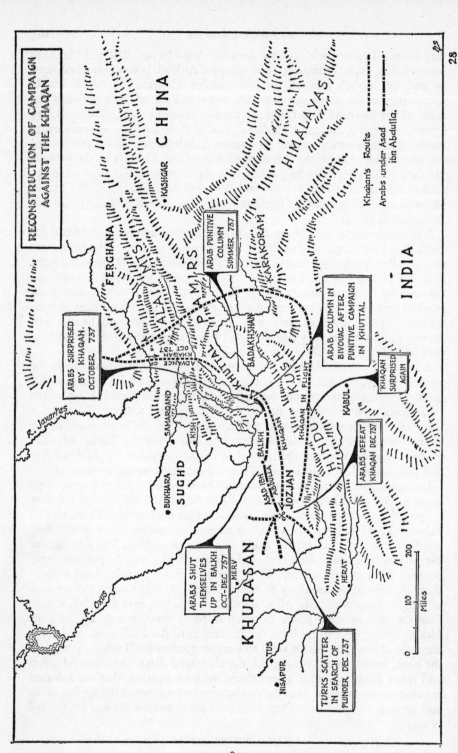

RECONSTRUCTION OF CAMPAIGN
AGAINST THE KHAQAN

CHINA

FERGHANA

KASHGAR

ALAI MTS.

ARAB PUNITIVE
COLUMN
SUMMER 757

PAMIRS

KARAKORAM

HIMALAYAS

ARABS SURPRISED
BY KHAQAN.
OCTOBER 737

ADVANCE OF
KHAQAN OCT 737

BADAKHSHAN

KHUTTAL

R. Jaxartes

SAMARQAND

KISH

ARAB COLUMN IN
BIVOUAC AFTER
PUNITIVE CAMPAIGN
IN KHUTTAL

HINDU KUSH

INDIA

KHAQAN SURPRISED
AGAIN

BUKHARA

SUGHD

KHAQAN IN FLIGHT

KABUL

ASAD IBN
ABDULLA

BALKH

KHAQAN

JOZJAN

ARABS DEFEAT
KHAQAN DEC 757

ARABS SHUT
THEMSELVES
UP IN BALKH
OCT-DEC 757

MERV

R. Oxus

HERAT

200

100

Miles

TUS

NISAPUR

KHURASAN

TURKS SCATTER
IN SEARCH OF
PLUNDER DEC 757

0

Khaqan's Route ....
Arabs under Asad
ibn Abdulla ----

28

184

While dividing the plunder of Khuttal, Asad had already sent his heavy baggage on towards Merv, before the Turks had appeared. Next morning, peering anxiously from their lines through the grey dawn, the Arabs could see no Turks at all. The Khaqan had marched by night in pursuit of the Arab baggage column. The Turks had raised a great army—unknown to the Arab intelligence which must have been remarkably careless—and Asad found himself heavily outnumbered. He followed with some circumspection, but the Khaqan had already seized the baggage column, though the Arab army, manoeuvring cautiously without coming to action, was able to recover some of the survivors. Asad then retired and shut himself up in the city of Balkh, leaving Khurasan wide open to the enemy. The Arabs called a frightened council of war, some advised the governor to remain inside the walls of Balkh and send messengers to the khalif for reinforcements. Some suggested that they slip out, pass the Turks by forced marches and occupy Merv, the capital of Khurasan, before the Khaqan could get there. Others, bolder, were for giving battle, even at a numerical inferiority.

In December 737, the Khaqan moved westward towards the heart of Khurasan—but here the timidity of the Arabs turned to their advantage. The Khaqan, who is alleged to have had 30,000 men, had conceived such a contempt for the apparently panic-stricken troops who had taken refuge in Balkh, that he scattered most of his army in raiding and foraging parties. Doubtless the winter was severe and supplies were a problem. Each Turk had set out from home with a bag of salt meat hung from his saddle, but these provisions had now been eaten.

Asad caused one of the gates of Balkh to be opened and his own tent to be pitched on the open plain outside. Several of his commanders came to him and said, "May God prosper the ameer.[3] Do not overstrain our obedience by keeping us shut up in Balkh. Lead us out to victory."

The army commander called the troops to prayers. After completing the prescribed ritual, he turned to the men and cried out, "Let every soldier pray God for victory." The prayers were long and earnest. Then Asad rose to his feet and, facing the troops again, he called three times, "You will be victorious, by the Lord of the Kaaba."

The Arabs marched light and swiftly. The Khaqan with a small force was camped in complete confidence at Kharistan in Jozjan, his men scattered far and wide, plundering the fertile countryside. Suddenly a cloud of dust was reported from the north. The Khaqan was in doubt and misgiving. Could it be the timid Asad from Balkh? Scouts galloped out to identify the oncoming horsemen, while the Turks hastily armed and mounted. The Arabs came straight on and formed their line of battle without halting. Although surprised, the Turkish right wing charged with such effect that the Arabs were thrown into confusion. But, on the other flank, the tribal contingents of Azd and Beni Temeem bore all before them. Soon the Turks were swept from the field, and the Khaqan was fortunate to escape with some four hundred horsemen and some of the loot and camp-followers. One hundred and fifty-five thousand sheep were rounded up by the victors.

3. This was the regular way of greeting a senior officer.

The Khaqan escaped into the wild mountain valleys to the east. Here at last he thought himself safe. Camp was made, fires lighted, the women cut up the meat and hung the great cauldrons over the flames. The Khaqan was able to stretch his legs and relax, perhaps to blame himself for the over-confidence which had plunged him so suddenly from triumph into defeat.

But a local tribesman had offered to guide the Muslims to the Khaqan's mountain resting place. A party of Arabs crept up the mountain track and from a commanding ridge, saw the Khaqan's lager in the valley below, the cauldrons boiling over the camp fires. The alarm was given, the Turkish drums beat the retreat but the Arabs were all around them. The Khaqan's horse fell on the muddy track but the chief escaped unrecognized. The flee-ing Turks left everything behind, including their own women and many captured Arab girls. The Khaqan made good his escape and, returning to his country, prepared to renew the war, but was shortly afterwards murdered by another Turkish tribal leader, possibly at the instigation of the Chinese. The confederation, which had been made possible by his leadership, fell apart and the Turkish tribes returned to their previous occupation of fighting one another.

Asad despatched a messenger post haste to carry the news to Damascus. Exhausted and travel-stained, he stood outside the door of the palace and called, "Allahu Akbar! Allahu Akbar!" Ushered into the presence of the khalif, he cried, "Victory Victory! O Prince of the Faithful." When he had told his story, Hisham stepped down from his couch and prostrating himself on the ground, offered up to God the Prayer of Thanksgiving.

*   *   *

Of all the races conquered by the Arabs, the Berbers of North Africa offered the most stubborn resistance. As we have seen, they seemed to have been finally pacified by Musa ibn Nusair when he, in 712, crossed over into Spain, leaving his son Abdulla to act for him in North Africa. Thereafter an increasing number of Berbers became converted to the Muslim religion. But their change of faith did not make them resigned to Arab domination. On the contrary, it added to their discontents the same grievance as we have already seen leading to revolt in Khurasan—the complaint that the Arabs denied social equality to Berber converts to Islam.

The Kharijites have already been frequently described, their puritan fana-ticism, their search for the rule of God alone, their denunciation of the iniquity of princes, their stern ascetism, their savage fighting qualities and their claim that all Muslims not of their sect should be put to death. After the reign of Abdul Malik, during which they had been forcibly suppressed in Arabia, they began to infiltrate into North Africa. Among the Berbers they met with immediate success, for both communities hated the Umaiyid government. Moreover the Kharijites recognized the equality of all Muslims, irrespective of race, and thereby secured the enthusiastic support of the Berber converts to Islam. The Berbers were simple, earnest and credulous and, lacking that cynical streak which has always characterized the Arabs, were roused to intense fervour by Kharijite enthusiasm.[4]

In their former risings, the Berbers had begun by renouncing Islam. Now the Kharijites told them that they were truer Muslims than the Prince of the Faithful himself. By a strange reversal of rôles, the Berbers were now ready to revolt in the name of the Muslim faith against the Sunnis who had originally converted them to Islam. When Hisham was proclaimed khalif in 724, Arab rule in North Africa was again in a precarious condition. In 740, a general revolt broke out, which included all the Berbers from Tangier to Qairawan. The rebels encountered the Arab forces in a great battle in the Wadi Shelif between Algiers and Oran.[5] Surrounded by the greatly superior numbers of Berber tribesmen, the Arabs once again gave proof of one of their noblest qualities—that they always knew how to die. They fought on until they were completely exterminated. So many leaders lost their lives in this battle that it was thereafter known to the Arabs as the Battle of the Nobles.

So enraged was the Khalif Hisham to hear of this reverse that he swore that he would teach these Berbers a lesson. An army of 27,000 men was raised in Syria and reached Ifriqiya in the summer of 741. It advanced as far as the province of Tangier, where, however, it was completely defeated by the Berber tribes at Bagdoura[6] in the Wadi Sebou. The whole of North Africa west of Qairawan seemed once more to be lost.

But Hisham refused to give up. In 742, a new army arrived from Syria under Handhala ibn Safwan, and inflicted a defeat on the Berbers. The rebels returned, however, and the new governor found himself besieged in Qairawan by immense numbers of Berber tribesmen. No further relief from Syria was to be hoped for and supplies in the city were soon running low. The resolute Handhala resolved on a desperate sortie. Weapons and armour were issued from the magazine to all male citizens. Then, at the first pale light of dawn, the garrison formed up in the square of the town, while the innumerable watch fires of the Berbers twinkled all over the plain which surrounded the city.

As the daylight grew clearer, every man drew his sword and threw away the scabbard. The gate was thrown open and the garrison sallied forth led by the gallant Handhala, a man as conspicuous for the nobility of his character as for his courage. The Arabs attacked with the fury of despair, the hand-to-hand struggle was long and desperate but at length the Berbers began to give ground, then broke and fled. Many thousands were killed in hot pursuit, the siege was raised and Handhala returned in triumph to thank God for this well-nigh miraculous deliverance. In 743, Arab rule was once again established in Ifriqiya and the Maghrib.

*   *   *

4. Dozy has a vivid phrase to describe the process. "The Calvinists of Islam," he writes, "had at last found their Scotland." *The Moslims in Spain*.
5. Some authorities place this battle in what is now Northern Morocco.
6. Or Nafdoura.

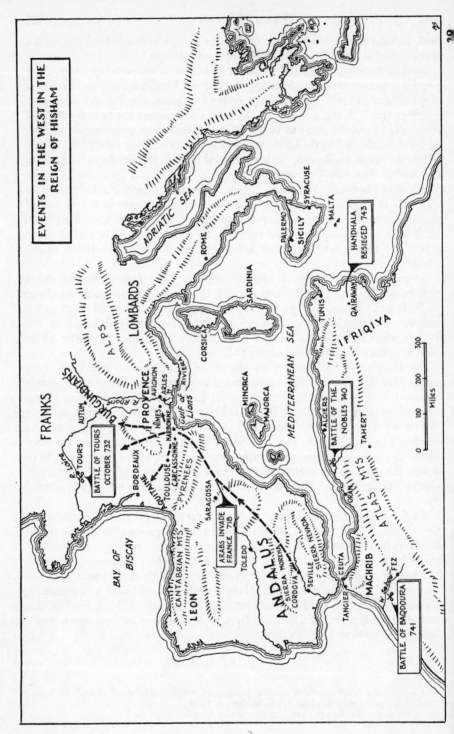

EVENTS IN THE WEST IN THE
REIGN OF HISHAM

FRANKS

BURGUNDIANS

LOMBARDS

ALPS

R. Rhône

AUTUN

BATTLE OF TOURS
OCTOBER 732

R. Loire

TOURS

BORDEAUX

AQUITAINE

TOULOUSE

CARCASSONNE

NARBONNE

PYRENEES

PROVENCE

AVIGNON

ARLES

NÎMES

RIVIERA

Gulf of Lions

ADRIATIC SEA

ROME

CORSICA

SARDINIA

MINORCA

MAJORCA

MEDITERRANEAN SEA

PALERMO

SICILY

SYRACUSE

MALTA

BAY OF BISCAY

CANTABRIAN MTS

LEON

SARAGOSSA

ARABS INVADE
FRANCE 718

TOLEDO

SIERRA MORENA

CORDOVA

SEVILLE

SIERRA NEVADA

ANDALUS

CEUTA

TANGIER

MAGHRIB

ATLAS MTS

FEZ

W. Sebou

BATTLE OF BAQDOURA
741

ORAN

ALGIERS

BATTLE OF THE
NOBLES 740

TAHERT

TUNIS

QAIRAWAN

IFRIQIYA

HANDHALA
BESIEGED 743

0   100   200   300

Miles

We left Spain in the year 714, when Musa ibn Nusair had been recalled by the Khalif Waleed, leaving his son Abdul Aziz as his deputy in the governorship of Spain. We have also seen how the Khalif Sulaiman had sent assassins who successfully murdered Abdul Aziz in the great mosque of Cordova. Spain remained, in theory at least, a province subordinate to the governor of Ifriqiya in Qairawan, who, however, found sufficient to keep him occupied in the unending wars with the Berbers.

Thus the Muslims of Spain, Arabs and Berbers, were left very largely to fend for themselves. This they did at first with some success, for they were still full of initiative and spirit. In 718, they broke through the eastern end of the Pyrenees and occupied Carcassonne and Narbonne, whence they proceeded to raid as far afield as Aquitaine and Burgundy. In 721, however, they were repulsed from the walls of Toulouse by Eudes, Duke of Aquitaine. The Frankish kingdom was at the time at a low ebb. The Merovingian dynasty, which had been founded by Clovis (481–511), was effete. The last kings had lost their authority, which had been usurped by their so-called Mayors of the Palace. As a result, Duke Eudes was at first left to defend himself unsupported against the Muslims.

In 725, the Arabs made a further advance occupying the whole countryside as far as Nimes, from whence they raided northwards up the Rhone valley, ultimately reaching Autun, from which they returned laden with plunder. In 732, the Arabs, under their governor, Abdul Rahman ibn Abdulla, besieged Bordeaux, defeated Eudes, and ravaged the country as far north as the Loire. Eudes appealed to Charles Martel, the Mayor of the Palace of the Frankish kingdom, who marched southwards. A pitched battle was fought in October 732 between the Arabs and the Franks near Tours. Abdul Rahman ibn Abdulla was killed and the Arabs were repulsed, Charles remaining master of the battle-field. The Franks, however, seem to have suffered such heavy casualties that they made no attempt to pursue but themselves also retreated. In 735 Eudes died and Charles added Aquitaine to the Frankish dominions. He, however, made no attempt to attack the Arabs, who were holding Arles.

It is idle to speculate what would have happened had the Arabs defeated the Franks at Tours. Would they have pressed on a further two hundred and fifty miles to the Straits of Dover? Or would they have turned eastwards into Italy and marched on Rome? As it proved, however, Tours was to be the high-water mark of their expansion.

For four years the Muslims seem to have occupied the entire shore of the Gulf of Lions, cutting off the Franks from the Mediterranean. In 737, the Arabs occupied Avignon, but Charles Martel retook the city, advancing even as far as Narbonne. It is difficult to follow all these campaigns. The country which we now know as France was not at this time united under the Franks —Aquitaine was often independent and at times openly hostile to Charles. The Burgundians and the people of Provence were also inimical to him.

In 738 the Arabs were apparently again holding Arles and were even threatening the frontiers of Italy on what we call the Riviera coast. Liutprand, King of the Lombards in Northern Italy, found it necessary to march against them and drive them back. The Arabs, for more than twenty years, held a large area in France, amounting at its greatest extent to half the country. Their ultimate failure was due firstly to the genius of Charles Martel and secondly to their own internal discords in Spain.

From 732 to 741, Uqba, a son of Hajjaj ibn Yusuf, was governor of Spain and the country appears to have been reasonably quiet. Uqba, however, died in January 741, and was succeeded by a certain Abdul Malik ibn Qatan, a native of Medina. After the Battle of the Nobles, in which the Syrian army in Africa had been almost exterminated by the Berbers, several thousand Syrian survivors had taken refuge in Spain. The Battle of the Nobles had been fought in Ifriqiya in 740. The following year, inspired by the success of their brethren in North Africa, the Berbers of Spain rose against the Arabs and a bitter Muslim civil war ensued. After heavy fighting, the rising was suppressed, but immediately afterwards fighting broke out among the Arabs themselves—the people of Medina who, ever since the Battle of the Lava in the reign of Yezeed I, had always opposed the Umaiyids, engaged in hostilities with the Syrians, thereby transferring to Spain the bitter feuds of Arabia. Eventually the Medinese were worsted, a new governor arrived from Ifriqiya, and order was restored. Here, in 745, we must leave the Arabs of Spain to return to events in Damascus.

*   *   *

In 740 occurred another muddled tragedy at Kufa. Zeid, a grandson of the martyred Husain, had gone to Kufa, ostensibly in connection with a lawsuit. But after its settlement, he had stayed on for a year in the city secretly enrolling partisans.

The hereditary succession from Ali ibn abi Talib did not rest with Zeid but had been with his elder brother Muhammad, now deceased. Jaafar, surnamed the Truthful, the son of Muhammad, was now the Shiite imam. A deputation from Kufa had visited Jaafar in the Hejaz to enquire what were his instructions regarding Zeid and had apparently been told to support him. The 6th January, 740, was chosen by Zeid for the rising in Kufa and his supporters were notified of the date. The governor of Kufa was soon made aware of the plot and summoned the people of the town to a meeting in the great mosque a few hours before the appointed time. The doors of the mosque were then closed, and a great part of the conspirators found themselves interned.

At the appointed hour, Zeid presented himself to the public. A few supporters raised the cry of "O Victorious!" "Ya Mansoor!", but only a few scattered individuals appeared in arms. At length three hundred horsemen had collected and Zeid rode forth at their head. Skirmishing lasted for about forty-eight hours, a few people were killed and wounded. Finally Zeid himself was killed by an arrow and his followers hastily dispersed. The head of the rebel was cut off and sent to Hisham in Damascus. His dead body was crucified outside Kufa. Thus ended in fiasco one of the earliest attempts made by the descendants of Ali ibn abi Talib to seize the khalifate. Many more were to follow, nearly all of them politically inept. English people may well be reminded of the Stuarts, whose very lack of success increased their romantic appeal.

The rebellion of Zeid in 740 has a peculiar interest because it gave birth to the Zeidi sect, which still exists, particularly in the Yemen, where the royal family belonged to it. Hasan, a son of this Zeid, took refuge in the mountains at the southern end of the Caspian Sea, where he subsequently set up a Zeidi state. The Zeidis are considered to be an offshoot of the Shia.

* * *

Meanwhile another subversive movement was gaining greater and greater impetus. The propaganda of Beni Abbas was conducted on lines which remind us of the revolutionary movements of our own time. The network of its secret cells covered Iraq and Persia, but was strongest of all in unruly Khurasan. The authorities were now aware that underground sedition was active. Every now and then, a few men were arrested and put to death, their hands and feet having previously been cut off, and others were detained in prison, though the numbers detained were negligible compared to the occupants of concentration camps in the totalitarian movements of our own times. As so often occurs in the case of underground movements, the authorities were never able to obtain evidence against suspects.

In 742, Bukair ibn Mahan, an official who had been secretary to the governor of Sind and was one of the principal organizers of the Abbasid campaign, passed through Kufa, where a number of his coadjutors were detained in the castle. A slave boy by the name of Abu Muslim was engaged in waiting upon these prisoners. Hearing the detainees discussing the evils of the times, he appeared deeply moved and shed tears. His emotion was perceived by Bukair, who bought him for four hundred dinars. We shall hear more of Abu Muslim later.

* * *

The Khalif Hisham died at fifty-three or fifty-four years of age. He had been a wise and intelligent ruler, who worked diligently at the administration of the empire. He carefully checked the revenues of the treasury, and was extremely painstaking in his judicial decisions. "I never saw one of the khalifs to whom the shedding of blood was more hateful than Hisham," said one of his contemporaries. He kept his sons under careful discipline and sent them on military raids into the Byzantine Empire. When one of them, who had been absent from Friday prayers, gave it as his excuse that his horse was dead, the khalif replied that that was no excuse for not coming to prayers, and ordered him to walk to the mosque every Friday for a year.

Another son wrote to him (they seem to have been unable or afraid to address him verbally) that his mule was too weak to ride, and asked if he could have another. Hisham replied unsympathetically that his mule was doubtless weak because he left its feeding to a groom. "Measure out its food and give it to it yourself," the stern father enjoined, "and you will find that your mule will soon be strong again."

He personally supervised everything, including the cultivation of his lands, and instructed the farm workers to pick the olives by hand and not to beat the trees with sticks to make the fruit fall, a process still often followed and still forbidden by the officials of the Syrian and Jordan governments. How little has changed since the 740's!

Hisham, as a result of his carefulness, earned the reputation of being a miser. Yet we may accept this charge with reserve. Generosity amounted almost to a vice among the Arabs and the lavish expenditure of many of the khalifs went far to weaken the empire. Hisham had a squint and was coarse and thickset—what we should perhaps call a "farmer type". He was passionately fond of horses and organized many race meetings in Damascus. He strengthened the defences of the frontiers and built water channels and cisterns on the pilgrim road to Mecca. In brief he was hardworking, careful about money, active and practical.

An amusing anecdote seems to indicate that, even at this time, considerable democratic freedom of speech was used towards the khalif, a point worthy of note in view of what was to follow. The Khalif Hisham one day held a review of the troops in Homs. As he rode up, the horse of one of the officers shied violently—"What made you choose a horse that shies like that as your charger?", enquired the khalif.

"No, by God, O Prince of The Faithful," replied the officer, "he is not a shier. The trouble is that our vet Ghazwan has a squint just like yours and so he mistook you for him."

"God damn you and your horse," replied 'Farmer George'[7] Hisham gruffly but apparently without resentment.

Beni Umaiya, writes Masudi, produced three great statesmen, Muawiya I, Abdul Malik ibn Merwan, and Hisham ibn Abdul Malik. The latter, if not a genius, was at least capable, hard-working, reliable and successful. He died on 6th February, 743, leaving the empire victorious and at peace, after a prosperous reign of nineteen years.

*   *   *

The end of the reign of Hisham, with the Arabs still at the height of their military power, is perhaps the opportune moment for the inclusion of a note on their methods of war.

They had conquered their immense empire in an amazingly short time, although they had no previous tradition of military operations as a Great Power. We are doubtless justified in assuming that this initial career of conquest must be principally attributed to religious enthusiasm. We must not forget, however, that after their early victories from 634 to 654, they remained indisputably the greatest military Power of the world for two hundred years, as long as, let us say, from Wolfe's capture of Quebec until today. To maintain their military superiority for so long a period cannot be attributed to an outbreak of wild enthusiasm. It means that they must have been the leading scientific soldiers of their time for two centuries.

7. It is I, of course, who have coined this nickname to convey an idea to my English-speaking contemporaries.

Unfortunately our information on their military operations during the great days of the Umaiyids is extremely scanty. Nevertheless certain interesting facts can be collated. We are inclined to expect Arab tactics to consist of wild mounted charges at full speed, carried out in a state of frenzied and reckless excitement. It is therefore surprising to discover that the Arabs preferred to remain on the defensive at the beginning of a battle. For this purpose their infantry formed up in successive ranks. The pikemen kneeled on one knee, thrust the butt end of their pikes into the ground and covered their bodies with long shields, thereby presenting a solid wall of points and shields. The rear ranks consisted of swordsmen and behind them of archers. In this formation, they received the enemy's attack. If they repulsed it, they might advance but if so, they moved forward extremely slowly, a yard at a time, presumably with the object of keeping their line absolutely solid. We have seen the Syrian army employing these tactics against the Kharijites outside Kufa.

Equally surprising is the fact that the cavalry were told not to charge at full gallop and not to lose cohesion and become involved in a wild pursuit. Once the enemy's formation had been broken up, the cavalry were to reform and return to their original station in the line of battle.[8] Throughout all descriptions of military operations, we find the emphasis laid on the fact that military bravery does not consist in dash but in patient endurance.

It seems impossible to discover the date on which tribes gave way to regular units. As early as the Battle of Siffeen in 657 there was a unit of four thousand men, who all wore green headgear as a uniform. The organization of the army was doubtless originally copied from the Byzantines, who had centuries of experience behind them.

The Arabs commonly made considerable use of ambushes in a pitched battle. The night before an engagement, detachments would be sent out under cover of darkness and told to lie up in concealment, only posting look-out men to watch the progress of the action. The main Arab army would then draw up at dawn in view of the enemy. At a suitable moment in the battle, the ambushers would suddenly emerge and attack the enemy in flank and rear. The first mention of this manoeuvre is in 640 at the Battle of Heliopolis, the Arab commander being Amr ibn al Aasi.[9]

The Arabs took great precautions to ensure their own security against such surprises. When on active service, the army marched in order of battle, with its advanced guard, flank guards, main body and rear guard. Scouts and spies preceded the whole army. When the enemy was believed to be within five days march, the troops marched with all their standards unfurled ready for instant action. The standards, as rallying points, played an essential part in battle.

Then, as now, armies were costly. The Arab soldier seems to have received considerably more pay than his Byzantine counterpart. He also drew rations. The tradition that the plunder was divided among the troops was still observed. In the case of the annual summer raid into Byzantine territory, the

8. Cromwell's cavalry, in his New Model Army, were trained in the same manner.
9. *The Great Arab Conquests.*

loot was often valuable. In addition to these perquisites, the pay of the Arab troops was, at this period, less often in arrears than with the Byzantines. The average pay of the Arab soldier was about 500 dirhems a year, the cavalry receiving twice as much in return for providing their own horses.

The soldier's personal weapons had not changed much since the days of the Prophet, except that the army had become regular and weapons and armour were standardized. In addition to a helmet and a coat of chain-mail, the cavalry now had pieces of plate armour (greaves) on their legs. In the time of Waleed, they are mentioned as carrying maces as well as lances. Every night the army laid out its camp in a standard manner and fortified it with a ditch. Whenever possible, if a general engagement were imminent, the baggage was placed in a fortified camp behind the battle line before the action began.

A great deal of expensive equipment was required for the siege train, including mangonels and catapults for throwing pieces of rock and arrows against the walls of, or into, the besieged city. The "artillery" was accompanied by stone-masons, who cut the rocks from the neighbouring mountains and shaped them to a size suitable for throwing. The Arabs had learned all the technical methods of siege warfare. There were battering rams for attacking the city gates, with overhead protection from projectiles thrown down from the walls. Saps, trenches and tunnels under the walls were also used. Convoys of camels were employed to carry baggage, tents, rations, arms, equipment and the siege train. Mules were also used as pack animals.

Great sums of money were spent on fortification. On the Byzantine front Tarsus, Adana, Massisa, Marash and Malatia were the chief fortresses, but there were also many smaller forts. Although more money was spent on the fortification of the Byzantine border than elsewhere, yet the same methods were everywhere in use, at the Gates of Derbend against the Khazars and all over Khurasan and Trans-Oxiana.

In brief the Arabs, with their usual adaptability, had completely changed the wild methods of tribal war practised in the days of the Prophet. They had quickly mastered the scientific methods of the Byzantines and the Persians. For two hundred years they were to be the world's greatest military Power, extremely technical and professional. Moreover their military methods were characterized by deliberation, method, regularity and organization. On the battlefield itself, their tactics were slow, cautious and precise. Above all the need for patience, endurance, perseverance and caution was constantly emphasized.

At sea, Arab supremacy was as great, or perhaps greater, than on land. This was the more surprising because, until the year 650, most of them were almost entirely ignorant of the sea. Among the conquered races, however, notably on the sea coast of Syria and to a less extent in Egypt, there were many sailors with an ancient tradition of service in merchant ships.

In the early years, say from 650 to 700, the ships were rowed and navigated by the men of these races, while the Arabs took their stations on deck, ready to fight. The captain, who was responsible for the fighting, was an Arab. The Rais, possibly a Lebanese or an Egyptian, was responsible for the navi-

gation and for command of the crew. After 750 most of the sailors are found
to be Muslims and racial distinctions seem to have disappeared.

The Arab ships, which were principally built in the harbours of Lebanon,
were doubtless imitated from those of the Byzantines. Ifriqiya and Andalus
built their own ships. The chief means of propulsion was by rowers. In the
larger vessels, there were normally a hundred rowers on two decks, seated
on twenty-five seats, two men on each. At the bow of the ship rose the castle,
where soldiers stood, either to shoot at the enemy with bows and arrows or
ready to board. In some of the larger ships, the upper deck may have been
entirely occupied by troops, with the rowers below.

The Arab tactics at sea were to make straight for the enemy, grapple ship
to ship with grappling hooks and fight it out with swords on deck. Sometimes, as we have seen, Byzantine ships were fitted with nozzles from which
liquid fire was discharged. The Arabs had no adequate answer to this
weapon and their fleet was totally defeated during the siege of Constantinople.
Yet we hear no mention of flame-throwers in ships in the naval battles in the
Mediterranean. Perhaps the liquid fire was not fitted to ships sailing the high
seas, lest one be captured or wrecked and the secret of this formidable weapon
be revealed to the enemy. Suffice it to say that the Arabs enjoyed naval command of the Mediterranean for some four hundred years, as long as from the
Spanish Armada to our own times.

NOTABLE DATES

Arab Invasion of Southern France	718
Hisham proclaimed khalif	724
Arabs occupy Nîmes	725
Rebellion in Khurasan	728
Khazars invade Adharbaijan	730
Battle of Tours	732
Defeat of Khaqan of the Turks at Kharistan	Dec. 737
Arabs seize, then lose, Avignon	737
Rising and death of Zeid ibn Ali in Kufa	740
Berber revolt in North Africa	} 740
Battle of the Nobles	
Battle of Bagdoura in Africa	741
Defeat of the Berbers outside Qairawan by Handhala	742
Arab rule re-established in North Africa	743
Death of Hisham	743

PERSONALITIES

The Khalif Hisham ibn Abdul Malik
Maslama ibn Abdul Malik, brother of Hisham,
    commander-in-chief
Merwan ibn Muhammad left by Maslama as governor of
    Adharbaijan
Khaqan of the Turks—"old bothers"

Handhala ibn Safwan, governor of Ifriqiya

Eudes, Duke of Aquitaine

Charles Martel, Mayor of the Palace to the Frankish king   717–741

Abdul Rahman ibn Abdulla, Arab commander defeated and
    killed at Tours

Zeid ibn Ali, grandson of Husain, killed in rebellion at Kufa

Abu Muslim, ex-slave in Kufa, recruited to help in Abbasid
    propaganda campaign

XI

The Débâcle of Beni Umaiya

Hitherto Damascus had formed the stronghold of the Ommeyades. Under Walid II, for the first time, a fatal change set in. His devotion to music and horse-racing, . . . his profligacy and his open defiance of the rules of morality, alienated his best supporters. . . . They rose in angry revolt and were joined by the populace of Damascus. . . . His head severed from the body was paraded in the streets of Damascus.   AMEER ALI, *History of the Saracens*

Vicissitudes of Fortune, which spares neither man nor the proudest of his works, which buries empires and cities in a common grave.   EDWARD GIBBON

XI

THE DÉBÂCLE OF BENI UMAIYA

YEZEED ibn Abdul Malik, Hisham's predecessor, had died young at a time when his eldest son Waleed was only fifteen years of age. Unable to appoint so young a successor, Yezeed nominated his brother Hisham but had caused the people to swear an oath of allegiance to the young Waleed as the ultimate successor of Hisham.

Waleed, the son of Yezeed II, after the death of his father, had turned out badly. (Yezeed himself, the owner of the beautiful Hababa, had scarcely been a great ruler.) Waleed was notorious as a heavy drinker and as a cynic, scoffing at religion. He openly expressed intense hatred for his uncle Hisham, whom he avoided as much as he could, living as far from Damascus as possible. Hisham admonished Waleed and lectured him on his profligate way of life, but the younger man replied only with ribald verses and insulting remarks, referring to his uncle as "that damned old squint-eye". It was even alleged that Waleed had said that he wished to perform the pilgrimage to Mecca in order to hold a drinking party on the roof of the Kaaba.

Hisham desired, with some justification, to cut Waleed out of the succession and to bequeath the khalifate to his own son. The usual difficulty, however, arose. The principal men in the state had bound themselves by an oath of allegiance to recognize Waleed as khalif after Hisham's death. They could not be released from that oath unless Waleed himself were to absolve them, which he emphatically refused to do. As a result, on the death of Hisham, Waleed II succeeded to the khalifate without opposition.

Although he was continually drunk and openly impious (he was reported to have used the Qoran as a target for his archery), he was open-handed and prodigal, whereas Hisham had been accused of parsimony. Doubtless intentionally, Waleed endeavoured to make his conduct a complete contrast to that of his hated uncle. The pay of the army was immediately increased by ten per cent. Poets, singers and musicians, who had earned little under Hisham, were loaded with gifts and flocked to Damascus to reap a golden harvest. He was himself an accomplished poet in a ribald and erotic vein.

> "The Imam Waleed am I. In all my glory
> Of trailing robes I listen to soft lays.
> When proudly I sweep on towards her chamber,
> I care not who inveighs.
>
> There's no true joy but lending ear to music,
> Or wine that leaves one sunk in stupor dense.
> Houris in Paradise I do not look for:
> Does any man of sense." [1]

1. Nicholson. Op. cit.

Another of Waleed's passions was horse-racing and he organized race meetings outside Damascus on an unprecedented scale.

Soon after Waleed's assumption of the khalifate, Yahya, the son of Zeid [2] ibn Ali ibn Husain, raised the standard of rebellion in Khurasan, whither he had fled when his father had been killed in Kufa. He carried on hostilities for some time but was eventually killed by an arrow in a battle with government troops. His dead body was publicly exposed, nailed to a cross. According to Masudi, every male child born that year in Khurasan was called by its parents either Zeid or Yahya, so great was the sympathy felt by the local people for the two Aliid martyrs.

Soon revolt broke out in Damascus itself. Yezeed, a son of Waleed I, [3] placed himself at the head of the rebellion, and Waleed II was besieged in a castle outside the capital. With only a handful of supporters, the khalif in vain terminated a life of drunkenness and debauchery by a sudden desperate display of physical courage. But it was too late. His castle of refuge was quickly carried by assault and Waleed himself was killed. The next day, 17th April, 744, his head, raised on a lance, was paraded through the streets of Damascus. His khalifate had lasted one year and three months.

*　　*　　*

Yezeed, the son of Waleed I, had led the revolt and was himself immediately proclaimed khalif in Damascus. He was the third of that name to become Prince of the Faithful. The previous Yezeeds had both been idle and frivolous —the pot-bellied Yezeed I in whose reign Husain had been killed, and the amorous Yezeed II, the lover of Hababa. Yezeed III seemed to promise a more conscientious attitude to his duties.

His mother had been the grand-daughter of Yezdegird, the last king of Persia. A great-great-grandmother had been the daughter of a Byzantine Emperor, while another grandmother had been the daughter of the Khaqan of the Turks. In a boastful poem, Yezeed had claimed:

"I am the son of Chosroes, my ancestor was Merwan,
　　Caesar was my grandsire and my grandsire was Khaqan."

It is ironical to remember that the second khalif, Umar ibn al Khattab, lived in a great fear of behaving like a king. "Am I a king or a khalif?" he was alleged to have asked a party of his companions. "A khalif does not take anything except lawfully," one of them replied, "and you, praise God, are like that. But a king oppresses people." Things had changed indeed when a khalif could boast of his descent from kings and emperors, none of whom had been Muslims.

In spite of his pride in his ancestry, however, Yezeed III appears to have been of a serious disposition. In his initial sermon in Damascus, he claimed that he had only acted in the service of religion, which had been insulted and almost extinguished by the vicious Waleed. He undertook to serve only the

2. This was the Zeid who had rebelled in Kufa. Page 190.
3. Genealogical tree of Umaiyids, page 64.

public interest and the true religion and promised to abdicate his charge if any more worthy candidate should present himself.

One of his first actions was to prohibit singers and musicians, who had been so generously encouraged by his predecessor.[4] It will be remembered that Waleed II had been reckless in his expenditure and had sought to gain support by increasing the pay of the army. The careful and conscientious Yezeed III thought that the rise in the army's pay had been too great, or more than the treasury could afford, so he ordered a reduction. The soldiers immediately dubbed him "Reduction Yezeed", and it is by that name that he has come down to us in history.

On the whole, Yezeed III might well have made a successful khalif and have restored, for a time at least, the fortunes and prestige of Beni Umaiya. Unhappily he was not to live long enough to enable him to stave off disaster.

* * *

It will be remembered that Maslama ibn Abdul Malik had, for many years, been the leading military commander of the empire. Four of his brothers had been khalifs, Waleed I, Sulaiman, Yezeed II and Hisham, but Maslama had never shown any interest in politics or any desire to rule. Lean, brown and active ("that yellow locust", Yezeed ibn Muhallab had called him), all his interests were devoted to the army and the camp. When he grew middle-aged, he had trained his cousin, Merwan ibn Muhammad ibn Merwan, in the same way of life. We have already seen that, in 732, Maslama had handed over to Merwan his task of governor of the Jezira and of Adharbaijan.

The appointment was no sinecure. It included a long stretch of the Byzantine frontier on the west and that of the Caucasus, occupied by the warlike Khazars, on the north. In 737, in a brilliant campaign, Merwan passed the Derbend Gates, completely defeated the Khazar army, overran the country and took the capital, Itil.[5] The Great Khan of the Khazars was at the mercy of the Arabs. At his wits' end, he agreed publicly to profess Islam. It was apparently the only means which the Khazars could devise to secure the withdrawal of the Arab army from their country.

The daughter (or possibly the sister) of the Khan was married to the Byzantine Emperor Constantine V, and pressure was already being exerted upon him from that quarter to become a Christian. Eventually he was to abjure Islam and profess Judaism, on the grounds that being a Jew would not bring him under the influence of either of the Great Powers. Judaism, therefore, he thought, would be the most comfortable faith for a small country.

Merwan spent many years in almost continuous military operations. Like his former commander, Maslama, he was heart and soul a professional soldier. His endurance and courage had earned for him the nickname of "The Ass of the Jezira", for to the Arabs the ass represents not a foolish but a

---

4. The repeated orders for the banishment of professional singers seem to confirm the charges brought against them by historians that they were all sexually immoral and led the younger generation into immorality.

5. Map 7, page 30.

patient animal, long-suffering under hard work and lack of food. The nick-name would perhaps be better rendered in English as "The Pack-Mule of the Jezira".

No sooner did Merwan hear of the murder of Waleed II than he abandoned the frontier of the Caucasus and marched southwards at the head of twenty thousand men. Yezeed III, despairing of victory over so famous and experienced a general, offered to compromise. An agreement seemed to be in sight when Yezeed III suddenly died, on 12th October, 744, after a reign of only six months.

Everything was again in confusion. Ibrahim, a brother of Yezeed III and son of Waleed I,[6] was proclaimed in Damascus. While Merwan had been apparently willing to negotiate with Yezeed, he refused categorically to recognize Ibrahim, and declared his support for the two young sons of the drunken Waleed II, both of whom had apparently been imprisoned in Damascus. An additional irritant lay in the fact that in Damascus Ibrahim was supported by the Yemenites, while Merwan favoured the Qaisite faction.

With the speed of action which had always characterized his military operations, Merwan marched from Harran. Taking Qinisreen and Homs in his stride, he advanced by forced marches on the capital. At Ain al Jurr, between Baalbek and Damascus, the khalif's army barred the way. Merwan was heavily outnumbered, but his was a professional army, long inured to war and victory against the Byzantines and the Khazars, and led by an outstanding general. Merwan engaged Ibrahim's army in front, while at the same time secretly despatching a column to take it in the rear. The frontal battle lasted nearly all day, but as soon as the flank atttack went in, Ibrahim's army disintegrated, suffering a terrible slaughter at the hands of Merwan's veterans. Ibrahim fled from Damascus, but, before doing so, caused Hakam and Othman, the two young sons of Waleed II, to be murdered in prison. Merwan had ostensibly rebelled in defence of the rights of these two boys who were now dead. Inevitably Merwan himself was acclaimed in Damascus with the title of Merwan II, on 23rd November, 744.

Only two years before, when Hisham was reigning, the Umaiyid dynasty still seemed secure, but in the two years from 743 to 745, Beni Umaiya had lost almost everything. The spectacle first of the drunken and profligate Waleed II and then of the civil wars between the different members of the clan had destroyed the credit of the family for ever. Merwan was a fine fighter, an experienced commander and a man of ascetic life. If he had succeeded to the khalifate directly after Hisham, all might have been well. But in 745 it was already too late.

Before describing the final agony of Beni Umaiya, it may be worth while to summarize the various and bitter internal feuds, which were tearing apart the vitals of the great Empire of the Arabs.

Firstly, the most prominent at this actual moment, was the feud between the northern and the southern Arab races, Adnan and Qahtan, or, as we have called them, Qais and Yemen. It would almost appear as if the khalifs themselves had been the chief irritant, for with their various wives, they had

6. Genealogical tree, page 64.

sometimes married Qaisites and sometimes Yemenites. Perhaps, amid the jealousies of rival wives, the youthful Umaiyids had grown up to detest their half-brothers, the offspring of some hated rival Qaisite or Yemenite woman. Suffice it at any rate to say that the later Umaiyid khalifs were often bitterly hostile to their own relatives in accordance with their attachment or hostility to one or the other faction. Perhaps in the Byzantine Empire, the feud between the Blues and the Greens was, to our thinking, equally meaningless, though not quite so disastrous to the state. In European history the rivalry between Guelphs and Ghibellines is to us almost as difficult to understand.

But the Yemenite-Qaisite feud was not the only one which threatened to destroy the empire. There was also the schism dividing the eastern and western halves, the Iraqi against the Syrian, or perhaps the former Persian against the former Byzantine territories. This was a far more real incompatibility than that between the Qais and Yemen Arabs, for it was the line between east and west which still haunts us today. Before the Arab conquest a hundred years earlier, the Byzantine Empire had been Christian, the Persian Zoroastrian, and the difference between the two religions had given rise to two distinct cultures. The Arabs had imposed themselves on both as a ruling class, but their readiness to marry the women of the conquered races meant that, after four generations, the "Arabs" of Syria and Palestine were half-Byzantine, while those of Iraq and the east were half-Persian.

The third source of discord was due to religion, principally in the form of disputes over the succession to the khalifate. Here there were four groups in the field. On the one hand, there were the supporters of Beni Umaiya, in general the orthodox or Sunnis. Against them was the Shia, or the party which claimed that the legitimate succession was limited to the descendants of Ali ibn abi Talib. Although the Shia originated over a dispute regarding the succession, the lack of material success achieved had already begun to transform the Shia into a passionate half-mystic religious cult rather than a practical political movement.

In addition to those who advocated the claims of Beni Umaiya or of the family of Ali, the supporters of the descendants of Abbas had recently entered the field. More skilful and more "modern" than the Shia in their technique, they had built up a widespread underground organization, which had honey-combed the eastern half of the empire with secret cells. Indeed so secret and so centrally controlled was the organization that many of its adherents were not even aware of its objectives and believed that they were working for the family of Ali. Finally, in the religious field, stood the Kharijites, who professed themselves disgusted with the vices and ambitions of princes.

Another cause of dissension arose from the discontent of the conquered races. Nationalism as we know it did not exist in the eighth century, that is to say, people did not believe that differences of racial origin were necessarily a reason for antagonism. They did, however, in all the conquered countries, intensely resent the arrogance of the Arab ruling class. Many Persians, Syrians, Egyptians, Berbers and Spaniards had, whether for religious, social or financial reasons, adopted the Muslim religion, but had nevertheless—and contrary to the theory of Islam—been denied social and financial equality with the Arabs.

All these causes of discontent were, as if by a sudden coincidence of circumstances, to unite now against Merwan. Known to favour the Qaisites, he was opposed by the Yemenites. An Umaiyid, the advocates of Beni Ali and Beni Abbas necessarily hated him. As a prince the Kharijites wished to overthrow him. As an Arab, the subject nationalities would rise against him. Above all, the accumulated resentments against Beni Umaiya were to burst into flame in the belief that the luck had turned and that the Umaiyids were on their way out.

* * *

Before relating the incidents which were to lead to the fall of the Umaiyid dynasty, we may pause for a moment to review the ninety years during which Beni Umaiya had ruled the Empire of the Arabs.

The reader is now referred to the list of the Umaiyid khalifs. It will be seen that three of them—Muawiya, Abdul Malik and Hisham—were rulers of outstanding personality or ability. Moreover the combined reigns of these three amounted to fifty-eight years out of the ninety years of Umaiyid rule or very nearly two-thirds. In addition, Waleed the first, who reigned ten years, may also be called a very adequate khalif, and Sulaiman his brother was popular, while Umar ibn Abdul Aziz was wise, pious and beloved, if financially inept. If we add these three reigns to the original three, we find that the Umaiyids ruled capably for seventy-three years out of ninety. Yezeed I and Yezeed II were frivolous, sensual and to some extent ineffective. Their reigns totalled seven years. Waleed II was definitely a drunken vicious brute, but he only reigned for just over a year. The reigns of Merwan I and Merwan II were occupied by civil wars, though both were capable men. As individuals, therefore, Beni Umaiya were probably as capable as any dynasty in history.

The absence of any accepted system for choosing the successor to the khalifate gave rise to almost all the civil wars and also to the sects, some of which divide Islam to this day. The long civil wars between Muawiya and Ali ibn abi Talib and then between Merwan I, Abdul Malik and Abdulla ibn Zubair stopped the Arabs in their full career of conquest. If these two civil wars had not occurred, and they had continued the victorious expansion on which they had embarked under Umar ibn al Khattab and Othman, there is no means of estimating where their conquests might have ended. But the civil wars not only kept them preoccupied for several years, but they also destroyed the idealism and the sense of brotherhood which had fired the early Muslims. In addition, great numbers of their bravest warriors were killed in this fratricidal strife.

It may be worthwhile to summarize briefly the history and development of the procedure for selecting the khalif's successor. The original theory, during the Medina period, was that the khalif should be chosen by acclamation of the whole Muslim community. This might have been feasible as long as that community was virtually limited to the people of Medina, but

TABLE TO SHOW THE UMAIYID KHALIFS

Name	Length of Reign in Years	Qualities	Remarks
MUAWIYA I Son of Abu Sofian 661–680	19	Statesman of outstanding quality—the first khalif not chosen for purely religious reasons.	Fought for the khalifate in civil war against Ali ibn abi Talib.
YEZEED I Son of Muawiya I 680–683	$3\frac{1}{2}$	A rather shallow and frivolous character, obese and pot-bellied.	In his brief reign occurred the massacre of Husain and his comrades at Kerbela.
MUAWIYA II 683	2 months	A weak and sickly boy, he was believed to be virtuous and well-disposed.	He was already ill when he was proclaimed khalif, possibly of tuberculosis.
MERWAN I	2	He rebelled against Abdulla ibn Zubair and spent two years in civil war against him.	Legally Merwan never was khalif though he was proclaimed in Damascus. Technically he was merely a rebel against Abdulla ibn Zubair.
ABDULLA IBN ZUBAIR 683–692	9	Not of Beni Umaiya. He spent all his reign in civil wars.	He was recognized by all provinces after death of Muawiya II. Eventually killed in the siege of Mecca in the reign of Abdul Malik.
ABDUL MALIK IBN MERWAN 685–705	20	A great ruler and statesman. Blamed because he offered unquestioning support to Hajjaj in Iraq.	He commenced his reign with the civil war against Abdulla ibn Zubair. He only became sole legal khalif in 692 on the death of Abdulla.
WALEED I Son of Abdul Malik 705–715	10	A good serious ruler, under whom the empire achieved its maximum military extension. A great builder. He also supported Hajjaj.	
SULAIMAN IBN ABDUL MALIK 715–717	2	Not an outstanding personality, but interested in the army. Constantinople besieged in his reign. A gluttonous eater.	"The young king" in green silk before his mirror.

Name	Length of Reign in Years	Qualities	Remarks
UMAR IBN ABDUL AZIZ 717–720	3	A deeply pious but also wise and conscientious ruler. Under his quiet justice, the many internal feuds which were rending the empire were stilled.	A good khalif.
YEZEED II Son of Abdul Malik 720–724	4	A somewhat unimpressive character. Frivolous though not evil or vicious —the owner of the slave girl Hababa.	
HISHAM IBN ABDUL MALIK (Farmer George) 724–743	19	The fourth of Abdul Malik's sons to succeed. An outstanding ruler of a rough and ready practical type.	
WALEED II Son of Yezeed II 743–744	1 year and 3 months	A drunken libertine, murdered after a year and 3 months.	The immediate cause of the ruin of the dynasty.
YEZEED III Son of Waleed ibn Abdul Malik 744	6 months	We know scarcely anything about him. He led the revolt against Waleed the Drunkard. He claimed to be religious but his opinions were unorthodox.	"Reduction Yezeed".
IBRAHIM Brother of Yezeed III. Son of Waleed ibn Abdul Malik 744	2 months	Little is known of him, though most people seem to have thought him unfit to be khalif.	He was deposed by Merwan, to whom he subsequently swore allegiance.
MERWAN II Son of Muhammad ibn Merwan 744–750	6 years	A good and enthusiastic soldier but no politician. Anyhow things had already gone too far as the result of the reigns of Waleed the Drunkard, Yezeed III and Ibrahim.	Merwan the Ass.

"acclamation" was obviously meaningless where a great empire was involved. Moreover as all the powers of the government were concentrated in the khalif, it was not possible to allow a long period to elapse after the death of the khalif, such as would have been necessary if all the distant provinces were to be consulted. There were indeed Muslim jurists who actually advocated an imperial plebiscite but the idea was purely theoretical and could not have been carried out. Thus, in practice, "acclamation" was soon limited to the leading notables at court, members of the reigning family and their dependents, senior officials, temporal and spiritual, and commanders of the troops in the capital.

The danger of civil war on the death of the khalif was so great that the custom early appeared of designating his successor before his decease. This method, moreover, made it possible to obtain the consent of the provinces. Even so, however, there was no adequate machinery for obtaining the approval of the public as a whole. What happened was that the governor, senior officials, army commanders and notables in the provinces were asked to swear allegiance to the successor before the death of the ruling khalif. These oaths of allegiance were taken extremely seriously and, as we have seen, the majority of those who had taken them felt absolutely bound by them.

A curious anomaly was presented by the fact that the successor, to whom oaths were thus to be sworn in advance, was normally chosen by the ruling khalif. It was, therefore, never clear to what extent the khalif had the right to nominate his successor, a completely autocratic system, and to what extent the public had the right to elect him, a completely democratic system. Sulaiman ibn Abdul Malik, as we have seen, nominated Umar ibn Abdul Aziz as his successor in a sealed letter not to be opened until after his death—yet he was extremely doubtful whether his wishes would be carried out.

The Arab dislike of the system of primo-geniture is emphasized by the fact that, out of fourteen Umaiyid khalifs, only four were succeeded by their sons. The Arab system, according to which the successor should be the most suitable member of the ruling family, dated from before Islam. The average age of the Umaiyid khalifs when they died was forty-three, with the result that, in many cases, their sons were not yet grown-up. As it was generally admitted that a child could not be khalif, this shortness of life often precluded the succession of a son.

In marked contrast to the Abbasids who were to succeed them, the mothers of the Umaiyid khalifs were almost all Arab wives. Merwan the Ass, whose mother was a Kurdish slave concubine, was an exception. In general, therefore, the Beni Umaiya khalifs were true Arabs of the original peninsula stock.

In brief, we may conclude that, although the ability of the reigning khalif to nominate his successor tended to increase, yet the theory of popular election continued to receive lip-service and doubtless to influence the selection of the successor. The khalif was well-advised to choose a man acceptable to the public, if revolts and civil wars were to be avoided.

The autocracy of the Umaiyids is especially striking because the pre-Islamic Arabs were, of all the people on earth, perhaps the most wedded to their personal freedom. The original Arab conquerors had been nomadic tribes-men from the desert. Their chiefs, although owing to their lineage they received a certain amount of respect, enjoyed no authority whatever. The reason for this was obvious. A man whose property consisted of animals and whose dwelling was a tent loaded on those animals, was perfectly mobile. If he disliked the community in which he was living, or the chief attempted to coerce him, he had only to load his tent on a camel and move away to join another group. The tribal tent-dweller, therefore, was really a free man. He was little interested in what the chief ordered or in what the majority of his community wanted. He was quite literally a law unto himself.

The citizens of Britain and the United States claim today to be free men and to live in free countries, but their freedom is only relative. In practice they have agreed to a compromise. They have consented to surrender their freedom to a vague entity known as the majority, which can make laws which others must obey. In other words, men who live in settled communities are not personally free. In order to enjoy a limited amount of freedom under such circumstances, they agree to surrender the remainder.

The fact that, under this system, we still claim to be free, makes us fail to comprehend what freedom meant to a nomadic Arab. He knew nothing of the majority. He claimed the right to do as he wished, even if every other man on earth disapproved of such action. The nomad really was free, and the key to his perfect freedom was mobility. As soon as these men came to live in cities and acquired immovable property, they lost their mobility and there-fore their perfect freedom. But they did not of course think the matter out in this manner. Personal freedom had become to them an instinct. Although living now in houses and in cities, they were not prepared to take anyone's orders. Those who were trying to organize and rule an empire with such subjects soon found the task impossible.

Faced with this situation, two alternatives presented themselves to the ruler. These violent and anarchic free men must either be persuaded or coerced into the surrender of part of their freedom. Religion came powerfully to the support of Abu Bekr and Umar, the first two khalifs. Their fellow citizens, they claimed, were not serving them but God. While the religious enthusiasm lasted, the argument was sufficient to ensure obedience, or at least order. It fell to Muawiya, when religious enthusiasm was cooling, to replace it by political persuasion. He never arrogated to himself despotic authority. He never appeared to be more than the first among his peers, the chief adviser of the Arab people. He spent endless hours talking and discussing with the notable men of the community and accepted with apparently imperturbable good humour the rude remarks of his enemies delivered to his face. Significantly he was the only khalif against whom there was never a rebellion.

No race has ever produced a dynasty consisting solely of geniuses. The situation was extremely difficult for a khalif of frivolous character or inferior intellect. If everything depended on the patience and persuasive powers of the khalif, the system broke down when the ruler was stupid. Thus those khalifs who had not the personality or the intellect to persuade were often faced with revolts. In general, it was during the reigns of the weak khalifs that the most savage forms of coercion were used.

The Central Arabians, although devoted to personal freedom, followed with devotion a man whom they considered personally fitted to rule. When the khalif did not so impress them, he was obliged to resort to extreme and arbitrary measures to keep order. In brief, the fact that the Arabs, the most personally free of all peoples, gradually fell under an autocratic government is not entirely illogical. Even in our days, it often occurs that too much freedom leads to confusion, and thence to dictatorship.

A secondary factor leading to despotic rule was the fact that the Byzantine and Persian Empires had both been governed in this manner. Suddenly burdened with the task of ruling an empire, the Arabs were at first obliged to make use of the civil officials left behind by their predecessors. All these people were accustomed to a system of autocracy. It was the only kind of government they had ever seen.

It appears to us that one of the principal errors of policy made during the Umaiyid period was the refusal to admit non-Arab Muslims to social equality —yet this mistake may be attributed to the pride of the Arab race as a whole, rather than to the policy of the khalifs. It is a problem which every empire has had to face, before and after the Arabs, and to which none has yet found a perfect solution.

When using the word Arab so freely, it may be well to add the caution that the Arabs of the Umaiyid period—though already a good deal diluted with other races—still showed in general the characteristics of the early conquerors, who were the tribesmen of what are now Saudi Arabia, the Yemen and Hadhramaut. The many and diverse peoples who today call themselves Arabs bear little or no relationship to these original conquerors. Their culture, however, has come down to them from the early years of Islam and thus, although of different racial origins, they show certain of the passionate, chaotic qualities of the early Arabs, including the habit of oscillating between anarchic freedom and dictatorship.

Heavy taxation was one of the causes of dissatisfaction with the Umaiyids. As already explained, the system dated from the Prophet and the first two khalifs. In their efforts to raise more money, however, the Umaiyids sometimes superimposed various pre-Muslim or Persian taxes, on top of the regular Muslim system. The fact that conversions to Islam reduced the revenue introduced further complications.

In assessing the performance of Beni Umaiya, we must give them credit for their military exploits. The Arab empire more than doubled in size during the ninety years of Umaiyid rule. More striking still is the fact that, after their fall, the empire not only ceased to expand but began immediately to contract and was for ever afterwards on the defensive.

NOTABLE DATES

Accession of Waleed II	743
Rebellion of Yahya ibn Zeid ibn Ali in Khurasan	743

Deposition and Death of Waleed II   }

Accession of Yezeed III   }   17th April, 744

Death of Yezeed III   12th October, 744

Battle of Ain al Jurr   November, 744

Accession of Merwan II   23rd November, 744

PERSONALITIES

Waleed II, son of Yezeed II—"The Libertine"

Yezeed III, son of Waleed I—"Reduction Yezeed"

Ibrahim, brother of Yezeed III

Merwan II ibn Muhammad ibn Merwan I—Merwan "The Ass"

XII

The Revolution

"O Allah, Owner of the Kingdom, Thou bestowest the kingdom on whom Thou pleasest and takest away the kingdom from whom Thou pleasest to take it away. Thou dost exalt and Thou dost abase as Thou wilt."   *Qoran* III, 25

He hath stripped me of my glory and taken the crown from my head. He hath destroyed me on every side. His troops come together and raise up their way against me and encamp round about. . . . My kinsfolk have failed and my familiar friends have forgotten me. I called my servant and he gave me no answer; I entreated him with my mouth. All my inward friends abhorred me; and they whom I loved are turned against me.   *Job* XIX, 9 to 19

Western Asia was in a state of chaos. On all sides there was an expectant waiting for the convulsion that was in the air.

AMEER ALI, *History of the Saracens*

We . . . look for new heavens and a new earth, wherein dwelleth righteousness.

2 *Peter* III, 13

XII

THE REVOLUTION

ABBAS, the uncle of the Apostle of God, had seemed to play a rather doubtful rôle during the latter's lifetime, assisting the Prophet's enemies, while at the same time sending information to Muhammad himself. We have already mentioned the son of this early Vicar of Bray, Abdulla ibn Abbas, a friend of Husain, whom he had endeavoured to deter from his fatal expedition to Kerbela. Ali, the son of Abdulla,[1] was a man distinguished for his affability, piety and learning. He had passed the greater part of his life in Damascus, where he had for many years been the close friend of the Khalif Abdul Malik. He had fallen into disfavour, however, by marrying a wife previously divorced by that khalif. Abdul Malik appears to have been merely annoyed, but his son Waleed I was, for reasons unknown to us, deeply angered by the incident. When he succeeded to the khalifate, he had caused Ali ibn Abdulla ibn Abbas to be flogged and paraded through the streets of Damascus. Thus, to vent their private spites, the Umaiyids brought their own Quraish relatives into contempt.

Ali survived his persecution and did not die until 735 in the reign of Hisham but he and his children withdrew themselves from the court into rustic obscurity. Muhammad, the son of Ali, bitterly resented the manner in which his father had been treated and nursed the apparently fantastic ambition to overthrow the reigning dynasty. Living in a remote village, he commanded no popular support but conceived the idea of a clandestine political campaign. The propaganda was conducted, through a widespread underground network, in the name of "the family". This equivocal slogan deluded many supporters into the belief that they were working in favour of the descendants of Ali, a misunderstanding which the missionaries were in no hurry to dispel. Against the time when the truth would have to be exposed, however, the Abbasid missionaries prepared a story to the effect that the imamate had descended from Ali ibn abi Talib to Muhammad ibn al Hanafiya, a son of his by a wife other than Fatima. This man had bequeathed it to his son Abu Hashim, who, however, having no son of his own, had then made it over to Ali ibn Abdulla ibn Abbas (the man flogged by Waleed in Damascus.) By this means the imamate had been transferred from the descendants of Ali to those of Abbas.[2]

Although Muhammad ibn Ali the Abbasid was of course an Arab of the Arabs, his emissaries encountered their greatest success in Iraq and Persia, particularly in the stormy province of Khurasan. Not only were the people

1. Genealogical tree, page 222.
2. According to Shiite dogma, the imamate passed from father to son in the descendants of Ali. The imam was inspired by the Spirit of God, and passed the inspiration to his son.

of that area renowned fighters but there were also among them great numbers of non-Arab converts to Islam, who chafed under the contempt of the Arab aristocracy. In 743, in the reign of the drunken Waleed the Libertine, Muhammad ibn Ali died, bequeathing the leadership of the movement to his son Ibrahim, who became known thenceforward as Ibrahim the Imam.

Meanwhile, as we have seen, Merwan had made himself master of Damascus in 745, and showed himself a strong partisan of the Qaisite faction. As a result of the khalif's known partiality fighting broke out in many places between the Qaisites and the Yemenites. In Bahrein and Oman, tribal warfare had already commenced. In Fars and Khuzistan, the Yemenites declared their rejection of Merwan. Seeing the whole country in confusion, the Kharijites of Iraq seized Kufa and expelled the governor. Other Kharijites from the Yemen invaded the Hejaz and actually occupied Mecca and Medina. Even nearer home, Homs rose in revolt.

Merwan, the old soldier, faced all his enemies. He marched swiftly on Homs, took it by assault before the malcontents knew he was coming, and crucified five hundred dead bodies outside the walls. But while he was marching on Homs, Damascus had risen. Before the insurgents could organize themselves, Merwan's army was back in the capital, the disturbance was over and its leader hung. Believing Syria to be cowed, the khalif marched to Raqqa, having ordered his forces to concentrate there for the reconquest of Iraq.

Sulaiman, a son of the Khalif Hisham, had commanded the Damascus army which had been defeated at Ain al Jurr by Merwan. He had, however, subsequently sworn allegiance to Merwan, and now accompanied him on his staff to Raqqa. On arrival there, however, he received Merwan's permission to return to Syria. On his way back, he encountered a force of ten thousand men, marching up to reinforce Merwan. Although Sulaiman had sworn allegiance only a few days earlier, he seduced this force from their loyalty, proclaimed himself khalif and occupied Qinisreen.

Abandoning the invasion of Iraq, Merwan returned, but the mutineers threw themselves into Homs, and delayed the khalif for nearly a year before he could reduce the city by siege. Meanwhile Sulaiman the son of Hisham, who had engineered this revolt, seems to have abandoned the mutineers in Homs and escaped to Iraq, where he joined the Kharijites, the fanatical enemies of all princes.

These Iraqi Kharijites, who had seized Kufa in June 745, had now seized Wasit also. Then they marched northwards—while Merwan was still besieging Homs—and occupied Mosul in September 746. From there they sent forward columns to besiege Raqqa and Nisibin. At this moment, however, Merwan at last succeeded in taking Homs and, marching swiftly eastwards, defeated the Kharijites in a great battle at Kufar Tutha, thirty miles west of Nisibin.

The Kharijites, with whom was Sulaiman, the son of the Khalif Hisham, retired on Mosul, where they entrenched themselves on the west bank of the Tigris. Merwan, following close upon their heels, was unable to take their camp by assault and was obliged to besiege it. One day, in a Kharijite sortie,

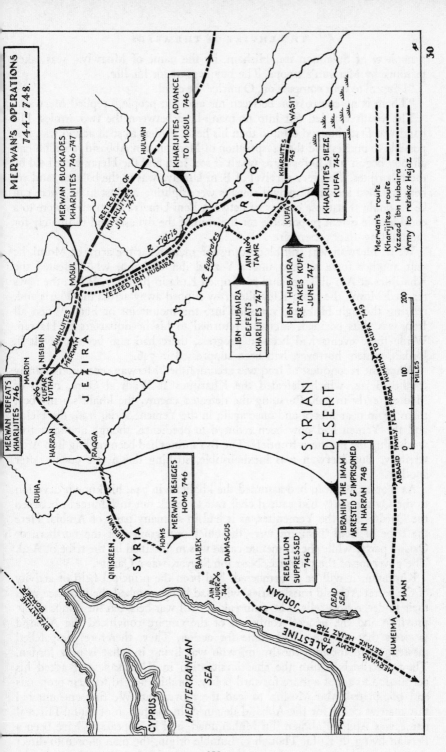

MERWAN'S OPERATIONS
744-748.

MERWAN BLOCKADES
KHARIJITES 746-747

KHARIJITES ADVANCE
TO MOSUL 746

RETREAT OF KHARIJITES
JULY 747

KHARIJITES SIEZE
KUFA 745

YEZEED IBN HUBAIRA
747

IBN HUBAIRA DEFEATS
KHARIJITES 747

IBN HUBAIRA
RETAKES KUFA
JUNE 747

MERWAN DEFEATS
KHARIJITES 746

MERWAN BESIEGES
HOMS 746

REBELLION
SUPPRESSED
746

IBRAHIM THE IMAM
ARRESTED & IMPRISONED
IN HARRAN 748

ABBASID FAMILY FLEE FROM HUMEIMA TO KUFA 749

Merwan's route
Kharijites route
Yezeed ibn Hubaira
Army to retake Hejaz

IRAQ

JEZIRA

SYRIAN DESERT

SYRIA

PALESTINE

JORDAN

MEDITERRANEAN SEA

CYPRUS

DEAD SEA

BYZANTINE BORDER

HULWAN

WASIT

KUFA

AIN AL
TAMR

MOSUL

R. Tigris

R. Euphrates

NISIBIN

MARDIN

KUFAR
TUTHA

HARRAN

RAQQA

RUHA

QINISREEN

HOMS

BAALBEK

DAMASCUS

AIN AL
JURR
744

MAAN

HUMEIMA

MERWAN'S RETREAT TO HEJAZ 748

KHARIJITES

MERWAN

MERWAN

0   100   200
MILES

215

30

a nephew of Sulaiman ibn Hisham, by the name of Muawiya, was taken prisoner by Merwan's troops. The boy begged for his life.

"I appeal to your compassion, O uncle," he cried.

"There is no compassion between me and you people," replied Merwan.

The youth was led out into no-man's-land between the two armies. His hand was first chopped off and then his head. Pitiless as such action was, it is possible to understand the exasperation of Merwan. An Abbasid rebellion had already begun in Khurasan, as we shall see. Iraq and the Hejaz were held by the Kharijites. The very survival of Beni Umaiya was in the balance, and yet here his own jealous Umaiyid cousins were fighting against him. There can be no doubt that these civil wars between Beni Umaiya themselves were to a considerable extent responsible for the ruin of the dynasty and ultimately for the splitting up of the empire.

While Merwan was still blockading the main Kharijite army at Mosul, he sent another force to Iraq under Yezeed ibn Hubaira, who defeated the Kharijites at Ain al Tamr and reoccupied Kufa in June 747. When the news reached Mosul, the main Kharijite army slipped away across the Tigris and, retiring through Hulwan, vanished into the mountains of Fars. When all Iraq was thus pacified, Merwan returned to his headquarters in Harran. While these events had been in progress, there had also been a revolt in Jordan, which, however, had been suppressed in 746.

When the reconquest of Iraq was accomplished Merwan sent another army to the Hejaz, which defeated the Kharijites at Wadi al Qura, north of Medina, early in 748. Pursuing the defeated enemy, the khalif's army beat them again near Mecca and once again in the Yemen. Syria, Iraq, the Hejaz and the Yemen had now been reduced to obedience, though at the cost of weakening the northern frontiers. The Byzantines had been raiding into Arab territory. But Merwan was inexhaustible, striking down one enemy after another.

As soon as Merwan had assumed the khalifate in 744, his known devotion to the Qaisite party had caused civil war to break out in Khurasan between the Qaisites and the Yemenites, as it had in so many parts of Arabia. Here the tribe of Beni Temeem were the chief protagonists of the northern or Qaisite party, while the Yemenite cause was maintained by the tribe of Azd. The governor of the province, Nasr ibn Sayyar, was a Qaisite.

Khurasan, it will be remembered, had been the principal field of activity of the secret Abbasid missionaries, who had honey-combed the province with their underground cells. The outbreak of civil war between the Arabs of the province and the general confusion of the empire convinced the Abbasid workers that the time had come for action. They, therefore, despatched messengers to Ibrahim the Imam, who was living in what is now Jordan. They described to him the chaotic situation in Khurasan, and asked his permission to adopt a more forward policy. Ibrahim agreed to their proposals and nominated Abu Muslim to lead the movement. We first encountered this man working for the Abbasid detainees in the prison of Kufa. His real name was Abdul Rahman ibn Muhammad, and he appears to have been a Persian living in Kufa. Though of humble origin, the man chosen to direct the Abbasid revolution was a born leader. Small in stature, of a dark complexion, with handsome features and a persuasive manner, he was never seen to laugh. The gravest events could hardly disturb his serenity, the greatest victories produced in him no sign of joy and the most disastrous reverses never destroyed his calm.

When he had first arrived in Khurasan, his youthful appearance had created doubts concerning his adequacy, but his manifest capabilities soon silenced criticism. He had thrown himself heart and soul into the organization of the movement. Leaders were appointed to every group and cell. The confusion and misery of unending civil wars had rendered the people ready for any new régime which might produce the much-longed-for saviour who would introduce the reign of peace and justice. The movement developed a Messianic preaching exactly suited to this public longing. The organization wore a religious Muslim appearance, preaching devotion to Beni Hashim, the Prophet's family, from whom the promised imam was to come. The blood-drenched Beni Umaiya, who from the first had been the bitterest enemies of the Apostle of God, would be finally overthrown, and the reign of peace at last be established.

But in spite of this appearance of piety, Abu Muslim was prepared to be all things to all men. Although the townspeople of Persia were by this time mostly Muslims, many of the peasants still clung to the belief of the old religion, such as the transmigration of souls and the idea of creation as a struggle between light and darkness. To such people Abu Muslim conveyed the impression that he believed there might be a good deal in their view. So tactful was he to the heretical sect of the Khurramites, that they subsequently adopted him as their messiah. Some of the promises and misconceptions which the propaganda employed were to produce bitter reactions later but by that time the Abbasids were firmly in power.

Although the majority of the secret adherents of the party were non-Arab converts to Islam, there were many Arabs also among its enthusiastic supporters. The fact that the initial propaganda spoke of the family of the Prophet, without specifically mentioning the descendants of Abbas, secured the adherence of many of the Shiites, who believed themselves to be working for the descendants of Ali.

In June 747, while Merwan was still blockading the Kharijites at Mosul, Abu Muslim received in Khurasan a letter from Ibrahim the Imam, ordering him to come out into open rebellion, using the slogan of "The Family". Two war-banners were also sent and were immediately hoisted on lances. The revolution had begun.

In the province of Khurasan, the new rebels armed and collected and established themselves in a number of entrenched camps. When Abu Muslim ordered all the faithful to appear dressed in black, the many adherents who had joined the secret organization became for the first time apparent.

Asad ibn Abdulla, who had defeated the Khaqan in 737, had died the following year and had been succeeded as governor by Nasr ibn Sayyar, a man who had served for thirty years in Khurasan and had a thorough knowledge of the country. Under his wise administration, the whole of

Trans-Oxiana was reoccupied, including Shash and Ferghana. It is noticeable that when the population of Khurasan joined Abu Muslim in rebellion, the peoples of Trans-Oxiana remained loyal to Nasr.[3] The latter now wrote desperately to Merwan, describing the chaotic condition of the province and the growing danger to be apprehended from Abu Muslim, and begged for reinforcements. But Merwan could only answer with excuses and advice. He had no army to spare. When Nasr read the khalif's reply, he could only comment bitterly to his staff, "Our friend seems to be virtually admitting that he just cannot win."

Meanwhile civil war was still going on in Khurasan between the Qaisites and the Yemenites. At length Abu Muslim declared openly his support for the Yemenite faction against the governor. A general battle took place, the Yemenites were victorious but their leader was killed. The governor was compelled to abandon Khurasan and withdrew to Rei. Nothing could have suited Abu Muslim better. The Yemenites, his allies, held the field but were now without a leader. In March 748, he installed himself in the governor's palace at Merv and became the ruler of Khurasan. Twenty-six years had elapsed since Muhammad ibn Ali the Abbasid had initiated his secret propaganda campaign.

Meanwhile Ibrahim the Imam was still living in seclusion in the village of Humeima near Maan in modern Jordan. Only a handful of the leaders of the rebellion knew that it was he who was to be the expected mehedi. Then, for a moment, the luck seemed to favour Merwan, who intercepted a secret letter from Ibrahim to Abu Muslim, in which the former urged the latter to press on with the rebellion. Ibrahim the Imam was arrested and thrown into prison in Harran.[4]

No sooner had Abu Muslim established himself in the palace at Merv than he exacted an oath of allegiance from the people in the name of Beni Hashim. As there was no specific mention of Beni Abbas, the Shiites took the oath willingly. A certain Qahtaba ibn Shabeeb, an Arab of the Tai tribe, had brought the two war-banners already mentioned from Ibrahim the Imam. Abu Muslim now nominated this Qahtaba to be commander of the army which he was raising. Meanwhile he appointed his own governors to the districts of Khurasan and to the country beyond the Oxus, and proceeded to collect taxes and enlist troops, as though he were the legal government. Two of his subordinates are worthy of mention. One, Muhammad al Ashath, was a descendant of that Abdul Rahman al Ashath, chief of the tribe of Azd, who had raised a rebellion against Hajjaj in Iraq. The Ashath family, living in Persia, had ever since been inspired by hatred of Beni Umaiya. The Arab tribe of Azd, being Yemenites, played a leading part in the revolution. The other was a certain Khalid ibn Barmak, a native of Balkh, of whom we shall hear more.

Living as we do at an epoch when the human race is believed to be divided into a number of different races, we tend to interpret the movements of history in terms of nationality. Yet it is improbable that the actors in the

3. H. A. R. Gibb. Op. cit.
4. Map 30, page 215, for Humeima in Southern Jordan and Harran in Northern Syria.

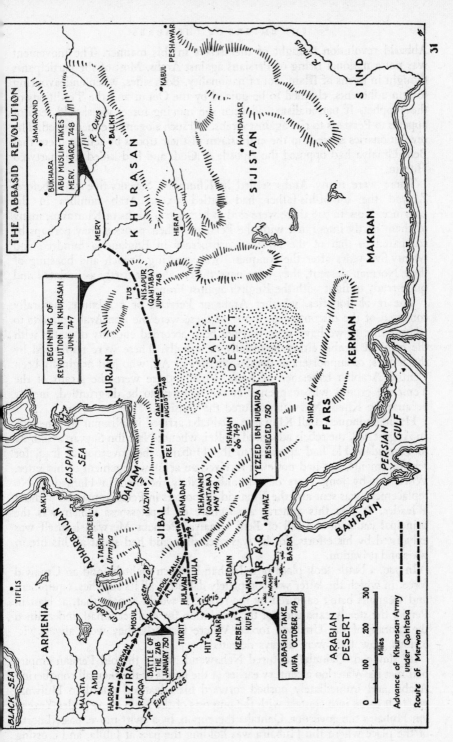

THE ABBASID REVOLUTION

BLACK SEA

ARMENIA

TIFLIS
BAKU
CASPIAN SEA
ARDEBIL
L. Urmiya
TABRIZ
ADHARBAIJAN
MALATIA
AMID
MOSUL
Greater Zab
Lesser Zab
MERWAN
HARRAN
RAQQA
JEZIRA
R. Euphrates
TIKRIT
HIT
ANBAR
KERBELA
KUFA
WASIT
MEDAIN
SWAMP
BASRA
I R A Q
AHWAZ
R. Tigris
JALULA
HULWAN
HAMADAN
ABDUL MALIK AL AZDI
KAZVIN
DAILAM
JIBAL
REI
NEHAWAND (QAHTABA) MAY 749
ISFAHAN
JURJAN
SALT DESERT
QAHTABA AUGUST 748
TUS
MERV
KHURASAN
BALKH
R. Oxus
BUKHARA
SAMARQAND
NISAPUR (QAHTABA) JUNE 748
HERAT
SIJISTAN
KANDAHAR
KABUL
PESHAWAR
R. Indus
SIND
MAKRAN
KERMAN
FARS
SHIRAZ
BAHRAIN
PERSIAN GULF
ARABIAN DESERT

ABU MUSLIM TAKES MERV. MARCH 748

BEGINNING OF REVOLUTION IN KHURASAN JUNE 747

YEZEED IBN HUBAIRA BESIEGED 750

BATTLE OF THE ZAB JANUARY 750

ABBASIDS TAKE KUFA. OCTOBER 749

Miles
0   100   200   300

Advance of Khurasan Army under Qahtaba
Route of Merwan

31

219

Abbasid revolution thought of themselves in this manner. The movement was not a national rising of Persians against Arabs. Most of the participants thought in terms of Islam, not of nationality. Both sides, when endeavouring to win adherents, claimed to be guided by the Qoran and the Traditions of the Prophet. If nationalism had been the moving force, we should read of appeals to Persians to rise against Arabs. No such slogans are mentioned. The revolutionaries stirred up the enthusiasm of their troops by telling them that Beni Umaiya had opposed the Apostle of God, and had killed the martyred Husain.

There were many Arabs settled in Khurasan. Seventy-five years before, Zayyad the son-of-his-father had settled 50,000 Arab families in the province. Now in 748 there were said to be 200,000 Arabs in Khurasan, many of them partly integrated with the Persians. Their position may perhaps be compared to that of the Norman aristocracy in England a hundred and twenty-five years after the conquest. Still speaking French and boasting of their Norman descent, they were nevertheless already partly assimilated and quite ready to fight with the English against France.

The revolutionaries, whether Arabs or Persians or a mixture, naturally consisted of the discontented. Many of these were the non-Arab converts to Islam, who, as we have seen, had not been accorded equality of status with the original Arabs, either financially or socially. These were reinforced by the Shiites, or supporters of the descendants of Ali, who had originally been Central Arabian tribesmen of Kufa. Finally there were the Arabs of the Yemenite groups who happened at the moment to be disgruntled, merely because the Khalif Merwan favoured the Qaisites.

Having conquered all Khurasan, Qahtaba arrived in Nisapur in June 748. In August 748, the rebels advanced on Rei, whence Nasr ibn Sayyar withdrew to Hamadan. He had appealed to Ibn Hubaira, the governor of Iraq, for reinforcements, but had not even received an acknowledgement of his letter. Worn out by long years of war and anxiety, he died in Hamadan. No replacement was sent and the Umaiyid supporters in Persia remained without a leader. It was this general atmosphere of hopelessness which was the principal cause of the fall of Beni Umaiya. Perhaps Merwan himself was exhausted by his efforts, for he was over sixty and had spent all his life in wars and privation.

In 749, a battle took place near Isfahan between Qahtaba and an Umaiyid force, in which the latter was completely defeated, all its supplies, equipment and weapons being captured by the rebels. It would appear that, at least in Persia, the steady expansion of the revolution for two years had undermined the morale of the Umaiyid forces. Where formerly they were always victorious, now they were always defeated.

In May 749, Qahtaba captured Nehawand, where the old Persian empire had met its Waterloo a century earlier at the hands of the then all-conquering Arabs, and immediately pushed forward his advanced guard to Hulwan, where it came into contact with the outposts of the Kufa army under Yezeed ibn Hubaira the governor. Qahtaba thereupon, by a swift move, passed north of the place where Ibn Hubaira was holding the pass at Jalula, and crossing the Tigris and the Euphrates, moved down the latter river towards Kufa. It was the month of August 749. Seeing his position turned, Ibn Hubaira hastened back to defend Kufa. A confused action took place on the Euphrates in the dark, Qahtaba being killed, but the Khurasan army under his son Hasan pressed on and occupied Kufa, Ibn Hubaira retiring to Wasit. By this time, however, everything in southern Iraq was in confusion, with the Khurasan army everywhere in hot pursuit.

It will be remembered that the Imam Ibrahim had been arrested by order of Merwan and thrown into prison in the castle of Harran. Such a possibility seems to have been foreseen, for Ibrahim had already prepared a document bequeathing the imamate to his brother Abdulla. We have already seen this Abdulla, years before, a newly born baby, shown in his father's arms to the emissaries from Khurasan.

No sooner was Ibrahim marched off to prison than Abdulla and all the family abandoned their home at the village of Humeima. They set out across the desert for Kufa, where they were received and concealed by a supporter, unknown to the authorities or to the people of Kufa. When the rebel army entered the town, an attempt was made by the Shia to produce an Aliid candidate to the khalifate. The Khurasan army, however, objected. The new Abbasid imam then appeared and rode in triumph to the great mosque of the city. Here he prayed the midday prayer at the head of the congregation and delivered a sermon, denouncing the wickedness of Beni Umaiya. He then proclaimed the advent to power of the Prophet's family, who would henceforward spread the rule of religion and justice over all the earth. Abdulla, at the end of his speech, sat down exhausted but his uncle Daood ibn Ali then spoke. Claiming that the family of Abbas would be guided solely by religion, he added "from now onwards we, the family of the Prophet, will rule until we hand over our charge on the Last Day to Jesus the son of Mary at His second coming." [5]

The situation was somewhat precarious, for the majority of those present had been of the Shia, that is to say supporters of the descendants of Ali, not of Abbas. The slogans of "Beni Hashim" and "The Prophet's Family" which the revolution had used, left the matter intentionally in doubt. Beni Abbas, however, had been wiser in their generation than the descendants of Ali. They had not come helplessly to appeal for support from the people of Kufa, as Husain had done. On the contrary, they had not shown their hand until the Khurasan army had already occupied Kufa. Confronted with a *fait accompli*, the Kufans greeted with enthusiasm their new khalif who, even if he were not a descendant of Ali, had at least defeated and driven out Beni Umaiya and the hated Syrians. For the remainder of the day, from noon until dark, dense throngs of Kufans followed one another to swear allegiance between the hands of the new imam. It was 28th October, 749.

Meanwhile another army had been despatched from Khurasan by Abu Muslim. When Qahtaba had turned south to take Kufa, this force, under Abdul Malik ibn Yezeed al Azdi, had moved on Mosul. (The fact that the revolution did not originate as a national rising of Persians against Arabs

5. Duri, *Al Asr al Abbasi al awal*.

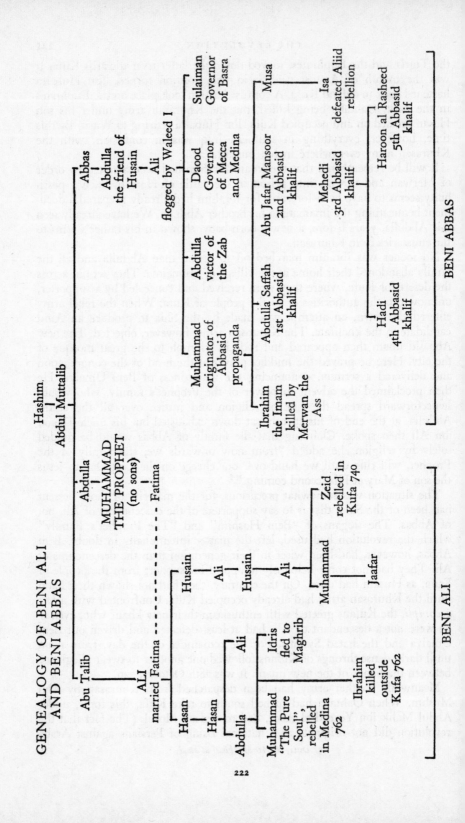

GENEALOGY OF BENI ALI AND BENI ABBAS

is shown by the fact that both commanders of the Abbasid armies were Arabs
—Qahtaba ibn Shabeeb of Tai and Abdul Malik ibn Yezeed of Azd.)

It is difficult to understand why the Khalif Merwan, who had shown such
remarkable energy when he first achieved power, had remained until now
immobile at Harran. Now, however, he roused himself and set out with his
army to meet Abdul Malik al Azdi. When news reached Kufa that the khalif
was advancing, all the troops available were sent to reinforce the northern
rebel army, and the command was entrusted to Abdulla ibn Ali ibn Abdulla
ibn Abbas, uncle of the new imam and younger brother of the late
Muhammad ibn Ali, who had inaugurated the movement. If Merwan had
moved before the rebels took Kufa, he could have defeated the northern rebel
army alone. By delaying until the fighting in southern Iraq was over, however, he allowed the greater part of Hasan ibn Qahtaba's army to join the
northern force against him.

Merwan was the first to reach Mosul, while Abdulla ibn Ali drew up his
army on the River Zab, a tributary of the Tigris some eighty miles below
Mosul. On 25th January, 750, the khalif advanced to meet the enemy.
Accounts of the battle are contradictory and unreliable. The extraordinary
successes already won by the revolution had undermined the morale of the
Umaiyid soldiers, some of whom may themselves have been half-convinced
that it was God's will that the Prophet's family should rule. Many units of
the Umaiyid army refused to attack, and Merwan's orders were disobeyed
at the critical moment of the battle. Other narratives suggest that the
Yemenites in the khalif's army refused to fight. Masudi mentions a report
that, presumably due to the general government confusion, the pay of the
troops was in arrears. Yet if the Umaiyid cause had been in the ascendant,
these elements would not have dared to hang back. Thus their reluctance to
fight, if it existed, was probably also due to the impression that the revolution
was winning.

Whatever the real events of the battle may have been, the Umaiyid army
met with a decisive defeat. Merwan had crossed the Zab to engage the enemy,
with the result that when the Syrian army broke, many were drowned in
trying to escape across the river. It is frustrating to be unable to follow the
course of events in the Battle of the Zab, for it was one of the decisive battles
of the world. In fact the Abbasid victory was due rather to their propaganda
than to their military prowess. The morale of the Umaiyid army had been
undermined before the battle began.

The Battle of the Zab not only changed the whole shape of the Empire of
the Arabs but, in so doing, it profoundly affected the future of Europe also.
Unlike the Umaiyids, the Abbasids were to neglect the Mediterranean and
to devote their attention to Persia and the East. The threat of an Arab conquest, which had been hanging over Europe for a century, was, as a result,
to come to nothing.

*   *   *

When Merwan retired to Mosul, the city closed its gates to him, so he
passed on with a small escort to his original residence in Harran. The

Abbasid army, however, was in hot pursuit and Merwan was obliged to hasten on through Homs to Damascus and then still on to Jordan and Palestine. As the triumphant Abbasid army swept on in pursuit, city after city opened its gates, the citizens pouring forth, all dressed in black, to swear allegiance to their new masters. Only Damascus, for ninety years the royal capital of Beni Umaiya, closed its gates and obliged Abdulla ibn Ali to make his dispositions for a siege. But soon differences arose within the walls. Fighting broke out between those who desired to surrender and those still faithful to the defeated dynasty. In June 750, the gates were opened, the white banner of the Umaiyids was torn down and the black Abbasid flags flew from the ramparts. Abdulla ibn Ali celebrated the fall of Damascus by a massacre of Umaiyids and of those who had been loyal to them.

The débâcle was complete and irretrievable. Abandoned by all, the unfortunate Merwan reached Egypt, but still continued his flight with the enemy horse close on his heels. Pausing to rest the night of 5th August, 750, in the little village of Busir in the Faiyum, he was surprised in the darkness by a detachment of cavalry. The khalif's escort fled, and Merwan, who had been sleeping in the village church, came out almost alone to face his enemies who had run him to ground at last. In a few minutes he was dead, and the severed head of the enemy of God was sent off by a special galloper to Abdulla ibn Ali, who had occupied Palestine with his army.

Merwan was in his sixties when he was killed. Most of his life had been passed in the northern Jezira and in Armenia and in military operations against the Byzantines and the Khazars. He lived a frugal and active life, almost always in the field with his troops. Asked by one of his intimates why he had no use for women or perfumes or other sensual pleasures, he had replied by telling a story of the Khalif Abdul Malik.

"One day Abdul Malik ibn Merwan," said he, "received a letter from Hajjaj during the Ashath rebellion reporting that the two armies were face to face at Deir al Jumajim and that a major battle was imminent. While he was still reading the letter, a girl slave was brought in, who had been sent to him as a present by the governor of Ifriqiya. She was, in face, figure and manner, the most beautiful woman he had ever seen.

" 'By God, you really are as perfect a girl as any man could wish to set eyes on,' said Abdul Malik, looking up for a moment and then returning to the despatch he was reading.

" 'Why don't you seem to want me if I am as you say,' asked the young woman, perhaps mortified at the khalif's lack of attention.

" 'How could I think of a woman, by God,' replied Abdul Malik, 'while Hajjaj and Ashath are drawn up in line of battle and the leaders of the Arabs are about to slaughter one another?'

"That is why I too have never had any time for women," added Merwan the Ass.

His statement was true. He had spent his life in campaigns and battles, and his leisure in the study of history and of the wars of the great kings and commanders of past ages.

Assuming the khalifate at about sixty years of age, he was perhaps too ignorant of courts and politicians to be able efficiently to rule a great empire. He was unable to dissemble with his enemies, or to play off one against another to gain time. Perhaps too he was hard and lacking in sympathy, at least to the outside world.

He never lived in Damascus, but even when he was khalif he preferred to remain in Harran where he had passed most of his life. His military activity during the first three years of his rule was energetic and efficient, but the political situation was already too far undermined for it to be restored by force. Only a real statesman of the highest quality would have enjoyed a chance of success, and Merwan's intellect and character were too limited for so immense a task. As a ruler, however, his most crude mistake lay in identifying himself with the Qaisite faction. As a result, he not only found enemies in the people of Khurasan, the Shia and the Kharijites, but he alienated the Yemenites, who formed half the Arab tribes.

In the field of military tactics, he was credited with the reorganization of the Arab armies, which, ever since the days of the Prophet, had always fought in line. Merwan is alleged to have trained them to fight in columns, more mobile and manoeuvrable than a continuous line, a change not unfamiliar to us who remember the continuous lines of trenches of the First World War and have seen them change into the mobile columns of the blitzkrieg.

* * *

While Abdulla ibn Ali, the uncle of the new khalif, was engaged in pacifying Jordan and Palestine, the people of Qinisreen in northern Syria suddenly "put on white". Black and white had become the respective colours of the Abbasids and the Umaiyids and each city signified its attachment by the colour of the garments of its citizens. Some Abbasid troops, it appeared, had misbehaved in the country round Qinisreen and had assaulted a number of women. The inhabitants had retaliated by killing several of the soldiers and then, fearing punishment, had put on white, the movement spreading rapidly to Homs and Palmyra. Abdulla ibn Ali marched northwards, but no sooner had he passed Damascus than the capital rose in revolt. After heavy fighting in July 751, the Qinisreen rising was repressed, the people changing once more into their black garments. Meanwhile, however, the people of the Jezira had donned white garments and many months of operations were needed before Raqqa, Harran, Ruha and Mardin [6] were once again brought to terms and resumed their black clothing.

It will be remembered that Yezeed ibn Hubeira had been Merwan's governor of Iraq and that, when the Khurasan army occupied Kufa, Ibn Hubeira had retired to Wasit where he was besieged by an Abbasid force. Ibn Hubeira had been an old comrade in arms of Merwan in his many campaigns in the Caucasus and in Asia Minor. Though all the world had surrendered to the new régime, he continued to maintain, month after month, an active defence of Wasit. The Khalif Abdulla, also known as Abu al Abbas, eventually sent his brother Abu Jafar to press the siege. The latter opened negotiations with Ibn Hubeira and, after the siege had lasted for a year,

6. Map 30, page 215.

terms were agreed upon. Abu Jafar gave safe conduct to Ibn Hubeira and the garrison, the gates were thrown wide and the besieged camped in the open beside their former besiegers. But the Khalif Abu al Abbas wrote to his brother Abu Jafar to put Ibn Hubeira to death, a suggestion which Abu Jafar strongly resisted. The khalif's orders, however, could not ultimately be rejected, and, in spite of the pledge of safe conduct, Ibn Hubeira and his officers were treacherously executed.

The Khalif Abu al Abbas had indeed amply earned his title of As Saffah, or the Shedder of Blood, by which he has come down to us in history and by which in future we shall refer to him. He gave orders that every member of Beni Umaiya be put to death, by fair means or foul. A number had been massacred in Basra and their bodies left for the pariah dogs to devour. But worst of all was the action of Abdulla ibn Ali, uncle of the Shedder of Blood, and victor of the Battle of the Zab.

The Khalif Saffah had nominated his uncle governor of Syria, with specific orders to kill all the Umaiyid family. This he did by suggesting to them an amnesty and inviting all Beni Umaiya to a great banquet at which they were to take the oath of allegiance. When the hall was full, a signal was given to the troops and between eighty and ninety Umaiyids were massacred in cold blood. Scarcely was the carnage over than Abdulla ibn Ali called for the banquet to be served, before the bodies of the dead and the dying had been removed. It seems incredible, but appears to be true, that the Abbasids and their supporters indulged in the banquet, while the floor of the hall was still covered with blood-soaked bodies, and the revelries of the living were interrupted by the groans of the dying. Daood ibn Ali, brother of Abdulla ibn Ali, was sent by the Khalif Saffah as governor of Mecca and Medina with orders to extirpate the brood of Umaiya in the holy cities by the same methods.

The choice of a site for the capital of the empire was one which perplexed the new dynasty. The Syrians had been too long faithful to Beni Umaiya for it to be safe for the Abbasids to place themselves in their power. Saffah had been proclaimed in Kufa, but the people of that city were too fickle to make it suitable as the imperial capital. The new khalif first resided in a castle near Kufa, which he named the Hashimiya, but in 753 he moved to the town of Anbar, a hundred miles further up the Euphrates. The ultimate position of the capital, however, still remained in doubt.

While these stirring events were being enacted in Iraq, Syria and Egypt, Abu Muslim, the engineer of the original revolt, remained as governor of Khurasan and Jibal. In 750, surprisingly enough, a Chinese military force had actually appeared in Ferghana on the Jaxartes and had attacked Shash, the ruler of which had appealed to Abu Muslim for help. As a result, an Arab force crossed the Jaxartes and, in July 751, completely defeated the Chinese at Talas, two hundred miles beyond the river.[7] Soon afterwards, civil war broke out in China, where the T'ang dynasty was in decline. The Battle of Talas marks the end of Chinese intervention in Trans-Oxiana. Under the Abbasids, the province was to enjoy a long period of prosperity and to produce a brilliant Muslim civilization of its own.

7. Map 17, page 101.

In 753, Abu Muslim wrote to the Khalif Saffah asking permission to visit him, and arrived in Iraq early in 754. It so happened that the khalif's brother, Abu Jafar, was also in Anbar, whither he had come from his post as governor of Armenia and the Jezira, with a view to leading the annual pilgrimage to Mecca.

The victory of the revolution had been to a great extent due to the Khurasan army, the troops of which were now deployed in Syria, the Jezira and Iraq as well as in Persia. Indeed the safety of the régime seemed still to depend on the loyalty of the Khurasanis. It was true that Beni Umaiya had been exterminated but the Shia were still a doubtful quantity. Many had supported the rebellion against the Umaiyids in the belief that a descendant of Ali would be made khalif with the result that they were now disillusioned. In so uncertain a situation, the prestige of Abu Muslim with the Khurasan army was dangerously great.

Abu Jafar approached his brother the khalif with the suggestion that Abu Muslim should be murdered. "If you do not lunch off him today, he will dine off you tomorrow," he said. The Blood-Shedder hesitated, not indeed from conscientious scruples, but from the fear that such an action might precipitate the very crisis which both brothers feared, a mutiny of the Khurasan army. Abu Jafar and Abu Muslim continued to eye one another with suspicion.

In May 754, Abu Jafar set out on the pilgrimage to Mecca, accompanied by Abu Muslim. Before the departure of the convoy, Saffah nominated his brother as his first successor in the khalifate, with his nephew Isa ibn Musa after him. In the same month Abdulla ibn Ali, the governor of Syria and massacrer of Beni Umaiya, marched northwards with an army. His object was to prove the religious fervour of the new dynasty by resuming the old Umaiyid custom of an annual summer raid into Byzantine territory.

The Khalif Saffah died of small-pox on 9th June, 754, while his brother and heir was still absent on the pilgrimage. He was thirty-four years of age and had ruled for four and a half years.

* * *

We may well be horrified at the brutality of the Umaiyids, the chopping off of heads, hands and feet and the cold-blooded massacres of prisoners taken in battle, particularly when they too were Arabs and Muslims. The Abbasid missionaries had never ceased whispering to their sympathizers that the family of the Prophet would come and put an end to all these horrors. In their messages, they drew an almost Messianic picture of the Hashimite Saviours, who would establish over the whole earth the reign of peace, charity and justice. In those blood-soaked times, it was largely these dreams which had swept the Abbasids triumphantly into power.

There is irony in the fact that the first representative of the family which was to have ushered in this new millennium was the cold and calculating Saffah, the Blood-Shedder.[8] In fact the Abbasids, at the height of their power,

8. Profesor Duri thinks that the title the Blood-Shedder should more properly be applied to Abdulla ibn Ali, the perpetrator of the Damascus massacre.

were to rule by force even more ruthlessly than the Umaiyids. Disillusion-
ment was not long in spreading, even in spite of the propaganda which the
new dynasty continued to use.

"Would that we could bring back the 'oppression' of Beni Merwan,
        And consign the 'justice' of Beni Abbas to hell-fire."
sang Abu al Attar, a contemporary poet.

Beni Umaiya had indeed done their share of blood-letting but they had
been violent rather than treacherous. In general they had clung to the old
Arab traditions of hospitality and the sacred inviolability of the guest. We
have seen how Sulaiman ibn Abdul Malik appealed to his brother Waleed I
not to disgrace him by arresting his guest, Yezeed ibn Muhallab. Yet the
first Abbasids deliberately invited all Beni Umaiya to a banquet of reconciliation in order to massacre them. It is interesting to recollect that their ancestor
Abbas, the Prophet's uncle, seems also to have been of a somewhat tortuous
character.

It is indeed distressing to mark the progress of treachery in the empire.
The early Muslims were extremely scrupulous in honouring all their obliga-
tions to the letter, even when to do so reacted to their own disadvantage.
Moreover they observed the same rigid and simple honesty in their dealings
with Jews, Christians and heathen as with their fellow Muslims. As the
Umaiyid period advanced, there were a few cases of a perhaps slightly doubtful character, but nothing in the records of Beni Umaiya could be compared
with the massacre at the Damascus banquet or the killing of Yezeed ibn
Hubeira at Wasit.

A peculiar feature of Saffah, as it had been of Merwan, was his indifference
to women. He had only one wife, whom he consulted frequently on current
affairs, but he never took a second nor made use of slave-girls or concubines.
He was generous with money and had pleasant manners. He enjoyed witty
conversation and would sit up nearly all night with his intimates, telling and
hearing anecdotes, reciting poetry or discussing the history of the great kings
of antiquity. Perhaps we may conclude that Saffah was purely an intellectual,
guided by logic, and lacking in emotions or the weaknesses bred by affection
or pity. All accounts agree that he was a man of a most determined personality.

*   *   *

We must, moreover, avoid the mistake of comparing the crudities of Arab
rule in the seventh century with the régimes of modern states and deducing
that they were unfit to govern. To place these events in due perspective, we
may briefly notice certain contemporary incidents in Byzantium. The Qoran
sanctioned the principle of retaliation, an eye for an eye and a tooth for a
tooth, though Muhammad added that the man who could voluntarily forego
his revenge would gain merit thereby. But the Byzantines professed Christianity, the religion of love, the religion of the Sermon on the Mount. Here
then are a few incidents in the history of Byzantium, which, at the time,
claimed to be the most civilized state in the Mediterranean world.

The Empress Irene, widow of Leo IV and mother of Constantine VI deposed and blinded her own son. Leo V, the Armenian, was proclaimed emperor by the army. He had a favourite by the name of Michael the Amorian. But Leo became suspicious of his friend Michael, and caused him to be arrested on Christmas Eve on a charge of conspiracy. He was immediately sentenced to have an ape tied to him, the pair of them being fastened to a pole. He was then to be thrown into the furnace which heated the palace baths. The next morning, however, the Emperor Leo was assassinated in church, while singing the Christmas office. Michael the Amorian found himself suddenly dragged from a dungeon to the purple. Fearing lest they should ever attempt to regain their father's throne, Michael gave orders for the castration of the four sons of Leo. One of them died during the operation.

The Emperor Michael II, like the Khalif Waleed II, was constantly drunk. Like Waleed also, he amused himself by mocking at religion and was alleged to have dressed up a pig (or perhaps some boon companion nicknamed The Pig), as a bishop and made it conduct divine service. This Michael II was assassinated by Basil the Macedonian, who then succeeded him as emperor.

The Emperor Nicephorus Phocas was murdered in his sleep by his wife. Three hours after the murder of her husband, the Empress caused her lover John Zimisces, to be proclaimed emperor.

When the Emperor Basil II defeated the Bulgars, he took 15,000 prisoners of war, all of whose eyes were put out before they were sent back to their people.

Such incidents as these and many more, in the history of their Christian neighbours, may help us to see the brutalities of the Arabs in the light of the general morality of their times.

NOTABLE DATES

Accession of Merwan II	23rd November 744
Kufa seized by Kharijites	June 745
Mosul occupied by Kharijites	746
Battle of Kufar Tutha	746
Rebellion in Jordan suppressed	746
Abu Muslim comes out in open rebellion	June 747
Ibn Hubeira reoccupies Kufa	747
Hejaz reconquered from Kharijites	748
Qais–Yemen civil war in Khurasan	745–748
Abu Muslim ruler of Khurasan	March 748
Rebels under Qahtaba take Rei	August 748
Battle of Isfahan	Spring 749
Qahtaba captures Nehawand	May 749
Imam Ibrahim executed by Merwan	August 749
Qahtaba takes Kufa	October 749
Saffah acclaimed khalif in Kufa	28 October, 749
Battle of the Zab	25 January, 750
Fall of Damascus	June 750
Death of Merwan	5 August, 750
Death of Khalif Saffah	9 June, 754

PERSONALITIES

The Khalif Merwan II, surnamed "The Ass"

The Imam Ibrahim, son of Muhammad ibn Ali the Abbasid

Yezeed ibn Hubeira, Merwan's governor of Iraq

Abu Muslim, organizer of the Abbasid rebellion in Persia

Qahtaba ibn Shabeeb, commander of the Abbasid army in Persia

Khalid ibn Barmak of Balkh, one of his subordinates

The Khalif Saffah (Abdulla abu al Abbas), the Shedder of Blood

Abdulla ibn Ali the Abbasid, victor of the Zab, governor of
   Damascus, uncle of Saffah

Abu Jafar, brother of the Khalif Saffah

XIII

Old Farthings

Whereas the Umaiyids had been little more than the heads of a turbulent Arabian aristocracy, their successors reverted to the old type of Oriental despotism with which the Persians had been familiar since the days of Darius and Xerxes.　　　　　NICHOLSON, *Literary History of the Arabs*

Kings will be tyrants from policy, when subjects are rebels from principle.
　　　　　　　EDMUND BURKE

In 762, Al Mansur laid the foundation stone of his new capital, Baghdad. As if called into existence by a magician's wand, this city fell heir to the power and prestige of Ctesiphon, Babylon, Nineveh, Ur and other capitals of the ancient Orient, and attained a degree of prestige and splendour unrivalled in the Middle Ages, except perhaps by Constantinople.
　　　　　　　HITTI, *History of the Arabs*

XIII

OLD FARTHINGS

ABU JAFAR was still on the Meccan pilgrimage when news reached him of the death of the Khalif Saffah. He returned hastily to Kufa and then to Anbar, being proclaimed khalif with the title of Mansoor,[1] The Victorious, and accepting the oaths of allegiance of the citizens. Meanwhile his uncle, Abdulla ibn Ali, had, as already mentioned, set out to raid the Byzantine Empire. Before he reached the frontier, however, he too learned of the death of Saffah. Summoning his officers to a conference, he announced his own candidature and was forthwith acclaimed by his army as the new Prince of the Faithful. Turning their backs on the enemy, the troops marched back to the Jezira.

In this crisis, the Khalif Mansoor had recourse to Abu Muslim whom, three months earlier, he had advised his brother to have murdered. For there were many Arabs and Syrians in the army of Abdulla ibn Ali and the khalif realized that, once again, he must depend for victory on the Khurasan army, over which Abu Muslim enjoyed unrivalled authority. The two armies confronted one another near Nisibin in the Jezira, but so equally were they matched that both hesitated to risk all in a pitched battle. After several months of manoeuvring, a general engagement eventually took place in December 754, in which, as a result of Abu Muslim's superior generalship, the khalif's army gained a complete victory.

"What are we to do now?" exclaimed Abdulla ibn Ali to an Arab supporter, as his army broke into flight.

"I remember," replied his candid companion, "how you said after the Battle of the Zab, 'May God curse Merwan, for he was afraid and ran away.' It seems to me that, after that remark, you had better fight on till you are killed." The advice was rejected, however, and the khalif's wicked uncle hastened from the field and eventually sought refuge with his brother, Sulaiman ibn Ali, who was governor of Basra.

Yet Abu Muslim's great victory did nothing to reassure the Khalif Mansoor, as I shall henceforward call him, for he was more afraid of Abu Muslim than he had been of his uncle Abdulla ibn Ali. Abu Muslim was dangerous owing to his influence in Persia and with the Khurasan army. The khalif accordingly wrote him a flattering letter, congratulating him on so glorious a victory and informing him that he had nominated him governor of Syria and Egypt.

Abu Muslim, however, was far too acute to be taken in by so obvious a manoeuvre, intended to separate him from the troops from Khurasan, with

1. All the Abbasids were in the habit of taking a new title when they were proclaimed khalif, a practice confusing to the English reader. The custom was borrowed from Persia.

whom he possessed such high prestige. He accordingly replied briefly that he was returning to Khurasan. Should he do so, thought Mansoor, he would be in a position to defy the khalif, for most of the troops on whom the Abbasids now relied were Persians. He therefore sent him a deputation of the younger members of Beni Abbas, with fulsome invitations to visit him on his way.

Abu Muslim was suspicious. His officers advised him not to go. In the end, after long deliberations, he decided to accept. Mansoor was sitting alone in a tent to receive him, having first concealed four trusted men of his body-guard behind the curtains. When he clapped his hands, they were to step out and strike. When Abu Muslim entered, the Prince of the Faithful began to reprove and to scold him but he replied apologetically and endeavoured to kiss the hand of the khalif, who, however, eluded the gesture and clapped his hands together. The four soldiers emerged and fell upon their victim, while Mansoor screamed, "Strike him. Strike him." Abu Muslim's last words were alleged to have been, "Forgive me," but whether he was seeking pardon from God or from Mansoor cannot now be known. His body was rolled up in a carpet and dropped into the Tigris on the banks of which the camp had been pitched near Medain.

Some anxiety was felt as to the attitude of the army, but the khalif distributed sums of money among a number of senior officers and the affair passed without any immediate unfortunate reactions. Having disposed of the man to whom he owed his throne, the Prince of the Faithful felt more confident. Whether Abu Muslim was in reality a menace to the dynasty or a selfless and dedicated servant, we shall now never know.

The name of Abu Muslim was long remembered and venerated in Persia, particularly by the sect of the Khurramites, of whom we shall hear more in a later chapter. Some of these sectaries even believed that he would return one day to the earth as the promised mehedi who would usher in the reign of peace and justice.

The Abbasids had been so fully engaged in the revolutionary struggle and then in disposing of Abu Muslim, that summer raids into Byzantine territory had been discontinued. In the first summer after the accession of Mansoor, the Emperor Constantine V Copronymus (whose-name-is-dung) turned the tables upon the Arabs. It was the Byzantines who carried out the summer raid and captured and destroyed Malatia. The following year the town was rebuilt by the Arabs but there were to be virtually no more summer raids into Byzantine territory for another seven years to come.

Mansoor's uncle, Abdulla ibn Ali, had laid claim to the khalifate for himself on the death of Saffah but had been defeated by Abu Muslim and had taken refuge with his brother Sulaiman ibn Ali in Basra. From thence he had sent his oath of allegiance to the khalif. In 756, the latter invited Abdulla ibn Ali and the principal officers who had supported him to come to him in Kufa under safe conduct. No sooner did they arrive than Abdulla was thrown into prison and most of the remainder of the officers were beheaded. Abdulla was later murdered in custody.

Curiously enough, although it was an army of Khurasanis which had been the means of raising the Abbasids to supreme power, dissidence in the province continued, as it had in Umaiyid days. There was a note of pathos in the rising in Khurasan, in which the rebels alleged that they had brought the Prophet's family to power in order to establish the rule of mercy and justice, not in order to raise another régime of blood-thirsty tyrants. Such insolent remarks on the part of subjects could not be tolerated, and the movement was quickly suppressed. The Messianic dreams which had given rise to the general revolution against the Umaiyids had doubtless now been dispelled. If the Abbasids were no worse than the Umaiyids, they certainly did not seem to be any better. But at any rate they were now firmly in the saddle, and regrets were no longer of any value.

One class of men had certainly gained by the change and these were the Persian converts to Islam, to whom, under the Umaiyids, social equality with the Arabs had always been denied. Now they held many of the most important government positions, including that of chief collector of taxes, which was filled by Khalid ibn Barmak, a native of Balkh who, as we have seen, had come to Iraq in the army sent by Abu Muslim.

* * *

In the almost universal massacre of Beni Umaiya, one youth had escaped. His name was Abdul Rahman ibn Muawiya, and he was a grandson of the Khalif Hisham. It will be recollected that Abdulla ibn Ali had issued a proclamation offering an amnesty to Beni Umaiya and inviting them to a banquet in Damascus. Some eighty Umaiyids had accepted and had been butchered in the banqueting hall. Abdul Rahman and his brother Yahya were suspicious of the proffered armistice and did not go to the palace. Their absence was noticed, however, and troops were immediately sent to apprehend and kill them. Yahya was seized and put to death, but by a fortunate coincidence Abdul Rahman was out hunting when the soldiers arrived. Warned by a faithful retainer, he was able to escape to a country house which he owned on the Euphrates. But a few days later the black banners were seen approaching and the prince had only just time to escape on foot with a younger brother and lie up in a wooded copse on the river bank. A slave, however, guided the soldiers to the hiding place of the fugitives and soon a troop of cavalry arrived at a gallop and surrounded the wood. The two princes threw themselves into the Euphrates, but the younger of the two brothers was soon exhausted. The soldiers called to him to come back, promising not to harm him and the youth turned in to the bank. No sooner did he struggle out of the water than he was immediately beheaded. Abdul Rahman emerged alone and exhausted on the other bank.

Travelling by himself, he reached Palestine unrecognized, and was there joined by two devoted servants, Bedr and Salim, who also brought money and jewels concealed in their clothing. Reaching Egypt, the three wanderers, after many narrow escapes, arrived in Barqa, where, for a time, they lay hidden. The ruler of Ifriqiya at the time was one Abdul Rahman ibn Habeeb, who had seized power in the confusion caused by the Abbasid revolution. A great-grandson of the famous Uqba ibn Nafi, founder of Qairawan, he hoped in the general anarchy to establish for himself an independent kingdom in

Ifriqiya. Discovering two other Umaiyid fugitives, sons of the dissolute Khalif Waleed II, Ibn Habeeb seized and killed them. Warned by the fate of his relatives, Abdul Rahman and his faithful servant Bedr (for Salim had gone back to Syria) took refuge with the Berbers of the Atlas mountains. Finally after five years of penniless wandering, the two hunted fugitives reached Ceuta near the Straits of Gibraltar, and conceived the idea of crossing to Spain, where there were many chiefs and freedmen of Beni Umaiya. We have already seen that, in Arab society, freedmen were under a moral obligation to serve, from generation to generation, the descendants of the man who had first given his freedom to their slave ancestor.

Bedr accordingly crossed to Spain to sound the readiness of the Syrians and the Umaiyid freedmen established there to support the fugitive prince. The freedmen, as was their sacred duty, immediately declared themselves ready to sacrifice their lives for their patrons. The governor of Spain at the time was of the Qaisite faction, so two chiefs of the freedmen made tentative approaches to that party but with no success. The Yemenites, however, being as it were out of office, offered their willing assistance. Bedr hastened back to Africa where, after an absence of several months, he was welcomed by his anxious master. An immediate embarkation for Spain was decided upon, and, in September 755, Abdul Rahman landed at Al Munecar, some forty-five miles east of Malaga.

The governor of Andalus [2] was Yusuf al Fihri, who also claimed descent from the famous Uqba ibn Nafi, the early conqueror of Ifriqiya. When Abdul Rahman landed in the south, Yusuf had been campaigning in the Saragossa area, but returned to his capital in Cordova on hearing of the prince's arrival. He was a man lacking in decision and, instead of instantly attacking the invader and his handful of supporters, he sent emissaries to negotiate, offering the hand of his daughter and a landed estate to Abdul Rahman, if he would undertake not to lay claim to the position of ruler of the country. The negotiations failed, the mission returned to Cordova, but, as the winter had set in, the governor postponed military action until the weather should be favourable.

In the spring, Abdul Rahman was the first to take the field. It was fortunate for him that the southern area of Andalus was largely inhabited by Arabs of Syria, including the divisions of Damascus, Homs and Jordan. Many of these joined his forces as did also the majority of the Yemenites, and in the middle of March he occupied Seville, where he accepted the oaths of allegiance of many adherents. By this time, however, Yusuf the governor was marching on Seville, following the northern bank of the Guadalquivir, the Arabic Wadi al Kabir, which means the Great River.

On Friday, 14th May, 756, the two armies faced one another at Musara, on the bank of the river. The struggle was of brief duration. The supporters of the Umaiyid prince rapidly pierced the enemy's line, the governor took refuge in flight and Abdul Rahman entered Cordova in triumph, led the prayers in the great mosque and preached the sermon to the assembled

---

2. The name Andalusia seems to have been derived from the Vandals who had conquered it three hundred and fifty years before.

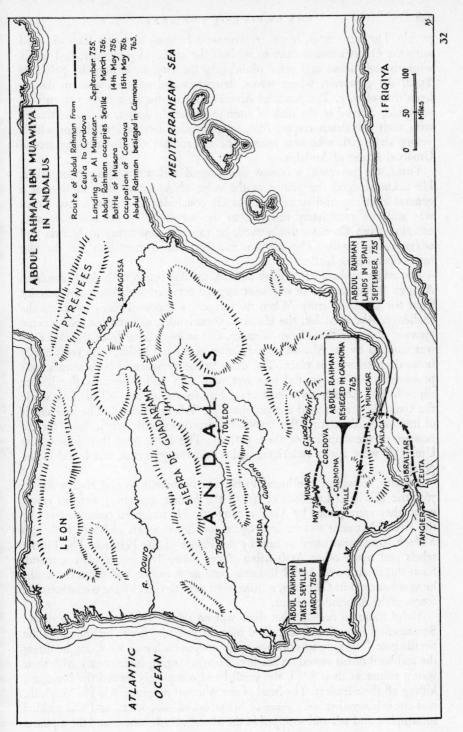

ABDUL RAHMAN IBN MUAWIYA
IN ANDALUS

Route of Abdul Rahman from
Ceuta to Cordova.   September 755.
Landing at Al Munecar.   March 756.
Abdul Rahman occupies Seville   14th May 756.
Battle of Musara   15th May 756.
Occupation of Cordova
Abdul Rahman besieged in Carmona   763.

PYRENEES

SARAGOSSA

R. Ebro

LEON

ATLANTIC
OCEAN

R. Douro

R. Tagus

SIERRA DE GUADARAMA

TOLEDO

MERIDA

R. Guadiana

A N D A L U S

R. Guadalquivir

CORDOVA

MUSARA
MAY 756

SEVILLE

ABDUL RAHMAN TAKES SEVILLE
MARCH 756

CARMONA

ABDUL RAHMAN
BESIEGED IN CARMONA
763

MALAGA

AL MUNECAR

GIBRALTAR

CEUTA

TANGIER

ABDUL RAHMAN
LANDS IN SPAIN
SEPTEMBER. 755

MEDITERRANEAN SEA

IFRIQIYA

0   50   100
Miles

32

people. The Yemenites, however, who were fighting to satisfy their old feud with the Qaisites rather than to support the Umaiyid pretender, had meanwhile broken loose and were plundering the city, including the palace of Yusuf the governor, whose wives, daughters and servants were in danger from the soldiery. The youthful Abdul Rahman, for he was only twenty-six years old, arrived in the nick of time to rescue the ladies, whom he treated with such chivalrous respect that, in gratitude, they presented him with a young slave girl, who was later to be the mother of Hisham, the second Umaiyid Ameer of Andalus.

Yusuf, the governor, was now discouraged and was willing to negotiate. He acknowledged the prince as the ruler of Andalus, on condition of a general amnesty, and peace was quickly concluded in July 756. But Yusuf was still not completely resigned to the surrender of his authority and, escaping from Cordova unobserved, he raised a new army at Merida and advanced on Seville. The garrison marched out to meet him and the two forces drew up for battle.

According to the ancient Arab custom, the day began with single combats. A huge Berber freedman of Yusuf stepped forward and defied any warrior from the Umaiyid army. When no volunteers appeared ready to accept the challenge, Abdul Malik, the Umaiyid commander, ordered his son to come forward and save them from disgrace. But as he stepped from the ranks, he was stopped by an Abyssinian freedman of Abdul Malik, who respectfully insisted on taking his place. The duel, in the presence of both armies, was prolonged, but the ground was wet with rain and eventually the Berber slipped. The Abyssinian leaped upon him in a flash and killed him, while the Umaiyid army raised a great shout of "Allahu Akbar". The incident is of interest as illustrating the devotion of freedmen and their jealousy for the honour of the families of their patrons. The battle was then joined, the Umaiyids were again victorious, and Yusuf the governor was killed in the pursuit.

Andalus, however, continued to be rent by rebellions and civil wars. In 763, the Fihrites (the tribes of Yusuf the former governor) were in revolt when they were joined by Ala ibn Mughith. He had been commissioned by the Khalif Mansoor to take over Spain for the Abbasids and bore with him a black banner entrusted to him by the Prince of the Faithful. The Fihrite rebels and many other Arab tribes placed themselves under his command. Soon the situation of Abdul Rahman became desperate and for two months he was besieged in Carmona, a little town near Seville, by the overwhelming forces of the Abbasid governor.

Abdul Rahman decided that there was no alternative but victory or death. Summoning seven hundred picked men, he caused a fire to be lighted by the Seville gate. The gate was thrown open, and, as each man went out, he threw the scabbard of his sword on the fire. Then, charging impetuously with their young prince at their head, the small band completely routed the besiegers, killing all their leaders. The head of the Abbasid nominee, Ala ibn Mughith, was cut off, together with those of his principal supporters, and was pickled in camphor and salt and wrapped in the khalif's black banner and the diploma appointing Ala to be governor of Andalus. A label was attached to one ear of each head, stating the name and rank of its former owner. Wrapped up in a sack, the gruesome parcel was despatched by a well-paid messenger and eventually reached the Khalif Mansoor, who is alleged when he received it to have thanked God that so grim an enemy as Abdul Rahman the Umaiyid was so far away beyond the sea. Thus only thirteen years after the seizure of power by the Abbasids, the empire was already beginning to break up.

*　　*　　*

In 762, there occurred yet another of those inefficient but tragic risings of the descendants of Ali ibn abi Talib. It will be recollected that Abu Muslim's propaganda had employed the slogan of "The Family", which many Shiites had assumed to mean the family of Ali. When, therefore, the revolution terminated in the khalifate of the family of Abbas, the adherents of Ali considered themselves to have been deceived. There were two young men in Medina at the time, Muhammad and Ibrahim, the sons of Abdulla ibn Hasan ibn Hasan ibn Ali ibn abi Talib, who were alleged to have expressed themselves forcibly on the subject.[3]

Mansoor, as we have seen, had gone to Mecca on the pilgrimage in 754 and was still so engaged when he was notified of the death of Saffah and of his own elevation to the khalifate. When he was in Mecca on this pilgrimage, he noticed that neither Muhammad nor Ibrahim had called on him to pay their respects.

In the year 761, the Khalif Mansoor again performed the pilgrimage and, when in the Hejaz, demanded the presence of Muhammad and Ibrahim, to whom he offered safe conduct. Muhammad, however, in his reply, enquired bitterly whether the safe conduct was the same as that offered to Ibn Hubaira, to the Khalif's uncle Abdulla ibn Ali, and to Abu Muslim. When the two young men did not give themselves up, their father and twelve other men descended from Hasan the son of Ali ibn abi Talib were arrested. Some were flogged up to one hundred lashes, their property was seized and they were sent to prison in Kufa. Abdulla ibn Hasan, father of the two youths, was actually flogged in the presence of the Khalif Mansoor, remarking defiantly, "This is not the way we treated your prisoners at Bedr."[4] Seeing the violence of the khalif against them, the two youths took to the mountains of the Hejaz. Many of the descendants of Hasan died in prison.

Muhammad, in his propaganda, had pointed out that he was descended from Fatima, the Prophet's daughter, whereas Mansoor's mother was a Berber concubine. Mansoor's retort was that the Shia themselves believed that the imamate descended from father to son. Thus descent through females did not count. Eventually Muhammad raised the banner of revolt in the Hejaz at the end of September 762, quickly seizing Medina and Mecca. Ibrahim had left for Basra, intending to raise a revolt there also. The supporters of Beni Ali appeared dressed in white.

3. Genealogical tree, p. 240.
4. The remark had a peculiar sting. Bedr was the first battle fought by the Prophet Muhammad against the unbelievers. Abbas, ancestor of the Abbasid khalifs, was fighting for the heathen and was taken prisoner by Muhammad, but was well-treated.

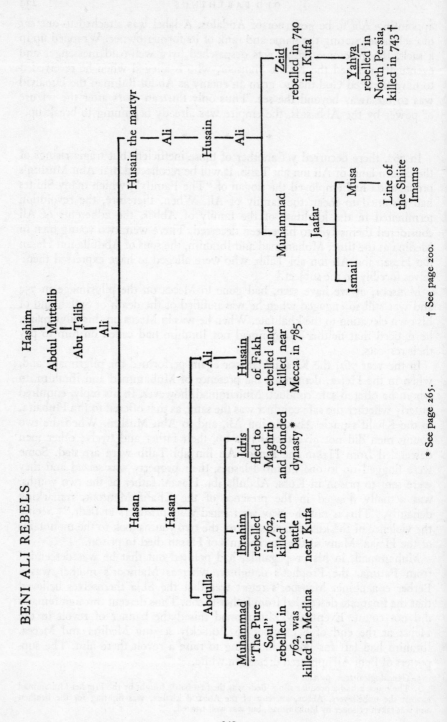

BENI ALI REBELS

* See page 265.

† See page 200.

Mansoor, when he received the news of the rising, is said to have consulted a veteran commander of the wars of Merwan as to what military action he should adopt. Informed that the centre of the revolt was in Medina, the old man replied, "Praise God! A place where is neither food, nor arms nor men. Send one of your freedmen to Wadi al Qura and cut off their communications with Damascus and it will all peter out."

This eighth-century summary of the situation is of especial interest to us because in the First World War the Turks concentrated a large force in Medina. The Ameer Feisal and T. E. Lawrence operated in the area north of Wadi al Qura and caused the Turkish operations to peter out by cutting their communications with Damascus. So little had strategy changed in the intervening twelve centuries.

The Khalif Mansoor, however, was not prepared to starve the rebels into surrender. He despatched his nephew, Isa ibn Musa ibn Muhammad,[5] with a large army from Kufa across the Arabian desert. A considerable part of the force consisted of Khurasanis.

Muhammad ibn Abdulla ibn Hasan, proclaimed khalif in Medina, was soon in difficulties. One of his supporters urged him to march on Egypt, which he could possibly have seized and which would have provided him with the sinews of war. But he declared that, as a descendant of the Prophet, he would defend the Prophet's city against the enemies of God. Nearly a century and a half earlier, Muhammad himself had defended Medina against an attack by the unbelievers and to do so had dug a ditch. Apparently for religious reasons, the Prophet's ditch was redug, though such a measure was useless against the Abbasid regular army.

At the end of December 762, Isa ibn Musa appeared with his army outside Medina, and summoned the rebels to surrender. Both sides invited the other to accept God's book and the Traditions of the Prophet, almost a routine formality for, of course, both claimed that they were already doing so. The Abbasid army then took up its battle positions round the city and a one-hour bombardment by mangonels and arrows followed. As the rival forces drew nearer to one another, champions rode forward challenging to single combat. A knight, clad in armour, emerged from the Abbasid line, but from the Medina force a man on foot came out to meet him, inviting the knight to dismount, as his challenger had no horse. The invitation was accepted, the man in armour dismounted, sent back his horse and was killed by his rival in a duel on foot.

When the single combats were over, Humaid ibn Qahtaba, son of the commander who had led Abu Muslim's army from Khurasan to Kufa, was placed in charge of the attack. When the column reached the ditch, a number of doors, wrenched from neighbouring houses, were used to bridge it to enable the cavalry to cross. The two armies then joined in a desperate hand-to-hand struggle which lasted from morning till the late afternoon.

Muhammad, with surprising generosity, had absolved from their oaths all those who had sworn him allegiance and had informed them that they could flee if they wished. Many people of Medina, gathering their women and

5. Genealogical tree, page 222.

children, escaped to the surrounding mountains, fearing a bombardment or the sack of the city. The Abbasid army, wrote an eye witness, was all dressed in black, and as it moved in a great mass towards the city, it looked as if the lava-strewn slopes of the volcanic Hejazi mountains were flowing across the plain.

By the afternoon it was evident that resistance could not continue much longer. Muhammad—a curiously modern touch—burned his secret correspondence and the nominal roll of his supporters. The tribe of Juheina had been one of the first to support the Prophet Muhammad and had now rallied to his descendant. Three hundred men of the tribe prepared to make a last stand. Muhammad gave them permission to escape but they refused. As they rode towards the enemy, the black Abbasid banner floated out over the Prophet's mosque behind them. Another enemy column had turned their flank and had broken into the city. The heroic three hundred dismounted, each man hamstrung his horse to make it impossible for him to escape, and threw away his scabbard. Three times they charged the black ranks with ever-dwindling numbers and then they were overrun. Muhammad was slashed across the head with a sword. He dropped to his knees with a bitter cry, "Alas, I am the son of your Prophet, wounded, persecuted and denied." Then a soldier ran him through. Humaid ibn Qahtaba hastened up to cut off his head, which was sent back to Isa and by him, by a special messenger, to the Khalif Mansoor. We do not know much about Muhammad ibn Abdulla ibn Hasan, who was nicknamed "The Pure Soul", but he appears to have been genuinely religious. A brother of his, Idris[6] ibn Abdulla, was to escape to Africa, where we shall hear of him again.

In accordance with the orders of the khalif, Isa ibn Musa declared an amnesty and prevented all looting. The Umaiyids had earned too much hatred by their severity to the Prophet's city to encourage the Abbasids to follow their example. Only the property of the descendants of Hasan the son of Ali was confiscated. It was December 762, the rebellion had lasted a little less than three months, and had shown all the typical heroism and ineptitude of Beni Ali.

Meanwhile Ibrahim, the brother of Muhammad, was to have raised a simultaneous rebellion in Basra. Instead of crossing the desert, he appears to have travelled through Damascus and Mosul and down the Tigris. Owing to the length of the journey, Ibrahim did not reach Basra until December 762, when the Abbasid army was already in Medina. As soon as the standard of revolt was raised in Basra, the Khalif Mansoor summoned Isa ibn Musa back in hot haste to Kufa.

Ibrahim seized Ahwaz and even the Persian province of Fars and marched on Kufa with a considerable army. Isa ibn Musa arrived in the nick of time, when Ibrahim's rebel army was only a few miles from Kufa, and the Khalif Mansoor was completing his preparations to escape to Rei in Northern Persia. In a battle outside Kufa, Ibrahim's first attack drove back the Abbasid army and victory, for the first time, seemed to be almost within the grasp of the descendants of Ali. Then a man somewhere drew a bow at a venture. A

6. Pronounced Idrees.

stray arrow struck Ibrahim in the throat, and he fell forward, embracing the neck of his horse. His followers hastily dismounted and laid him on the ground, but in a few minutes he was dead. His troops fell into confusion and the Abbasids counter-attacked. Next morning in Kufa, the Khalif Mansoor received his guests at a levée with the severed head of Ibrahim, great-great-grandson, of the Apostle of God, resting in his hands.

* * *

When Muhammad and Ibrahim had raised their rebellion against Mansoor, the former had sent one of his sons to Sind, the governor of which, Umar ibn Hafs, was believed to be favourable to the cause of the descendants of Ali. Umar, who enjoyed a high reputation as a soldier, welcomed the message and a day was fixed on which he agreed to appear in public with his staff in white clothing and to renounce his loyalty to the family of Abbas. The day before the coup was to take place, however, news was received of the defeat of the rebels and of the death of Muhammad. The white clothes and banners were secreted away and the son of Muhammad took refuge with a Hindu prince in India.

But news of the intended *coup d'état* in Sind had reached Mansoor, who despatched an angry reproof to the governor. Umar ibn Hafs collected his relatives about him and read out to them the khalif's letter, inviting their opinions as to the safest course to pursue. A young member of the family volunteered to sacrifice himself. He suggested that the governor arrest him and put him in prison, and then write to the khalif laying the blame for the conspiracy on him. "If he kills me," said the youth, "I shall know at least that I have died to save you all"—a remarkable example of family loyalty. After some hesitation the suggestion was adopted and the report sent. The khalif replied, ordering the despatch of the prisoner in chains. He no sooner arrived than Mansoor ordered his immediate execution.

But Mansoor was still uneasy about the loyalty of the governor of Sind and was casting about in his mind for a suitable candidate with whom to replace him, when a certain Hisham ibn Amr of the tribe of Taghlib asked for an audience. When admitted he began, "I have been noticing my sister in the house lately, and what I have seen of her beauty, her intelligence and her piety have made me think that she might make a worthy wife for the Prince of the Faithful." The khalif dismissed his visitor, promising to notify him of his decision later, and then turning to one of his confidants, remarked, "I would like to marry that girl, if it were not for a verse of the poet Jareer.[7]

" 'Don't take Taghlib as brothers-in-law,
For as in-laws the negroes are more noble than they.'

"I am afraid, if I married this girl, that she might bear me a son and that people would put him to shame by reciting this verse. But go after Hisham and tell him that I am grateful for his thoughtfulness. I do not need another

7. Jareer had been court poet to Hajjaj in Iraq, and subsequently to the Khalif Abdul Malik ibn Merwan.

wife at the moment, but you can inform him that, in return for his kindness, I have made him governor of Sind."

The story is of interest, not only as showing how governors were chosen by the Abbasids, but as illustrating the extraordinary fear which the Arabs always entertained of being disgraced by the sarcasms of a poet. Even the Prophet himself had been sensitive to these attacks. Taghlib was one of the oldest and the noblest of the Arab tribes and the poet's vituperation had been completely unjustified. Hisham the Taghlibi was, however, sent as governor to Sind. Umar ibn Hafs was transferred directly from Sind to the governorship of Ifriqiya, where we shall hear of him again in the next chapter.

* * *

The most famous act of Mansoor, and one which affected the whole future of the Arab Empire, was the founding of Baghdad. During the thirteen years since their seizure of power, the Abbasids had been without a capital. Damascus, so long devoted to the Umaiyids, would have been too precarious. The Abbasids had been brought to power by an army from Khurasan. Mansoor, as we have seen, had intended to withdraw to North Persia in the event of his defeat by Ibrahim the Aliid. He only felt safe when his Persian supporters were near at hand, yet, with an empire extending westwards to the Atlantic, a capital situated behind the mountains of Persia would have been too far removed from the centre of his dominions. These considerations indicated the fertile valley of the Tigris and Euphrates as the solution, and Saffah, as we have seen, began his reign in a palace outside Kufa and then moved to Anbar. The Kufans, however, were too unreliable to be pleasant neighbours, in addition to which many of them were Shiites.

Mansoor undertook long personal reconnaissances, extending as far north as Mosul, to find the ideal site for a new capital, eventually selecting a position on the west bank of the Tigris, where the city of Baghdad still stands. The Euphrates and the Tigris at this point approach to within twenty miles of one another. In the eighth century the navigable Isa canal from the Euphrates joined the Tigris at this point. Thus the products of Syria could reach Baghdad by water down the Euphrates from Aleppo and Raqqa, for the river appears in those days to have been readily navigable.[8] In the same manner, the trade with India and the Persian Gulf could come up the Tigris by ship, while vessels bearing grain and foodstuffs from the Jezira could sail down the Tigris from Mosul. On the east, the main road from Persia descended from Hulwan on to the plains opposite the new capital. Thus Mansoor was right in praising the central position of Baghdad and in congratulating himself on his perspicacity in being the first to remark it.

But while Baghdad was central between Syria and Persia, it was far from being central between Spain, Morocco and Persia. As has already been explained, the boundary between East and West in the eighth century (and to some extent even today) did not lie along the Mediterranean coast but extended from the upper Euphrates to the Caucasus, the centuries-old frontier

8. It is now no longer navigable for practical purposes, as I can testify by experience, for I descended it in an Arab boat in 1924 with no little difficulty.

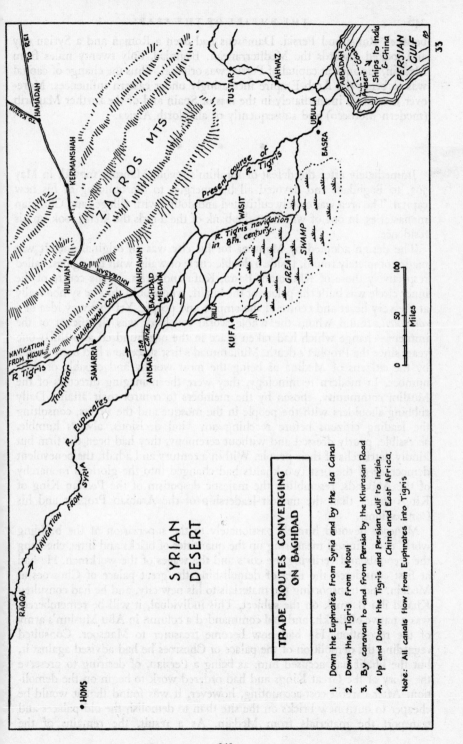

SYRIAN DESERT

HOMS

RAQQA

NAVIGATION FROM SYRIA

R. Euphrates

ThartharCanal

SAMARRA

ANBAR CANAL

ISA CANAL

HILLA

KUFA

BAGHDAD
MEDAIN

NAHRAWAN CANAL

NAVIGATION FROM MOSUL

R Tigris

HULWAN

KHURASAN RD

NAHRAWAN

KERMANSHAH

ZAGROS MTS

HAMADAN

TO REI

TO KAZVIN

Present course of R. Tigris

R. Tigris navigation in 8th century.

WASIT

GREAT SWAMP

BASRA

TUSTAR

AHWAZ

UBULLA

ABADAN

PERSIAN GULF

Ships to India & China

Persian Coast

0   50   100
Miles

TRADE ROUTES CONVERGING ON BAGHDAD

1. Down the Euphrates from Syria and by the Isa Canal
2. Down the Tigris from Mosul
3. By caravan to and from Persia by the Khurasan Road
4. Up and Down the Tigris and Persian Gulf to India, China and East Africa.

Note: All canals flow from Euphrates into Tigris

33

between Rome and Persia. Damascus had been a Roman and a Syrian city and looked towards the Mediterranean. Baghdad, only twenty miles from Medain, the ancient capital of Persia, was oriental. Thus the change of capital was to bring the Arab Empire increasingly under eastern influences. Moreover it resulted immediately in the loss of Spain and of the further Maghrib (modern Morocco) and subsequently of all North Africa.

*   *   *

Immediately after the defeat of Ibrahim's revolt, Mansoor moved, in May 763, to Baghdad, and devoted all his energies to the building of his new capital. The area was closely cultivated and dotted with villages and Christian monasteries, in one of which on the bank of the Tigris the khalif took up his residence.

The design adopted by Mansoor for his city was an original one. It was made completely round, inside a double circle of walls, with four gates, called respectively those of Khurasan, Basra, Kufa and Syria. In the centre of the inner circle was built the palace of the khalif, who would thus be symbolically at the very heart and centre of the empire and people. Yet this very idea of a *roi soleil*, round whom the whole world revolved, was significant of the immense change which had taken place in the one hundred and thirty-one years since the Prophet's death. Muhammad's first successors had been chosen by the citizens of Medina as being the most worthy and capable of their number. In modern terminology, they were the managing directors of the Muslim community, chosen by the members to control their affairs. Daily rubbing shoulders with the people in the mosque and the streets, consulting the leading citizens before reaching any vital decisions, always humble, accessible, poorly dressed and without ceremony, they had been the firm but kindly patriarchs of their people. Within a century and a half, the benevolent democracy of the first two khalifs had changed into the glorious monarchy of the Abbasids, resembling the majestic despotism of the Persian King of Kings rather than the modest leadership of the Arabian Prophet and his Companions.

Mansoor devoted himself passionately to the supervision of the building work, even himself measuring up the quantities of bricks and lime, checking the accounts and verifying the costs and the wages of the workmen. He had at first considered the idea of demolishing the great palace of Chosroes at Medain, and transporting the materials to his new city, and he had consulted Khalid ibn Barmak on the subject. This individual, it will be remembered, was a native of Balkh, and had commanded a column in Abu Muslim's army of the revolution. He had now become treasurer to Mansoor. Consulted regarding the demolition of the palace of Chosroes he had advised against it, but the khalif had accused him, as being a Persian, of desiring to preserve the glory of the Great Kings and had ordered work to begin on the demolition. After careful cost-accounting, however, it was found that it would be cheaper to burn new bricks on the site than to demolish the old palaces and transport the materials from Medain. As a result, the remains of the

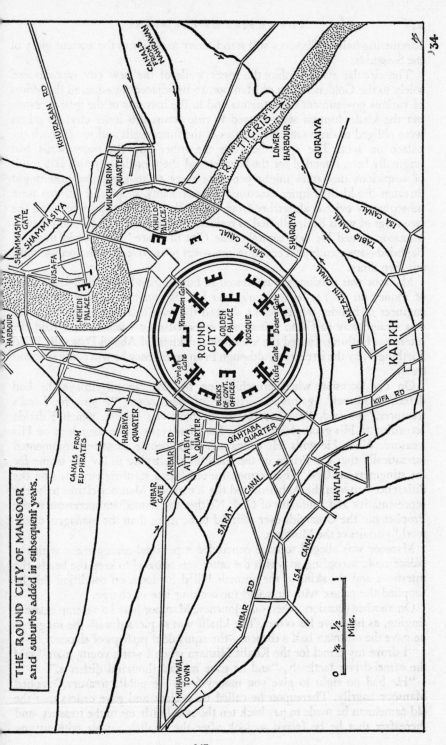

THE ROUND CITY OF MANSOOR
and suburbs added in subsequent years.

1   ¾   ½   ¼   0
Mile.

CANALS FROM KHARASAN NAHRAWAN

KHURASAN RD

MUKHARRIM QUARTER

SHAMMASIYA GATE

SHAMMASIYA

RUSAFA

KHULD PALACE

MEHEDI PALACE

UPPER HARBOUR

R. TIGRIS

LOWER HARBOUR

QURAIYA

SARAT CANAL

SHARQIYA

ISA CANAL

TABIQ CANAL

BATZIYIN CANAL

Khurāsān Gate

ROUND CITY

GOLDEN PALACE

MOSQUE

Syrian Gate

Dasra Gate

Kufa Gate

BLOCKS OF GOVT. OFFICES

KARKH

HARBIYA QUARTER

ANBAR RD

ATTABIYA QUARTER

ANBAR GATE

GAHTABA QUARTER

KUFA RD

HAYLANA

SARAT CANAL

ISA CANAL

ANBAR RD

MUHAWWAL TOWN

MUHAWWAL

247

34·

banqueting-hall of Chosroes still stand today to testify to the ancient glory of the Sassanids.

The circular space within the inner walls of the new city was devoted solely to the Golden Palace of Mansoor, to its adjacent mosque, to the offices of various government departments and to the barracks of the guards. None but the khalif himself was allowed to ride across this inner city; all others were obliged to dismount at the gates of the inner walls and to approach the palace on foot. The space between the inner and the outer walls had originally been intended for the bazaars and shops of the city but, as a result of suspicions that spies might penetrate there or that popular riots might threaten the khalif's inner sanctum, the merchants, shops and citizens were subsequently evicted altogether from the walled city, the space between the two rings of walls being allotted to residential houses for officers and officials. Mansoor named his new capital "The City of Peace" but the old name of Baghdad—apparently of Persian origin—was to survive in common use until our own times.

Mansoor was passionately interested in building and spent very large sums of money on it. Yet he was notorious for his parsimony. Woe betide any engineer or builder whose books showed the least financial irregularity. He was straightway cast into prison and emerged only when he had paid the uttermost farthing. Indeed the khalif was nicknamed Abu al Dawanik, "Old Farthings", by the irreverent, although in an emergency he was ready to spend freely.

On one occasion when preaching on the Meccan pilgrimage, he had defended himself against the charge of parsimony. "I am the Lord's treasurer," he said. "He has placed me over His tribute, which I divide according to His good pleasure. The Lord has verily made me a lock on His treasure. When He wills, He opens me." The people, however, commented sarcastically that the Prince of the Faithful was trying to lay the blame for his stinginess on God. This sermon indeed lays a startling emphasis on the difference between the Abbasids and the Umaiyids. Mansoor claims to be the representative and confidant of God. Neither the immediate successors of the Prophet nor the Umaiyids ever claimed to be more than the managers of the worldly affairs of the Muslims.

Mansoor was alleged to have concluded a personal arrangement with the palace cook, according to which the latter was allowed to keep the heads, the intestines and the skins of the animals killed for food, on condition that he supplied the palace with firewood for cooking free of charge.

On another occasion, when on a journey, Mansoor heard a veteran retainer singing, as he drove his camel. The khalif was so pleased with the song that he gave the old man half a dirhem—the equivalent perhaps of sixpence.

"I drove my camel for the Khalif Hisham when I was a young man," said the camel-driver tactlessly, "and he gave me ten thousand dirhems."

"He had no right to give you money from the public treasury," replied Mansoor angrily. Thereupon he called up a clerk and gave orders that the old camelman be made to pay back ten thousand dirhems to the treasury, and thereafter that he be forced to look after the khalif's camels without any wages at all. When speaking to a ruler, it is tactless to enlarge upon the virtues of his predecessor.

NOTABLE DATES

Accession of Mansoor	754
Abdul Rahman ibn Muawiya lands in Spain	755
Rebellion of Muhammad and Ibrahim, sons of Abdulla ibn Hasan	762
Abdul Rahman established as Ruler of Spain	763
Foundation of Baghdad	763

PERSONALITIES

The Khalif Mansoor
Abu Muslim, the leader of the revolution
Khalid ibn Barmak, the first of the Barmecids
Abdul Rahman ibn Muawiya, the Umaiyid who seized Spain
Ala ibn Mughith, appointed by Mansoor to be governor of Spain
Umar ibn Hafs, governor of Sind

XIV

Mehedi and Hadi

Amidst the riches of the East, the Abbasids soon disdained the abstinence and frugality of the first caliphs, and aspired to emulate the magnificence of the Persian kings.   GIBBON, *Decline and Fall of the Roman Empire*

To the Alids the Abbasid caliphs were usurpers, the rightful caliphs being the descendants of Ali and Fatima. The Alids never ceased to exercise a disruptive influence on the body politic of Islam.   HITTI, *History of the Arabs*

The ascendancy of the Persians over the Arabs, that is to say of the conquered over the victors, had already for a long while been in course of preparation; it became complete when the Abbasids, who owed their elevation to the Persians, ascended the throne. These princes made it a rule to be on their guard against the Arabs, and to put their trust only in foreigners.

DOZY, *Histoire de l'Islamisme*

XIV

MEHEDI AND HADI

WHEN we last considered Ifriqiya, we left Handhala ibn Safwan in charge as governor, after his gallant sortie from Qairawan, which had resulted in the suppression of the Berber rebellion of 740–742. Handhala remained governor until 745, when the outbreak of civil war between the Khalif Merwan and the Abbasids threw everything once more into confusion. Handhala seems to have left for Syria and a certain Abdul Rahman ibn Habeeb seized power, hoping, in the general anarchy, to found an independent dynasty. We have seen him arresting Umaiyid fugitives, whom he suspected as competitors in the foundation of an African kingdom.

In 755, however, Ibn Habeeb was assassinated, and Ifriqiya again descended into chaos, the Abbasids being too pre-occupied to spare any time for the distant provinces. A Berber tribe from the desert took Qairawan, the long-suffering people of which were subjected once again to massacre and plunder. Another Berber tribe, this time from Tripoli, drove out the first and established itself in Tripolitania and Qairawan.

It was not until August 761 that Muhammad ibn al Ashath, appointed Abbasid governor of Egypt under the Khalif Mansoor, at the head of an army of 40,000 men defeated these Berbers at Tawargha, between Barqa and Tripoli. He then re-occupied Qairawan and was able to establish control of Ifriqiya.

In 768, Mansoor appointed to the governorship of Ifriqiya that same Umar ibn Hafs, whom we have seen planning a *coup d'état* in Sind, in favour of the descendants of Ali. Umar was a descendant of the great Muhallab, once chastiser of the Kharijites and governor of Khurasan. Three years later, however, another general rising of Kharijite Berbers took place, and Qairawan was again surrounded, Umar ibn Hafs defending the unfortunate city with immense heroism. Eventually supplies were exhausted, and the garrison was reduced to the last extremity, while every night the whole plain outside the walls as far as the eye could reach, glittered with the camp fires of the innumerable hosts of the Berbers. But in spite of the demoralization of the garrison and the citizens alike, the dauntless courage of Umar ibn Hafs refused to admit the possibility of surrender.

Then one day in October 771 a messenger arrived, having crept through the Berber lines. He bore a letter to the gallant governor from his wife, informing him that the Khalif Mansoor was dissatisfied with his services and was sending a new governor with a fresh army to supersede him. Probably the Prince of the Faithful still suspected the loyalty of the former governor of Sind.

EVENTS IN IFRIQIYA & MAGHRIB
742-772

CASPIAN SEA

CAUCASUS

BLACK SEA

MOSUL

BAGHDAD

KUFA

ABBASIDS

ANQARA

BYZANTINE EMPIRE

MALATIA

TARSUS

SYRIA

DAMASCUS

CYPRUS

CONSTANTINOPLE

GREECE

AEGEAN SEA

RHODES

CRETE

ALEXANDRIA

FUSTAT

EGYPT

RED SEA

MEDITERRANEAN SEA

ADRIATIC SEA

ROME

SICILY

SYRACUSE

BARQA

Berbers defeated by Yezeed Ibn Hatim 772 & Qairawan recaptured

Berbers defeated by Ibn al Ashath. 761

TRIPOLI

TAWARGHA Aug 761

JENBI

Qairawan besieged & defended by Umar Ibn Hafs 771

QAIRAWAN

IFRIQIYA

ATLAS MTS

TAHERT

Independent Kharijite Principality of Ibn Rustem

SAHARA DESERT

GENOA

MARSEILLES

PARIS

TOURS

AUTUN

BORDEAUX

TOULOUSE

PYRENEES

SARAGOSSA

TOLEDO

ANDALUS

UMAIYID DYNASTY

CORDOVA

SEVILLE

TANGIER

WALILA (FEZ)

FEZ

TAZA

TLEMCEN

MAGHRIB

IDRISID DYNASTY

Independent Kharijite Principality of Ibn Medrar

SIJILMASSA

ATLANTIC OCEAN

0   100   200   300
Miles

254

After the heroic labours which Umar had endured for three years in Qairawan, his dismissal was a bitter disappointment. He decided not to survive the disgrace. Donning his armour and mounting his horse, he rode, lance in hand, out of the gate of the city, which for many months he had so gallantly defended. Charging alone into the innumerable Berber hordes, he fought single-handed until overwhelmed and killed. After the death of Umar ibn Hafs, Qairawan surrendered to the Berbers on terms.

When the news of this disaster reached him, the Khalif Mansoor went in person to Damascus and from there to Jerusalem, to organize the army which was to reconquer Ifriqiya. The command was entrusted to Yezeed ibn Hatim, who marched from Palestine to Egypt at the head of an army of 50,000 men. In 772, he gained a decisive victory over the rebellious Berbers at Jenbi in Tripolitania.

Yezeed ibn Hatim inflicted a terrible punishment on the dissident tribes. "Thereafter", writes the historian Ibn Khaldoun, "the spirit of heresy and of revolt which had for so long inspired the Berbers of Ifriqiya subsided completely." Yezeed ibn Hatim was to continue to rule the province with a strong hand for another fifteen years, from 772 until 787.

But the area in which resistance had been stamped out covered only Ifriqiya. No attempt was made to subjugate the high Atlas, where independent Berber Kharijite principalities were established, notably at Tahert and Sijilmassa. At Tahert, Abdul Rahman ibn Rustem, an Arab possibly of Persian descent, established a Berber Kharijite principality, which his descendants were to continue to rule for a hundred and thirty years. The subjects of this little mountain state were all fanatical Kharijites, leading lives of asceticism and contemplation. Ibn Rustem ruled with the religious title of imam. Their society was equalitarian in the extreme, and observed the highest standards of puritan morality—one bowl of milk every three days is alleged to have been sometimes considered sufficient nourishment for the prince.[1] The whole community lived in a religious fever, and passed much of its time in theological argument, thereby perhaps emphasizing the difference between Arabs and Berbers. The religion of the former always took the practical form of good works and rarely extended to metaphysical speculation.

Another remarkable little Kharijite state, founded in 757 during the khalifate of Mansoor, was that of Sijilmassa. It lay in the semi-desert area of steppe and oasis south of the Atlas mountains and on the northern fringe of the Sahara. This little principality maintained its independence for one hundred and forty years under the leadership of the family of Ibn Medrar. The town of Sijilmassa appears to have been the "landfall" of caravans crossing the Sahara from Nigeria and Ghana, for it was said to be rich in iron, lead, quicksilver, black slaves, amber, silk and cloth. Presumably some of these articles were coming from West Africa to the Mediterranean, while the remainder were Mediterranean products going southwards to black Africa. Sijilmassa was the market and exchange for this trade. It enjoyed an ample water supply and around it and in the other oases south of the Atlas,

1. Julien, *Histoire de l'Afrique du Nord.*

dates, fruit and vines were cultivated. The whole city of Sijilmassa was surrounded by lofty walls and during its century and a half of prosperity, it was said to have been one of the richest and most prosperous cities in all North Africa.

A remarkable feature of Berber intransigence at this time and later was the fact that, although constantly in rebellion against Arab rule, they readily accepted Arabs as their leaders, both in religion and in politics—thus in spite of the almost invincible military persistence of the Berbers, they seem readily to have accorded intellectual pre-eminence to the Arabs. It was Arab dissidents, Kharijites, Shiites or unsuccessful claimants to the khalifate who again and again roused the conquered races to rebellion against the Arab Empire, until they eventually succeeded in dismembering it.

*　　*　　*

When the Khalif Saffah had nominated his brother Mansoor as his successor, he had also exacted an oath of allegiance to his nephew Isa ibn Musa, as successor to Mansoor. The latter now determined to name his own son Mehedi[2] as heir-apparent to the exclusion of Isa ibn Musa, although by defeating the Aliid rebels, Muhammad and Ibrahim, Isa had saved Mansoor's throne. The principal leaders of the empire, however, had already sworn allegiance to Isa ibn Musa in the days of Saffah. They had declared in these oaths that, if they betrayed their allegiance, their wives would automatically be divorced and all their slaves set free. (To swear by the divorce of their wives is still a practice among the Arabs.)

As a result of these solemn vows, the only manner by which the succession could be changed was by the voluntary withdrawal of Isa. The latter was at first unwilling to abandon his claim, with the result that every device of palace intrigue was turned against him. Requests having elicited no response, he was threatened. His son was half strangled, the soldiers of the bodyguard were secretly instructed to mob him in the streets, while simultaneously immense sums of money were offered to him as an inducement. The resourceful Khalid ibn Barmak was active in these measures and was apparently largely responsible for their success. Isa ibn Musa, harassed by these persecutions and doubtless in fear of assassination, eventually capitulated and abandoned his claim to the succession. Mehedi, the son of Mansoor, was then nominated as the heir to the khalifate.

The fact that the surrender of Isa ibn Musa had been largely engineered by Khalid ibn Barmak was to have important repercussions. It meant that Mehedi, when he became khalif, was to be under a debt of gratitude to Khalid, who thereby attained supreme influence in the state. He was to found the family known to this day in the West as the Barmecids.

Mehedi, who had now been declared heir-apparent to the khalifate, had been engaged in the suppression of a revolt in Herat, Sijistan and Khurasan.

2. The word Mehedi means the Guided One and it was the title used to describe the Muslim "Messiah" who was ultimately to return to the earth and usher in a millennium. In the case of the son of Mansoor, the word was used as a personal name. It is normally spelt in English Mahdi with the result that people at times pronounce it Mardi. In reality the vowels are all short and the h is pronounced. The nearest approach to it in English is Me-hed-di.

In 768, he returned to Baghdad, at the head of his victorious army. Mansoor assigned an area on the east bank of the Tigris as a cantonment for Mehedi's army, fearing, it was whispered, to admit them to the City of Peace, which was garrisoned by his own guards. Having completed the building of his capital, the khalif commenced the erection of the Rusafa palace on the east bank as a residence for Mehedi.[3]

This anxiety regarding the loyalty of the army serves to emphasize another outstanding difference between the Umaiyids and the Abbasids. The troops employed by the earlier dynasty had been almost entirely Arab, whereas the army which had carried the Abbasids to power had been raised in Khurasan and North Persia. We must, it is true, avoid the error of attributing to these peoples the mentality of modern nationalism and of thinking of them as Persians and Arabs. The fact remains, however, that, dating from Abu Muslim's Khurasan army, the great majority of the khalif's troops did come from North-East Persia. The Arab tribes, which alone had conquered this vast empire, eventually ceased to be used as soldiers. The nomads withdrew once more into their deserts, while such of their members as had settled in the cities became absorbed in the population of the empire.

A few years after the completion of the Round City of Mansoor, the suburbs had already spread far up and down the west bank of the Tigris. The names of the recipients of land-grants in the suburbs, and the allotment of cantonments to the troops, are extremely instructive, for scarcely an Arab name is to be found among them. Properties are listed in the names of beneficiaries from Balkh, Merv, Bukhara, Khiva and Sughd, obviously supporters of the Abbasid revolution to whom the dynasty owed a debt of gratitude. The cantonments appear to have been occupied principally by troops from Persia and by Turkish mercenaries. Mansoor's chief of police was a native of Balkh. The khalif, however, still retained some Arabs among his guards in the Round City.

Building had become the principal passion of the ageing khalif. After completing the Rusafa palace on the East bank of the Tigris as a residence for his son Mehedi, he built himself a new palace on the west bank, immediately overlooking the river. It was named the Khuld or palace of immortality, the suggestion being that the gardens which surrounded it resembled the gardens of paradise. The khalif took up his residence there in 775, not long before his death. He also caused the cities of Kufa and Basra each to be surrounded by walls and a moat.

In August 775, Mansoor set out with a large convoy across the Arabian desert to perform the pilgrimage to Mecca. He had suffered for some years from digestive troubles and had consulted many doctors without result.[4] After leaving Kufa, his pains became more acute, but he struggled on across the desert until within a day's march of Mecca. He died at dawn in his tent on the day on which he had hoped to reach the Holy City. It was the beginning of October 775. He was sixty-four years of age and had reigned twenty-two years.

Mansoor was tall, thin and of sallow complexion. When he first assumed

3. Plan of Baghdad, page 247.   4. He may have had gastric ulcers.

the khalifate, he put a great many people to death, and it is difficult to excuse the deliberate and cold-blooded murder of Abu Muslim, the man more than any other to whom the Abbasids owed their elevation. Once his throne became firmly established after the suppression of the Aliid rebellion of Muhammad and Ibrahim, he became less bloodthirsty.

Mansoor was of a serious disposition, well-read and interested in literature. He would not permit music and frowned on every kind of frivolity. Once his authority was undisputed, he was careful in the enforcement of justice and would not permit provincial governors to carry out the death sentence without reference to himself. He was undoubtedly a capable ruler and a painstaking administrator.

On one occasion, Mansoor was told that a victim of his had said that "he applied punishment as though he had never heard of such a thing as pardon". But the khalif replied, "because the bones of Beni Merwan have not yet rotted and the swords of the descendants of Ali ibn abi Talib have not yet been sheathed. We are in the midst of a people who, only yesterday, knew us as fellow citizens. Today they see us as khalifs, and the fear of us will not grip their hearts unless we ignore pardon and pursue chastisement."

The story contains the key to the history of the first Abbasids. Having seized power from their fellow-Qurashites, they lived in constant fear of plots against themselves such as they had successfully hatched against the Umaiyids. This obsession led them to neglect foreign conquests, for they believed their real enemies to be at home.

In spite of the overt political propaganda to the effect that Beni Umaiya had been the enemies of God, Mansoor entertained a great admiration for the Khalif Hisham ibn Abdul Malik (who, it will be remembered, was also accused of parsimony.) On more than one occasion, he sent for old men who had served under Hisham, and cross-questioned them regarding his administration.

Mansoor's mother had been a Berber concubine. Curiously enough, the mother of Abdul Rahman, the Umaiyid prince who had seized Andalus, was of the same origin, so that it was said that the sons of two Berber women ruled the world.

The long reign of Mansoor saw many marked changes in the spirit of the empire, as compared with what it had been in Umaiyid days. It was in his time that the first historians of Islam began to write, Ibn Ishaq dying during his reign. The Basra schools became famous for their grammarians of the Arabic language—a subject important for the study of the Qoran—and many religious jurists and traditionists flourished.

While interest in book-learning was on the increase, military aggressiveness showed a marked decline. The empire was everywhere on the defensive and there is no longer any mention of plans for new conquests. There was indeed plenty of fighting, but in every province the principal tasks of the army were the suppression of revolts. Apart from the rising of the Aliids, the rebellion of Ustadh Sees in East Persia and the mass revolt of the Berbers in Africa resulted in long and desperate campaigns. The Khazars carried out a terrible invasion of Armenia and Adharbaijan which went unpunished. There was spasmodic fighting against Byzantium, which, however, lacked the aggressiveness of the Umaiyid invasions.

It is difficult to attribute these changes to any single factor. On the one hand, the empire was reaching maturity and was moving away from sheer military aggressiveness towards culture, literature and the arts. Yet the peculiarities of the families of Quraish seem to have played some part in the transformation. The Umaiyids had been forthright soldiers, the Abbasids were politicians, statesmen and men of letters, the Aliids were other-worldly mystics. Such definitions are of course over-simplifications, yet, by and large, they represent genuine characteristics of the rival clans.

One factor in the policy of Mansoor established a precedent which was in the future to prove disastrous. It was doubtless his constant fear of the Umaiyids, and then of the Aliids, which caused him to distrust the Arabs. As a result, he made increasing use of his own freedmen in positions of responsibility. These freedmen—that is, former slaves—were of course always non-Arabs, for Arabs could not be slaves. Thus the number of Arabs in power became gradually reduced, both in the central administration, in the army and in the provinces. We have already more than once mentioned Khalid ibn Barmak as one of his chief ministers. His agents in addition bought Turkish slaves on the northern frontiers for employment in the khalif's service.

In the end, as a result of this policy, the Abbasids were to fall between two stools. An Arab dynasty, they deprived themselves of the loyalty of their own nationals, relying on the hired services of Persians and Turks, who were, in the long run, themselves to seize power when the Arabs, whom the dynasty had intentionally weakened, were unable to resist.

* * *

Mehedi, the son of Mansoor, succeeded to the khalifate in October 775 without opposition. He was thirty-three years old, young, handsome, generous and popular. He was the great-great-great-grandson of Abbas, the uncle of the Prophet. The year after his accession, a powerful expedition was sent by sea from Basra to invade India. It captured the town of Barabad, the present location of which is uncertain. One account alleges that the expedition was a punitive operation against Indian pirates who had been attacking Arab merchant ships. Many of the troops died of disease, some of the ships were wrecked, and the expedition would appear to have been only partially successful.

In the year 777, another rebellion broke out in Khurasan, under the leadership of a certain Yusuf al Baram. After some sharp fighting, the revolt was suppressed, and Yusuf and his chief supporters were brought in chains to Baghdad. Their hands and feet were cut off and then they were beheaded, their dead bodies being then crucified on the upper Tigris bridge. Hereafter the heads or the bodies of rebels were regularly exposed on the bridges over the river, as they used to be in London on Temple Bar. It is curious to note the rebellions in Khurasan against the Abbasids, in view of the many Khurasanis in high office and in the army. Mansoor indeed, shortly before his death is alleged to have enjoined upon Mehedi always to care for the people of Khurasan "on whom his throne depended".

In September 777, Mehedi performed the pilgrimage to Mecca, accompanied by a caravan of camels carrying snow in containers in order to cool the drinks of the Prince of the Faithful in those deserts of Arabia which, only a hundred and fifty years before, had been the home of his hardy ancestors.

The civil war between the Abbasids and the Umaiyids, followed by the parsimony of the Khalif Mansoor, had weakened the Arab forces on the Byzantine frontier, and had allowed the energetic Emperor Constantine V, son of Leo the Isaurian, to force back the frontier to the east, the Byzantines obtaining possession of the Taurus passes. In 778, the Arabs suffered a defeat near Marash, well to the east of the Taurus. In 780, the Byzantines again assumed the offensive, though the Arabs eventually succeeded in retaking Hadeth. Mehedi determined to recover the initiative and prestige which the Arabs had enjoyed throughout the Umaiyid period. The khalif's second son Haroon was placed in command of the operations, with Khalid ibn Barmak and his son Yahya, as his chief political advisers.

In the summer of 781, Haroon invaded Byzantine territory. Though nothing very striking was accomplished the Arabs held the initiative throughout the summer. The Arab operations were greatly facilitated by the death of the Emperor Leo IV, son of Constantine V, in 780 and by the assumption of power by his widow, the Empress Irene, in the name of his young son, Constantine VI.

In February 782, Haroon set out once more with a great army of some 95,000 men, equipped at lavish expense. Sweeping across the whole of Asia Minor, he reached the Bosphorus and gazed across the narrow seas at the walls and towers of Constantinople itself. Irene, at her wits' end, sued for peace. Delegations passed between her and Haroon. At length an agreement was concluded, according to which the empire was to pay the khalif an annual tribute of 70,000 dinars. By this humiliation of Byzantium, the khalifate recovered the dominating military position which it had maintained under the great Umaiyids. Haroon returned from the war in an aura of glory, and was made governor of Armenia and Adharbaijan. Yahya ibn Barmak remained as his principal secretary.

In 782, Mehedi caused oaths of allegiance to be taken to his two sons as his successors, at the same time giving each a title. Musa the eldest was to be called Al Hadi, while Haroon was given the designation of Al Rasheed. In 783 disturbances broke out in Jurjan and Tabaristan at the southern end of the Caspian and Musa al Hadi was sent with an army to restore order.

In July 785 the khalif appears to have conceived the idea of placing Haroon next in the succession, superseding his brother Musa al Hadi, but Al Hadi refused to agree. As in the previous case of Isa ibn Musa, the representatives of the people had sworn allegiance to Musa al Hadi and they could not be released from their oaths unless he himself declared his voluntary withdrawal. In August 785, the Khalif Mehedi was in the Persian mountains some fifty miles south of Kermansheh, apparently on his way to North

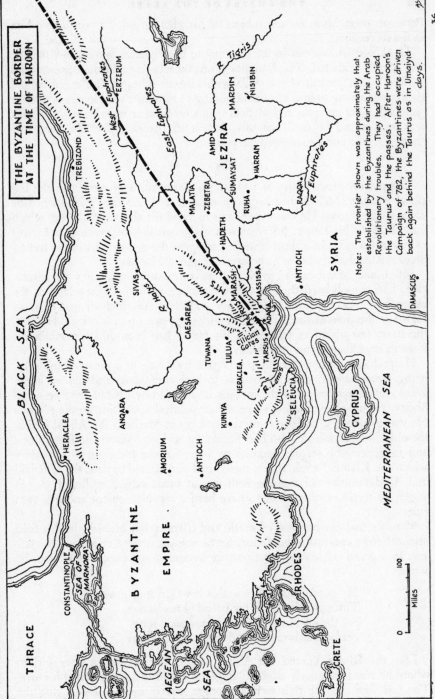

THE BYZANTINE BORDER
AT THE TIME OF HAROON

Note: The frontier shown was approximately that
established by the Byzantines during the Arab
Revolutionary troubles. They had occupied
the Taurus and the passes. After Haroon's
Campaign of 782, the Byzantines were driven
back again behind the Taurus as in Umaiyid
days.

THRACE

BLACK SEA

CONSTANTINOPLE

SEA OF MARMORA

HERACLEA

ANQARA

TREBIZOND

ERZERUM

West Euphrates

R. Tigris

MARDIN

NISIBIN

JEZIRA

AMID

SUMAYSAT

HARRAN

RUHA

RAQQA

R. Euphrates

East Euphrates

MALATIA

ZEBETRA

HADETH

R. Halys

SIVAS

CAESAREA

TAURUS MTS

MARASH

MASSISSA

ADANA

ANTIOCH

SYRIA

DAMASCUS

TUWANA

LULUA

Cilician Gates

TARSUS

HERACLEA

KUNIYA

SELEUCIA

R. Lamis

AMORIUM

ANTIOCH

BYZANTINE

EMPIRE

CYPRUS

MEDITERRANEAN SEA

RHODES

AEGEAN SEA

CRETE

0   100
Miles

261

Persia to meet Musa on the subject of his plan to put Haroon before him in the succession.

The khalif had set out in the morning to hunt gazelle, a sport to which he was greatly addicted. The hounds—probably saluqis or Persian greyhounds —were in hot pursuit of a gazelle with Mehedi riding at full speed behind them, when they passed a ruined building. The khalif's horse seems to have galloped under an arch, and Mehedi struck his head or was thrown. His back was broken and he died instantly. It was 4th August, 785. He was forty-three years old and had reigned ten years.

*   *   *

The parsimonious Mansoor had left immense sums of money in the imperial treasury. Mehedi had been a handsome and debonair prince when he came to the throne. He seemed anxious to avoid the charge of avarice, which had clung to his father. So great was his generosity, or perhaps rather his extravagance, that in a short time he had spent the greater part of the money accumulated during the long and careful reign of Mansoor.

Saffah and Mansoor had grown up as conspirators and, after the revolution, had consolidated their power with much bloodshed, especially at the expense of their cousins Beni Umaiya and Beni Ali. Mehedi had been an infant at the time of the revolution and had grown up as a prince. He was, therefore, less afraid of plots than his father had been and less vindictive towards the Umaiyids and the Aliids.

He probably sought and enjoyed popularity, being of a pleasant and easy-going temperament. He took trouble to hear complaints and redress grievances and caused many of the persons imprisoned by his father to be set at liberty, including even those suspected of political opposition to the régime. He was generous to the surviving descendants of Maslama ibn Abdul Malik, the old Umaiyid soldier who had fought for so long against the Byzantines, and in general he seemed anxious to atone for the bloodthirsty massacres which the Khalifs Saffah and Mansoor had perpetrated against the Umaiyid and Aliid families. Though Mehedi was at times subject to fits of violent anger, he seems on the whole to have been a capable, lenient and generous ruler.

Mansoor had disapproved of music and frivolity but Mehedi, in this field also, offered a contrast to his father, for he enjoyed luxury, wine, and the fair sex. In a poem celebrating his favourite freedman and boon companion, he wrote:

> "My good fortune I pray that my God may prolong
> Through Abu Hafs, the friend of my leisure.
> For the joy of my life is in wine and in song,
> Perfumed slave girls and music and pleasure."

Like the Khalif Yezeed ibn Abdul Malik, Mehedi had a slave girl to whom he was particularly attached and who is said to have returned his love. The girl slaves of the rich were no longer merely means of satisfying the passions of their owners. They were often expected to be accomplished musicians and mistresses of the art of Arabic poetry. At any moment Mehedi was liable to say to his companion, whether male or female, "This is a pleasant evening," or "We have had a good day's hunting. Extemporize some verses to me, celebrating the occasion." The khalif himself was gifted with considerable literary talent. His intimates needed both a good education and considerable poetic genius to enable them to produce extempore verses of the required standard.

The propaganda of Abu Muslim, which had raised so great a revolution against the Umaiyids, had denounced their wine-drinking khalifs and had promised a return of true religion under the rule of the Prophet's family. These pledges had proved to be mere election promises, forgotten as soon as Beni Abbas were well established in power.

During the ten years of his reign, Mehedi had, without abandoning his father's reliance on the Khurasanis, shown considerable favour and generosity to the Arabs. Unlike most of the Abbasids, his mother was an Arab Yemenite princess married to Mansoor and not a slave concubine. He built himself a palace at Raqqa on the Euphrates and greatly enlarged the courtyard of the Kaaba in Mecca, causing many houses to be demolished in order to extend the open space surrounding the House of God. He also commenced the work of establishing guard posts and cisterns for water along the pilgrim routes leading across Arabia to Medina and Mecca.

Although Mehedi enjoyed the pleasures of luxury, religion was treated outwardly with great respect. During his reign, the new sect of the Zindeeqs appeared in Khurasan and spread rapidly. Its tenets appear to have consisted of a mixture of Islam with influences from older oriental faiths, though the word came to mean any heretic. Mehedi showed his orthodoxy by an active persecution of these sectaries.

Mehedi in some ways differed substantially in character from his father, but the general trend towards orientalization continued. The move of the capital to Baghdad had surrounded the court with Persian influences and cut it off from the Mediterranean and the Roman world. It is noticeable, when reading the innumerable anecdotes which the Arab historians love to retail, that the khalifs tend more and more to choose their intimates and boon companions not from the Arab aristocracy but from their own freedmen, slaves and concubines. The Persian system of government had surrounded the ancient kings with an aura of semi-divine glory, a status inacceptable to the cynical Arab mind, which invariably wished to criticize, and even to mock, its leaders. The weakening of the Arab chiefs and the increase of Persian influence was already surrounding the Abbasids with an adulation which Arabs rarely consent to give, but which was readily conceded by freedmen and slaves.

One of the outward and visible signs of this trend towards despotism was the increasing use of the khalif's servants in important posts, including governorships of provinces. At the same time, the central government in Baghdad became more organized. What correspond to our modern departments of Justice, Finance, and Defence were already established under the name of diwans, and employed great numbers of government officials. A chief minister of the government, known as the wazeer, was now placed in control of all departments, and was answerable only to the khalif. This innovation, which owed its origin to Mehedi, was ultimately to prove disastrous for the Abbasids, who tended more and more to abandon affairs of state to their wazeers. Many senior officials and provincial governors were freedmen of the khalif. We have seen that freed slaves were considered to be morally bound to serve the interests of their liberators all their lives. The extensive use of freedmen in positions of power, therefore, meant that their loyalty was not to the Muslim community but to the khalif alone. Even, however, if the officials were not freedmen, they were career officials, with, in many cases, no social position except that derived from their offices. In Umaiyid times by contrast the government had been served by an aristocratic class, consisting partly of Arab tribal chiefs and partly of descendants of the Companions of the Prophet. These members of great families were always proud and often insubordinate, but their existence kept the khalif in the position of the first among his peers. The replacement of this aristocracy by career officials, many of them former slaves, left no one in the empire who ventured to criticize or oppose the will or the whim of the khalif.

The aristocracy of Arab chiefs had not been particularly enlightened and indeed had spent most of its time in war. It had, however, by its very existence, constituted a check on the despotism of the khalifs. Not for the first time in history, the disappearance of an aristocracy and the creation of a classless society, had opened the way for unchecked dictatorship.

While, however, we may lament this increase in despotism, we must recognize that in other directions the Abbasids represented progress. Mehedi was intelligent and well-read. Knowledge, science and literature continued to expand rapidly. The maturing character of the empire was further emphasized by the increasing importance attached to commerce and industry and the growth of a wealthy merchant class, of which we shall hear more in the years to come. Chivalry, war and conquest had dominated the Umaiyid period, commerce, the arts and industry were to be the features of that of the Abbasids.

* * *

Musa al Hadi succeeded to the khalifate on the death of his father. Whereas Mehedi—in contrast to Mansoor—had behaved generously towards the Aliids, returned their property confiscated by his father and allotted them pensions, Hadi cancelled these privileges and treated them with severity. As a result, nine months later, another Aliid rebellion took place in Mecca, this time in the name of Husain [5] ibn Ali ibn Hasan ibn Hasan ibn Ali ibn abi Talib. The rising was quickly suppressed, and Husain killed in a minor engagement at Fakh, six miles outside Mecca. When the head of Husain was sent to the Khalif Hadi in Baghdad, he burst into tears. "You come in to me calling, Good News! Good News!" he said, "as though you had brought me the head of a Turk or a heathen. Do not you know that this head belongs

5. Genealogical tree, page 240.

to a great-great-great-grandson of the Apostle of God?" Yet it was apparently his policy which had provoked the revolt.

But though Hadi was thus compassionate, the inevitable torturings, executions and confiscations were carried out in Mecca and Medina. It was after this revolt that Idris ibn Abdulla ibn Hasan [6] escaped from Mecca. He was the brother of Muhammad and Ibrahim, who had rebelled in 762 against Mansoor. Accompanied by only one freedman, he made his way to Egypt. Here he was assisted by Wadhih, a freedman of the khalif's family, who was in charge of the department of posts and intelligence in Egypt. The descendants of the Prophet through his daughter Fatima still commanded the veneration of many loyal and simple-minded Muslims, and it was probably for such conscientious reasons that Wadhih facilitated the passage of the fugitive to Tangier. When he learned of Wadhih's action, the khalif Haroon was to order his immediate execution and the crucifixion of his body.

From Tangier, Idris moved to Volubilis, an ancient Roman city in the foothills of the Atlas, where the remains of broken colonnades and ruined temples still, in our own days, attest the departed splendour of Rome. To the Arabs, Volubilis was known as Walila.[7] Here Idris met with a cordial welcome. The Berber tribes, already Muslims, received him with veneration as a descendant of the Apostle of God, and an enemy of the existing government, for the Berbers, like the proverbial Irishman, were invariably in opposition to whatever government was in power. Soon he was joined also by a number of Arabs who, for one reason or another, were enemies of the Abbasid dynasty.

Idris must have been a man of remarkable personality, for, within three or four years, he had secured the allegiance of several other Berber tribes of the Atlas region, and had extended his authority over the whole area of modern Morocco and as far east as Tlemcen in modern Algeria. Finding Walila too small, or perhaps desirous of founding a capital of his own, he commenced to build the city of Fez, more properly spelt Fas. The site of Fez was well chosen. Situated on the western foothills of the Atlas, with an ample water supply, it commanded the Taza gap— the pass leading from Ifriqiya between the mountains of the Reef and the Atlas, into the Maghrib or modern Morocco.

Thus all three of the rival Quraish clans had, for the moment, seized an independent state. In the Maghrib, Idris ibn Abdulla of the family of Ali ruled with the title of imam, a word originally used to designate only the leader of the congregation at prayers, but to which the Shia had now attached a mystic significance. In Andalus, Abdul Rahman ibn Muawiya, the Umaiyid, governed as an independent monarch with the rank of ameer, while the Abbasids in Baghdad still retained the bulk of the empire with the title of Prince of the Faithful.

* * *

Whatever may have been his attachment to slave girls, there was one woman who had largely dominated the Khalif Mehedi. Her name was

6. Genealogical tree, page 240. 7. Map 35, page 254.

Khaizuran and she had originally been a slave concubine. It was she who was the mother of the new Khalif Hadi and of Haroon. So great had been her influence over Mehedi that courtiers, army commanders and officials had been in the habit of soliciting her favour, in the hope that she would speak to the khalif on their behalf.

When Hadi succeeded his father, Khaizuran continued to receive the visits of prominent men, to interfere in public affairs to secure the advancement of her protégés and to offer her advice—or perhaps issue her orders—to her son. The young khalif eventually revolted against the maternal authority and an angry scene took place between mother and son. Hadi forbade any officer or official to visit his mother, while Khaizuran swore that never again would she speak to her eldest son. Meanwhile, however, tension had also arisen between the Khalif Hadi and his brother Haroon.

Mehedi, it will be remembered, had caused oaths of allegiance to be sworn to Hadi as heir-apparent and to Haroon as successor to Hadi. The latter now determined to disinherit Haroon and to secure the oath of allegiance to his own son Jaafar. Once again this could not be done unless Haroon voluntarily withdrew, thereby releasing from their oaths those who had sworn allegiance to him as successor to Hadi. Khaizuran, after her quarrel with Hadi, supported Haroon. Yahya ibn Barmak, or the Barmecid, was also busy canvassing in support of his patron, Haroon, until Hadi put him in prison. In these difficult circumstances, Haroon seems to have behaved with quiet tact. While refusing to abdicate his right to the succession, he acted modestly towards Hadi and promised to care for his sons, marry them to his own daughters and treat them all as his children.

With matters in this state, Hadi suddenly fell ill of pains in the stomach and four days later he died. Some reports allege that he suffered from gastric ulcers but, in view of the family tensions, it was inevitable that rumour should say that he had been poisoned by his mother. Yet she was by his bedside in his last illness and he died with his hand in hers. He had been khalif for only one year and two months and was twenty-six years old. His death occurred on 15th September, 786.

Hadi was in appearance tall, fair and handsome. His good looks gave him a certain prestige but he seems to have been dissipated and extravagant, though perhaps pleasant and well-meaning. He was completely dominated by his mother Khaizuran, until at last he rebelled, and temperamental family scenes ensued.

It is interesting to note that, in the year of the khalifate of Hadi, the pilgrim route across Arabia from Baghdad to Mecca was rendered unsafe by the depredations of the nomadic Arab tribes. For one hundred and fifty years, from the death of the Prophet to the reign of Hadi, they had been the supporters of religion and the mainstay of the empire. Now the increasing domination of non-Arab officials had thrust them once more into opposition to the government, a condition in which they were to remain almost until our own times. Ever since the overthrow of the Umaiyids by the Abbasids thirty-five years earlier, the language of the historians had begun to change. Whereas in earlier days they quoted the praises of the free Arabs of the desert, now references to stupid, ignorant tribesmen begin to appear, remarks couched in the same words as we hear today among the governing classes in Baghdad, Damascus and Cairo.

During the last year of Mehedi's life, the Byzantine government had denounced the humiliating agreement concluded three years earlier between Haroon al Rasheed and the Empress Irene. The change of policy was due to the fact that Constantine VI, the son of Irene, had come of age and had taken over control from his mother. Military operations of a desultory nature were resumed on the frontier in Hadi's reign.

NOTABLE DATES

Umar ibn Hafs appointed Governor of Ifriqiya	768
Death of Umar ibn Hafs and surrender of Qairawan	771
Battle of Jenbi—Berbers subdued	772
Death of Mansoor, elevation of Mehedi	775
Haroon al Rasheed's campaign to the Bosphorus	782
Death of Mehedi, elevation of Hadi	785
Rebellion of Husain ibn Ali at Mecca	786
Death of Hadi	786

PERSONALITIES

Umar ibn Hafs, Governor of Ifriqiya	768–771
Yezeed ibn Hatim, Governor of Ifriqiya	772–787

The Khalif Mehedi ibn Mansoor

Musa al Hadi ⎫
Haroon al Rasheed ⎬ Sons of the Khalif Mehedi
 ⎭

Khalid ibn Barmak

Yahya son of Khalid ibn Barmak

Husain ibn Ali, Aliid rebel in Mecca, killed at Fakh

Idris ibn Abdulla, Aliid rebel who fled to Morocco

Khaizuran, favourite concubine of Mehedi, mother of Hadi and Haroon al Rasheed

Byzantine Emperors

Leo III the Isaurian	716–741
Constantine V whose-name-is-dung	741–775
Leo IV	775–780
Irene (as regent for Constantine VI)	780–785
Constantine VI	785–797

XV

The Golden Age

God gave them the reward of this world and a good reward in the world
to come. For God loves those who do good.   *Qoran* III, 147

And many a sheeny summer-morn,
Adown the Tigris I was borne,
By Bagdat's shrines of fretted gold,
High-walled gardens green and old . . .
For it was in the golden prime
Of good Haroun Alraschid.

Down-droop'd, in many a floating fold,
Engarlanded and diaper'd
With inwrought flowers, a cloth of gold
Thereon, his deep eye laughter-stirred
With merriment of kingly pride,
    Sole star of all that place and time
    I saw him—in his golden prime,
    The good Haroun Alraschid.
                    TENNYSON, *Recollections of The Arabian Nights*

Power tends to corrupt and absolute power corrupts absolutely. Great men
are almost always bad men.   LORD ACTON

XV

THE GOLDEN AGE

O N 15th September, 786, Haroon al Rasheed was proclaimed khalif in succession to his brother Hadi. He was twenty-two years old when he was raised to the khalifate and was to reign for twenty-three years and to become one of the most famous princes of all time. Hadi, as we have seen, had endeavoured to disinherit Haroon and to replace him in the succession by his own son Jaafar, to whom he had obliged a number of people to swear allegiance. But Jaafar was still a child and opposition to Haroon evaporated in the first twenty-four hours.

Yahya the Barmecid had been thrown into prison by Hadi for his intrigues in support of Haroon's right to the succession. The first act of the new khalif was to send to the prison and release his friend and former tutor and to make him his chief minister. "I have placed the responsibility for my subjects on your shoulders," the young Haroon was alleged to have told his wazeer, "rule them as you think best, appoint and dismiss whom you will. Here is my signet ring, which I entrust to you."

The khalif's mother Khaizuran was delighted at the elevation of her favourite son and the disappearance of the obstinate Hadi, and recommended her constant interferences in the affairs of state. But Yahya the Barmecid seems to have got her measure and, while accepting her orders with obsequious respect, co-operated with her in return for her support. It was perhaps a relief that the imperious concubine died not long afterwards.

Those in disgrace with the former government were pardoned, a generous donative was issued to the troops and the new reign seemed to have commenced under the best possible auspices. The need for a cash distribution to ensure the loyalty of the army—so reminiscent of the later Roman emperors —was, however, significant. It emphasized the fact that most of the troops were now mercenaries, the majority Turks or Persians, who fought neither for God nor for their country, but for money. We have seen how Charlemagne, for lack of cash, had been obliged to pay his troops in land (the feudal system) instead of in money. Under the great Abbasids we see the opposite process. As a result of the abundance of wealth, the khalifs built up armies which fought solely for payment and not for religion or patriotism.

In the summer of 791, Haroon al Rasheed succeeded in nominating his son Ameen as heir-apparent, though he was only five years old. The incident provides one more example of the continually widening breach with Arab, and even with Muslim, tradition. The Arabs, even before Islam, had always been resolutely opposed to the principle of primogeniture. The chieftainship of an Arab tribe passed to the most capable member of the leading family not necessarily to the eldest son of the previous incumbent, and never to a child.

After Islam, the theory had been accepted that the khalif should be the most capable member of the tribe of Quraish and of the Muslim community. If people were to be asked to swear allegiance to a five-year-old child, the theory of the most worthy citizen had obviously been discarded. Moreover in the early days of Islam, the khalif had been chosen by the faithful to manage the mundane affairs of the Muslim community. It was a responsibility rather than a privilege. The nomination by Haroon of his infant son as his successor smacked more of the half-mystic aura which surrounded eastern royalty than of the simple matter-of-fact manager of the affairs of the early Muslim state. In Khurasan the nomination of Ameen was only accomplished after a number of distributions of cash donatives to the troops.

*   *   *

It will be remembered that a certain Idris[1] ibn Abdulla, a descendant of Ali ibn abi Talib, had escaped from Mecca and reached the Maghrib in 788, where he had established himself as the head of an independent state and had laid the foundations of a new capital at Fez. To despatch an expeditionary force from Baghdad to the Maghrib was beyond the power of the Abbasid khalif, whose interests in any case lay increasingly in the east. But to allow the continuance of an independent Muslim state under Aliid rule might be dangerous. Were it to grow strong, it might conquer Ifriqiya and Egypt and encourage revolts among the many Shiites in Arabia and Persia. To conquer the Berbers was impossible, but to dispose of Idris might well be practical politics.

With this object a certain Shamakh, a freedman of the late Khalif Mehedi, was sent to the Maghrib, where he passed himself off as a doctor of medicine, and ingratiated himself with Idris. Having won the confidence of his intended victim, he prescribed for his indispositions and accompanied him wherever he went in his visits of inspection to the various districts of his kingdom. One evening in 792 Idris sent for the doctor and complained to him of toothache. Shamakh gave him some tooth-paste which he had mixed with a deadly poison and told him to make use of it at dawn the following morning. Then, withdrawing from the presence of his patron, he mounted a fleet mare which he had held ready for precisely such an emergency, and galloped all night at full speed for the east.

At dawn, the unfortunate Idris applied the paste to his teeth, repeating the process at intervals in the hope of securing relief from the pain of his toothache. In a few hours, he began to feel unwell and before midday he was dead. The death of the imam and the sudden disappearance of the doctor aroused suspicion and a party of horsemen set out in pursuit. Shamakh, however, though almost overtaken in a wild gallop, arrived safely in Qairawan. He was eventually rewarded by Haroon al Rasheed with the post of chief of the department of posts and intelligence in Egypt.

Idris died childless but Kenza, one of his Berber concubines, was pregnant.

1. Genealogical tree, page 240.

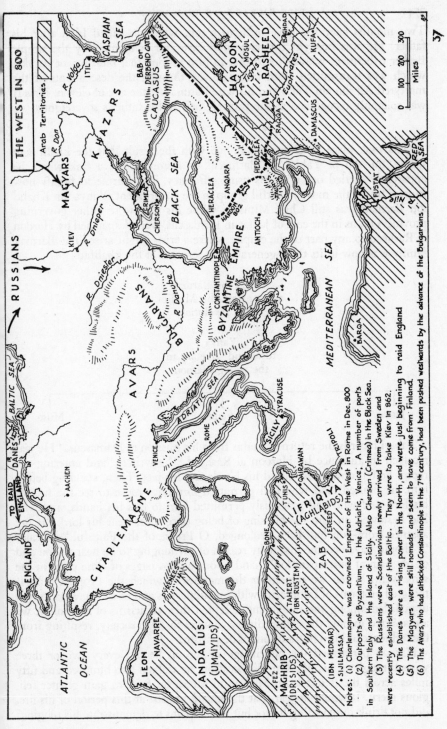

Two months later she gave birth to a son, who was called Idris after his
father. He was brought up with fond care and veneration by the simple
Berber tribesmen, who believed that in him resided that blessing, or baraka,
which was transmitted from father to son through the descendants of the
martyred Ali ibn abi Talib and his wife Fatima. At the age of eleven, Idris II
was solemnly recognized as the princely heir to his father's sovereignty.

*   *   *

Riots took place in Damascus in 796 with the result that the khalif sent
Jaafar, the son of Yahya the Barmecid, to restore order, a task which he
apparently carried out with his usual efficiency. The Barmecid family now
formed by far the most powerful group in the government. Yahya ibn Khalid
ibn Barmak was still Chief Minister, while his sons were either governing
provinces or, as in the case of Jaafar in Damascus, were despatched by Haroon
al Rasheed to any part of the empire where a crisis might arise. The Barmak
family was now in its third generation as servants of the khalifate.

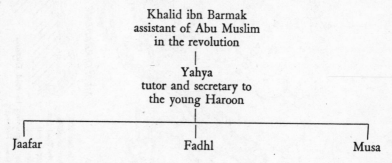

Khalid ibn Barmak
assistant of Abu Muslim
in the revolution

Yahya
tutor and secretary to
the young Haroon

Jaafar   Fadhl   Musa

Tabari records the return of Jaafar from his mission to Damascus. "He was
received in audience by Haroon al Rasheed," he writes, "and entering the
room, he fell down and kissed his hands and his feet. Then, standing before
him, he praised God who had permitted him once more to see the face of
his lord and who had graciously permitted him to kiss his hands, and who
had bestowed on him the blessing of being once more near his lord. "If my
absence from you had been prolonged, O Prince of the Faithful," he said,
"I should have become insane by reason of my longing to be near to you and
of my pain at our separation"—and so on for two pages of close print in the
same vein. When we remember the manner in which the Prophet himself
mingled on terms of familiarity with his supporters and how Muawiya moved
unguarded among the public and accepted their criticisms of his policy, we
are amazed to note the extraordinary changes in Arab society, resulting from
the influence of Persian traditions of despotism.

Haroon performed the pilgrimage in 796, as he did every two or three
years throughout his life. On this occasion, he walked two hundred and fifty
miles across the desert from Medina to Mecca on foot, to gain greater religious merit. It would appear that the khalif, at least at this period of his life,
did not drink intoxicating liquor but was at pains to demonstrate his religious

orthodoxy. It is stated that he prayed with a hundred prostrations every day, whereas only seventeen prostrations constituted the compulsory ritual. The historians represent him as weeping when he thought of the heavy responsibilities which rested on his shoulders.

Throughout the year he was endlessly on the move, visiting Mosul, then Medina and Mecca, then across the desert to Basra, spending forty days in Kufa, back to Baghdad and finally to a new palace which he had built for himself at Raqqa on the Euphrates. He was still only in his early thirties and full of energy and enthusiasm. There can be no doubt that his great reputation was largely due to his constant activity in the field and to the personal visits which he paid to so many cities. He reorganized the defences of the Byzantine frontier, unifying the command of the border fortresses under the name of the Awasim. In 798, Haroon appointed his second son Mamoon to be next in the succession to his eldest son Ameen.

In 799, the Khazars, who for more than a hundred years had been a thorn in the side of the Arab Empire, emerged once more from beyond the Caucasus and over-ran Adharbaijan and Armenia, looting, burning and raping. For seventy days, they ravaged the country unopposed, driving off great numbers of Muslims into slavery. When an army arrived to expel them, they vanished once more behind the Caucasus.

* * *

Mention has already been made of Yezeed ibn Hatim, the strong man of Ifriqiya, who governed that province with a high hand for fourteen years. In 787, Yezeed died and his son Rouh attempted to assume his father's responsibilities—but the young man did not command the prestige of the veteran and the province was soon once more in disorder. In 800, Haroon al Rasheed appointed Ibrahim ibn al Aghlab to be governor. His father had held an important post in Ifriqiya under Mansoor and had been killed in the disturbances of those times. Ibrahim had also served in that province throughout the period of the governorship of Yezeed ibn Hatim and had held senior appointments. When fresh disturbances broke out on the death of Yezeed, Ibrahim approached the authorities in Baghdad, offering to mediate in the troubles of the province. His offer was accepted and he was made governor of Ifriqiya.

He concluded an arrangement with the khalif, under which he undertook to keep the province quiet without any requests for armed intervention by the khalif's forces, on condition that he be given a completely free hand. Haroon was perhaps glad to be quit of direct responsibility for North Africa, a country in which he was not deeply interested and which constituted a constant drain on the imperial treasury.

The Aghlabid dynasty was to rule Ifriqiya for a hundred years, in reality enjoying complete independence, but careful always verbally to acknowledge the suzerainty of the orthodox khalif in Baghdad. This simple arrangement was satisfactory to all parties. The Abbasids enjoyed the prestige arising from the inclusion of Ifriqiya in the list of imperial provinces, without incurring any anxiety or expense. The Aghlabids established themselves as virtually independent monarchs, but their profession of loyalty to the orthodox khalifs gave them prestige and perhaps an occasional royal bounty or subsidy from the imperial treasury.

Yet Haroon's acceptance of such a *modus vivendi* was yet a further indication of the change of spirit in the capital. How far we have travelled from the time when Uqba ibn Nafi rode his horse into the Atlantic Ocean, declaring his readiness to march on to the ends of the earth, striking down those nations which refused to acknowledge the Unity of God, or from the day when Musa ibn Nusair had conceived the idea of conquering France and Italy and returning to Damascus by way of Byzantium. The Arab Empire had become orthodox, comfortable and cultured. Its rulers were no longer unlettered and simple-minded enthusiasts. Music, art, history, philosophy, literature and sensual luxury had transformed the rude conquerors into sophisticated and cultured aristocrats.

The boundaries of the Aghlabid state were difficult to define, for Arabs have always reckoned their dominions in terms of people rather than of territory.[2] In general they appear to have governed the coastal populations, who were orthodox or Sunni Muslims and who included the descendants of the Arab conquerors, among a population of mixed races. In the east, the town of Tripoli owned allegiance to the Aghlabids, though the Berber tribes of the neighbourhood were independent and Kharijites. To the south, the Jereed and the Zab marked the approximate boundary between the government and the tribes, while on the Mediterranean coast the authority of the Aghlabids did not in reality extend much beyond Bone, perhaps between fifty and a hundred miles into modern Algeria. The Berbers of the Atlas were independent, intensely Kharijite, and hence hostile to the orthodox Aghlabids, much as the Scottish highlands were once Jacobite and Catholic, while the lowlands were Free Church and Hanoverian.

The early part of the ninth century was marked by intense Muslim religious activity, in Ifriqiya as elsewhere. This enthusiasm, however, now took the form of asceticism on the one hand and of theological discussion on the other. Whatever might be the political rivalries of the different Muslim states, students from Cordova and Qairawan flocked to Mecca, Medina, Baghdad and Basra to sit at the feet of the most famous theologians and grammarians of this age of increasing intellectual activity. Abstruse problems of theology, it is said, formed the principal subject of conversation among the young men of Qairawan. The Kharijites of the Atlas remained, it is true, outside the direct influence of the orthodox schoolmen, but we have already seen that amongst them also religious fervour and asceticism were often at white heat.

One of the most remarkable institutions which found its origin soon after this time in North Africa was that of the ribats. These may perhaps best be described as Muslim monasteries, to which the pious could withdraw, free from worldly distractions, to concentrate upon prayer and meditation. Reference has already been made to the manner in which the Mediterranean, from being the Roman highway, had become a field of battle between Islam and

2. Map 37, page 273.

Christianity. The ribats became not only houses of prayer and fasting, but also fortresses, garrisoned by dedicated Muslim warriors, not unlike the monastic military orders of Christendom.[3] "We, in North Africa," a learned Muslim of Tunis said to me, "have always been more devoted to our faith than have the people of Syria, Iraq or Arabia. They were surrounded by other Muslims, but we have for a thousand years held the front line of Islam against Christendom."

In spite, however, of this unending state of holy war, there were still, in the days of the Aghlabids, many Christians in Ifriqiya, the remains of the Roman and Byzantine communities. They do not appear to have suffered persecution, though the gain in social prestige achieved by conversion to Islam offered great temptations. It is perhaps significant that ultimately no native Christians survived in Ifriqiya, though considerable Christian communities have persisted until today in Palestine, Jordan, Lebanon, Syria and Iraq. In the cities of North Africa, the Jews formed a wealthy and intellectual community.

*   *   *

In the year 802, Haroon caused oaths of allegiance to be taken to his third son giving him the title of Mutamin. The eldest son, Ameen, was made governor of Syria and Iraq, the second, Mamoon, of Persia and the third, Mutamin, was placed in control of the Jezira and the Byzantine border. These appointments were purely nominal, for all three boys remained in Baghdad. Haroon is perhaps to be blamed for the fact that he did not allow his sons to play a more active part in public affairs, with the result that, when he died, they were still lacking in experience and fell under the influence of their ministers.

The nomination of three of his sons as heirs-apparent—albeit in theory one after the other—and the division of the empire between them as governors, seemed to observers at the time to expose the state to the risk of civil war. This danger was made more acute by the increasing tendency to look upon the empire as the property of the family, instead of as the community of Muslims, ruled by the khalif as first citizen of the state. Unfortunately, considerable rivalry had already developed between the khalif's two eldest sons, Ameen and Mamoon. Haroon was anxious concerning the future of the empire after his death and held frequent discussions on the subject with his confidants.

In the year 802, he went on the pilgrimage to Mecca, accompanied by both Ameen and Mamoon. There, in the sacred building of the Kaaba, long and complicated undertakings were drawn up between the two brothers. Whereas Ameen was to succeed his father as khalif, he was also to leave Mamoon as governor of all Persia east of Hamadan, and was not in any way to interfere with his control. In the same manner, neither Ameen nor Mamoon were to interfere with Mutamin's governorship of the Jezira. In reality such a settlement seemed virtually to divide the empire into three

3. Monks, however, took their vows for life, while Muslims could remain for a time in the ribats and then withdraw.

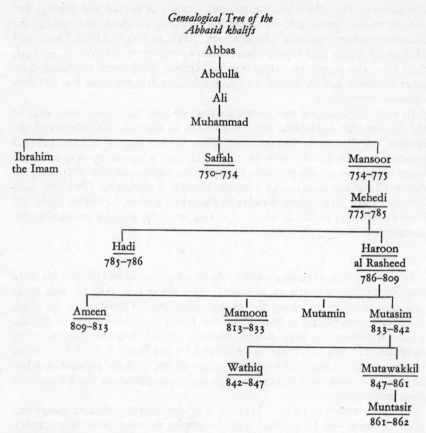

*Genealogical Tree of the
Abbasid khalifs*

Abbas

Abdulla

Ali

Muhammad

Ibrahim
the Imam

Saffah
750–754

Mansoor
754–775

Mehedi
775–785

Hadi
785–786

Haroon
al Rasheed
786–809

Ameen
809–813

Mamoon
813–833

Mutamin

Mutasim
833–842

Wathiq
842–847

Mutawakkil
847–861

Muntasir
861–862

NOTE: Names of khalifs are underlined.

independent princedoms. Many imprecations were called down on the heads
of any who contravened the terms of the settlement, while the leading
courtiers, chamberlains, generals and qadhis were called to witness the
transactions and then to broadcast the details of the settlement to all the
pilgrims. A copy of the document was suspended in the Kaaba itself, but
shortly afterwards blew down, so that observers remarked sarcastically that
it was an agreement which would soon be blown away.

* * *

Haroon al Rasheed had now ruled for seventeen years, during which time
his most trusted advisers and officials had been Yahya the Barmecid and his
sons. Jaafar had been born within a day or two of Haroon himself and so
intimate had been the two families that it was said that Khaizuran had often
suckled Jaafar, while the wife of Yahya the Barmecid did the same for
Haroon. During the anxious year of Hadi's khalifate, when the latter was

determined to disinherit Haroon in favour of his own son, the Barmecids had supported Haroon and had suffered imprisonment for his sake.

When Haroon al Rasheed ultimately was raised to the khalifate, he was not slow to show his gratitude and to hand over the government of his empire to Yahya the Barmecid and his sons Fadhl, Jaafar and Musa. As far as we can perceive, they appear to have rendered loyal and devoted service to their patron, but in the process they had become extremely wealthy. Accurate accounting had not as yet been established and officials who controlled the revenues of the state were expected to grow rich, as the Barmecids certainly did. Their wealth was immense, their palaces were as sumptuous as those of the khalif, their domestics and freedmen as numerous. Wielding almost unlimited power, as they did for many years, they achieved immense patronage and their generosity and hospitality were magnificent. "As generous as Jaafar the Barmecid," passed into a proverb.

It is doubtless impossible to rule an empire without incurring enemies and the Barmecids were no exception. Naturally many courtiers were jealous of this dynasty within a dynasty. They were always ready to assist complainants, or themselves to drop a word here and there intended to poison the mind of Haroon against his favourites, or to provoke his jealousy. Yet, for seventeen years, all the efforts of their rivals were unavailing. The Barmecids belonged to a noble Persian family. Although the Arab historians refer to Khalid as Ibn Barmak, it appears that Barmak was the title held by the high-priest of the Magian fire-temple at Balkh. The presence of Persians in the highest offices of the state may have assisted in the integration of the Persian and Arab races, which was already taking place. Nevertheless a number of Arabs in court circles resented the power wielded by the Persians. One of their principal opponents was Fadhl ibn Rabia, chamberlain of the palace.

The Barmecids were great patrons of literature. The following verses are said to have been addressed by Yahya to his son Fadhl:

> "Seek glory while 'tis day, no effort spare,
> And patiently the loved one's absence bear;
> But when the shades of night advancing slow
> O'er every vice a veil of darkness throw,
> Beguile the hours with all thy heart's delight:
> The day of prudent men begins at night.
> Who but a fool his pleasures would expose
> To spying rivals and censorious foes?" [4]

—sentiments doubtless shared by the khalif as well as his ministers.

Haroon's evening parties were characterized by a great deal of humour, conviviality, poetry and music. Jaafar the Barmecid was among the boon companions with whom he shared his evening revels. He was also extremely fond of his unmarried sister Abbasa and frequently called for her company. According, however, to the conventions of the society of those days, Abbasa could not appear unveiled in the presence of Jaafar, so that Haroon was obliged to limit his company to one or the other of them.

4. R. A. Nicholson, *Literary History of the Arabs.*

To overcome the difficulty he one day suggested to Jaafar that he marry Abbasa, a process which would enable her to appear unveiled without scandal, but he stipulated carefully that the marriage must only be a formality to allow them both to join in his musical evenings. Jaafar was not to be entitled to any other intimacies with the khalif's sister. Jaafar swore to observe the conditions and then went through the marriage ceremony. Thereafter Haroon, Jaafar and Abbasa were able to enjoy their evenings together.

According to Masudi, it was Abbasa who persuaded Jaafar to break his oaths to the khalif. However this may have been, Abbasa one day became aware that she was pregnant. Seized with panic, she obtained permission to perform the pilgrimage to Mecca and, while there, gave birth to a son, who was secretly entrusted to a foster-mother in the Holy City. Abbasa returned to Baghdad and everything went on as before, until one day she became angry with one of her maids. The resentful girl revealed the whole scandalous story to Haroon. When the latter went on the pilgrimage during which he suspended the agreement between his sons in the Kaaba, he caused enquiry to be made after Abbasa's child. Under examination the foster-mother broke down and confirmed the maid's story. Haroon was furious and returned to Baghdad bent on revenge.

On arrival in the capital, the khalif sent Masroor, one of his trusted servants, with a detachment of troops to arrest his former companion and servant. The unfortunate Jaafar was drinking with a few friends when Masroor called him out and escorted him to the palace where he confined him in chains and reported to Haroon. "Bring me his head," said the khalif curtly. Masroor returned to the wretched Barmecid and told him his orders. "Try to gain time," begged the formerly all-powerful minister. "He may change his mind or perhaps he is drunk and will regret his order when he is sober." Masroor went back to his master, who, however, merely repeated his orders. A few minutes later, Masroor returned with the bleeding head of the khalif's chief servant. Jaafar was thirty-seven years old when he met his death.

Without lying down to rest, the khalif ordered the arrest of Yahya ibn Khalid, the father of Jaafar, of Fadhl his brother and of every member of the family, their servants, agents, slaves, freedmen and clerks, and the confiscation of all their property. The day after his execution Jaafar's head was exposed on the middle bridge over the Tigris. His body was then divided in half, one half being nailed to a post on the upper bridge and the other on the lower bridge. History does not record the fate—or the emotions—of Abbasa. It would appear, however, that, even before this event, Haroon was already tiring of the Barmecids. Yahya, the father of Jaafar, had the keys of the khalif's harem and kept the women under a strict discipline, concerning which they complained to Haroon more than once. It is even suggested that the finances were so entirely in the hands of the Barmecids that the khalif at times found himself short of cash and was obliged to beg Jaafar or Yahya to let him have some money.

Yahya the Barmecid and his two sons ruled the empire for seventeen years, during which their wealth and power were so great that they would have been more than human if they had not taken too much for granted. Jaafar.

for example, had spent twenty million dirhems from public funds to build himself a palace. Their rivals also accused the family of Shiite leanings, a charge which seemed to be corroborated when an Aliid rebel, Yahya ibn Abdulla, was released from prison by Jaafar's order without the knowledge of Haroon al Rasheed.

Whether or not there was a scandal involving the khalif's sister, there seems to be no doubt that Haroon was becoming increasingly tired of the Barmecids for four or five years before their final fall. The family had built up an immense system of patronage and many people who had profited from their generosity lamented their fall. Even the dissolute court poet Abu Nuwas mourned them:

> "Since earth has put you away, O sons of Barmak,
> The roads of morning twilight and evening twilight
> Are empty. My heart is empty, O sons of Barmak."[5]

* * *

We have already seen that Haroon al Rasheed, during the lifetime of his father Mehedi, had reached the Bosphorus with a great army and had dictated terms of peace and tribute to the Empress Irene, who was then acting as guardian to her young son, Constantine VI.

The Byzantine Empire was at this time again torn by religious controversy. The point at issue was the use of images and icons. The iconoclasts insisted on the destruction of images, the iconodules with equal vehemence on their retention. As always in Byzantium, the religious schism led to political rivalries. The great Emperor Constantine V, nicknamed "whose-name-is-dung", who had ruled from 741 to 775, had been a violent destroyer of images. His son Leo IV had reigned only five years, from 775 to 780, when he died leaving his widow Irene and his young son, Constantine VI. Irene was a passionate iconodule, and the images removed during the reign of Constantine V were replaced during the regency of Irene. It was during her regency also, 780–785, that she had agreed to pay tribute to the khalif.

In 785, however, Constantine VI came of age, assumed power and denounced the tribute agreement. It was the last year of Mehedi's reign, to be followed by that of Hadi, who was pre-occupied, as we have seen, with attempts to supersede Haroon in favour of his own son. Spasmodic hostilities took place on the frontier.

In 797, however, the Empress Irene tired of her son's rule and arranged a *coup d'état* in which he was overthrown. His eyes were put out and his heartless mother assumed power in her own right with the title of Augusta. She, thereupon, renewed her former agreement with Haroon al Rasheed, and image-worship became again the orthodox tenet.

The career of the Empress Irene was extraordinary in many ways. Other women had governed the empire but always in the name of, or as regent for, an emperor. Irene was the first who, from 797 to 802, governed as empress in her own right. The fact that she caused her own son to be blinded in order to secure power for herself, is sufficient comment on her character. Her

5. Translation by E. Powys Mathers.

inability to lead her armies in person was the greatest handicap suffered by a female ruler. Irene secured peace at the price of the payment of tribute not only to the khalif on her eastern boundary but also to the Bulgarians in the north.

In 802, after five years of rule as empress, Irene was herself deposed by another revolution and a member of the aristocracy assumed the purple under the title of Nicephorus I. It would appear that subservience to the khalif had been one of the charges brought against the Empress Irene. It, therefore, appeared to be incumbent on the new emperor to reverse her policy. Nicephorus[6] accordingly in 804 despatched an ambassador to the khalif bearing a letter in the following terms:

"From Nicephorus King of the Romans to Haroon King of the Arabs.

"The queen who preceded me on the throne looked upon you as a castle and herself as a pawn.[7] She paid out to you her wealth, whereas in reality you should have paid twice the amount to her, but that was due to the weakness and foolishness of women. On reading my letter, therefore, you must pay back that which you unjustly took from her or else the sword will decide between us."

On reading the letter, the face of the khalif became distorted with fury. Calling for a pen and ink, he turned over the letter of Nicephorus and wrote on the back with his own hand,

"In the name of God, The Compassionate, The Merciful—From Haroon, the Prince of the Faithful to Nicephorus, the Roman dog. I have read your letter, you son of a heathen mother. You will see and not hear my reply."

The very same day orders were issued for the concentration of the army, and the khalif placed himself at the head of his troops. The army was alleged to be 135,000 strong, exclusive of volunteers or camp-followers who were not on the nominal roll. Pouring across the frontier, the Arabs carried fire and sword across Asia Minor until they reached Heraclea on the Black Sea,[8] only a hundred and fifty miles from Byzantium. Utterly unprepared for so violent a reaction to his boastful challenge, Nicephorus was fain to solicit a humiliating peace on condition of the continued payment of the annual tribute. Haroon al Rasheed returned from the campaign to enjoy a period of rest in his palace at Raqqa, which had now become his principal residence.

The withdrawal of the Arabs and the advent of the winter, when the Taurus passes were blocked by snow, emboldened Nicephorus to denounce the new agreement a few weeks after its signature, but once more he had underestimated his enemy. Haroon immediately reconcentrated his army, passed the Taurus again in spite of the snow and ice, and once more advanced across Asia Minor.

6. There is a curious tradition that Nicephorus was descended from Jebela ibn al Aiham, Prince of Ghassan, an Arab who migrated to Byzantium. *The Great Arab Conquests.*

7. The simile is from the game of chess. The original word used was rook but I have translated it castle, as the term more generally in use today for the same piece.

8. See Map 37, page 273. There were two Heracleas. One was on the Black Sea and one on the western slopes of the Taurus.

The Byzantine army was completely vanquished and the whole country from the Black Sea to the Mediterranean was abandoned to fire and sword, to plunder, captivity and slavery. Once more the trembling Nicephorus was obliged to crave for peace. In the ensuing agreement, as an added humiliation, it was stipulated that the coins in which the emperor would pay tribute to the khalif would be stamped with the names of Haroon and his three sons. In addition, all Muslim prisoners in Byzantine hands were to be returned. While these operations had been in progress on land, a naval expedition landed another army in Cyprus.[9] Sixteen thousand Christian captives formed part of the loot and were subsequently sold as slaves in the markets of Syria.

In view of the fact that inability to lead her armies had been the chief cause of Irene's downfall, it was unfortunate that Nicephorus, unlike most of those who usurped the throne of the Caesars, was not a soldier. His past career had been that of a civilian official and a Minister of Finance. During the nine years of his reign, he exercised strict supervision over the departments of the administration. He was alleged to have been of a crafty and treacherous disposition.[10]

It was, however, his lack of skill as a general which proved his ruin. After suffering two humiliating defeats at the hands of Haroon al Rasheed, he engaged in hostilities against the Bulgarians, to whom also Irene had paid tribute. After a number of alternate successes and defeats, he set out in May 811 with a large army, and captured the enemy's capital at Pliska. But on the return march, his army was ambushed in a mountain pass. On 26th July, 811, the Byzantine army was exterminated, Nicephorus himself being killed. His skull, lined with silver, was henceforward used as a drinking bowl by the kings of the Bulgarians.

It is perhaps significant that, although he achieved such an overwhelming military superiority over the Byzantines, Haroon made no attempt to take Constantinople, to annex Asia Minor or to take any measures to ensure the long-term continuance of Arab supremacy. As a result, sixty years later, the Byzantines were able to resume the initiative and obtain their revenge.

*   *   *

According to Frankish records, Haroon exchanged embassies with the Emperor Charlemagne, who received handsome gifts from "The King of Persia, Aaron", including a water-clock and an elephant.[11] The Arab historians, however, do not mention such an incident.

*   *   *

The Abbasid army on the march in time of war must have been an impressive sight. The advanced guard consisted of the light cavalry, dressed in chain-mail, with steel helmets on their heads and lances in their hands. The Arab lance was flexible, up to twenty feet long and decorated with ostrich

9. Cyprus had been originally captured by the Arabs in the reign of the Khalif Othman in 649 but had been lost again in the civil wars. Retaken by Haroon in 802, it was to remain Arab until 963.

10. J. B. Bury, *History of the Eastern Roman Empire*.

11. Hitti, *History of the Arabs*.

feathers. In the main body of the column marched the infantry, armed with pike, sword and shield, and the archers with their long bows. In the centre of the convoy, thousands of camels slouched along, loaded with provisions, tents, weapons and equipment. Ambulances and a form of sedan-chairs were carried for the sick and wounded. The siege train, consisting of mangonels, catapults and other engineering equipment was transported on camels, mules and pack-horses.

In the midst of the troops rode the Prince of the Faithful, on a magnificent charger streaming with pearls and gold, surrounded by his household and the senior officers of the army. The splendour of the scene was enhanced by the brilliant uniforms of the royal guards, dressed in bright colours, covered with gold embroidery. Over the whole army waved a forest of banners and standards also embroidered heavily with gold thread. Behind the khalif's retinue moved the eunuchs and a line of thickly veiled palanquins, in which travelled a number of selected ladies of the khalif's household.

When the army reached the site selected for the night's encampment, the advanced guard had already dug trenches and put the area in a state of defence. In a short time tents were unloaded and, a few minutes later, a canvas town had sprung up with streets, markets and squares. Everywhere camp fires flamed up and the great cooking-pots were soon on the boil. After a simple meal, groups of men gathered round each fire and whiled away the evening with stories, poetry or songs, accompanied by the lute or the rebec, the Oriental viol. Only after midnight did stillness and silence steal over the great canvas city, until the loud rolls of the kettle-drums announced the commencement of another day's campaigning.[12]

*   *   *

The popular indignation against the Umaiyids, as a result of which the Abbasids had obtained power, had been largely due to heavy taxation. The new dynasty, however, continued the same methods. It was not only the sums taken by the government which caused resentment but the greedy and tyrannical methods of the tax-collectors, who did not hesitate to employ flogging and torture to extract more money from the peasants. In Egypt particularly the oppressions of the tax-collectors exceeded all bounds, in spite of orders issued periodically by various khalifs, prohibiting the use of violence or torture by tax-collectors.

*   *   *

Haroon al Rasheed is chiefly known to English readers from the pages of the Arabian Nights, in which he figures as rather a convivial figure. The impression thus produced scarcely does justice to so great a man, and one so remarkably active. In actual fact, he ceased to reside in Baghdad in the last years of his reign and rarely visited the city even for a night.

His principal residence was now at Raqqa on the Euphrates, half way between Iraq and Syria. In the year 804, the people of Baghdad petitioned the khalif, asking him to reside in his capital. In his reply, Haroon expressed

12. I have borrowed part of this description from Von Kremer, op. cit.

his deep affection for the city of his fathers, but excused himself on the grounds of the war against Byzantium and the fact that Raqqa was near the frontier. Were it not, he added, for these considerations, he would never have left his well-beloved city of Baghdad. It is indeed possible that he had discovered by experience that Baghdad was too much under the influence of Persia and too far from the Mediterranean and the western provinces. Raqqa indeed would have been a more central capital for the empire than Baghdad, but unfortunately it was situated in semi-desert country, which could not support a great city.

In the year 807, there was more trouble in Khurasan. The governor of the province was Ali ibn Isa ibn Mahan, like the Barmecids a descendant of one of the Abbasid emissaries to Khurasan in the days of Abu Muslim. This Ali ibn Isa had (also like the Barmecids) acquired immense wealth owing to the royal favour but had done so by the use of oppression and extortion. After ten years as governor of Khurasan, he is said to have accumulated a fortune of eighty million dirhems. The fact that the tyranny of Ali ibn Isa had become notorious suggests some negligence on the khalif's part. Eventually a rebellion broke out in Trans-Oxiana and began to gain ground, with the result that Haroon decided to visit the area in person.

Coming from Raqqa, he passed through Baghdad in February 808, and moved up into North Persia. It is said that he was already suffering from an internal complaint and wore a silk belt bound round his stomach to ease the pain. He was aware that all three of his sons had spies in his entourage, who watched his health, "counting his very breaths", he said. It was already obvious that these sons were only waiting for his death to engage in a fratricidal struggle to secure the khalifate. With all his immense prestige and glory, he must have been saddened and anxious concerning the possible outbreak of civil war after his decease.

He travelled across Persia, reaching Jurjan at the south-eastern end of the Caspian in November 808. From there, feeling increasingly unwell, he travelled to Tus in Khurasan. Here his illness increased until he was unable any more to rise, but he sent on his second son Mamoon, who had accompanied his father and was to be governor of Khurasan, to establish his headquarters in Merv, the capital of the province.

On 23rd March, 809, Haroon al Rasheed, the greatest of the Abbasids, and the greatest emperor of his time, passed away in a Persian garden a few miles from Tus. He was forty-five years of age and had been khalif for twenty-three years.

*   *   *

The reign of Haroon is generally recognized as marking the highest pinnacle of glory achieved by the Abbasids, perhaps even by the Arab Empire throughout its history. In fact, however, the empire was more extensive and militarily more aggressive under Waleed ibn Abdul Malik the Umaiyid, who had reigned a century earlier from 705 to 715. When Haroon came to power, Spain had already been lost and the Maghrib was lost during his reign. In fact, if not in theory, Ifriqiya was lost also and the boundary of imperial administration had returned to Barqa in Cyrenaica. Haroon's apparent lack of interest in North Africa is remarkable in view of the immense efforts he devoted to fighting against the Byzantine Empire.

The military prestige of the khalifate had fallen greatly after the disappearance of the Umaiyids and, during the reigns of Saffah and Mansoor, it was the Byzantines who retained the initiative. Haroon completely restored Arab military domination. On eight different occasions, he invaded the Byzantine Empire at the head of his armies. The speed and energy with which he reacted to the defiant challenge of Nicephorus and his subsequent crossing of the snow-covered Taurus with his army in winter, bear witness to the forcefulness of his character and to his power of leadership. Far from being the drunken reveller of Baghdad, his untiring energy kept him continually on the move. Nine times he performed the pilgrimage to Mecca and Medina, involving weeks of monotonous travel by camel. Several times he visited Khurasan and the Persian provinces.

The laudatory verses pronounced in his honour by a contemporary contain little exaggeration. Referring to the khalif he said:

> He who would see our prince must distant lands explore,
> Or towards the Holy Cities set his face.
> There he, on prancing steed, directs the war,
> Here sways to the tall camels rhythmic pace.

Yet he was no mere rough soldier, more at home in the camp than in the city. Well educated in both religion and literature, he was a patron of the learned and of poets. He sought out the company of ascetics, and religious teachers on his visits to Mecca and Medina and would refer to them the religious difficulties which at times confronted him. He is said to have been much addicted to long prayers and to weeping when he heard a pious sermon.

He was always extremely orthodox in his religious professions. His reign was an age of great intellectual activity, particularly in the field of theology and religious jurisprudence. The early Arabs had been content to accept Islam simply, without any desire to split hairs. But now, two centuries after Muhammad's flight from Mecca, the Muslims had learned to argue the complicated problems of theology. Great numbers of men of learning were engaged in writing books, in compiling traditions of the Prophet, in commenting on the Qoran and in studying grammar and language. Two of the greatest of Muslim jurists, Abu Hanifa and Muhammad ash Shafei, were alive during Haroon's reign. Bukhari, the greatest of all compilers of the traditions of Muhammad, was born the year after Haroon died.

There was also a great deal of free religious speculation, some of which was denounced as heretical. The khalif would cry out in indignation whenever such heresies were mentioned. It is impossible now to form an estimate as to how genuine was his religious devotion or whether his piety was tinged with policy.

Though as a young man he did not drink, he undoubtedly indulged in alcohol in middle life, a practice forbidden to Muslims. Yet his evening entertainments were not mere drunken debauches. Like the eighteenth century in Europe, it was an age in which conversation and culture were regarded as an art and intellectual discussions of high quality formed part of the recreation of the educated classes. Both the poetry and the music were of a high order. There were many famous poets at the court of the khalif and Ishaq al Mosuli was said to be unrivalled in his singing to the accompaniment of the lute.

The two most famous poets at the time of Haroon were probably Abu Nuwas and Abu al Atahiya. The former was a libertine, who was more than once imprisoned for drunkenness and immorality.

> "Ho! a cup and fill it up and tell me it is wine,
> For I will never drink in shade when I can drink in shine!
> Curst and poor is every hour that sober I must go,
> But rich am I whene'er well drunk I stagger to and fro.
> Speak, for shame, the loved one's name, let vain disguise alone:
> No good there is in pleasures o'er which a veil is thrown."

Abu al Atahiya, on the other hand, was of a serious and religious disposition:

> "Get sons for death, build houses for decay!
> All, all, ye wend annihilation's way.
> For whom build we, who must ourselves return
> Into our native element of clay?
> O Death, nor violence nor flattery thou
> Dost use, but when thou com'st, escape none may."[13]

The following verses have been attributed to Haroon himself:

> "An early dew woos the half opened flowers,
> Wind of the south, dear child,
> Close clings about their stalks for drunken hours;
> And yet your eyes, dear child,
> Cool pools which rise, dear child,
> High in the mountains of my soul,
> These, these the lips have drunken whole
> And yet your mouth, dear child,
> Your mouth, dear child, is envied of the bees."[14]

Haroon al Rasheed is said to have had the idea of digging a canal to join the Mediterranean to the Red Sea, approximately on the same alignment as the Suez Canal which was dug more than a thousand years later. It is alleged that Yahya the Barmecid dissuaded him on the grounds that the Byzantine Mediterranean fleet would thereby be enabled to enter the Red Sea and threaten Mecca. If the story be true, it shows the Barmecid, on this occasion

13. Nicholson. Op. cit.
14. Translated by E. Powys Mathers in *An Anthology of World Poetry*.

at least, to have been less of a statesman than his master. Indeed in an age without maps to have chosen the same alignment for the canal as that selected by De Lesseps in the nineteenth century would have been an extraordinary tribute to the mind of the great khalif.

*   *   *

When first he was raised to the khalifate, Haroon seems to have been an open-hearted and generous young man, possibly also genuinely religious. Twenty-three years of despotic power, surrounded by the servile flattery which had now become the custom of the court, could not fail to cause a deterioration in his character. Yet he never seems to have been as cruel or as treacherous as Saffah or Mansoor.

The bedouin tribes of Arabia today have a curious proverb—"The best of my sons is the one you have heard about." The suggestion is that fame implies something remarkable in a man. Judged by this standard, Haroon al Rasheed stands far above any other khalif. Of the fifty-four khalifs who reigned from the time of the Prophet to the overthrow of The Arab Empire, his is the only name familiar to Western readers today. In the Arab countries, even the most illiterate peasant or shepherd is familiar with the stories of Haroon al Rasheed and his wife, the Lady Zubaida. His nocturnal escapades in Baghdad, his glorious campaigns against the Byzantines, the poems of Abu Nuwas, the amatory adventures of the palace set, the gold, the silver, the jewels, the priceless carpets, the splendid horses—all have passed into history, legend and romance, to build up the picture, perhaps the dream, of the Golden Age of the City of the Khalifs.

*   *   *

As soon as Haroon al Rasheed breathed his last, a messenger was despatched post haste from Tus to Baghdad, where the heir-apparent had been left in charge during the absence of his father. The oaths of allegiance were duly administered to the members of the Abbasid family in the capital, to their freedmen, servants and officers and to the troops of the garrison who, according to the now established custom, received a handsome royal donative. Thus was Ameen, the son of Haroon al Rasheed, declared Prince of the Faithful, without any murmur of dissent, in the capital of the empire. Meanwhile his brother Mamoon was still in Merv, the capital of Khurasan.

NOTABLE DATES

Accession of Haroon al Rasheed	15th September, 786
Establishment of Idris ibn Abdulla in the Maghrib	788
Death of Idris I by poison	792
Ibrahim ibn al Aghlab made governor of Ifriqiya	800
Fall of the Barmecids	803
Haroon's campaigns against Nicephorus	805
Death of Haroon al Rasheed	23rd March, 809

PERSONALITIES

The Khalif Haroon al Rasheed
Ameen ⎫
Mamoon ⎬ his sons
Mutamin ⎭
Yahya ibn Khalid the Barmecid
Jaafar ⎫
Fadhl ⎬ his sons
Musa ⎭
Idris ibn Abdulla, Prince of the Maghrib
Idris II, his son
Ibrahim ibn al Aghlab, governor of Ifriqiya
Abbasa, sister of Haroon

BYZANTINE EMPERORS

Leo IV	775–780
Irene, widow of Leo IV, as regent for her son	780–785
Constantine VI, son of Leo IV, and Irene	780–797
(From 780–785 Constantine was a minor and his mother Irene acted as regent)	
Irene, in her own right, after blinding her son, Constantine VI	797–802
Nicephorus I	802–811

XVI

Fratricidal Feuds

O that my head were waters, and mine eyes a fountain of tears that I might weep day and night for the slain . . . of my people. Take ye heed every one of his neighbour and trust ye not in any brother: for every brother will utterly supplant.

Jeremiah IX, 1 and 4

Give not thy strength unto women, nor thy ways to that which destroyeth kings. It is not for kings to drink wine; nor for princes strong drink. Lest they drink and forget the law, and pervert the judgement of the afflicted.

Proverbs XXXI, 3–5

XVI

FRATRICIDAL FEUDS

FIFTY years have elapsed since we last mentioned the history of Andalus, where in September 755, the Umaiyid Prince Abdul Rahman ibn Muawiya had landed on the coast. In 763, it will be remembered Abdul Rahman had defeated Ala ibn Mughith, whom the Abbasid Khalif Mansoor had appointed to reconquer Spain for the khalifate.

But though he had thus triumphed over the Abbasids, Abdul Rahman was by no means firmly seated on his new throne. As already explained, the Qaisites had held the power in Andalus at the time of Abdul Rahman's arrival with the result that the Yemenites readily rallied to the pretender—they did so, however, in the hope of being able to replace the Qaisites in power. No sooner was Abdul Rahman victorious and established in his own right than the Yemenites rose against him.

Depicted by the historians as originally a handsome, brave and debonair young pretender, the unending revolts of his new subjects seem to have embittered his character, and done away with any scruples he may once have possessed. The leader of the Yemenite confederation, one Abu Sobbah, was given safe conduct and invited to a conference, whereupon he was treacherously assassinated in the palace of Cordova.

The Berbers had played a leading, if not the chief, part in the conquest of Spain, but when it came to the division of the spoils, the Arabs had seized for themselves the fertile lands of the south and had allotted to their Berber allies the arid plateaux of Estremadura and Castile. While thus nursing a permanent grievance against their Arab overlords, the Berbers, as we have seen in Ifriqiya, were of a simple and credulous mentality. A Berber schoolmaster proclaimed himself a descendant of Ali ibn abi Talib, and raised a mass revolt of his compatriots in Estremadura and on the upper Tagus. Desultory hostilities against the Berbers lasted for six years until the rebels were gradually pushed northwards into the mountains of Castile. Thither Abdul Rahman was about to pursue them, when the Yemenites chose the moment to rise in revolt, to avenge the blood of their chieftain Abu Sobbah. Abandoning his campaign against the Berbers, the prince returned hot foot to Cordova to confront the Yemenites. As skilful as a diplomat as he was courageous as a soldier, he sent secret emissaries to sow dissension in the ranks of the insurgents. When he advanced to the attack, a large part of the rebel forces deserted to his side. The Yemenites were defeated with—it is alleged—a loss of thirty thousand dead, doubtless an exaggerated estimate.

The Berber rising in the north was still dragging on when a far greater danger suddenly threatened the unhappy Abdul Rahman. Sulaiman al Arabi, the governor of Barcelona and a Yemenite, conspired with ibn Habeeb,

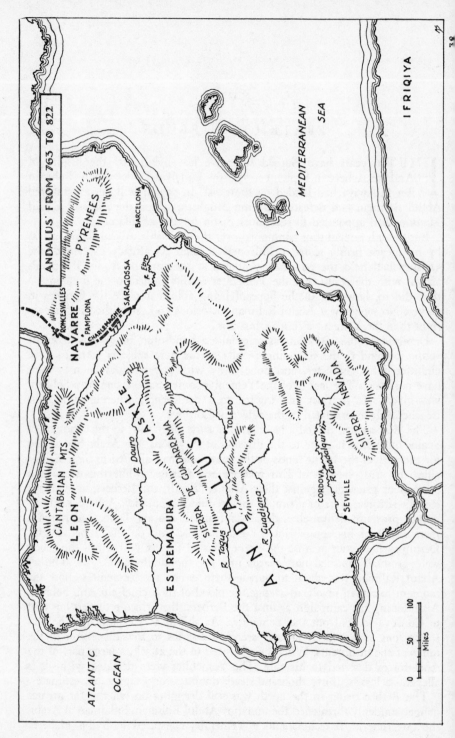

ANDALUS FROM 763 TO 822

PYRENEES

BARCELONA

NAVARRE

ROMCESVALLES
PAMPLONA
CHARLEMAGNE
778
SARAGOSSA
R. Ebro

CANTABRIAN MTS

LEON

CASTILE

R. Douro

ESTREMADURA

SIERRA DE GUADARRAMA

TOLEDO

R. Tagus

R. Guadiana

A N D A L U S

SIERRA NEVADA

CORDOVA
R. Guadalquivir
SEVILLE

ATLANTIC
OCEAN

MEDITERRANEAN
SEA

IFRIQIYA

0   50   100
Miles

son-in-law of Yusuf al Fihri, the governor of Spain at the time of Abdul Rahman's arrival. Unable to face the Umaiyid prince in the field, they conceived the idea of bringing in foreign aid. In 777, the conspirators went to Paderborn, where the Emperor Charlemagne was holding an assembly of his nobles, and suggested to him an invasion of Andalus. Just as Christian Spain had been handed over to the Muslims through the hatred of Count Julian for King Roderic, so now the discontented Yemenites and Fihrites were ready to hand the country back to the Christians to gratify their spite against Abdul Rahman. (In Baghdad the Khalif Mehedi, father of Hadi and Haroon al Rashid, was on the throne.)

Charlemagne had recently defeated the Saxons, who had expressed themselves willing to adopt Christianity. The Saxon king, Wittekind, had fled from his country and had taken refuge in Denmark. The emperor's dominions were at peace and he readily fell in with the idea of conquering Spain from the Muslims, and marched through the Pyrenees with a great army. Sulaiman al Arabi had meanwhile seized Saragossa with the assistance of Husain ibn Yahya, a man of Medina and a direct descendant of one of the Helpers and Companions of the Apostle of God. But when the Frankish army appeared before the walls of Saragossa, Husain could not bring himself to surrender the city to the enemies of his religion and his nation, and Charlemagne found himself obliged to lay siege to the fortress which was occupied by his supposed allies.

At this critical moment, news reached Charlemagne that, profiting by his absence, Wittekind had returned to his country, that a general rising of the Saxons had resulted and that their army, devastating the country as it went, was already approaching Cologne. Abandoning the Spanish venture, Charlemagne set out by forced marches for the Rhine. Passing through the narrow defile of Roncesvalles in the Pyrenees, the Frankish army had become unduly strung out in a long column. The Basques, inveterate enemies of the Franks, were lying in ambush. Allowing the main body to pass unmolested, they fell upon the rearguard, under the command of Roland. While the main body marched on, unaware of the disaster, the rearguard was exterminated. At the height of the battle, Roland blew his great horn as a sign of distress, but the sound did not reach the main body and no answering call came to cheer the doomed soldiers.

> "Dieu! Que le son du cor
> Est triste au fond des bois."[1]

The death of Roland gave rise to a whole literature of romance and chivalry. He appears in reality to have been killed by the Basques, but tradition has hallowed his death by attributing it, at least in part, to the Muslims. When the Norman knights advanced, three centuries later, to the battlefield of Hastings, they sang the *Chanson de Roland* to stimulate their martial spirit.

*   *   *

---

1. "God! How sad is the sound
   Of that horn in the depth of the woods."
   Alfred de Vigny.

Fortune had again smiled on Prince Abdul Rahman and this formidable invasion of his country had been brought to nought without his striking a blow. At last, after incredible adventures, the young man who, as a desperate fugitive, had swum the Euphrates and wandered like a vagabond among the Berber tribes of Africa, had established himself firmly on the throne of a wealthy and beautiful country. But happiness still eluded him. He had fought against every group of his subjects in turn, Qaisites, Fihrites, Yemenites and Berbers. He had fought with incredible courage, determination and ferocity, by treachery and in open battle. His subjects were cowed but many of them were secretly his implacable enemies.

To increase his adherents, to add lustre to his capital, perhaps also out of family affection, he had invited the scattered remnants of the Umaiyid clan —some of whom were still wandering in Africa—to take refuge at his court. But instead of showing gratitude for his protection, they, on two occasions, conspired to assassinate him and place another of their number on the throne. Unable to trust any of his subjects, he sought to ensure the safety of his rule by the use of mercenary troops. He bought slaves and enrolled them as soldiers, and enlisted many Berber tribesmen whom he brought over from Africa. By this means, he built up an army of 40,000 men who owed loyalty to his person alone.

But while Abdul Rahman lamented the fact that all his worldly success had not brought him happiness, it had nevertheless gained him the grudging admiration of even his bitterest enemies. In far-away Baghdad, the Khalif Mansoor had once asked his courtiers who they thought deserved the title of the falcon of Quraish. "You yourself, O Prince of the Faithful," replied the courtly flatterers. "No, it is not I," replied the khalif. Some suggested Muawiya and others Abdul Malik ibn Merwan. "No," replied Mansoor, "The falcon of Quraish is Abdul Rahman in Andalus. The man who, after wandering solitary through the deserts of Asia and Africa, had the boldness to seek his fortune without an army, in lands unknown to him beyond the sea. Having naught to rely upon save his own wits and perseverance, he nevertheless humiliated his proud foes, exterminated rebels, secured his frontiers against the Christians, founded a great empire, and reunited under his sceptre a realm which seemed already parcelled out among petty chieftains. No man before him ever did such deeds."

Yet Ibn Hayyan, the Arab historian of Andalus, gives us a different picture. "Abdul Rahman," he writes, "was kind-hearted and well disposed to mercy. He was eloquent in his speech and endowed with a quick perception. He was very slow in his decisions, but constant and persevering in carrying them into effect. He was active and energetic; he would never lie in repose or abandon himself to indulgence. He was a brave warrior, always the first in battle. Terrible in anger, his countenance inspired awe. He visited the sick and mixed with the people in their rejoicings."

Abdul Rahman died in 788, two years after Haroon had assumed the khalifate in Baghdad, and was succeeded by his son Hisham, who was thirty years of age when he came to the throne. The new prince differed remarkably from his father in character. Even in his youth, his chief pleasure had been in the society of the learned. When he assumed power, his principal anxiety was to further the cause of religion and to secure justice for all his subjects. The agents whom he sent out to all parts of his dominions were charged, not to uncover conspiracies, but to seek out cases of injustice or the activities of the exploiters of the people. In him the poor and the oppressed always found a friend and a protector. He himself would often go out at night to visit the sick or to carry food to the houses of the deserving poor—a tradition established long before in Medina by Umar ibn al Khattab, the second successor of the Prophet. Yet he was no unpractical bigot. He increased the strength of the bodyguard of soldier-slaves and fought in person against the Christians in the north.

Unfortunately for his country, he died after a reign of only eight years and was succeeded in 796 by his son Hakam. When discussing the reign of Ibrahim ibn al Aghlab, who in 800 had assumed the government of Ifriqiya, we have already heard of the intense religious and intellectual activity of the time. From Cordova, as much as from Qairawan, students flocked to Medina to study religion under the great masters of the age. Especially famous was the school of religious jurisprudence founded there by Malik ibn Anas, who died in 795. The majority of the theological students from Andalus who went to Medina were not Arabs but Spanish converts. As so often happens, their piety was more ardent than that of the Arabs who had converted them.

The non-Arab converts to Islam in Andalus nursed the same grievances as had given rise to the Abbasid revolution in the East. Although in theory all Muslims were equal, the haughty Arabs insisted on treating their non-Arab co-religionists as members of a lower social class. But now the sons of these Spanish converts were returning from their studies in Medina, more pious, more ardent and better informed than their arrogant Arab rulers. These developments passed unnoticed during the pious reign of Hisham, but the young Hakam, who now ascended the throne, was of a cheerful and sociable disposition, fond of hunting and a drinker of wine. He was not indeed openly irreligious, but on the contrary he was punctilious in fulfilling his duties. He showed respect to religious teachers and entered into discussions with the theologians. To us, the pleasures of the young Hakam might appear innocent but, as the result of the influence of the theological students who had studied in Medina, the country was in the throes of an ascetic and puritan revival. To the Malikite saints, Hakam was soon the man of sin personified. The leader of these revivalists was Yahya ibn Yahya, a Berber who had studied in Medina.

As has already been indicated, the Muslim state ideal was not self-government by the people but observance of the Qoran and the Traditions of the Prophet. The ruler was the administrator of laws laid down by God himself and the theologians considered themselves to be the persons best qualified to explain those laws. The khalif, sultan or ameer was merely the executive officer whose task it was to see that the divine rules—as interpreted by the theologians—were duly observed. It was a system which gave the religious an excuse for interference in politics, which Yahya ibn Yahya was ready to exploit. Both the Berbers and the Spaniards converted to Islam already resented the refusal of the Arabs to grant them social equality. Thus Cordova, the capital, was in a constant turmoil, the prince's African mercenaries being barely able to prevent a revolution

The city of Toledo had been the capital of Spain under the Visigoths and doubtless resented the removal of the government to Cordova. "Never," writes an Arab historian, "were the subjects of any monarch so unruly and seditious." In 808, Hakam determined to teach them a lesson. His son was sent to Toledo on a visit and was instructed to invite all the principal men to a banquet in the castle, to be held the morning after his arrival. During the night a great ditch was dug in the courtyard of the fortress. Next morning the guests were admitted one by one. As each entered, his head was struck off and his body was pushed into the ditch, until all the leading men of Toledo, amounting to several hundred, had been executed. Deprived in a few hours of all their leaders, the people of Toledo henceforward abandoned all attempts at revolt. The incident was long remembered as the Day of the Ditch.

Hospitality was, and still is, the supreme Arab virtue, in which they excel all other races. The ragged dwellers in the tents of the desert not only welcome every passer-by to share their frugal meal, but are prepared to risk their lives to protect their guest from danger or even from discomfort. It seems to us strange that less than two centuries after their emergence from their desert home, Arabs could be found so foully to betray that very quality of hospitality which had formed the chief pride of their forbears.

Six years after the Day of the Ditch in Toledo—in May 814—revolt broke out in the capital city of Cordova, and the sultan found himself besieged in the castle, which appeared to be in imminent danger of being carried by storm. But if power had made Hakam cruel and treacherous, it had not deprived him of courage. With perfect self-possession, he drew up his plan. The garrison was not numerous enough to drive the insurgents back but a small party of cavalry would be strong enough to break through. These the prince instructed to gallop through the crowd of rioters and set fire to the suburbs. The gate was thrown open, the cavalry slashed their way through the mob and soon smoke was billowing up to the sky from the residential quarters of the town. The men attacking the castle turned their backs and hastened away down the streets to rescue their families and their property from the flames. Thereupon the African mercenaries sallied out in pursuit and cut them down unmercifully as they fled.

The rioters were completely defeated and were ordered to leave Andalus within three days with their wives and families. Some sailed to Egypt, and seized the city of Alexandria, whence they were to be driven out eleven years later in 825. They thereupon conquered Crete, where they established their own government which lasted for nearly a century and a half, until the island was reconquered by the Byzantines in 961. Another eight thousand families of Cordovan exiles crossed to the Maghrib, where they were welcomed by Idris and settled in his new city of Fez. The curious part about the exiles from Cordova was that few of them were either Arabs or Berbers. They consisted principally of Spanish converts to Islam.

Hakam died in 822, after ruling Andalus for twenty-six years. During the last eight years of his reign, the country enjoyed peace and prosperity. The prince himself became benign and merciful when the turbulence of his subjects abated. In a poem composed shortly before his death, he claimed that he had used his sword as a tailor his needle, to sew together the provinces of his kingdom. "If I spared not the wives and children of the rebels, it was because they threatened my family and myself. He who cannot avenge insults offered to his family is devoid of honour."

Arabs, while constantly demanding freedom and ever ready to oppose whatever government attempts to rule them, yet have a genuine admiration for a man who, by fair means or foul, can triumph over all opposition. Hakam had perhaps for this reason won their respect and passed the last years of his life in peace and honour.

Having carried the story of Andalus up to the death of Hakam in 822, we must return to the Prince of the Faithful in Baghdad.

*   *   *

GENEALOGY OF BENI ABBAS KHALIFS
after MANSOOR

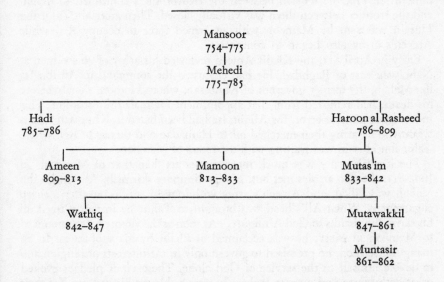

As soon as, in March 809, the news of Haroon's death reached Baghdad, Ameen and Mamoon exchanged friendly letters and it seemed for a short time as though the complicated arrangements made by the late khalif would actually be put into effect. But certain courtiers in Baghdad, notably the Chief Minister, Fadhl ibn Rabia, feared the ultimate succession of Mamoon to the khalifate and suggested to Ameen the appointment of his son Musa as heir-apparent. Ameen at first seemed inclined to execute the wishes of his late father but gradually allowed himself to be persuaded. His first step was to remove his brother Mutamin from the governorship of Armenia and the Jezira, which Haroon al Rasheed had bequeathed to him. He then gave orders for the name of his son Musa to be included in the Friday prayers, at first after those of the three brothers Ameen, Mamoon and Mutamin, but then in conjunction with his own name alone. It will be remembered that on his last visit to Mecca, Haroon had caused the document setting out his will regarding his sons, to be hung in the Kaaba. Ameen now sent a messenger to remove his father's testament and to bring it to Baghdad, where it was destroyed. He then wrote to Mamoon, instructing him to remit the surplus revenues of Khurasan to Baghdad and informing him that he—Ameen—was appointing certain officials to posts in that province. These measures certainly appeared to be contrary to Haroon's settlement, which virtually made Mamoon independent of Baghdad. Yet it must be admitted that Haroon's arrangements were probably impossible of execution.

Mamoon was alarmed and inclined to surrender but his minister, Fadhel ibn Sahel, persuaded him to resist. He accordingly replied in respectful terms but took the precaution of placing outposts on the roads coming from Iraq, with orders to arrest all propagandists, emissaries or intriguers, who might come from Iraq to Khurasan to seduce the people from their allegiance to himself. In 810, the tension between the two brothers continued to mount and the frontier between them was virtually closed. Then a certain Tahir ibn Husain was sent by Mamoon with an armed force to occupy Rei, while Ameen's army also began to concentrate.

Early in April 811, the Khalif Ameen reviewed his army of 40,000 men at Nahrawan east of Baghdad. He had entrusted the command to Ali ibn Isa ibn Mahan, the former governor of Khurasan, whom Haroon, shortly before his death, had removed from that appointment for maladministration. This in itself was a major error, for Ali ibn Isa had been hated in Khurasan for his tyranny. The army then marched off to Hamadan and thence to Rei, where Tahir ibn Husain was waiting with the forces of Mamoon.

The khalif's army was much more numerous than that of Mamoon. In June 811, the two armies met but, in a preliminary skirmish, Ali ibn Isa ibn Mahan was killed, and Ameen's army withdrew in confusion after a sharp engagement. When Ali's head was brought to Tahir, he instantly freed all his slaves "in thanks to God Almighty". As soon as the victory was announced to Mamoon in Merv, he was acclaimed as khalif by his supporters. In an inaugural sermon, he promised to govern only in the interests of religion and to devote himself to the service of God alone. These pious pledges evoked great enthusiasm and were to be largely responsible for his victory. Yet their ultimate effect was to be disastrous, for when he became khalif, he forgot them. Meanwhile Ameen in Baghdad, having sent off his army to Persia, was giving himself up to frivolous pleasures.

The news of the defeat and death of Ali ibn Isa at the hands of the much smaller force of Tahir ibn Husain, caused consternation among the supporters of Ameen. The mercenary troops seized the opportunity to mutiny and to demand an advance of pay. The khalif, instead of appealing to God or to

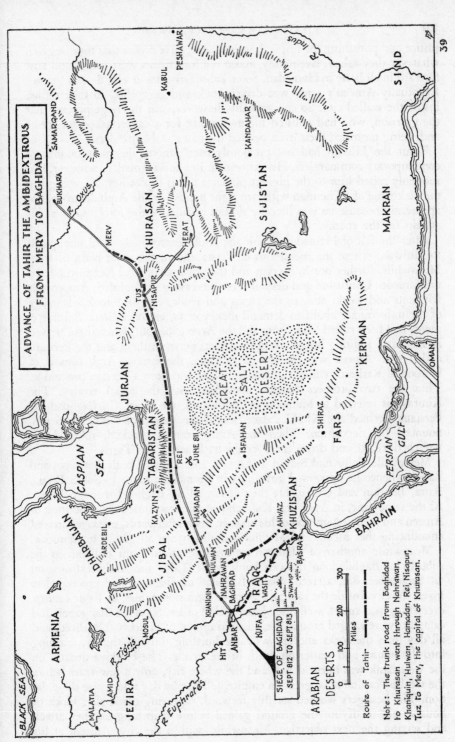

ADVANCE OF TAHIR THE AMBIDEXTROUS
FROM MERV TO BAGHDAD

SIEGE OF BAGHDAD
SEPT 812 TO SEPT 813

0   100   200   300
Miles

Route of Tahir

Note: The trunk road from Baghdad
to Khurasan went through Nahrawan,
Khaniquin, Hulwan, Hamadan, Rei, Nisapur,
Tuz to Merv, the capital of Khurasan.

39

301

justice and punishing the disloyal, immediately gave orders that they be given whatever they asked. Eventually 20,000 reinforcements were raised and sent forward in all haste to Hamadan. Soon Tahir arrived and a battle was fought. Eventually Ameen's army was driven back and compelled to take refuge inside the walled city. So energetically, however, was the siege pressed that the garrison, who had enlisted for money not for a cause, asked for terms and, being promised their lives, opened the gates to the invaders.

Tahir ibn Husain had not previously been among the most famous of contemporary commanders. His victories at Rei and Hamadan, however, had suddenly raised him to the highest pinnacle of his profession. He was given the nickname of "The man with two right hands" or the Ambidextrous, not apparently because he was literally so, but because of the forcefulness of his attacks on the enemy.

After the fall of Hamadan, Tahir the Ambidextrous advanced unopposed to Hulwan, where the mountains of Persia end in the great plain of Iraq. Meanwhile, further north, Kazvin and the province of Jibal had surrendered to Mamoon. Confusion and despair were increasing in Baghdad. Ameen was frivolous and weak, and, in the chaos and panic, everyone took advantage of the unfortunate khalif to demand money or other concessions. Reinforcements had been raised from Syria and the Arab tribes but, when these arrived in Baghdad, fighting broke out in the streets between them and the Persians and Turks. Ameen was the son of Zubaida, the famous Arab consort of Haroon al Rasheed, while Mamoon's mother had been a Persian concubine. Thus the two brothers became identified with the racial rivalry. The Khurasanis referred to Mamoon as "the son of our sister". In Baghdad the Persians stormed the Khuld Palace, seized the person of Ameen and pronounced his deposition. Then the Arabs counter-attacked, released the wretched khalif and drove the Persians back across the Tigris.

Meanwhile Tahir had moved to Ahwaz, and occupied both that town and Basra, whence he appointed governors in Mamoon's name to South Persia, Basra, Bahrein and Oman. He then advanced on Baghdad through Wasit. At the same time, in April 812, Kufa and Mosul proclaimed the deposition of Ameen and their recognition of his brother. Soon afterwards, messages arrived announcing that Mecca and Medina had also sworn allegiance to Mamoon.

Meanwhile another of Mamoon's armies advanced from Hulwan to the suburbs of Baghdad on the east bank while Tahir the Ambidextrous, on 1st September, 812, arrived outside Baghdad on the west and proceeded to invest the city. Inside the capital, all was in confusion, while, in Tahir's camp, everything was smart, well-disciplined and in order. Soon the mangonels and catapults were ranged around the splendid capital of Haroon al Rasheed, and all day long the rocks and arrows came hurtling through the air, crashing into the houses and scattering death in the streets. The Harbiya quarter on the west bank was burnt down, and the whole city, only a few years before the wealthy capital of so great an empire, fell day by day into worse dilapidation. The besiegers worked steadily forward, capturing block after block of houses, and fortifying the ground gained before launching another attack and seizing the next objective. Meanwhile, within the city, Ameen, at his

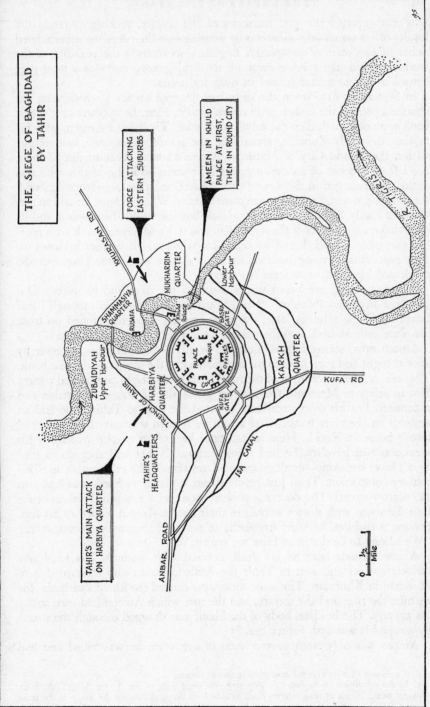

THE SIEGE OF BAGHDAD
BY TAHIR

FORCE ATTACKING
EASTERN SUBURBS

AMEEN IN KHULD
PALACE AT FIRST,
THEN IN ROUND CITY

R. TIGRIS

KHURASAN RD

SHAMMASIYA
QUARTER

MUKHARRIM
QUARTER

RUSAFA

Lower
Harbour

Khuld
Palace

BASRA
GATE

ZUBAIDIYAH
Upper Harbour

HARBIYA
QUARTER

TRENCH OF TAHIR

PALACE
MOSQUE
GOV'T
OFFICES

KUFA
GATE

KARKH
QUARTER

KUFA RD

TAHIR'S
HEADQUARTERS

TAHIR'S MAIN ATTACK
ON HARBIYA QUARTER

ISA CANAL

ANBAR ROAD

0   ½
    Mile

wits' end, opened the vast treasuries of the empire, seeking to retain the loyalty of his remaining adherents by pouring into their laps the accumulated riches of the years of prosperity. Baghdad, so recently the paradise of the world, arrayed like a bride awaiting the bridegroom, now—as a local poet bewailed—lay torn and ruined in dust and ashes.

In September 813, when the siege had dragged on for a whole year, the attackers pressed the assault with renewed zest. First the quarters on the east bank were occupied, then the suburb of Karkh. The Khalif Ameen, with his mother the Lady Zubaida, abandoned the Khuld palace and took refuge within the Round City of Mansoor. Ameen's uncle, Ibrahim ibn Mehedi, has left an account of an evening which he spent with the khalif, who was at the time besieged in the Round City. "I received a message from Ameen," the old man wrote, "asking me to come to him. When I came, he said to me, 'What a lovely night it is, Ibrahim. Look how beautiful the moon is and its reflection on the waters of the river. Will you stay and have a drink with me?' 'As you like,' I replied, and he called for wine, which was set between us. The unfortunate young man called for a girl to sing something, but she displeased him and he ordered her away.

"Then suddenly we heard voices down by the river and he asked, 'Did you hear anything, Ibrahim?' 'No, I heard nothing,' I replied, though I had heard it. A few minutes later, the noise recurred, and he jumped up from his place and ran back into the palace. Two nights later, he was killed."

Ameen now, seeing himself deserted by all, decided to cross the river by boat at night and surrender to the commander of the troops on the east bank. This officer was a freedman of the royal family who, he hoped, would convey him in safety to Mamoon, from whose generosity he hoped for pardon and a pension. But his own attendants betrayed the plan to Tahir, who laid an ambush on the river bank. After a scuffle, Ameen was seized and dragged into a house in Karkh. Here he sat, once lord of an empire which, by his weakness and frivolity, he had thrown away. "What will they do to me? Don't leave me alone—don't go away—I am afraid," he kept repeating to his solitary companion. Then just before dawn, a clatter of hoofs was heard in the narrow streets. The door was pushed open and a group of Persians broke into the room with drawn swords in their hands. Ameen leaped to his feet. Seizing a cushion, he tried frenziedly to ward off the sword points, crying "We belong to God and to Him we return."[2]

A few seconds later he lay dead, covered with wounds. His head was quickly cut off and sent to Tahir the Ambidextrous, who forwarded it to Mamoon in Khurasan. The same messenger carried the khalif's insignia, the mantle, the ring and the sceptre, and the mat which Ameen had used to say his prayers. The headless body of the khalif was dragged through the streets by a rope.[3] It was 25th September, 813.

Ameen was only twenty-seven years of age when he was killed and had

2. A common Muslim expression of piety in face of disaster.

3. In the revolution in Baghdad in July 1958, the dead body of the Ameer Abdulillah, heir-apparent to the throne of Iraq, was reported to have been dragged through the streets in the same manner.

reigned four years and eight months. He was famous for his handsome looks, being tall, fair and of fine physique. He was well-educated, eloquent, accomplished and wrote good poetry—but his character was weak and frivolous and he was badly advised by ministers who sought only their own interests. He was pleasant and affectionate with his intimates, but he failed in leadership. Instead of providing a moral cause for which men would fight, his only idea was to give money to buy support. It was by the advice of his minister, Fadhel ibn Rabia, that he disinherited Mamoon and substituted his own son as heir-apparent, though the infant was still at his mother's breast, so that a lampoonist of Baghdad wrote:

> The Minister's a traitor and the Prince a profligate,
> For Fadhel[4] is the Minister and head of all the state.
> But what is even stranger and harder far to bear
> Is that we are expected allegiance now to swear
> To a baby which is still in arms and cannot wipe its nose
> Nor even leave its nurse's lap to put on its own clothes.

*   *   *

Mamoon's chief adviser and minister in Khurasan had been Fadhel ibn Sahel. No sooner did information reach Merv of the death of Ameen than Hasan ibn Sahel, the brother of Fadhel, was sent to take over control of Iraq and Arabia. Tahir the Ambidextrous was ordered to hand over everything to Hasan and to withdraw to Raqqa. Abu Muslim, who, more than any other, had raised the Abbasid family to the khalifate, had been murdered by the Khalif Mansoor. Tahir the Ambidextrous, who had enabled Mamoon to achieve the supreme power, was already regarded with suspicion. To a despotic ruler, the presence of a man to whom he owes his power cannot fail to be uncongenial. The elevation of Fadhel and Hasan, sons of Sahel, to the two highest offices, nevertheless provoked great resentment in Baghdad, especially among the members of the Abbasid family themselves.

In February 815, commenced a whole series of risings led by various descendants of Ali ibn abi Talib. The first began in Kufa, in support of a great-great-great-great-grandson of Ali, and was followed by similar outbreaks in Mecca, Medina, Wasit and Basra, all of which cities were seized by different groups of rebels. Then the Yemen was also occupied by the Shia. The following year, Mamoon caused Ali ibn Musa ibn Jaafar, the leading descendant of the martyred Husain, to be brought to him in Khurasan, where he received him with honour. In Kufa, Basra, Mecca and Medina, the property of the Abbasids and their supporters was plundered, their houses were burned down and any men seen wearing black clothes were killed. It may well be that the Aliids in this made a tactical error, for their appeal to the public could only be one based on religion. By displaying vindictiveness towards their enemies, they forfeited their only asset. Arab resentment at the fact that Mamoon owed his victory to Persian support also undoubtedly

4. Curiously enough the Chief Ministers of both Ameen and Mamoon were called Fadhel. That of Ameen was Fadhel ibn Rabia, an Arab, the man referred to in this rhyme. That of Mamoon was Fadhel ibn Sahel, a Persian.

played a part in these rebellions. More than a year elapsed before order was restored.

Meanwhile Mamoon, although he had now been everywhere recognized as khalif, remained in Merv, while hatred of his viceroy in Iraq, Hasan ibn Sahel, continued to increase. At length the populace of Baghdad rose in revolt, and Hasan was obliged to flee to Wasit, the troops also being in a state of mutiny owing to arrears in their pay. It is noticeable that the one man who seemed to be capable of riding these storms, Tahir the Ambidextrous, was engaged in unimportant duties in Raqqa. In January 817, the populace of the capital endeavoured to acclaim Mansoor ibn Mehedi, an uncle of Mamoon, as khalif, declaring that they would not have a Magian to rule them. The opprobious term (the Persians had been Magians or fire-worshippers before Islam) referred to the viceroy, Hasan ibn Sahel, who was not only a Persian but a recent convert to Islam.

Mansoor ibn Mehedi, however, refused to accept the position of khalif, but agreed to be governor of Baghdad in the name of Mamoon. Thus a ridiculous situation arose, in which there was virtually civil war in Iraq, between Hasan ibn Sahel, viceroy of Mamoon, and Mansoor ibn Mehedi, uncle of Mamoon, who also claimed to be acting in his name. Meanwhile administration was at a standstill, taxes could not be collected, and the villages of lower Iraq were constantly plundered by the mercenary troops of one side or the other. Conditions in Baghdad had become unbearable. Bandits and unpaid soldiers swarmed in the streets, carried off women, robbed on the highways and blackmailed citizens and landowners, who were obliged to pay the gangs to secure immunity for their possessions.

With everything in Iraq thus out of control, in March 816, the viceroy Hasan ibn Sahel (who was still living in Wasit unable to enter Baghdad) received a letter from Mamoon, informing him that the Prince of the Faithful had appointed, as heir-apparent to the khalifate, Ali ibn Musa ibn Jaafar ibn Muhammad ibn Ali ibn Husain ibn Ali ibn abi Talib. The khalif ordered oaths of allegiance to be taken everywhere to Ali ibn Musa. Moreover he also ordered that the use of black clothing and black flags—the Abbasid colour—should forthwith be discontinued and that all loyal subjects should wear green. This unexpected order burst like a bombshell in the chaotic streets of Baghdad. Some, presumably the Shiites, readily acquiesced, some refused indignantly to abandon the cause of Beni Abbas in favour of their bitterest enemies, Beni Ali. Some donned green, others categorically refused to abandon their black clothing. Eventually towards the end of July 816, it was decided in Baghdad to appoint Ibrahim ibn Mehedi to be khalif. (We last heard of him taking wine with the Khalif Ameen two nights before the latter's death.) Some, however, wished to declare Ibrahim heir-apparent to Mamoon, while others demanded the immediate deposition of Mamoon, on the grounds of his betrayal of the Arabs and the Abbasid clan. Others blamed the undue influence of Fadhel and Hasan, the sons of Sahel, the "Magian" advisers, on the youthful khalif.

Mamoon claimed that he had chosen Ali—commonly called Ali al Ridha—as being the most deserving character of either Beni Abbas or Beni Ali.

Professor Duri,[5] however, suggests that the appointment was due to a subtle intrigue by Fadhel ibn Sahel. Baghdad was essentially the city of the Abbasids and would never accept an Aliid ruler. Thus if Beni Ali provided the next khalif, a new capital would be chosen and it would be easy to arrange for one of the cities of Persia to be selected. Then indeed the Empire of the Arabs would become completely the Empire of the Persians.

Perhaps, also, finding himself in Khurasan, Mamoon was obliged to continue the appeasement of the Persians, who had grown rather disgruntled with the Abbasids. The resentment bred in Persia by the treacherous murder of Abu Muslim and the ruthless extermination of the Barmecids was still alive.

It is difficult to understand why Mamoon, after the death of Ameen, remained for a further four years in Khurasan, while the empire slid into anarchy. The only explanation seems to be that Fadhel ibn Sahel, the Chief Minister, kept the young khalif in ignorance. At length, early in 818, Ali al Ridha is said to have told him that civil war was in progress in Iraq between his uncle Ibrahim ibn Mehedi and his viceroy Hasan ibn Sahel and that Fadhel ibn Sahel had concealed from him the real situation. He immediately ordered preparations for the removal of the court to Baghdad. Soon after the commencement of the journey in February 818, a party of four armed men surprised Fadhel ibn Sahel in his bath and murdered him, with or without the prior knowledge of the khalif. The assassins were arrested and beheaded, loudly claiming that Mamoon himself had ordered the murder.

In October 818, Mamoon was still only at Tus, where he visited the tomb of his father, Haroon al Rasheed. Here Ali al Ridha, the Aliid claimant whom Mamoon had appointed as his heir-apparent, died suddenly after eating grapes. The Shiites claim that Ali al Ridha was poisoned—Tus, the place of his death, was renamed by them Meshhed, the place of martyrdom, and is still a resort of pilgrims, who invoke curses on Mamoon at the tomb. Thus Fadhel ibn Sahel the wazeer and Ali ibn Musa, the Aliid heir-apparent, the two men most responsible for Mamoon's unpopularity, had both "died" unexpectedly. Mamoon reached Hamadan in 819. At the news of his approach, the fickle troops and populace of Baghdad decided to depose Ibrahim ibn Mehedi, whom two years before they had acclaimed. The name of Mamoon, Prince of the Faithful, was once again mentioned in the Friday prayers in the mosques.

On 8th September, 819, the Khalif Mamoon made his entry into the city. His clothing and that of his attendants and all their flags and emblems were green. None were granted an audience in the palace unless they were dressed in green. So many protests reached him, however, from the Abbasid family and their supporters that after a week he relented and himself appeared in black. Within a few hours, all the green clothing in Baghdad had vanished. We may perhaps conclude that Mamoon had conceived the ambition of conciliating the family of Ali, but that he subsequently realized the depth of feeling on the subject among Beni Abbas, and wisely decided to give way in the matter of the colours.

5. Al Asr al Abbasi al awwal.

The Shia, as we have seen, had originally been a political party. Its members believed that the khalifate should, after the death of the Prophet, have passed to Ali and his descendants. Meanwhile, however, the descendants of Ali had grown increasingly numerous and the Shia itself had broken up into several sects, each supporting the claim of a different member of the family, or adopting some point of dogma rejected by the others. It has been alleged that, at one time or another, there have been no less than seventy different Shiite sects.

Although the origin of the Shia was therefore a political question regarding the legitimate successor of the Prophet, it became a passionate religious movement as time passed. The invariable defeat of the Shiites caused them to attach increasing importance to their secret spiritual dogmas, to the gradual renunciation of hope in the competition for worldly power.

According to the dogma which they elaborated, Muhammad had nominated Ali and his descendants to succeed him as "imams". Each successive imam appointed one of his sons as his successor. The Shiites believed that each imam in turn inherited from his predecessor some portion of divine immanence. The legitimate imam, at any given moment, was to a certain extent an incarnation of the spirit of God. Moreover, this being the case, the imam was incapable of sin or error, an infallible and impeccable being, indwelt by the divine essence.

This conception, it will be noticed, was fundamentally opposed to the orthodox or Sunni idea of the khalif. The latter was merely the chief of the Muslim community in so far as its mundane affairs were concerned. It was the duty of the Sunni khalif to see that the laws derived from the Qoran and the Traditions were properly observed. He managed the financial affairs of the Muslims and commanded them in war. He had no spiritual jurisdiction whatever. The Shiite imam by contrast was an emanation of the Deity Himself, wielding infallible spiritual authority .

Different sects of the Shia adopted different branches of Ali's descendants as the line of the legitimate imams. A new difficulty arose, however, when a legitimate imam died without issue, for the dogma laid down that the divine essence passed from the imam to one of his sons. This dilemma gave rise to the doctrine of the "hidden imam". An imam who died without issue was believed to be still alive, though hidden from mankind. This hidden imam was one day to return as the mehedi to usher in the reign of peace and justice in the world. The doctrine of the return of the mehedi is admitted also by the Sunnis but it plays with them a far less conspicuous part than in the Shiite dogma.

The Zaidis believed that Zeid, the grandson of Husain, killed in Kufa[6] was the hidden imam. The Ismailis claimed that the imamate was continued in the line of descendants of Ismail. Another group alleged that Muhammad, the son of Ismail, was the last imam and that it was he who would return as the mehedi. As Ismail was the seventh in descent from Ali, these people became known as the "seveners". The majority of Shiites, however, rejected the progeny of Ismail, and traced the chain of imams through the descendants

6. Page 190.

GENEALOGY OF THE SHIITE IMAMS

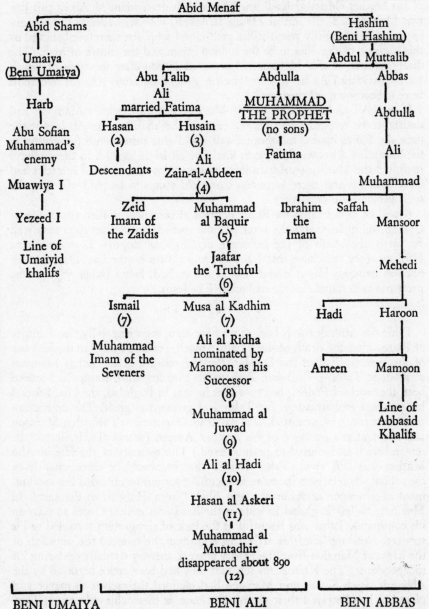

BENI UMAIYA   BENI ALI   BENI ABBAS

NOTE 1. No. 8 was the Ali ibn Musa recognized by Mamoon as heir to the khalifate.

NOTE 2. The numbers shown after the names give the succession to the Shiite imamate.

NOTE 3. Each Shiite imam had a title, such as the Truthful, the Accepted, the Generous, etc.

of his brother, Musa al Kadhim. The twelfth descendant of Ali in this line was Muhammad, the son of Hasan al Askeri, who was alleged to have disappeared mysteriously when still a youth, and who was therefore believed by this division of the Shia to be the hidden imam and the future mehedi. (The disappearance of this Muhammad occurred in 890 after the time of which we are writing.) As he was the twelfth generation from Ali, his adherents were to be known as "twelvers".

It was Ali al Ridha, the son of Musa al Kadhim, whom Mamoon had desired to be recognized as his successor in the khalifate. As Ali was at the time the Shiite imam, in whom dwelt the divine immanence (according to the Shia), his acknowledgment as khalif of all Islam should, in theory, have re-united the Muslim world. In fact, however, too many vested interests had been built up and there were too many old scores to be paid off, to make such a re-unification possible.

It will be noticed that the Shiite dogmas of incarnation, the immanence of God in the imams, and the return of the mehedi on the last day, may well be partly the result of the influence of Christian dogma. In some places Muslims seem to believe that Jesus also will return on the Last Day, the distinction between His role and that of the mehedi being rather vague. One party has even stated that the mehedi will be Jesus.[7]

*   *   *

Tahir the Ambidextrous had, as we have seen, been sent to live in obscurity at Raqqa after the death of the Khalif Ameen, perhaps owing to the jealousy of the wazeer, Fadhel ibn Sahel. After the murder of the latter, Mamoon summoned Tahir to Baghdad. Perhaps his banishment to Raqqa had indeed been the work of Fadhel, but now that he was in Baghdad, the khalif found his presence embarrassing, for Tahir had grown too great. The embarrassment, moreover, was mutual. One day it was reported to Tahir that Mamoon had wept at the memory of his brother Ameen (whom Tahir, it will be remembered, had caused to be murdered.) The memory of the fate of Abu Muslim was still vivid. Tahir decided that he would be safer away from the capital. By a large bribe to an influential courtier, he obtained the appointment of governor of Khurasan and Jibal, "from Hulwan to the east". In May 821, he left Baghdad in state at the head of a military force to take up his command. Tahir was resentful at the lack of recognition accorded to his services. Not long after his arrival in Khurasan, he ordered the omission of the name of Mamoon from the Friday prayers, thereby virtually declaring his independence. The Khurasanis felt that they had been twice betrayed by the Abbasids. Both Saffah and Mamoon had pledged themselves to justice and piety but had betrayed their promises as soon as they achieved power. They therefore welcomed a local dynasty, independent of Baghdad. Shortly afterwards, Tahir the Ambidextrous died, possibly poisoned by order of Mamoon, who, however, was obliged to recognize his son Talha as his successor.

To us who now know the whole story of the Empire of the Arabs, it is fascinating to see the causes of its ultimate dissolution gradually appearing

7. Encyclopaedia of Islam.

and growing, although to those living at the time, the state appeared to be at the height of its power and glory. The first four years of Mamoon's reign, with his Chief Minister apparently in sole control and the khalif ignorant of what was going on, seemed to foreshadow the age of the puppet khalifs which was to come.

The constant fickleness of the mercenary troops, whom during these years of confusion and civil war, all parties attempted to buy over with cash dona- tives, and who meanwhile looted and rioted of their own accord, foreshadows already the military *coups d'état* of the future. The seeds of all these troubles had been sown by the Abbasid revolution itself. In their struggle with their fellow-Arabs the Umaiyid and Aliid clans of Quraish, the Abbasids had mistrusted Arab soldiers and had won the khalifate with the arms of Turkish and Persian mercenaries, led by their own generals. When victory was achieved, the victorious troops occupied the chief positions in the state and the Arab tribal chiefs were evicted.

Western historians appear in most cases to have considered the decline of the Arab aristocracy as an advantage. Yet to rejoice at the suppression of these arrogant war-lords is to forget that political institutions are largely a matter of balance. The decline of the Arab aristocracy was to leave the field open to the foreign mercenaries, who were soon to become the real rulers. If the Arabs could have been retained in the political arena, they might have balanced the non-Arab troops and thus, even if unwittingly, protected the freedom of both the khalif and the people. As the power of the foreigners increases, the men who, a century and a half before, had conquered so im- mense an empire are now referred to by contemporary writers as "vagabonds, Arab tribesmen and other riff-raff".

The third reason for the disintegration which was to come was the prac- tice, on the part of the khalifs, of allowing some prominent man to become governor of a province and to pass on the appointment to his son. Even the great Haroon al Rasheed had, in this manner, allowed Ibrahim ibn al Aghlab to set up an almost independent dynasty in Ifriqiya. Now Tahir had estab- lished in Khurasan a semi-independent principality, similar to that of the Aghlabids in Ifriqiya.

Whatever lip-service these subsidiary dynasties might pay, the area under the effective control of the khalifs steadily diminished. This fragmen- tation of the empire was not due to local "independence movements". Such ideas were unknown in the ninth century. It was rather due to the idleness and the luxury of the khalifs who often welcomed the idea of farming out distant provinces from which they might receive tribute without the trouble of ruling, administering or sending troops. It is interesting to remember that, when someone asked Umar ibn al Khattab, the second successor of Muhammad, how he succeeded in ruling the Arabs, he replied, "by fre- quently changing their commanders". The idea of a regular civil service was unknown in the ninth century, but if the khalifs had been more careful to change their provincial governors at regular intervals, these minor dynasties could not have struck root.

The sect of the Khurramiya has already been referred to in connection with the death of Abu Muslim. Their name was derived from a place called Khurram, in the province of Ardebil, in Adharbaijan. They seem to have professed a corrupt form of Islam, which included belief in the transmigration of souls and in the future return of Abu Muslim as the mehedi.

The year 819 had been one of famine and epidemics in Persia, in which the poor suffered great hardships. Doubtless in protest at these conditions, a popular rebellion broke out in Adharbaijan under the leadership of a certain Babek of the Khurramiya sect. Operating in difficult mountain country, Babek, who must have been a splendid guerilla leader and a hero to the peasants, was to maintain his resistance against the empire for twenty-two years. We shall hear more of him in ensuing chapters.

In 825, Ibrahim ibn Mehedi, brother of Haroon al Rasheed, gave himself up, or was arrested. He had been in hiding for six years. It was he who had been acclaimed as khalif in Baghdad while Mamoon was still living in Khurasan. Mamoon welcomed him and pardoned him. It is indeed a relief during this reign to hear no more of the amputation of hands and feet and the cutting off of heads with which in the past we were so familiar. Mamoon pardoned almost all the rebels and political opponents who appeared during his khalifate.

In January 826, the Khalif Mamoon was married to Buran, the daughter of the chief minister, Hasan ibn Sahel. On the evening of the wedding day, a thousand pearls were scattered over the head of the bride. Hasan ibn Sahel was said to have spent fifty million dirhems on the festivities, while tickets bearing the names of one or other of the minister's country estates were thrown to the crowd to scramble for. Any who subsequently came forward with a ticket received an estate. It is curious to think that this immense wealth and ostentation had come to Beni Abbas on the basis of their descent from the uncle of the Prophet, who considered it to be wrong to lie down at night to rest if there were any food or money in the house. God, he believed, would each day provide the day's needs, so that even to store up a bag of dates was a sign of lack of faith.

The immense riches possessed by the khalifs and their ministers and often frittered away in idleness and luxury was of course the product of taxation. Yet we must not judge this system by our modern ideas of public finance, which are scarcely two or three centuries old. In earlier societies, public and private affairs were often confused in the mind of the people and of the ruler. It is only a little over two hundred years ago since Louis XIV said that the state was himself. There does not seem to be much evidence to show that the subjects of the Arab Empire had any idea that the public revenues should not be spent on the khalif's luxuries. They might disapprove of his wine-drinking on religious grounds but they had not conceived the idea that money raised by taxation should be spent separately from the khalif's privy purse.

Meanwhile the Jezira and Syria had risen in rebellion and Egypt was in confusion. We have already seen the evicted rebels from Spain seizing Alexandria and there setting up a government of their own. In 825, Abdulla, another son of Tahir the Ambidextrous, was sent with an army to re-establish the authority of the khalif. This he did without much difficulty, capturing

Fustat and later Alexandria. The Spanish rebels, as already mentioned, left Alexandria by sea and conquered Crete, where they established their own independent Muslim government.

When he had restored Egypt to the empire, Abdulla ibn Tahir was made viceroy of the Jezira, Syria, Palestine and Egypt, his brother Talha, being at the same time viceroy of Persia in succession to his father the Ambidextrous.

NOTABLE DATES

Andalus

Charlemagne's invasion of Spain Death of Roland at Roncesvalles	778
Death of Abdul Rahman ibn Muawiya of Spain	788
Death of Hisham son of Abdul Rahman	796
Death of Hakam, son of Hisham	822

The Khalifate

Accession of Ameen	809
Civil war between Ameen and Mamoon	811
Kufa, Mosul, Basra, Mecca and Medina declare for Mamoon	April 812
Tahir the Ambidextrous besieges Baghdad	Sept. 812
Fall of Baghdad Death of Ameen	Sept. 813
Numerous Shiite risings	815
Revolt in Baghdad Ibrahim ibn Mehedi acclaimed	816
Mamoon enters Baghdad	819
Rebellion of Babek in Adharbaijan	819
Tahir the Ambidextrous made Governor of Khurasan	821
Death of Tahir—his son Talha succeeds him	822
Abdulla, another son of Tahir, viceroy of Egypt	825

PERSONALITIES

Andalus

Prince Abdul Rahman I
Prince Hisham, son of Abdul Rahman
Prince Hakam, son of Hisham
Charlemagne, Emperor of the West

The Khalifate

Khalif Ameen, son of Haroon al Rasheed
Khalif Mamoon, son of Haroon al Rasheed
Tahir the Ambidextrous, general of Mamoon
Ali ibn Musa, Aliid claimant to the khalifate, and Shiite imam
Hasan ibn Sahel, Chief Minister of Mamoon
Babek, the Khurramite, rebel in Adharbaijan
Talha ibn Tahir
Abdulla ibn Tahir } sons of the Ambidextrous

XVII

The Age of Culture

It is a fruitless if pleasant pastime to analyse the characters of nations. The nation is too complex to admit of detailed statistical examination.

The first thing that strikes us is the unique assimilative power of Arab culture, often misrepresented as purely imitative. The Arab conquests united, for the first time in history, the millennial Mediterranean tradition and the rich civilization of Persia. Of the cohabitation of many peoples within Islamic society a new civilization was born, yet bearing the characteristic imprint of Arabic Islam.

PROFESSOR BERNARD LEWIS, *The Arabs in History* (slightly abridged)

He did not think . . . that it was necessary to make a hell of this world to enjoy paradise in the next. WILLIAM BECKFORD

XVII

THE AGE OF CULTURE

FROM childhood Mamoon had been fond of books and reading. He had studied jurisprudence and history, and he spoke and wrote elegant Arabic and was a proficient poet. As a young man, he had not been indifferent to the fair sex but he was not a sensualist.

On one occasion a slave girl was pouring water for the Khalif Haroon al Rasheed to wash his hands, when the young Mamoon, standing behind his father, threw her a kiss. She reproved him with a little frown and a quick smile, but, in doing so, she ceased for a few seconds to pour the water. Haroon looked up at her and said, "What's the matter?". The girl stammered and blushed and eventually murmured, "Nothing." The khalif was annoyed. "What is all this about?" he asked crossly. "Tell me the truth immediately, or I will have you punished or put to death."

Thus threatened, she admitted, much to Mamoon's embarrassment, that he had thrown her a kiss over his father's shoulder.

"Do you like her?" enquired Haroon amused. "If so you can have her, but only on condition that you improvise a piece of poetry on this incident." Without a moment's hesitation, Mamoon recited:

> I kissed her from afar, a fair gazelle,
> And with my eyes I told her all my heart.
> She frowned me nay—I knew she wished me well
> By that quick smile which oped her lips apart.
> I paid my court as warmly as could be,
> Nor left that room till she belonged to me.

A slave-dealer once offered Mamoon a girl for whom he was asking a thousand dinars. In justification of the price, he claimed that she was extremely expert at improvising poetry and was eloquent, well-mannered and a good chess player. "If," said Mamoon, "she can cap a verse which I will recite to her by a verse of her own, I will buy her for the price you ask." Then, turning to the girl, he recited:

> What wouldst thou say to one whom lack of sleep
> Hath rendered pale and thin for love of thee?

The girl immediately capped the verses with her own in the same rhyme and metre:

> If I found one who with me faith would keep
> By kindness I'd reward his love for me.

It may be interesting in passing to note that, at this period, the heirs to the throne of Byzantium selected their wives at bride shows. Imperial messengers were sent to scour all the provinces in search of suitable maidens whose exceptional beauty, wit and high morals made them worthy of an imperial throne. The physical measurements needed were apparently laid down in the regulations and the selection committee actually measured the faces, heads, figures and feet of the candidates. On the appointed day, all the competitors were assembled in a room of the palace, under the supervision of the reigning empress.

When the future Emperor Theophilus chose his bride, he was given a golden apple to present to the lady of his choice. Passing through this bevy of beauties, he stopped in front of a young woman by the name of Kasia and recited:

> "A woman was the fount and source
> Of all man's tribulation."

Kasia immediately capped the verse:

> "And from a woman sprang the course
> Of man's regeneration."

In spite of her quickness, Theophilus did not give Kasia the apple. He passed on and presented it to Theodora, whom he married.[1]

The incident provides one more example, of which there seem to be many, to show that we must not regard Byzantium and the Arab Empire as two utterly different and contrasting civilizations with nothing in common. Each profoundly influenced the other. They copied each other's fashions and architecture. The weapons and organization of their armies and navies were almost identical. Both seized as many captives as they could in war and sold them as slaves. Both made use of cruel tortures and mutilation. Both governments were constantly faced with rebellions. In the same manner, the capping of verses of poetry may have been a fashionable amusement with both. It was perhaps characteristic of the Byzantines that when they indulged in this pastime, an abstruse piece of religious dogma was the subject selected for the verses.

*   *   *

When Mamoon grew more mature in age, he applied himself to philosophy, and became the patron of poets. His lively intelligence was interested in all kinds of knowledge and he devoted himself to the study of astronomy and medicine as well as law, religion and philosophy. He was especially interested in the philosophy of ancient Greece and maintained a considerable staff of translators, who produced many Greek works in Arabic editions, of which we shall hear more later on.

Mamoon has been called the wisest of the Abbasids. He was more humane and tolerant than any of his predecessors and even rebels were rarely sentenced by him to death. He is alleged on one occasion to have exclaimed, "By God,

1. J. B. Bury, *History of the Eastern Roman Empire*.

I delight in pardoning to such an extent, that I fear that God may not reward me for it, because I do it for my own pleasure. If men knew how much I love pardoning, those guilty of crimes would all come to me."

As has already been indicated, he conceived, at the beginning of his reign, a great sympathy for the descendants of Ali ibn abi Talib, who for a century and a half had been involved in an endless succession of fruitless rebellions. He even, as we have seen, went so far as to name Ali al Ridha as heir after him to the khalifate. On his arrival in Baghdad, however, Mamoon was persuaded by the "experienced politicians" that such high-flown sentiments were not practical politics.

Towards the end of his life, his philosophical studies caused Mamoon to adopt the tenets of the Mutazilite sect. From the theological angle, Mutazilism arose from the attempt to define the position of the Muslim who had committed a capital sin. The Kharijites said that such a person had become an unbeliever. Others claimed that he was still a Muslim. The Mutazilites placed such a person in an intermediate category, neither a good Muslim nor a heathen.[2]

By Mamoon's time, however, the Mutazilites had acquired another main point of dogma. The simple minds of the first Muslims had accepted unquestioningly the dogma that the Qoran had existed from eternity in Heaven. The Mutazilites now asserted that the Qoran must have been created in time. If it had existed from eternity, the Oneness of God—the most fundamental of Muslim dogmas—would be imperilled, for something other than God would have existed from eternity.

Before his death, Mamoon adopted with enthusiasm the dogma that the Qoran had been created in time. He caused the leading theologians to be summoned to the capital and cross-questioned as to whether or not the Qoran had been created. After being threatened with decapitation, the great majority conformed by admitting that it was created.

It is, however, of interest to note that the heated discussions provoked by theology and philosophy represent another aspect of the departure from Arab ways of thought. In the early days of Islam, the Byzantines had been divided by bitter theological feuds, but the Arabs, essentially a practical race, had been concerned solely with what God wanted them to do. Now the interbreeding of the original Arabs with Greeks and Persians had introduced similar intellectual subtleties into the Arab Empire.

* * *

We have seen how the Emperor Leo V had ordered Michael the Amorian to be tied to an ape and thrown into the palace furnace and how Leo himself had been assassinated the next morning and Michael made emperor. The Amorian had been an army officer and his sudden elevation to the purple provoked the jealousy of his brother officers, a problem which has faced several military dictators in the Middle East in our own days.

Thomas of Gaziura had, in 803, been associated with Michael the Amorian in a military revolt against the Emperor Nicephorus. When the revolt failed,

2. *Encyclopaedia of Islam.*

Michael turned King's evidence, obtained favour at court and entered on that palace career which eventually resulted in his elevation to the throne. Thomas, perhaps less of an intriguer, had gone into exile in Syria, where he remained for ten years, from 803 to 813. In 820, however, Thomas headed another military revolt against Leo V, who was assassinated before it could be suppressed. When Michael the Amorian mounted the throne, his brother officer Thomas was still in revolt, and had collected a large army on the borders of Armenia. His first step, however, was not to march on Constantinople but to invade the Arab Empire. In 823, Mamoon was still insecure and the rebellion of Babek in Adharbaijan was in full flood. The khalif was scarcely in a position to embark on a campaign against Thomas.

Negotiations were opened, as, doubtless, Thomas had intended. Having lived for ten years in exile among the Muslims, he must have been familiar with their politics. Agreement was soon reached. Mamoon undertook to assist the rebel to make himself emperor, while in return Thomas agreed to surrender certain frontier fortresses and to pay tribute to the khalif. Thomas was then crowned Byzantine Emperor by the Orthodox Christian patriarch of Antioch in Arab territory.

One would have expected that such a transaction with the traditional enemies of his race would have lost Thomas the support of his countrymen, but the reverse proved to be the case. He was joined by nearly all the troops in Asia Minor and in December 821, he laid siege to Constantinople itself. The siege dragged on for fifteen months until the spring of 823, when the Bulgarians arrived on the scene, presumably at the request of Michael, and defeated Thomas in a pitched battle. Michael, thereupon, sallied forth to administer the *coup de grâce*. Thomas of Gaziura was taken prisoner. He was dragged in chains into the presence of Michael, who, not disguising his joy, trampled with his feet on the neck of his prostrate rival. He then ordered his hands and his feet to be cut off, and a stake to be hammered through his body.

The civil war between Thomas of Gaziura and Michael the Amorian is of interest to us in our study of the contemporary Arab Empire. Firstly it shows that the Christian Byzantine Empire was as subject to assassinations, civil wars and revolutions as was that of the Arabs. Secondly the fact that Thomas, as an ally of the Arab khalif, could command so much popular support seems to prove that the peoples of the Byzantine Empire did not regard the Arabs as hated, national enemies. Finally we may notice that the execution of Thomas was accompanied by the cutting off of his hands and feet and his impalement on a stake, with all the vindictive cruelties which disgust us when exercised by the Abbasids.

In 829, Talha the son of Tahir the Ambidextrous, died in Khurasan, and his brother Abdulla succeeded him as the ruler of East Persia. The khalif appointed another brother to be viceroy of Egypt and Syria. It is curious that the later Abbasids not only allowed their provincial governors to be virtually independent sovereigns but also frequently appointed members of the same family to several of the most important posts in the empire at the same time. In Adharbaijan the year 829 was marked by heavy fighting against the rebel Babek the Khurramite.

Apart from Mamoon's intrigue with Thomas, there had been no Arab inroads into Byzantine territory for some eighteen years, that is to say since the devastating campaigns of Haroon al Rasheed in Asia Minor. The civil war between Ameen and Mamoon, followed by the disturbances in Iraq and elsewhere, had fully occupied the khalif's attention. Nevertheless the summer raid on the Byzantine Empire was deeply embedded in Arab tradition. It may be taken as an indication of the secure establishment of Mamoon's authority that, in the summer of 830, he in person led a new invasion of Asia Minor. He entered enemy territory by way of Tarsus, while his son, Abbas ibn Mamoon, crossed the border east of Malatia, presumably by the Hadeth route, at the head of a second column. Several towns were captured and some of them destroyed before the Muslim armies withdrew across the frontiers in the autumn. On his return the khalif paid visits to Damascus and Egypt.

After his withdrawal, the Byzantines appear to have carried out some reprisals against Massisa, with the result that Mamoon returned to the attack the following year. Meanwhile, in Constantinople, the Emperor Michael the Amorian was dead and his son Theophilus had assumed the purple. Michael had been coarse and brutal but Theophilus was an intellectual. At Adana, the khalif was met by emissaries from the emperor seeking peace, but the plea was rejected, and Mamoon crossed the border in July 831, and advanced to Heraclea in Cilicia, which surrendered without resistance. The Muslim army then divided into two columns, carrying fire and sword into the heart of Asia Minor. In the autumn, Mamoon returned to Damascus and thence to Egypt, where disturbances had broken out.

In 832, Mamoon again crossed the Byzantine frontier. This time the Emperor Theophilus took the field with an army and, although no major battle took place, the campaign was not so entirely favourable to the Arabs as in previous years. In the autumn, a deputation came from Theophilus, seeking peace. Nevertheless, presumably to save his face, the emperor ended his letter with a threat, with the result that the khalif replied in similar terms and the war dragged on. Early in 833, Abbas ibn Mamoon established himself in Tuwana, west of the Taurus, where he built a great fortress.

In July 833, Mamoon again led an invasion of Byzantine territory through Tarsus, and captured a number of towns. After an apparently brief campaign, he returned towards the frontier and camped on a small stream flowing down from the snows of the Taurus. In the summer evening, the khalif was sitting by the stream with his brother Mutasim, both dangling their feet in the water. "Did you ever see such beautiful, clear, cold water?", asked Mamoon, inviting a courtier to join them.

As they sat paddling their feet, a mule convoy jingled up, laden with mail and with delicacies from home. Mamoon called to a servant to see if there were any new season's dates from Iraq and soon the domestic came running back with two baskets full of soft sweet dates, as fresh as if they had just been picked from the palm tree. The three men sat eating dates, dangling their feet and admiring the clear stream and the lovely summer evening. A servant

THE BYZANTINE BORDER
AT THE TIME OF MAMOON

The border with Byzantine
territory varied but over the
two centuries 661–861 the
approximate border line
is marked.

CASPIAN
SEA

CAUCASUS

BAKU

ARDEBIL

TIFLIS

BARDHAA

ADHARBAIJAN
R. Aras

TABRIZ
Urmia
Lake

JIBAL

IRBIL

MOSUL

BAGHDAD

KUFA

ARMENIA

MANZIKERT
Lake
Van

ERZERUM

R. Tigris

JAZIRA
IBN OMAR
SINJAR
NISIBIN
MARDIN
RAS AL AIN
AMID
SUMAYSAT
ZEBETRA

TREBIZOND

R. Halys

SAMSUN

CAESAREA

TUWANA
LULUA
TAURUS MTS.
HERACLEA
CILICIAN GATES
TARSUS
MASSISA

HISN
HADETH MANSUR
BAHASNA
MALATIA

ALEXANDRETTA

ANTIOCH

BALIS

R. Euphrates

IRQQA

SYRIA

DAMASCUS

LEBANON

CYPRUS

BLACK SEA

MEDITERRANEAN
SEA

0   100   200
Miles

41

jumped into the water and caught a large fish in his hands. "Have it fried right away and we'll eat it now," shouted the khalif in high spirits.

But before the fish could be served Mamoon felt unwell. Soon he was shivering with a high fever. They piled blankets on him and lit fires but he could not get warm. His pulse was racing, while the perspiration poured from the whole of his body. The court physicians admitted that there was nothing which they could do. For some time the khalif lay with his eyes closed. Then suddenly opening them, he cried, "O Thou who dost not die, have mercy on those who do die." A few seconds later he ceased to breathe. Sitting on a summer evening by a stream, it would seem possible that he may have caught some form of malignant malaria. It was 9th August, 833. Before dying, Mamoon nominated his brother Mutasim as his successor. The body of the khalif was carried back and buried in Tarsus, in Arab territory. He was forty-seven years old when he died and had reigned for twenty years and five months.

The two most splendid periods in the long centuries of the Abbasid khalifate were the reigns of Haroon al Rasheed and of his son Mamoon. Meanwhile, the empire had become increasingly commercial and industrial. Baghdad was a busy port, into and out of which poured an immense volume of trade up and down the Tigris and down the Euphrates from Syria. Great convoys of pack animals bore the commerce of the capital up the main road through Hulwan to Persia.

The rise of the Empire of the Arabs, as has already been explained, had shut off Europe from the rest of the world. But to the Arab Empire, its ships and its commerce, the whole world was open. In Europe this situation had killed commerce and resulted in the feudal system, under which wealth consisted of land not money, and the most powerful men were land-owning barons, not city merchants.

In the middle of the ninth century of which we are now writing, Arab ships were sailing regularly to Canton in China, and were trading with Malacca, Java and Sumatra, as well as Ceylon and India. There was a prosperous colony of Arab merchants near Bombay, where they had established a "factory", just as the British East India Company was to do nine hundred years later. Arab sailors and merchants were also familiar with the east coast of Africa as far south as Madagascar. The great commercial houses of Baghdad imported silks from China, spices and aromatics from India, tropical woods, coconuts and tin. The greater number of the Arab ships traded from Baghdad and Basra, but some came up the Red Sea to Qulzum (the modern Suez) and to other ports. Muslim merchants from the Maghrib and Ifriqiya obtained gold from the so-called Gold Coast, now Ghana.

One of the most remarkable features of the Arab Empire, especially under the Abbasids, is the extraordinary profusion of gold. Not only did the khalifs use it for coinage, but it seems to have been plastered over their weapons, the bits and buckles of the bridles on their horses and on their belts. They ate and drank out of gold and silver vessels and many of their utensils were inlaid with gold. At the same period, gold was almost unobtainable in Western Europe.

Remarkable discoveries have been made in this matter in recent years. Mr. Twitchell, an American mining engineer, discovered gold in Western Central Arabia. A team was sent out to reconnoitre and extensive fields of gold mines were discovered over a wide area. Modern mining engineers who examined the old workings reported that the ancient Arab miners must have been competent technicians. The mines ceased to be worked at the period of the weakening of the Abbasid dynasty, doubtless because law and order collapsed in Arabia and the bedouin tribes became hostile to the government.[3] These gold mines were abandoned for a thousand years until rediscovered in our own times.[4]

There was little or no trade between the Arab Empire and Europe, owing to the unending hostility between Islam and Christendom. The Mediterranean, in Roman times the greatest highway of trade in the world, had become a no-man's-land and only war fleets or pirates sailed on its blue waters. A commercial trickle passed from the Arab countries by the Black Sea to Byzantium, chiefly through the hands of the Khazars of the lower Volga.

The only "neutrals" between Islam and Christendom were the Jews, who were permitted to live and trade in the countries of both "blocs". They had the entry alike to France, Spain, Constantinople, Egypt, Syria and India. Individual Jewish merchants even travelled from France to Suez and thence to India and back.

More surprising perhaps to us was the extent of Arab trade with Russia and thence with Scandinavia. Great numbers of Arab coins have been found in Finland, Sweden and Norway and even as far afield as Britain and Iceland. The coins are dated from the time when Arab coins were first minted under Abdul Malik ibn Merwan (khalif from 685 to 705) until the decline of the empire in the eleventh century. The trade route went from the Oxus through Khwarizm to the Middle Volga, and thence northwards to the Baltic. The Arabs bought sables, ermines, fox furs, beavers, arrows, birch bark, fur caps, fish glue, amber, slaves and cattle.[5] Slavs with fair hair and white skins were in much demand as slaves. There was also direct trade with the Khazars, whose capital was at Itil at the mouth of the Volga, at the northern end of the Caspian Sea.

Such widespread commerce naturally required corresponding financial arrangements, and a system of banking, making use of letters of credit and cheques, was available to merchants. Indeed our English word cheque is derived from the Arabic sek.

The wealth of the Arab Empire, however, was not derived solely from commerce. Industry likewise was extremely prosperous and very highly skilled. Textiles were probably the most wealthy and advanced branch of industry. The Arab Empire was by far the world's greatest producer of silk fabrics, although, ironically enough, the wearing of silk had been forbidden as a worldly luxury by the Prophet. The great manufacturing cities are in

3. Psalm 72, Verse 15 says: "Unto him shall be given of the gold of Arabia," suggesting that these mines may have been worked in remote antiquity.
4. As far as I am aware, no historian has ever mentioned these Arabian gold mines.
5. The Legacy of Islam.

many cases revealed by words which have since become part of the English language. Fustian was derived from Fustat, on the site of modern Cairo. Muslins came from Mosul, damask from Damascus. Taffeta is a Persian word. Carpets were everywhere in use in the Arab Empire, though they were not to be spread on the floors of houses in Europe for several centuries to come. Cotton goods, rugs, tapestries, lacquer work from China, dyes, drugs, spices, alum, cloves, mirrors, glass and gold and silver jugs and dishes were in use in the cities of the empire. The French word jupe, a skirt, comes from the Arabic jubba.

In the finer arts, the Arab Empire was as far ahead as in the production of ordinary textiles. A very high degree of skill had been achieved in inlaid gold and silver work. Glazed coloured tiles had been produced in the Middle East from very early times, but the extent of the empire and its wealth gave an immense impetus to the art. Similarly glazed pottery and lustre work, wherever they may have originated (we know that the Abbasids imported porcelain from China), were in production in North Persia, Fustat and Andalus and the remains of these artistic industries are to be found over the whole Arab area. The immense extent of the empire resulted in the transfer of industries once limited to one country, to the great cities all over the empire from India to Spain. Even though Spain and parts of North Africa became politically independent, the possession of a common language and religion resulted in a parallel development of art, industry, commerce and learning in all the then Arabic-speaking countries.

One of the greatest industries of the Arabs was in painted and enamelled glass, the chief sources of which were in Syria and Iraq. Centuries later Venice learnt the industry from Syrian craftsmen, and is still famous for glass though it is said that, to this day, the Venetian craftsmen have never reached the standards achieved by the Arabs in their imperial days. The whole industry was literally shattered by Tamerlane in the Tatar invasions.

In the days when Muhammad first preached Islam in Arabia, his principal opponents had been, not Christians, but idolaters. He consequently forbade the reproduction of living forms in statuary or painting, lest the Muslims worship such images for their own sakes. This prohibition limited the field of Muslim art in one direction but at the same time encouraged an extraordinary development in tracery, and ornamentation with geometrical or flowered patterns. The letters of the Arabic alphabet also lent themselves to intricate design. The state robes of mediaeval German emperors often bore Arabic texts, interwoven with the rich designs of the fabrics.

The Arabs, who had long ago forgotten the desert, were as progressive in agriculture as in industry. To this day, the entire Spanish vocabulary on irrigation is said to be derived from Arabic, as also are the names of flowers, fruits, vegetables, trees and shrubs. Orange trees had first been brought from China to Persia, but the wide extent of the Arab Empire caused their cultivation to be carried to North Africa, Sicily and Spain. Sesame, carobs, maize, rice, lemons, melons, apricots and oranges were sedulously cultivated in the Arab countries and only subsequently passed from them to Europe. The Persians have always been gardeners and they were doubtless responsible for the gardens of the palaces of Baghdad. Lilacs, tulips and other flowers were, many years later, to reach Europe from the Arab Empire.

It is of interest to us today, to whom such matters are of deep concern, to learn that Arab industry was state-controlled but that commerce was left to private enterprise. Great fortunes were built up by merchants trading to the Far East, India, Africa or Russia, but industry was normally financed by the government. The craftsmen, who were often highly skilled and extremely prosperous, were organized in guilds. Although both the commerce and the industry of the Middle East were later on to be utterly destroyed by the Tatars, the Arab countries of today seem to be returning to the same system. Every Arab is a merchant but the new attempts at industrialization are all sponsored by the governments concerned.

The Arab contribution to architecture was almost as outstanding as in the other fields of civilized activity. Like ourselves, they inherited many styles from the past, their dominions straddling the ancient empires of Egypt, Rome and Persia and including part of India. They thus had an immense variety of styles, materials and skills from which to choose. Yet they amalgamated them into a distinctive style peculiarly their own.

Considering that so large a proportion of the pre-Islamic Arabs lived in tents or mud-built huts, it is astonishing that they took so rapidly to splendid architecture, for as early as Abdul Malik ibn Merwan, they were already building magnificent palaces, castles and mosques. The beautiful mosque of the Dome of the Rock in Jerusalem, a building with few equals in the world, was erected by Abdul Malik. The earliest mosques, such as that of Uqba ibn Nafi in Qairawan and the great mosque of Cordova, made use of Roman columns and capitals, but later they developed entirely original styles. The variety of minarets in the Arabic-speaking world, in stone, brick, marble or covered with glazed tiles, some round, some square, is worthy of a book in itself. Horse-shoe arches, pierced stone windows, intricate stucco tracery and, above all, the art of covering large surfaces with beautiful geometrical designs are all peculiar to their art.

The need for allowing space for recreation in the open air to the many women and girls in a large household, gave rise to a specific form of domestic architecture, in which the living-rooms were built round a central courtyard but showed a blank wall on the streets. With their trees, flowers, pergolas and splashing fountains, many of those inner cool, quiet courtyards seemed veritable earthly paradises. It is sad to see them now pulled down and succeeded by suburban villas, in which air-conditioning replaces the pergola of vines and the cool tinkle of the fountain.

In military architecture the Arabs were no less distinguished. Mediaeval European castles owed their battlements and machicoulis to the Arabs. The first example of a castle entrance with an angle or traverse to allow it to be covered by a loophole inside the building is said to have been in Mansoor's walled city in Baghdad.

*   *   *

But of all the arts, that which the Arabs held most dear from the earliest days before Islam to the final destruction of their civilization by the Mongols, was that of poetry. Some of the greatest early poets were probably illiterate but gifted with immense memories. They recited their compositions which were then memorized and passed on by word of mouth from country to country and from generation to generation.

The telling of romantic stories had always been a favourite Arab diversion, one indeed to which western European literature owes an immense debt. In the original Arabic form, the prose narrative was constantly interrupted by poetic recitations. At every crisis in the story, the narrator would say (as the hero charged into battle or pondered the vicissitudes of fortune) "And he said," whereupon a long poem would ensue. Some such story-tellers have survived to this day. I have myself sat up almost a whole night in a tent far out in the desert, listening to a man who told stories, and recited the accompanying poems, continuously for some eight or nine hours.

Even more curious perhaps, to our minds, is the fact that not only the romanciers but the serious Arab historians impute a poem to the historical figures whom they mention, at almost every crisis of their lives. As some early Muslim hero rides through the ranks of the unbelievers, slashing right and left with his swift sword, he cried—and a poem will follow. It is difficult now to decide to what extent the insertion of such poems was a literary convention or whether Arabs really did improvise poetry on such occasions. Whether or not, however, we believe that the Arab warrior composed poetry in the middle of the cut and thrust of a cavalry charge, there can be no doubt that they were capable of extraordinary skill in poetic improvisation, and that doing so was considered an essential civilized accomplishment. The historians record endless examples of such impromptu compositions on ordinary social occasions or of the khalifs and other great men ordering poets to recite immediately a poem on this or that subject. Even, as we have seen, girl-slaves and concubines were expected to be able to improvise Arabic verse to amuse their masters.

Whatever may have been the skill of the Arabs at improvising poetry, there can be no doubt that all of them, educated or illiterate, carried a vast amount of poetry in their minds, for they are represented as quoting apt lines from the poets on every occasion in ordinary life.

The original poetry of the desert, before and after Islam, had dealt principally with the favourite Arab themes of love, war and generosity, combined with descriptions of nature and animals. At the Abbasid court, however, love lyrics were developed into an ideal of Platonic love. This etherealization of poetry may have been due to the greater refinement of society or to the increase of Persian influence, for the Persians were less matter-of-fact than the Arabs. It introduced a chivalrous atmosphere into the relations between the sexes.

But under Mamoon learning and literature were by no means confined to poetry as they had been under the early Arabs. The khalif's own active intellect was constantly engaged in the pursuit of every kind of knowledge. A certain Hunain ibn Ishaq (807–877) was employed by him in Baghdad to translate Greek scientific and philosophical works into Arabic. Hunain was assisted by a considerable staff, and almost all the known Greek philosophical and scientific works were translated into Arabic. Most of the work had been done by Christians, many of them of the Nestorian sect, who had originally been driven from the Byzantine Empire by the persecution of the Greek Orthodox Church. Hunain was himself a practising physician and his ten treatises on the eye is the earliest known systematic text book of ophthalmology.

By Mamoon's time medical schools were extremely active in Baghdad. The first free public hospital was opened in the city during the khalifate of Haroon al Rasheed. As the system developed, physicians and surgeons were appointed who gave lectures to medical students and issued diplomas to those who were considered qualified to practise. Doctors, druggists, barbers and orthopaedists were subject to government inspection. The first hospital in Egypt was opened in 872 and thereafter public hospitals sprang up all over the empire from Spain and the Maghrib to Persia.

As has already been mentioned, Basra had produced a famous school of grammarians, so important in view of the intricacies of the Arabic language. Al Asmai (740–828) of Basra wrote books on natural history, both animal and vegetable, while other works appeared on mechanics, irrigation and engineering.

All this intense intellectual activity was greatly facilitated by the establishment of the first paper factory in Baghdad in 794. As already mentioned, the Arabs had learned how to manufacture paper in Trans-Oxiana, where they found a factory established by a party of Chinese. Soon paper was being manufactured in nearly all the provinces of the empire. The age of translations came to an end soon after Mamoon and thereafter original scientific works in Arabic began to appear.

The Arab mentality seemed peculiarly adapted to the study of mathematics and, in this field, they did much original work. They seemed to have a great gift of lucidity, and were remarkably clear organizers and classifiers, qualities essential to mathematics. Mansoor had collected many learned men at his court, particularly engineers and astronomers. He had also taken great interest in astrology, and frequently consulted astrologers about the future. In the khalifate of Mamoon, an astronomical observatory was established. An Arabic work, *The Compendium of Astronomy* by Al Ferghani, was in use in Europe until the sixteenth century.

The Arabs made algebra an exact science—the name itself is Arabic—al jubr. They also laid the foundations of analytical geometry.

"They were indisputably the founders of plane and spherical trigonometry which, properly speaking, did not exist among the Greeks."[6]

Some controversy has taken place on the question of who discovered Zero, and it would now appear probable that the Arabs obtained the idea from China or India. The use of zero enables us to reckon in tens and hundreds and is thus the very basis of modern arithmetic. Even if the Arabs did not invent it, they were using it two hundred and fifty years before it reached Western Europe.

Al Battani (817-918) seems to have discovered trigonometrical ratios and

6. Carra de Vaux in *The Legacy of Islam*.

invented sine and cosine, tangent and cotangent. "This brings us far beyond the point reached by the Greeks and really opens up the era of modern science."[7]

The fact that all this learning was widely diffused among the people is emphasized by the fact that there were at this time no less than one hundred bookshops in the Baghdad suburb of Karkh alone. There was also a library attached to every mosque. In 820, Mamoon founded a central library in Baghdad which he called "The House of Wisdom". In Cordova, at about the same time, there were no less than seventy libraries.

*　　*　　*

To those who have heard the musical programmes of most Arabic-speaking radio stations today, it may come as a surprise that Arab civilization at its height devoted great attention to music. The voice was more appreciated by Arabs than the orchestra, partly perhaps because the voice could combine music with the poetry which was the first love of every Arab. Military bands, however, were developed by the Arab armies.

To the wealthy Arab, singers were perhaps the favourite evening entertainment. Most of the singers were slave girls but many were eunuchs. The latter were extremely popular, both because they preserved their clear boys' voices and also because they were able to perform before the whole family, even veiled ladies being able to be present.

The manufacture of musical instruments had been carried to a fine art and they had both bow instruments of the violin type and also stringed instruments like the lute and guitar—both names being derived from the Arabic. They also manufactured organs, both pneumatic and hydraulic.

The evening party had always been one of the principal pleasures of the Arabs. During the day, men were inevitably preoccupied with their normal tasks but once the sun was set, they prepared themselves for the evening's enjoyment. Of quick intelligence, possessing a marvellously flexible and sonorous language and themselves fluent natural speakers, they devoted these nocturnal parties principally to conversation. This indeed is still true today, except perhaps in those circles which deliberately endeavour to mimic Western customs.

One of the most remarkable qualities distinguishing the real Arabs from other races is personal dignity. We must not, therefore, visualize the evenings of the khalifs, or of the rich, sophisticated classes as degenerating into riotous noise or singing or shouting. Members of the best society, whether under the Umaiyids in Damascus or the Abbasids in Baghdad, were experts in the art of gracious and luxurious living. Their conversation was witty and sometimes intellectual. The women were beautiful, the food was delicious, the recitation of poetry or the improvisation of verses suited to the occasion was a pastime in which the members of society were expected to be competent. Some, on these occasions, drank wine, others rosewater or coloured drinks made of various fruits. Slaves, gorgeously dressed in silks and gold lace, waited hand and foot upon the company.

7. Carra de Vaux, op. cit.

For these festive evenings, those invited would change their everyday clothes and appear in special garments of bright colours.[8] They sat on low couches, spread with carpets, cushions and other materials which were then manufactured in large quantities. The room was strewn with myrtle, jasmine and scented flowers, while musk, amber and other fragrant perfumes burned in gold and silver vessels, which were periodically held under the faces of the guests to enable them to inhale the perfumed smoke which imparted a delightful fragrance also to their hair, beards and clothing. Wine or sweet drinks were served in cups worked with filigree of gold and silver or in finely cut glass. An orchestra—if the hosts were wealthy—provided a musical background or beautiful girl slaves sang to the lute or the guitar. General conversation, poetry and story-telling wiled away pleasantly the long hours of darkness. Perhaps owing to the fact that the glaring heat of the day is sometimes oppressive, Arabs have always loved to prolong their evening pleasures far into the night.

*　　*　　*

In Chapter XII we gave a brief description of the earliest city of Baghdad, the Round City of Mansoor. A hundred years later, the capital presented a very different appearance. Scarcely was the Round City completed, than the suburbs began to grow in every direction. The most extensive of these was the Karkh suburb covering several square miles south of the city of Mansoor, down the west bank of the Tigris.[9] It was the principal commercial area and was divided into separate markets for the various trades. The navigable Isa Canal, coming from the Euphrates, ran through the Karkh quarter and into the lower harbour on the Tigris. North of the Round City lay the Harbiya quarter, largely inhabited by Turks and Persians, and one constantly giving trouble in riots and disturbances. After finishing the Round City, Mansoor had built the Rusafa Palace on the east bank for Mehedi, and then the Khuld Palace for himself, on the river bank.

The Shammasiya quarter lay outside that of Rusafa. Shammas is the Arabic for a deacon and the name commemorates the presence of a large Christian population. In Baghdad there were six Nestorian monasteries on the east bank of the Tigris alone. All were said to have been surrounded by pleasant gardens frequented by the citizens. On various occasions the khalifs themselves seem to have stayed in one or other of these monasteries. The Nestorian patriarch had an official residence in Baghdad, while most of the Christians appear to have lived in the Shammasiya quarter. The great Christian monastery called Deir al Roum seems to have been built in the reign of Mehedi. The Nestorian Patriarch was a personage of some importance, who sent Christian missionaries and appointed bishops as far afield as India, Central Asia and China. All this seems to indicate that the Christians enjoyed a high degree of toleration under the early Abbasids.

In the reigns of Haroon and Mamoon, Baghdad and Constantinople were the two greatest cities of the world. It is interesting to note that the Emperor Theophilus spent large sums enlarging and decorating the Great Palace

8. As people in England before 1914 used to "change for dinner" every night.
9. Map 34, page 247.

of Constantinople in an attempt to compete with the splendid buildings of Baghdad. He even constructed a suburban residence on the Asiatic shore opposite Constantinople, exactly modelled on that of the khalif, thereby silently acknowledging the supremacy of the Arabs in architecture.[10] Indeed, the city on the Tigris in its days of glory could bear comparison with ancient Rome, the Paris of Louis XIV or the London of the nineteenth century, as one of the great imperial capitals of history.

It has been the practice of many Western historians to decry the part played by the Arabs in the empire which they created and to point out that the artists, the philosophers, the historians or the scientists were individually of Persian, Armenian, Greek or Spanish origin. It is true, of course, that the original Arabs of Arabia who gave the first and decisive impulse to imperial conquest were far too few in number to populate an empire. Indeed, when the Arab dominions were at their greatest extent—from Abdul Malik ibn Merwan to the end of the Umaiyids—the original Arabs probably formed perhaps only two or three per cent of the total population of the empire, although they still constituted to a great extent the ruling class. When the Abbasids came to power, the Arabs lost their privileged position and became ordinary subjects, on the same social level as the innumerable other races of the empire. Thus if their talents were equal to those of the other peoples, they could only be expected to have produced two or three per cent of the famous men of the new cosmopolitan state.

Yet even such a statement as this is a gross over-simplification. For who were the Arabs two hundred years after the death of the Prophet? There were still, of course, nomadic tribes in Central Arabia, similar to the original conquerors but their isolation in the great deserts prevented them from playing any part in public life. Meanwhile, those of their ancestors who had been carried by the wave of conquests to Iraq, Persia, Africa or Spain had intermarried with women of innumerable other races. Every man was known by his descent on the male side, so that a man might carry an old Arab tribal name such as the Temeemi, the Kindi or the Taghlibi and yet have only five per cent or ten per cent of Arab blood in his veins. Even Quraish, even the khalifs, were no longer Arabs in the sense of being descended from the people of Central Arabia. We must therefore logically follow one or other of two courses. Either we must admit that the only real Arabs were those still living with the nomadic tribes of Arabia, and that virtually none of the people living in the cities of Iraq or Syria, in Egypt, Africa or Spain, were Arabs at all. Or else we must adopt a new definition of Arabs and apply the term to anyone who—for example—spoke Arabic as his native language, though he might now well be a Turk, a Persian or even a Visigoth. The system of classifying the men of those days into nationalities according to their names is entirely misleading.

In the attempt to evaluate the events of history, over-simplification is one of the commonest causes of error. In reality it is impossible to unravel the racial origins of the inhabitants of Iraq, Syria, North Africa or Spain, whether in the ninth century or today.

10. J. B. Bury, op. cit.

The fact remains that the original conquests which began in 633 were carried out purely by Arabs from Central Arabia. Fifty years later, in the reign of Abdul Malik ibn Merwan, a splendid empire had been built up, extending from India to the Atlantic, magnificent buildings were being erected, and wealth, commerce and enlightenment were increasing rapidly. It is, of course, possible to say that the engineers who constructed the buildings were Greeks, that the doctors were Christians or Jews, the government officials and secretaries Persians, with the result that no credit need be given to the Arabs. Such an argument is like saying that the members of the Board of Directors of a great engineering or shipbuilding firm today deserve no credit for the success of the company, because none of them are fitters, rivetters, painters or carpenters.

The magnitude of the accomplishment of the original Arab conquerors can be, to some extent, appreciated by a comparison with the Mongol conquests of the thirteenth, fourteenth and fifteenth centuries. Fifty years after the Arab tribesmen emerged from the desert they were ruling a splendid, expanding and progressive empire. When the Mongol conquerors withdrew from the same countries, they left nothing but heaps of smoking ruins and pyramids of skulls. They utterly obliterated an ancient cultured civilization, which to this day has never revived. Libraries, palaces, factories, industries, universities, hospitals, craftsmen, artists, professors, all were swept from the face of the earth, their skills destroyed, their knowledge lost, their irrigation systems wrecked to such an extent that after being a great civilization the victims were relegated for five succeeding centuries to the category of backward and subject peoples. The conquering tribes of Central Arabia were quarrelsome, warlike and ignorant, yet they must have been of remarkable intelligence and extraordinary adaptability. Instead of plundering and destroying, they quickly adapted themselves to a sophisticated civilization. Instead of massacring artists and scientists they employed them. Yet they did not merely imitate them, as the Goths did the civilization of Italy. They remained complete masters of the situation, great lords and nobles. Even in Abbasid times, when the old Arab families were largely displaced, their language, their customs and, to a great extent, the culture and the arts which they had evolved, were accepted unquestioningly by the many and ancient races of the empire.

"Islamic art", it has been said, "derived its spiritual complexion from Arabia; but its material texture was fashioned elsewhere." [11] The statement would be equally true if it were made to refer to Islamic civilization as a whole instead of only to art. Innumerable craftsmen, Persians, Greeks, Byzantines, Egyptians, Berbers, Goths and Romans all contributed to the erection of the splendid structure of Islamic civilization, but the original architect of the whole grandiose structure was the Arab.

NOTABLE DATES

Mamoon's invasions of the Byzantine Empire	830–833
Death of Mamoon	9th August, 833

11. A. H. Christie.

PERSONALITIES

Talha   ⎫ Sons of Tahir the Ambidextrous
Abdulla   ⎭ and rulers of Khurasan
Babek the Khurramite in rebellion in Adharbaijan
Hunain ibn Ishaq, chief translator of Greek classics
    into Arabic
Mutasim, son of Haroon al Rasheed, successor to Mamoon

XVIII

Mutasim sells the Pass

Mutasim collected a large force of Turkish military slaves and arranged to receive a large number annually as part of the tribute from the eastern provinces. The old Khurasani guards of the Abbasid Caliphs had become Arabised and identified with the local population. From this time on the Caliphs relied to an increasing extent on Turkish troops and commanders, to the detriment of the older cultured peoples in Islam, the Arabs and the Persians.　　　　PROFESSOR BERNARD LEWIS, *The Arabs in History*

XVIII

MUTASIM SELLS THE PASS

WE must now leave the Baghdad khalifate with the death of Mamoon in 833, and turn to Ifriqiya. We left that province in the year 800 under the virtually independent rule of Ibrahim ibn al Aghlab, the son of an Arab officer killed in 767 in the disturbances in North Africa. Ibrahim, who ruled the province from 800 to 812, was a man of exceptional ability. A wise statesman, a skilful politician, a successful soldier, his reign inaugurated an era of peace and of reviving prosperity. He established the far-seeing policy of recognizing the supremacy of the Abbasid khalif, whose capital in Baghdad was too far away to enable him to exercise any direct influence in Qairawan.

In Ifriqiya, the Aghlabids in general exercised virtually undisputed authority over the coastal plains from mid-Algeria (to use its modern name) to Tripoli. The Kharijite Berbers of the high Atlas maintained their sturdy independence, as did also the nomad tribes on the northern fringe of the Sahara. The minority of Jews and Christians in the coastal plains seem to have been treated with a wise tolerance.

Nevertheless, the period was one of intense religious enthusiasm among the Sunni Muslims of the coastal plains. Qairawan had become a centre of religious studies as famous as Cordova, Fustat or Baghdad, even if not as sacred as Medina or Mecca. The threat of naval attack from the Mediterranean gave rise to an immense line of coastal forts or ribats, extending from the Atlantic coast all the way to Tunis and Tripoli, at intervals of a few miles. There was also a remarkably efficient system of giving the alarm by the lighting of beacon-fires, each ribat containing a single tower especially designed to carry the fire.

The ribats were manned by garrisons of Muslims, who desired to gain merit by fighting for the faith. At first they appear to have been unpaid, but to have been relieved every three or four months. During their tours of duty in the forts, they kept a look-out to sea and for any beacon-fires which might give the alarm, practised weapon training and tactical exercises, and devoted themselves to prayer and meditation.

Ibrahim ibn al Aghlab died in 812 and was succeeded by his son, Abdulla I, who ruled from 812 to 817, and made himself unpopular by his avarice. Ziyadat Allah I, who was Ameer of Ifriqiya for twenty years from 817 to 838, was a poet and bon viveur.[1] In his reign, however, the dynasty embarked on a great new military adventure, the conquest of Sicily. The island had remained nominally subject to Byzantium, though the emperors usually had

---

1. For a list of the Aghlabids, see page 349.

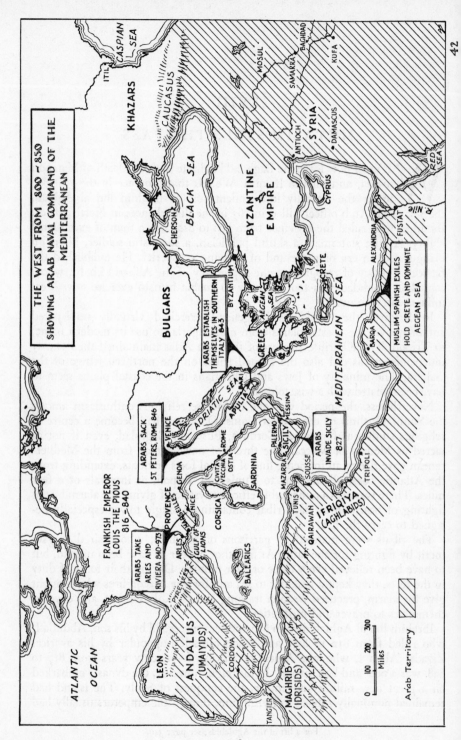

THE WEST FROM 800 ~ 850
SHOWING ARAB NAVAL COMMAND OF THE
MEDITERRANEAN

ATLANTIC OCEAN

CASPIAN SEA

ITIL

KHAZARS

CAUCASUS

MOSUL
SAMARRA
BAGHDAD
KUFA

BLACK SEA

CHERSON

SYRIA

BULGARS

ANTIOCH
DAMASCUS

BYZANTINE EMPIRE

BYZANTIUM

AEGEAN SEA

GREECE

CYPRUS

RED SEA

R. Nile

ARABS ESTABLISH THEMSELVES IN SOUTHERN ITALY 843

CRETE

ALEXANDRIA

FUSTAT

MEDITERRANEAN SEA

MUSLIM SPANISH EXILES HOLD CRETE AND DOMINATE AEGEAN SEA

ADRIATIC SEA

VENICE

APULIA

BARI

BARQA

ARABS SACK ST PETERS, ROME 846

ROME

OSTIA

PALERMO

MESSINA

GENOA

CIVITA VECCHIA

SICILY

FRANKISH EMPEROR LOUIS THE PIOUS 816~840

NICE

CORSICA

SARDINIA

MAZARRA

SOUSSE

ARABS INVADE SICILY 827

PROVENCE

MARSEILLES

ARLES

GULF OF LIONS

TUNIS

TRIPOLI

ARABS TAKE ARLES AND RIVIERA 840-975

PYRENEES

BALEARICS

QAIRAWAN

IFRIQIYA (AGHLABIDS)

LEON

ANDALUS (UMAIYIDS)

CORDOVA

ATLAS MTS

MAGHRIB (IDRISIDS)

TANGIER

Arab Territory

0   100   200   300
Miles

42

338

more than enough to occupy them at home and Sicily received little attention from the Byzantine government.

Just as Count Julian of Ceuta had invited the Arabs to invade Spain, so a seditious Greek officer suggested to the Aghlabids the conquest of Sicily. In 827, a fleet and an army sailed from Sousse and landed at Mazzara, under the command of Asad ibn al Furat, the qadhi of Qairawan, who had preached that the campaign would be a Holy War. Progress was slow, but Palermo was taken four years later and became the Arab capital. Apparently unexpectedly, a contingent arrived from Andalus, which at first gave fresh impetus to the operations, but later produced friction between the Spanish and the African contingents. In 843, Messina was captured and the Arabs began crossing to Southern Italy. In Ifriqiya, however, the Ameer Muhammad ibn al Aghlab (841–856) was passing his days in idleness and debauchery and no dynamic leadership from home assisted the expeditionary force in Sicily.

It is strange how frequently the character of an Arab ruler in these early centuries was in complete contrast to that of his predecessor, the reactions perhaps of dominated children against the qualities of their parents. The drunken Muhammad was succeeded by the virtuous Ahmed (856–863) and he again by Muhammad II, who passed most of his time in hunting and drinking.

The Arabs did not wait to complete the conquest of Sicily before passing on to invade Italy. In August 846, they took Ostia and appeared before the walls of Rome itself. They withdrew without attacking the city but only after sacking the shrine of St. Peter's on the opposite bank of the Tiber. Bari was occupied by an Arab garrison, which held no less than twenty-four fortresses in the province of Apulia alone. The establishment of the Arabs in Sicily and Southern Italy, at a moment when the Abbasids were weakening, gave the Muslims in 850 more complete naval control of the Mediterranean than ever before. At the same time Arab colonies were once more established in the South of France, while from Crete the Muslim refugees who had originally come from Andalus raided the islands of the Aegian, almost entirely destroying the sea-borne commerce of Constantinople.

Throughout the ninth century, Arab pirate squadrons terrorized the whole of the Gulf of Lions, some of them coming from Spain, others from Ifriqiya and from Sicily. Not only the Balearic Islands, Corsica and Sardinia, but Genoa, Nice, Civita Vecchia and Marseilles were sacked. In 842, and again in 850, the Arabs penetrated inland as far as Arles. In 890, they established themselves on the coast of the Riviera, and again dominated Provence and Dauphiné. It was not until 973 that they were finally expelled from Arles. When we realize that the continual invasions of Italy and the South of France were scarcely more than private piratical enterprises by local ameers, we cannot doubt that if the Abbasids had not lost interest in the West when they came under Persian influence, they could easily have conquered Italy and a great part of France.

Whatever the personal virtues or vices of the Aghlabids may have been, Ifriqiya during their century of rule enjoyed a revival of peace and prosperity, after the terrible Arab-Berber wars which had preceded it. The ameers were active builders, principally of splendid mosques but also of palaces for themselves, notably the Reqqada, outside Qairawan. The forts and castles which they constructed along the coast against sea-raiders and in the interior against the Berber tribes, are in many cases still visible today. Like almost all the Arab rulers of the centuries of empire, they did not rely solely on the loyalty of their own subjects. They, too, depended largely on a military force of slave-soldiers, though in their case they consisted principally of African negroes—a safer method than the employment of Greek, Turkish or Persian slaves, for they were less likely to seize power for themselves.

While the Aghlabids were not always models of piety, Ifriqiya as a whole, and Qairawan in particular, took its religion very seriously. It is possible that, by contrast with this highly-charged religious atmosphere, the worldliness of some of the ameers met with more criticism than did the frivolities of Damascus, Baghdad or Cordova. At any rate, in spite of their moral pecca-dilloes, they do not seem to have neglected their public duties. They never abandoned the administration to all-powerful chief ministers as the Abbasids did. They avoided the delegation of authority to insubordinate tribal chiefs and made use of professional civil servants. They appreciated the importance of water in a semi-desert country and the remains of the water-channels, aqueducts and cisterns which they built bear witness to this day to their diligence.

As the Arab Empire disintegrated, two channels were to open enabling the science, learning and skills of the Muslim world to be drawn back into Europe. It is amazing and fascinating to watch how these two channels of Spain and Sicily opened just in time to enable Europe to inherit Arab civilization. For the main sources of that civilization in Syria and Iraq were soon to be over-run by the hordes of Tatars and Turks, who were utterly to destroy the whole of that culture. The Eastern Arab countries have been a wilderness ever since and only in our own lifetimes have begun to regain consciousness after the six centuries of coma which resulted from the concussion.

But just before this shattering blow fell, the gateways of Spain and Sicily began slowly to open and the accumulated skill, learning and science of Arabia and the East, matured in Damascus and Baghdad and carried from thence to Qairawan and Cordova, poured into Europe at the very moment in which it was extinguished at its source. The perfect timing can scarcely be described as other than providential. No one now remembers the Aghlabids, yet in this, one of the greatest processes of history, their timely conquest of Sicily played a vital part.

It is true that the majority of European writers have considered the Muslim conquest of Sicily to have been a disaster. Yet it may be argued today that Christendom, in the long run, benefited from it more than did the Muslims. For if the Arabs had remained in Tunis and the Christians in Sicily, one of the principal channels through which Arab civilization enriched the life of the West would never have been opened.

* * *

We must now turn back to consider the history of Spain. We may, in a few lines, recapitulate the history of the Umaiyid rulers of Spain, already told in previous chapters. The first was Abdul Rahman ibn Muawiya, who escaped from the massacre of the Umaiyid family in Damascus, landed in Spain in September 755, and made himself ruler of the country. He died in 788, and was succeeded by his pious son Hisham, who reigned in justice and peace until 796, when he was succeeded by his son Hakam. The new prince, though not remarkably wicked, was not a devoted ascetic like his father, and so encountered opposition from the more fanatical Muslim religious teachers. Hakam ruled for twenty-six years and died in 822. It was at this time that we left our account of Andalus in Chapter XVI.

Hakam was succeeded by his son Abdul Rahman II. Though ruthless and treacherous in suppressing rebellion, Hakam had not been otherwise either an unjust or an incompetent ruler and he left the country peaceful and prosperous. The Umaiyids had now ruled Spain for some seventy years and had become generally accepted by all the people as their legitimate princes. More important still, one hundred and eleven years had passed since the Arab invasion of Spain. The difference between the Arabs, the Berbers and the Spaniards who had been converted to Islam, was no longer sharply defined. An Andalusian nation was taking shape. The Arab tribal rivalries between Qais and Yemen had disappeared. It is true that there was still a numerous Christian minority but the Muslims were wise and tolerant and the Christians were able to rise to high offices of state or to share fully, as merchants or as farmers, in the increasing prosperity of the country.

Abdul Rahman II of Andalus was the child of this new age of peace, wealth and civilization. In Baghdad, the Khalif Mamoon was presiding over the era of culture, literature, art and science, and the Umaiyids of Spain could not resist the temptation to compete with their rivals in the East. Abdul Rahman II, therefore, at peace with his subjects and his neighbours, set out to make Cordova a second Baghdad. His mind was cultured, his tastes were refined and he was of a pleasant and sociable temperament. Like all Arab princes, he was a devotee of poetry, composed his own verses and patronized poets and musicians. In these pursuits he was guided by his friend and protégé Ziryab, an Arab of Persian extraction, who had been a pupil of Ishaq of Mosul, the court musician of Haroon al Rasheed himself. Ziryab had even, on one occasion, himself performed before the great Haroon.

In Cordova, he became the Beau Brummel of Abdul Rahman II. He not only was the court musician, but he was obviously a man of varied and brilliant intellectual gifts. He could discourse on poetry, history and literature and, in daily social life, was famous for his witticisms and his quick and polished repartees. In dress, he was the model of elegance and set the fashion in the cut of his clothes, his manner of wearing his hair and the delicacies of his cuisine.

We, in the twentieth century, are so accustomed to the pre-eminence of Western civilization that we may be inclined to suspect that the refined civilization of Andalus was borrowed from France or Italy. Nothing could be further from the truth. The northern neighbours of the Arabs of Spain were ignorant country boors in comparison with the cultured gentlemen of the court of Cordova.

The court of Abdul Rahman II, however, was not distinguished merely by frivolities of music, poetry, dress and food. The translations from the ancient Greek authors, which had been so diligently executed under Mamoon, had spread to Andalus, where learned studies were actively pursued. The chain of inheritance by which Europe was to regain its civilization led from ancient Greece to Baghdad, from Baghdad to Cordova and from Cordova back to France, England and Western Germany. The Arabs, by cutting off Europe from the world, had caused the Dark Ages, at the end of which it was the Arabs also who gave back to Europe the light of knowledge.

Abdul Rahman II died on 22nd September, 852, after a happy reign of thirty years, during which Andalus had enjoyed peace, prosperity and an immense advance in culture, knowledge and refinement. Under the weak and miserly rule of his son, Muhammad, the Umaiyid dynasty of Spain seemed to be declining to its fall. But appearances were deceptive, for the golden age of the Arabs of Andalus was still to come. A hundred years after the time of which we are writing, Muslim Spain was to be, militarily and culturally, one of the Great Powers of the time. Much of the fine flower of the culture and the chivalry of Andalus was to be permanently absorbed into the civilization of Western Europe.

* * *

It is worthy of note that the Arabs established their most complete mastery of the Mediterranean in the century from 850 to 950, when the Abbasid khalifate was already tottering to its fall. This Western Arab sea power was established by the rulers of Spain and North Africa, without the assistance of Baghdad. Not that the Arabs of the East were poor seamen—on the contrary they were sailing regularly to India, China and Indonesia. The stories of Sindbad the sailor in the Arabian Nights, though embroidered with magic and fable for popular consumption, give some idea of this great age of commercial sea adventure. Abbasid naval weakness in the Mediterranean was due to their loss of interest in the West as a whole, which had been illustrated by Haroon's virtual abandonment of Ifriqiya to the Aghlabids.

The Franks never took to the sea, with the result that Byzantium and Venice and a few ports in southern Italy were the only non-Arabs who, however feebly, even attempted to resist Arab sea power. These operated a precarious coastal traffic round Greece and up the Adriatic, which, however, was just enough to maintain commercial communities in a few cities and to avoid the establishment in Greece and Italy of a complete agricultural and feudal system, such as had come into existence in France and England. The ninth and the first half of the tenth centuries were probably the lowest point of Christian sea power. Thereafter, and with the coming of the crusades, it began to revive. It is significant that, at the present day, all the most beautiful old mansions in England are on country estates. In Italy, the lovely palaces of the old families of merchant princes are to be found in the commercial and maritime cities, such as Venice and Genoa.

European seamanship was largely derived from the Arabs, though in the extreme north-west an independent school was being built up round the North Sea. Italian, Spanish and Portuguese seamen, however, the men who were to discover America and the sea route round the Cape of Good Hope, learned their trade from the Arabs.

*　　*　　*

On 9th August, 833, in the army camp where Mamoon died, his brother Mutasim was proclaimed khalif. He was the eighth son of Haroon al Rasheed and the third of his sons to become khalif. Abbas, the son of Mamoon, swore allegiance to his uncle.

Seventy years had elapsed since Mansoor had founded Baghdad and had settled in it the Khurasan troops on whom he relied. But the Khurasanis, after the disastrous civil war between Ameen and Mamoon, had abandoned their traditional devotion to the Abbasids. Mutasim felt himself obliged to seek elsewhere for loyal troops. He seems to have disliked the Arabs and placed almost all his reliance on Turkish mercenaries. Many of these were already in service but Mutasim greatly increased their numbers. He imported as many as he could from beyond the Oxus until he had built up a bodyguard of ten thousand of them. He dressed them in splendid uniforms, some of them being entirely clad in silk, while their belts and weapons were inlaid with gold and silver. The recruitment of Turks was entirely different from the previous employment of Khurasanis, for the Persians and the Arabs were Muslims and possessors of high cultures. The Turks came from tribes of barbarians.

Enjoying the favour of the khalif, the Turks became arrogant. They would gallop through the streets of Baghdad, splendidly mounted, knocking down women and children who failed to get out of the way. Any Turkish soldier who ventured alone down the backstreets of the city after dark was liable to be murdered in revenge by the enraged populace. Eventually relations between the people and the Turks became so strained that Mutasim decided to abandon Baghdad and to build himself a new city at Samarra, seventy miles higher up the Tigris.[2]

Being interested both in architecture and in agriculture, he devoted himself with energy to the erection of palaces and to the layout of gardens, orchards and plantations for his new capital. Mutasim was a man of great physical strength and of imposing presence, with a reputation for personal courage. He was lacking in culture and education, being in this direction the very opposite of Mamoon.

It is recorded that, when he was a small boy, one of the palace slaves used to do lessons with him. One day the little page boy fell ill and died, and Mutasim's father, Haroon al Rasheed, came to break the sad news. "Yes, my lord," replied the little Mutasim, "but at least he is now at rest and does not have to go to school any more." "Is school as bad as all that?" asked his fond father, and gave orders that the boy need not do lessons any longer, with the result that Mutasim grew up almost uneducated.

2. For the position of Samarra, see Map 33, page 245.

The rebellion of Babek the Khurramite in Adharbaijan has already been mentioned. The insurrection had begun in 816, during the period of general anarchy which had followed the death of the Khalif Ameen and while Mamoon was still in Khurasan. Subsequently sedition had spread to Hamadan and Jurjan. Now, twenty-two years later, Babek was as strong as ever.

The rebels took advantage of the wildness of the mountains, with every path and defile of which they were familiar. Avoiding pitched battles in daylight, their tactics had been to cut off caravans, ambush the mountain passes and to surprise detachments of troops at night. The army was obliged to move only in large formations and to escort every convoy which had to move across country. Any momentary relaxation of vigilance would lead to some regrettable incident.

The rebels, who enjoyed the sympathy and support of the country people, were kept constantly informed of every move of the regular army and would immediately pounce on any weak detachment. The army could still march through the country by day with drums beating and colours flying, but it was well-advised to bivouac early and strongly to fortify its camp. For as soon as it was dark, the insurgents assumed control of the whole area.

Mutasim, a keen soldier with no interest in culture to divert his attention, determined to put an end to this long-drawn-out small war. He sent his best general, Haider al Afsheen.[3] The new commander was an experienced but cautious soldier. He restrained the ardour of his more impatient subordinates and refused to take any risks with so enterprising an enemy. Gradually, yard by yard and mile by mile, he re-established control.

Babek soon realized that, this time, he was opposed to a commander who meant business. He accordingly wrote to the Byzantine Emperor Theophilus, informing him that the whole Arab army was concentrated against him in Adharbaijan and suggesting that this was the moment for a Byzantine invasion.

At last, in 837, Babek was brought to bay, his fortress capital was carried by assault and burned to the ground and Babek was sent in chains to the khalif in Samarra. His arrival was made the occasion for a day of public rejoicing. Babek was dressed up in splendid silken robes with a crown on his head and was led through the streets to the palace on an elephant. In the presence of the khalif, he was despoiled of his finery. His hands and feet were cut off, and swords were slowly thrust into his body, avoiding the vital organs in order to prolong his last moments of agony. Even his enemies admitted that he bore all his tortures with extraordinary fortitude, without even giving vent to a groan. His head was sent to Baghdad while his headless corpse was exposed, nailed to a wooden post, in Samarra. More than a century later, the place was still commonly known as "Babek's Post".

During the twenty-two years of his rebellion, Babek is alleged by the Arab historian to have killed 200,000 people. When his stronghold was finally captured it was found to contain seven thousand Muslim women and children working as his slaves. The numbers are doubtless unreliable but they suffice to show that his operations were on a considerable scale.

3. Afsheen seems to have been a title used in some parts of Trans-Oxiana.

Under the martial and energetic Mutasim, other successful campaigns imposed the khalif's will on the distant and mountainous provinces of Tabaristan, Tukharistan, Kabul and Kandahar. Those who remember the frequent punitive campaigns carried out in Afghanistan by the British army from India will be interested to learn that, a thousand years earlier, the Arab Empire was often obliged to undertake similar operations in the same country.

Meanwhile, the Emperor Theophilus had accepted Babek's suggestion and had marched with 70,000 men to the frontier of Syria, where in the summer of 837 he had besieged Zebetra, a town thirty miles south of Malatia. It so happened that Mutasim had been born in Zebetra, for Haroon al Rasheed was in the habit of taking some of his favourite concubines with him on his campaigns. The army was still in Adharbaijan and East Persia, but some of the historians relate that Mutasim sent a request to Theophilus to spare Zebetra, which had been his birthplace. Not only did Theophilus neglect the request, if it was ever made, but he appears to have acted with peculiar brutality towards that town, which was taken by assault and razed to the ground. More than a thousand Muslim women were driven off into slavery, not counting the children. The men of the city were all put to the sword.

The emperor then raided the surrounding country up to Malatia, carrying off the women. The eyes of the men were put out and their noses and ears were cut off. No sooner did the news reach Samarra than Mutasim moved into camp on the west bank of the Tigris and unfurled his war banners. Every available man was called up, from Egypt, Arabia, Syria and Iraq, over and above the regular Turkish units.

In the spring of 838, Mutasim moved off at the head of the greatest army ever commanded by any khalif. The total strength, which, however, must be accepted with reserve, is given by Masudi as 200,000 at the lowest estimate. The invaders crossed the Taurus in two columns. One, commanded by Mutasim in person, followed the coastal road through Tarsus. The other, under Afsheen, was to cross the mountains through the pass of Hadeth. The two columns were to rendezvous beyond the Taurus and march together to Anqara. As the two passes were nearly one hundred and fifty miles apart, the operation was not without risk.

The Arabs had now apparently acquired the secret of the Greek fire, which had saved Constantinople from the armies of Muawiya and Sulaiman ibn Abdul Malik. Special units of "oilmen" marched with Mutasim's army, trained to light and discharge the flaming liquid.

The Emperor Theophilus was already in the field with his army and was awaiting the Muslim invasion on the River Lamis. The Arab army passed the Taurus in June 838. The emperor received a report from his intelligence staff that another Arab column—that of Afsheen—was crossing the mountains further north at Hadeth. He quite rightly decided to destroy this northern column in detail, before the two Arab armies could unite. He accordingly slipped away from the River Lamis and marched rapidly northwards.

The disappearance of Theophilus was reported to Mutasim, who, however, was unable to pursue him owing to the fact that his siege train and baggage were still struggling through the mountains, but he despatched a warning

MUTASIM'S CAMPAIGN AGAINST
AMORIUM. SUMMER 838

THEOPHILUS DESTROYS
ZEBETRA. SUMMER 837

AFSHEEN DEFEATS
THEOPHILUS
JUNE 838

MUTASIM DESTROYS
AMORIUM. SEPT 838

THEOPHILUS
MAY 838

ARAB EMPIRE

JEZIRA

SYRIA

BYZANTINE
EMPIRE

BLACK SEA

SEA OF
MARMORA

AEGEAN
SEA

MEDITERRANEAN SEA

CRETE

CYPRUS

RHODES

CONSTANTINOPLE

ANQARA

ICONIUM

AMORIUM

SAMSUN

CAESAREA

TUWANA

LULUA

HERACLEA

TARSUS

ADANA

DANA

TAURUS MTS.

Cilician
Gates

R. Halys

MALATIA

ZEBETRA

HADETH

MARESH

ALEPPO

ANTIOCH

HAMA

RAQQA

MARDIN

R. Tigris

R. Euphrates

Mutasim's Advance
Afsheen's Advance
Theophilus' Route
Route of combined
Arab columns

0   100
Miles

43

346

post-haste to Afsheen. Before the message could reach him, Afsheen was surprised by the emperor and his column was at first thrown into some confusion. But Afsheen, who was an old campaigner, was equal to the emergency. Rallying his troops, he counter-attacked the Byzantine army and inflicted upon it a heavy defeat, as a result of which it withdrew westward in some disorder. This action took place at the end of June 838.

The two Arab columns joined at Anqara, and marched from there to Amorium (called by the Arabs Amuriya) which happened to have been the birthplace of Theophilus, or at least the native town of his family. (His father, it will be remembered, was known as Michael the Amorian.) Mutasim was therefore determined to raze Amorium, as the emperor had razed Zebetra. The siege train was quickly brought up and the heavy mangonels went into action. Theophilus and the Byzantine army had vanished. Soon a breach was made in the walls and the city was taken by assault. According to Arab reports, thirty thousand Byzantines were massacred and the city was razed to the ground. The siege had lasted fifty-five days, from the beginning of August to the end of September 838. Thirty thousand women and children, the Arab historians claim, were dragged off into slavery. Thus did Mutasim retaliate for the attrocities committed by Theophilus in Zebetra.

While the army was defiling back through the Taurus passes, a plot came to light. A number of senior officers had sworn allegiance to Abbas the son of Mamoon, apparently in resentment at the favour shown to the Turks. The conspirators were put to death, including Abbas, but Mutasim was still not to enjoy peace. Afsheen had reached the highest pinnacle of glory. It was he who had finally defeated Babek and, with his column alone, had routed Theophilus and the Byzantine army. The khalif could not do enough for his great general.

Mutasim had once or twice confided in Afsheen that he was not entirely satisfied with Abdulla ibn Tahir, the governor of Khurasan. A certain Maziar was in rebellion in Tabaristan. Maziar had been an ally of Babek and may have been a Khurramite. Afsheen was a Persian from Trans-Oxiana and apparently claimed descent from the ancient Kings of Persia.

Whether Afsheen, as a Persian noble, sympathized with Maziar or whether he hoped that he would himself be made governor of Khurasan if Ibn Tahir were defeated, is not certain. At any rate, Afsheen wrote to Maziar urging him to rebellion. Ibn Tahir, however, defeated Maziar and seized his correspondence with Afsheen. From these documents it was evident that the general had not only supported the revolt but also that he was definitely working to overthrow the Abbasid dynasty and to restore the Kingdom of Persia and the Majian religion. Afsheen died in prison.

In the course of the enquiries into the activities of Afsheen, a number of statements were taken which suggest that many of the khalif's mercenary troops were in reality not even Muslims. As Mutasim had bought many of them from Turkish tribes beyond the Oxus, the fact is perhaps not surprising. Yet there was irony in the situation, for the whole basis of the khalifate was religious, though the Prince of the Faithful was now using heathen troops to maintain his rule over his fellow Muslims. Yet, only two hundred years earlier, the first Muslim Arabs had swept the armies of the unbelievers before them like chaff.

Mutasim died on 5th January, 842, at the age of forty-seven. He was a man of great courage, devoted to war and to hunting and was a keen polo player. He was devoid of those cultural interests which had characterized Mamoon. His most notable characteristic was his infatuation with his Turkish troops. He was the first khalif who raised Turks to high offices of state.

Mutasim, with his fine physique and great courage, was a formidable figure who inspired fear. When a disturbance had occurred in the camp outside Amorium, Mutasim had come galloping across the field with his sword drawn in his hand, followed only by one mounted orderly. The troops had shrunk back in fear before this big man thundering up on his charger and the khalif had dispersed the rioters single-handed. But it might have been foreseen that these rough mercenaries would no longer be controllable if a weak khalif were to succeed that fierce dominating figure.

When he died, Mutasim was believed to have left eight million gold dinars in cash. In addition, the weapons and equipment of the Turkish troops were covered with gold. It is interesting to remember that Charlemagne, who had died a few years earlier in 814, had been obliged to use a silver currency owing to his inability to secure gold.

Thus when Mutasim died in 842, there did not appear to outsiders to be any indication of weakening in the empire. The khalif had by far the most powerful army in the world, one column alone of which had been enough utterly to rout the Byzantine army. The financial situation was extremely strong, trade and industry were booming, and the empire was at peace, at home and abroad. Mutasim had proved a powerful and capable ruler, yet he was to be the principal cause of the collapse of the empire which he had so boldly defended.

In the Empire of the Arabs, one-man rule had originated with the Prophet Muhammad himself, who had been the religious teacher, the military commander and the political head of his people. So great was his prestige that his successors had sought only to perpetuate his system. Yet, until the fall of the Umaiyids, a large measure of the old democracy and patriarchy had survived.

It was the Abbasid fear of their Qurashite rivals which led them to rely on Persians, to destroy the power of the Arab aristocracy and to neglect the Arab tribes as a source of army recruits. The Arab townsmen of Kufa, Basra and Damascus had lost their military virtues but the tribes had not.

The Abbasid reliance on Persians need not, however, have been fatal, for they were Muslims and well integrated into the empire. In fact, however, Persian influence was in the end disastrous because it led to unbalanced despotism. There was no longer anyone to oppose a khalif who made a major error of policy. As we have seen, the Turks imported by Mutasim were bitterly hated by the subjects of the empire, but there was no longer any group strong enough to prevent the khalif doing as he wished.

Yet why did the khalifs need foreign mercenaries at all? When we look at the Arabic-speaking countries today with their repeated military coups d'état, are we justified in suspecting that the khalifs felt themselves obliged to use foreign troops, because they could never entirely rely on the loyalty of their Arab armies?

The brief interval of time which intervened between the imperial glories of Haroon, Mamoon and Mutasim and the collapse of the khalifate seems at first surprising. If, however, we remember Louis XIV, we find that he also monopolized all the power of the state and reached an extraordinary pinnacle of glory. But when he died, he, like Haroon, left the government unbalanced. On the accession of a weak king, unable to bear such a load, the edifice, deprived of all other supports, collapsed in ruins.

For two centuries the Empire of the Arabs had been fighting back against the pressure of the northern barbarians just as Rome had done. Mutasim introduced into the very citadel of the empire an army of complete foreigners, many of whom could not speak Arabic and were scarcely even Muslims. Thereby he sold the pass to the enemy and committed the fate of the empire into the hands of men who were bound to it by no emotional or spiritual bond. To this day, the Arabic-speaking peoples have not recovered from the disasters which were to follow.

NOTABLE DATES

Ibrahim ibn al Aghlab made governor of Ifriqiya	800
Accession of Abdul Rahman II of Andalus	822
Arab Invasion of Sicily	827
Death of the Khalif Mamoon } Proclamation of Mutasim }	833
Defeat and death of Babek	837
Destruction of Zebetra by Theophilus	837
Destruction of Amorium by Mutasim	838
Death of the Khalif Mutasim	842
Arab capture of Messina	843
Arab sack of St. Peter's, Rome	850
Death of Abdul Rahman II of Andalus	852

PERSONALITIES

The Khalif Mutasim	833–842
Babek the Khurramite, the rebel of Adharbaijan	
Haider al Afsheen, commander-in-chief	

Sultans of Andalus

Abdul Rahman II	822–852
Muhammad	852–886

Aghlabid Ameers of Ifriqiya

Ibrahim ibn al Aghlab	800–812
Abdulla I	812–817
Ziyadat Allah I	817–839

Abu Aqal	839–841
Muhammad	841–856
Ahmed	856–863

Byzantine Emperors

Leo V, the Armenian	813–820
Michael II, the Amorian	820–829
Theophilus	829–842

XIX

The End of Greatness

The Turkoman chiefs were at this time the virtual arbiters of the fate of the Caliphate . . . The provincial governors gradually converted themselves into feudatories and the supremacy of the Caliphs dwindled into more or less nominal suzerainty.

AMEER ALI, *A Short History of the Saracens*

How are the mighty fallen and the weapons of war perished! 2 *Samuel* II, 27

Time is like a river made up of events. No sooner does anything happen than it is swept away, and another comes in its place, and will be swept away too.

MARCUS AURELIUS ANTONINUS

XIX

The End of Greatness

XIX

AN END OF GREATNESS

WATHIQ,[1] the son of Mutasim, succeeded his father without opposition on the day of his death, 5th January, 842. The Emperor Theophilus died in the same year and was succeeded by his widow, Theodora, as regent for his son Michael. In the year 845 died Abdulla ibn Tahir, the ruler of Khurasan.

In the year 845 also the Beni Sulaim bedouins of the Hejaz began robbing caravans and pilgrims proceeding to the Holy Cities of Mecca and Medina. A punitive force was sent against them, consisting largely of Turkish troops under their own generals. It also took action against Beni Hilal, Fazara and other Hejaz tribes, after which it invaded Nejed, where heavy fighting occurred. Familiar as we are with charges of Turkish mis-government of Arabia in the nineteenth century, we are surprised to find an army of Turks in Arabia in the ninth.

Wathiq abandoned the administration of the empire to his two principal ministers, Muhammad az Zayyat and Ahmed ibn abi Daood. He is said never to have issued an order without consulting them and never to have contradicted their opinions.

In many ways Wathiq offered a complete contrast to his violent, energetic and sometimes cruel father. Perhaps he had been dominated by Mutasim when a child, and had thereby been impelled to cultivate all the qualities diametrically opposed to those of his father. Instead of constantly issuing his orders, he abandoned the control of public affairs to others. He passed the whole of his reign in Samarra, never travelling, or visiting the provinces or embarking on a military campaign. He was kind and good-natured, considerate to the members of his household, benevolent towards his subjects, though he did not do anything practical to improve their lot. He was fond of eating and drinking and tended to over-indulgence in these pleasures.

Like his uncle Mamoon, he possessed an active and enquiring intellect and was always eager to hear different views or new ideas. The wise and the learned were welcome at his court and the conversation at his receptions was often of a high standard. He was interested in philosophy and enjoyed discussions on the qualities and the merits of the ancient and the contemporary philosophers. He was always anxious to hear of the latest developments in physics or natural history, and was particularly interested in medicine.

Wathiq had early shown literary talent and had become an accomplished poet. He was also extremely musical, himself played the lute and was said to have composed more than a hundred pieces of music. While his Persian and Turkish ministers and generals dealt with the affairs of state, the khalif was

1. The accent is on the first syllable, Waathick.

able to find time for these graceful pursuits and for the encouragement of science and literature.

After an uneventful reign of nearly six years, he died in 847 at the age of thirty-six. It was fortunate that, during his reign, the ruler of Byzantium was a woman, with the result that no hostilities took place.

The Abbasid khalifs were, of course, regarded as Arab rulers, but a simple calculation shows that by this time they were racially no longer Arabs at all.

(1) The Khalif Mansoor was the son of Muhammad ibn ali the Abbasid and a Berber concubine. He was therefore half Arab and half Berber.

(2) Mansoor married a Yemenite Arab woman. Their son, the Khalif Mehedi, was therefore three-quarters Arab and one-quarter Berber.

(3) Haroon was the son of Mehedi and Khaizuran, a Berber concubine. He was therefore three-eighths Arab and five-eighths Berber.

(4) Mamoon was the son of Haroon and a Persian slave-girl. He was therefore three-sixteenths Arab and thirteen-sixteenths non-Arab, and Mutasim was the same.

(5) Wathiq's mother was a Greek slave-girl. He was therefore approximately one-tenth Arab by race and nine-tenths non-Arab.

Genetics are doubtless too complicated a subject to be dealt with by such simple arithmetic. Nevertheless such a calculation does give some idea of how little Arab blood ran through the veins of the later Abbasids. Doubtless many of the men of the leading families, even those with Arab names, were of an equally mixed origin.

*   *   *

The general tendency of early Islam, as has already been noted, was to emphasize the external duties prescribed by religion, rather than to encourage any attempt by the individual soul to establish contact with God. Indeed the emphasis laid on the Unity, the Power and the Magnificence of God tended at least to imply His inaccessibility.

It is difficult to know precisely what the Prophet himself thought on this subject. In some passages the Qoran encourages Muslims to enjoy the good things of this world, verses eagerly quoted by many Arabs who, as a result of the great conquests, had acquired generous shares of these good things. Yet neither Muhammad nor his first two successors indulged themselves, except perhaps in a plurality of wives. The Prophet never accumulated wealth nor even made use of the most elementary comforts. His food, his clothing, his house and its furnishings were simple in the extreme, even when ample money was available if he had been interested in it.

After the establishment of the khalifate in Damascus, the official and orthodox view was that the enjoyment of worldly pleasures was perfectly legitimate, provided that the various rules laid down in the Qoran and the Traditions were correctly observed. In spite of this fact, however, there were always Muslim ascetics, even during the lifetime of Muhammad and his immediate successors. Some of these lived in the desert, practised austerity and poverty and gave themselves to long prayers. To some extent, fear of hell-fire, so vividly described in the Qoran, may have been responsible for these tendencies. Some of the early ascetics were called "weepers", because they wept so fervently through penitence and fear of punishment.

But gradually the ascetics went further and longed for some personal contact with God—even for some tenderness, for divine love, for a religion of the heart. The orthodox were unwilling to admit such possibilities. Islam conceived God as so splendid and so almighty that the idea of mutual affection between Him and a human being seemed to the orthodox to verge on blasphemy. Man, they said, was the slave of God. His duty was limited to witnessing to His Unity, to obeying His orders and to enduring the vicissitudes of life with patience and resignation. The orthodox canonists and theologians were even displeased at the emphasis placed by the ascetics on the searching of their own consciences. To the official teachers of religion, the Qoran and Traditions contained all that was necessary to salvation. For a man to consult his own conscience might well lead him into heresy.

One of the earlier teachers of this more interior form of Islam had been Hasan al Basri, who died in 728 in the reign of the Khalif Hisham. The Kharijites were extremely hostile to the mystic tendencies of the ascetics, who became known as Soofis, owing to their custom of wearing a single woollen garment, soof being the Arabic word for wool. The Shiites also denounced the idea of direct contact between God and man. According to their dogma, their own imams were charged with the rôle of teachers, intermediate between God and the human race.

Perhaps the orthodox theologians would have done better to adopt the soofis and then to control them. As it was, treated almost everywhere with hostility by the leaders of religion, some of them tended towards various forms of heresy. One of the most famous of these mystics of the early days was Dhu al Noon, a freed Sudanese slave, who had completely renounced the world. Having been denounced as a heretic, he was brought before the Khalif Mutawakkil loaded with chains. He spoke, however, with so much piety and resignation that the Prince of the Faithful was moved to tears and ordered his immediate release.

Political disasters, poverty and the hardships resulting from years of anarchy were to follow the reign of Mutawakkil. The resulting fears and sufferings of the people favoured the growth of a more spiritual and interior religion which the materialism of the years of prosperity had tended to stifle.

After reading so much of the worldliness and luxury of the court and of the khalifs, it is well for us to appreciate that a more spiritual form of religion did also exist. Throughout the whole period from 660 to 860, many differing threads of earnest ascetic religion were woven into the pattern of Muslim civilization.

* * *

Wathiq was succeeded as khalif by his brother Mutawakkil. During his predecessor's lifetime the new khalif had been out of favour at court and had suffered a good deal of humiliation at the hands of his brother and his ministers. No sooner did he assume power than he began to dismiss, to arrest and, in some cases, to torture the ministers of Wathiq. His tendency in everything was to reverse the policy of those who had bullied him before he came to power. His three predecessors had favoured the Mutazilite doctrines, so he cordially supported the orthodox dogma, an attitude which won him considerable popularity among the majority of his subjects.

Wathiq had been particularly considerate towards the descendants of Ali ibn abi Talib, seeking out any of them in financial distress and allotting them adequate pensions. Mutawakkil went to the opposite extreme and regarded the Shia with intense dislike. In 850, he gave orders for the tomb of the martyred Husain at Kerbela to be razed to the ground. Pilgrimages to the site were forbidden and the whole area was ploughed up and sown with crops. As a result, he was hated by the Shia. At night slogans reviling him for his impiety were scrawled on the walls and the mosques of Baghdad. Mutawakkil introduced humiliating regulations against the Christians, many of whom, until he came to power, had occupied high offices of state. He forbade their employment in government service. They were obliged to wear peculiar clothing, to ride on saddles with wooden stirrups and were subjected to other humiliations. It is noticeable that the Prophet Muhammad treated Christians with consideration, nor were they seriously molested during the early age of genuine religious enthusiasm. The less religious the khalifs became, the more the Christians were treated with obloquy.

The fact that the Abbasids neglected to maintain their naval command of the Mediterranean has already been mentioned. The Arab fleets which controlled that sea in the 850's were those of Ifriqiya and Andalus. The Abbasids had never shown much interest in North Africa, but the earlier and more virile khalifs had nevertheless visited Persia, Syria, Palestine and Egypt. Both Wathiq and Mutawakkil, however, were inclined to pass their lives at home in Samarra, surrounded by their Turkish guards and their favourites, eunuchs and concubines of the palace. They seemed to have lost interest in empire. The great khalifs had earned fame and popular loyalty by their frequent tours of the provinces, by being personally known to the public and by leading their armies in battle.

In 852, the government neglect of the Mediterranean was suddenly and strikingly emphasized by the arrival of a Byzantine fleet in the Nile Delta. Several thousand troops were put ashore and Damiettta was taken by assault. Many people were killed and great quantities of merchandise and other wealth was carried off, including six hundred women, some of them Muslims and some Christian Copts. Damietta was a prosperous industrial city, famous for its textiles. This shameful reverse was due entirely to the neglect of its duties by the central government.

*   *   *

Mutawakkil had nominated his three sons as his successors, according to their ages. Muntasir, the eldest, was declared heir-apparent and after him Mutazz and then Muayyad. Unfortunately the khalif was particularly infatuated with the mother of Mutazz, his second son. She was a Greek slave concubine by the name of Qabiha. One day this charming beauty had appeared before Mutawakkil with the name Jaafar written with musk upon her cheeks. (Jaafar was the khalif's personal name, Mutawakkil his title.) Thereupon the Prince of the Faithful lovingly improvised the following lines:

> Jaafar she wrote upon her cheek with musk,
> Rather from life than from that cheek I'd part.
> For she wrote with lines of musk upon her cheek
> But she wrote with lines of love upon my heart.

So potent were the charms of the fair Qabiha that Mutawakkil decided to disinherit his eldest son Muntasir and to name her son Mutazz as the heir-apparent. The usual complications ensued, for oaths of allegiance had been sworn to Muntasir and he refused to renounce his claim. Mutawakkil appears to have acted with a remarkable lack of wisdom in this affair. Perhaps he was afraid of what the fair Qabiha might say about his inability to secure obedience to his orders. Angry and frustrated, he summoned Muntasir to his presence and told him point blank that he was degraded from the succession.

No one seems to have anticipated a crisis. There was no feeling of tension and anxiety among the public, such as that which had preceded the final Umaiyid collapse. The Turkish troops, it is true, were hated and the power given to the Turks was resented, but the khalif and his troops lived in semi-isolation in Samarra and the people at large were perhaps not fully aware of the intrigues of the palace. It was indeed here that the danger lay. Ever since the inauguration of the empire, all power, religious, political and military, had been concentrated in the khalif. Innumerable rebellions had occurred, but these were not ostensibly directed against the institution of the khalifate, as a modern left-wing movement against a dictator might be. Nearly all the risings had taken the form of claims, not that the powers of the khalif should be limited, but that the existing khalif was not the man entitled to that office. None of the many malcontents had conceived the idea that, if the khalif were all-powerful, the way to supreme authority was to control the khalif.

Such a course was perhaps impossible as long as the Prince of the Faithful lived in his capital surrounded by his people. But Mutasim had deliberately moved from Baghdad to Samarra, accompanied only by his *corps d'élite* of Turks. He was not afraid of them—they were his darlings and the apple of his eye. But by establishing the khalifate in Samarra surrounded only by the "household troops", he was unwittingly placing his successors at their mercy. Nobody, of course, realized this, nor at first did the Turkish mercenaries themselves.

* * *

There were already intrigues among the Turkish officers in the hot-house atmosphere of Samarra. Some of them were jealous of Bugha ash Shurabi, a Turk who had become the most powerful man at court and in the khalif's confidence. Bugha had been a slave and the palace butler until promoted to high rank. And herein also lay a danger, for no man is a hero to his valet. Again and again in history, revolutions have been started by the privileged and pampered troops of the imperial bodyguard, although the despised and neglected common soldiers on the distant frontiers were still devotedly loyal to their emperor. Mutawakkil seems to have been an ordinary commonplace individual, and the Turks were too near to him. His infatuation with his concubines, his over-indulgence in drink and his inability to control his sons probably did not inspire respect at close quarters. Familiarity had already bred contempt.

The disgruntled officers informed Bugha by anonymous letters that the khalif intended to have him assassinated. At the same time, Mutawakkil was warned by the same means that Bugha was about to murder him. Thus both the khalif and his Turkish favourite were inspired with suspicion. The quarrel between Mutawakkil and his son Muntasir happened to boil up just at this moment. Bugha, believing that the khalif was about to have him murdered, decided to strike first and to make Muntasir khalif, after which he doubtless expected the empire to continue as before.

One afternoon a few days later, it happened that Mutawakkil was in an excellent temper and was chatting happily to his intimates. As the evening progressed, the Prince of the Faithful became more and more cheerful and kept calling for more wine until he was quite drunk. Or perhaps, Bugha, who was with him, had intentionally plied him with drink. When most of the courtiers had withdrawn, only Bugha and the khalif's favourite, Fateh ibn Khaqan, remained in the apartment. A page hovered around them to serve them.

Suddenly five Turks with drawn swords burst into the room. "What is this, Bugha?" cried the khalif in alarm. "These are the men on guard," replied the general. "They will be sleeping outside the door of my lord, the Prince of the Faithful."

The would-be murderers were taken aback at these words and at seeing Bugha amicably drinking with the khalif, for it was he who had told them to come at that hour and kill him. As a result, they withdrew in confusion. Bugha hastened after them and told them in forcible language to do their work.

The five ran back into the room and one slashed with his sword at the khalif's head but only cut off his ear. Somebody called, "Go easy, man. Aim properly—that's no good." One of the men then threw himself upon the terrified Mutawakkil, who tried to push him away with his bare hands. "For God's sake," cried Fateh the favourite, "it's the Prince of the Faithful." "Can't you shut up, you fool," shouted Bugha the Turk and ran him through with his sword. In a few seconds, the khalif and his companion lay motionless on the floor in pools of blood. The page had hidden behind the curtains and remained unhurt.

Slipping from the room, Bugha hastened down the palace passage, only to meet Muntasir running towards him. "What has happened?" cried the prince breathlessly. "All is well, O Prince of the Faithful," replied the general, saluting him as khalif. Quickly the courtiers and servants were summoned and told to swear allegiance to the Khalif Muntasir.

Next morning, 11 December, 861, a crowd collected outside the palace in Samarra and demanded the elevation of Mutazz. But Mutazz was not to be found, for he had already been imprisoned by the Turks. Bugha was in complete command of the situation and Muntasir was khalif—for as long at least as the Turks were pleased with him. This, in practice, proved to be not very long.

Six weeks later, the young Khalif Muntasir lay on his deathbed. The manner of his death has never been established but rumour inevitably suggested poison. It was said that he had annoyed the Turks by showing too much independence of thought. For some forty years, the Turkish mercenaries were to make and unmake khalifs at their whim. By then, the professional mercenary army built up by the masterful Mutasim had lost its cohesion. The khalifs returned to Baghdad and enjoyed a brief Indian summer of authority in Iraq, though the empire had broken up during the years of the Turkish usurpation of power.

* * *

It is noticeable that the Arab historians agree that the reign of Mutawakkil was a period of great happiness. The economic situation was still prosperous, commerce and industry were flourishing and there had been no major wars in the reigns of Wathiq or of Mutawakkil. The Emperor Theophilus, who had been active and aggressive, was dead. During the khalifate of Muta-wakkil, Byzantium had been quiescent under the regency of Theodora and the early part of the reign of her son, Michael the Drunkard. If Mutawakkil seems to us a somewhat feeble individual, he was none the less good-natured and benevolent and there were few rebellions in his time. Perhaps also the disasters which were to follow caused people later on to look back with nostalgia to the peaceful days of Mutawakkil, as so many in Europe used to look back to the years before 1914.

* * *

The assassination of Mutawakkil marking, as it did, the end of the despotic rule of the khalifs, may be taken as a convenient place in which to summarize the achievements of the great Abbasids, as we have already done for the Umaiyids. We have followed the story of the dynasty for a hundred and eleven years, from the accession of Saffah in 750 to the murder of Mutawakkil in 861. Of the ten khalifs who ruled during this period, Mansoor and Haroon al Rasheed were men of really outstanding all-round ability. Their two reigns totalled forty-six years or approximately two-fifths of the period. Saffah, Mehedi, Mamoon and Mutasim were all capable and active rulers in different ways. Their reigns totalled forty-three years, or approximately another two-fifths. Hadi and Ameen tended to be weak—especially Ameen—but the total of their two reigns was only five years. Both had the misfortune to have exceptionally capable brothers next to them in the succession, with the result that their brief reigns were passed in discord or civil war. In the whole period of the great Abbasids the most unhappy years were probably 811–813, the years of the civil war between Ameen and Mamoon and of the siege of Baghdad.

The last two khalifs of our period, Wathiq and Mutawakkil, whose reigns totalled nineteen years, were of a different nature. Neither of these two brothers were outstanding personalities. They both spent their reigns in the palace of Samarra, without visiting the provinces. During their reigns, the Empire of the Arabs continued to run peacefully on under the momentum imparted to it by their great predecessors. Their very inactivity seemed to increase the happiness of their subjects, for there were no wars and few rebellions. Trade and industry flourished and wealth, luxury and learning were widespread. Nobody realized that the heart of the empire had almost ceased to beat.

From the imperial point of view the Abbasids fell far short of the Umaiyids. Spain was lost soon after they came to power and in 800 Ifriqiya became virtually independent under the Aghlabids. In the reign of Mamoon, the descendants of Tahir the Ambidextrous made themselves very nearly autonomous in Khurasan.

The khalifs made no attempt to recover the lost provinces although, from Haroon to Mutasim, they commanded more powerful armies than any of their predecessors. The determination to maintain the empire had vanished, not the power to do so. Many imperial races in history have performed prodigies of valour to conquer their empires but, as soon as the conquests were completed, have lost interest in the maintenance of their vast dominions. Beni Abbas provide an example of this phenomenon.

*   *   *

On the night of 10th December, 861, the swords of Bugha and his five assassins had destroyed the mighty Empire of the Arabs. The murderers did not know this—they thought they were engaged in a local palace feud. What they really did was to open the eyes of the world to a new idea—that the road to world power lay through the seizure and control of the khalif. Thereafter an almost unbroken succession of military adventurers seized possession of the persons of the khalifs and maintained them in idle impotence in their palaces, while Persian and Turkish war-lords ruled in their name. It was a simple idea, yet one of which no one had thought until Bugha blundered into it by accident.

The Abbasids were to remain as puppet khalifs for another four centuries. But when it became obvious that the khalifate was no longer free but had become a mere tool in the hands of successive soldiers of fortune, the various countries which had constituted the empire broke away. The Arabs did not cease at once to be a leading nation. Arab culture, science and industry were to continue to advance and to achieve greater triumphs than ever. Various Arabic-speaking states were to become Great Powers and to wield influence in the councils of the nations. But they did so as separate governments. The khalifate had been the heart of the empire. When that heart was struck with paralysis, the Empire of the Arabs passed for ever from the stage of history.

NOTABLE DATES

Accession of the Khalif Wathiq	842
Death of the Khalif Wathiq ⎱	
Accession of the Khalif Mutawakkil ⎰	847

PERSONALITIES

The Khalif Wathiq
His brother the Khalif Mutawakkil
The Khalif Muntasir, son of Mutawakkil
Bugha ash Shurabi the Turk, palace slave and butler
    and then army commander

Epilogue

"T HE only thing we learn from history," it has been said, "is that men never learn from history." Whether or not we admit the truth of this epigram, we still find ourselves tempted to endeavour to deduce, from the experience of past ages, lessons which may help us to solve the problems of our own times. In considering the Arabs, the temptation is peculiarly strong because so little seems to be basically changed in their characteristics since the ninth century.

Firstly we can be quite clear that the peoples today called Arabs, extending from Persia to Morocco, are a medley of different races which, however, for thirteen hundred years, have professed the same religion and made use of the same language and culture. These facts have given them a superficially similar appearance, resembling the likeness which exists today between the nations of Europe, which enjoy the same religion and culture but often react very differently to any given situation.

Each Arabic-speaking country, moreover, is separated from the next by hundreds of miles of desert. Iraq, for example, is divided from Syria and Jordan by five hundred miles of uninhabited steppe—as far as from London to Switzerland. Jordan and Syria are separated from Egypt by the Sinai desert. Egypt in its turn is cut off from Tripoli by a thousand miles, which include the Western Desert. The politicians can now fly back and forth, but to the ordinary citizen these vast desert barriers are still all but impassable.

The Berbers of what is now Algeria resisted the all-conquering Arabs for sixty years just as they have recently opposed the French with equal per-severance. Others of the Arabic-speaking countries of today offered little or no opposition to the Arab conquerors of the seventh century and are to this day rarely successful in their military enterprises. All this is unchanged in the last thousand years.

But although the Arabic-speaking peoples of today are of many different racial origins, certain characteristics of the Arabs of the seventh century are traceable in them all. This phenomenon may probably be attributed to the fact that, in the early years, these peculiarities became inextricably integrated into the Muslim religion. Of these features two of the most remarkable are perhaps their admiration for generosity and hospitality and their determina-tion always to pay back an injury. This matter of revenge leads us on to that of personal honour, individual freedom and dignity and the passionate desire to wipe out an affront.

These same peculiarities characterized the peoples of Western Europe, especially the upper classes, in the Middle Ages. The fighting of duels between gentlemen has only ended in the last century and a half, not under the influence of Christian love, but as a result of the prevalence of commercialism over the idea of honour. The persistence of this individualism among the Arabic-speaking races gives rise to such incidents as the desertion of officers to the enemy, as a result of what they consider to have been some personal injustice. These passionate forms of personal individualism serve to keep the Arabic-speaking countries in a constant state of turbulence. Even if rival parties assume the name of socialists, communists or patriots, questions of personal pique will usually be found to be behind their mutual hostility, which is as likely to be settled with fire-arms as through the ballot-box.

Owing to what seem to us to have been accidental circumstances, the Prophet became in his lifetime both ruler, military commander and religious teacher. His successors sought only to imitate his example and thus one-man rule became the universal model for Muslim states. The ruler combined religious and political leadership, his post was not hereditary, his powers were almost unlimited but he was (at least in theory) democratic, accessible and patriarchal. This Arab conception of equalitarian one-man rule was nevertheless, as we have seen, at times discarded in favour of the Persian and pre-Islamic form of autocracy. Above all, in the whole history of Arab—and even of Muslim—government until the present century, there is no record of any country ever having been ruled by an elected legislative body. In this field our assumption that the methods of government which we have evolved must necessarily be welcome to the Arabs also can only be described as naïve.

One of the most striking features of the preceding narrative must surely be the amazing contrast between the asceticism and devotion of the Prophet and his immediate successors and the wealth, luxury and worldliness of the Arab rulers only thirty years after Muhammad's death. It is interesting to speculate whether the extraordinary speed with which the Arabs conquered their empire was not in reality a disaster for Islam. The three and a half centuries of persecution which Christianity underwent before it was adopted as the religion of the Roman Empire may have been a blessing in disguise. Were the Arabs too successful? Does it not still remain today as true as ever that mammon is the greatest enemy of God?

APPENDIX I

TABLE OF BYZANTINE EMPERORS

(*Contemporary with Umaiyids and Abbasids*)

Name	Method of Accession	Arab Contemporary	Dates of Reign
1	2	3	4
Dynasty of Heraclius			
Heraclius	Revolt	Muhammad and two successors	610–641
Constantine III		Umar ibn al Khattab	641–642
Constans II		Umar, Ali, Muawiya	642–668
Constantine IV		Muawiya, Yezeed I, Merwan	668–685
Justinian II Slitnose		Abdul Malik ibn Merwan	685–695
Leontius ⎱	Revolt	Abdul Malik ibn Merwan	695–698
Tiberius ⎰			698–705
Justinian II Slitnose (Second Reign)		Waleed I	705–711
Philippicus	Revolt	Waleed I	711–713
Anastasius II	Revolt	Waleed, Sulaiman	713–716
Theodosius III	Revolt	Sulaiman	716
Isaurian Dynasty			
Leo III the Isaurian	Revolt	Sulaiman, Umar, Yezeed II, Hisham	716–741
Constantine V Copronymus (whose-name-is-dung)		Yezeed III, Merwan the Ass, Saffah, Mansoor	741–775
Leo IV		Mehedi	775–780
Irene (as Regent)		Mehedi	780–785
Constantine VI		Hadi, Haroon al Rasheed	785–797
Irene (in her own Name)		Haroon al Rasheed	797–802
Nicephorus I	Revolt	Haroon al Rasheed, Ameen	802–811
Staurikius, son of Nicephorus		Ameen	811
Michael I (brother in law of Staurikius)		Ameen	811–813
Leo V the Armenian	Revolt	Mamoon	813–820
Amorian Dynasty			
Michael II the Amorian	Revolt	Mamoon	820–829
Theophilus, son of Michael II		Mamoon, Mutasim	829–842

Theodora (as Regent)		
for Michael III	Wathiq	842–856
Michael III the	Wathiq, Mutawakkil,	
Drunkard	Muntasir	842–867
(a minor from 842–856)		

NOTE: Emperors who seized the throne by violence are shown in column 2 as "Revolt". Where column 2 is blank, the emperor was the legitimate heir. Of 25 emperors, ten seized the throne by violence.

APPENDIX II

GENERAL CHRONOLOGY

from the Prophet Muhammad to the Khalif Mutawakkil

	YEAR A.D.
Birth of Muhammad	570
Muhammad migrates to Medina	622
Muslim capture of Mecca	630
Death of Muhammad	632
Battle of the Yarmouk and Conquest of Syria	636
Battle of Qadasiya and Conquest of Iraq	637
Conquest of Egypt	640–642
Battle of Nehawand and Conquest of Persia	642
Assassination of Khalif Othman	656
Civil war between Ali and Muawiya	656–661
Assassination of Ali	661
Foundation of Qairawan	670
First siege of Constantinople	670–677
Death of Muawiya I	680
Massacre of Husain's party at Kerbela	680
Death of Khalif Yezeed I	683
Abdulla ibn Zubair proclaimed khalif in Mecca	683
Merwan proclaimed khalif in Damascus	684
Abdul Malik proclaimed in Damascus	685
Rebellion of Mukhtar in Kufa	685–687
Death of Abdulla ibn Zubair	692
Pacification of North Africa	705
Death of Abdul Malik	705
Conquest of Spain	711–713
Qutaiba reaches Kashgar	712
Muhammad ibn Qasim's conquest of Sind	712
Second siege of Constaninople	716–717
Umar ibn Abdul Aziz, the good khalif	717–720
Arab invasion of France	718–720
Khalif Hisham	724–743
Battle of Tours	732
Defeat of Khaqan	738
Khalif Waleed II the Libertine	743–744
Accession of Khalif Merwan the Ass	744
Rebellion of Abu Muslim in Khurasan	747–748
Battle of the Zab	750

INDEX

Most Arabic names consist of the personal name of the individual followed by the personal name of his father. For example, John son of Thomas, Muhammad son of Abdulla.

It is the custom in England to index such names under the second name, that is under the name of the father. Thus John the son of Thomas is indexed as "Thomas, John the son of". This practice has in general been followed in the present index. In the case of important people, the name has been entered twice—for example under John and under Thomas, with a cross-reference. In the case of lesser characters, the name will usually be found under that of the father. Thus Musa son of Ameen is shown not under Musa but under "Ameen, Musa ibn".